Windows
Server® 2008
Implementation and
Administration

Windows Server® 2008
Implementation and Administration

Barrie Sosinsky

Wiley Publishing, Inc.

Acquisitions Editor: Tom Cirtin

Development Editor: Candace English

Technical Editor: Jim Kelly

Production Editor: Elizabeth Campbell

Copy Editor: Liz Welch

Production Manager: Tim Tate

Vice President and Executive Group Publisher: Richard Swadley

Vice President and Executive Publisher: Joseph B. Wikert

Vice President and Publisher: Neil Edde

Book Designers: Maureen Forys and Judy Fung

Compositor: Craig Johnson, Happenstance Type-O-Rama

Proofreader: Rachel Gunn

Indexer: Jerilyn Sproston

Cover Designer: Ryan Sneed

Cover Image: Ryan McVay, Digital Vision, Getty Images, Inc.

Library of Congress Cataloging-in-Publication Data

Sosinsky, Barrie A.

 Windows server 2008 : implementation and administration / Barrie Sosinsky. -- 1st ed.

  p. cm.

 ISBN 978-0-470-17459-3 (paper/website)

 1. Microsoft Windows server. 2. Operating systems (Computers) 3. Client/server computing. I. Title.

 QA76.76.O63S654736 2008

 005.4'476--dc22

                         2007043224

Dear Reader,

Thank you for choosing *Windows Server 2008 Implementation and Administration*. This book is part of a family of premium quality Sybex books, all written by outstanding authors who combine practical experience with a gift for teaching.

Sybex was founded in 1976. More than thirty years later, we're still committed to producing consistently exceptional books. With each of our titles we're working hard to set a new standard for the industry. From the paper we print on, to the authors we work with, our goal is to bring you the best books available.

I hope you see all that reflected in these pages. I'd be very interested to hear your comments and get your feedback on how we're doing. Feel free to let me know what you think about this or any other Sybex book by sending me an email at nedde@wiley.com. Or, if you think you've found a technical error in this book, please visit http://sybex.custhelp.com. Customer feedback is critical to our efforts at Sybex.

Best regards,

Neil Edde
Vice President and Publisher
Sybex, an Imprint of Wiley

This book is dedicated to my mother Thelma Sosinsky with special thanks for her help and support over the past years; and to the memory of my father Jack Sosinsky.

Acknowledgments

This book could not have been either started or completed without the active encouragement of some special people. First I want to thank Matt Wagner my longtime literary agent for suggesting me for this project and for smoothing the path along the way. Tom Cirtin was the acquisition editor at Sybex who championed the project, got the book commissioned, and herded me along down the road to completion. Without the encouragement of my friend Mark Hepburn this book simply would not have been done.

I started writing this book just before I began working at ICONICS documenting their latest GENESIS32 industrial automation software suite. My thanks go to Russ and Paula Agrusa for providing me the opportunity to come and learn about this area of technology. I've been surrounded by a talented group of very nice people who have become friends. They have made this year one of the most satisfying and educational period that I've had in quite a while.

Many people at Sybex have worked on this project along with me. Some I've worked with personally; while many others were unknown to me. Candace English served as the development editor on this project and improved the book's content and approach. Elizabeth Campbell was the production editor on the project, and brought this project in smoothly and professional.

A special thanks goes to Jim Kelly at Blue Rocket Writing for taking time away from his own writing to provide the technical editing for the book. An operating system book isn't an easy book to tech edit because the subject matter is so broad. Jim's suggestions were almost always on the mark, and valuable.

During this project I've come to expect and enjoy all the regular conversations I've had with Pete Gaughan, editorial manager at Sybex. These discussions about commitment, schedules, project management, staffing, the computer book market, and the zen of computer book authorship have gone a long way towards focusing my attention on getting this project done.

It's mind boggling how much time I've spent on this project, and there is one last group of people who require my thanks. Time spent on this book was time spent away from my family: my wife Carol Westheimer, and my daughter Allie and son Joseph; so with this book now done I'm looking forward to spending more time with you all. I wrote this book surrounded by the animal part of my family, my cats: Stormy, Shadow, Scamper, Smokey, Slate, Spats, and Slippers. From time to time my furry friends would walk across my keyboard looking for attention and treats—introducing typos, and bringing me back to reality. I love you all.

About the Author

Barrie Sosinsky is a Boston based author who has written over 30 books on computer technology and many articles in leading journals. He has an interest in operating systems, servers, networks, storage, and enterprise applications. He currently works as a senior technical writer for a company that creates automation software for large enterprises.

Contents at a Glance

Contents

Introduction

Microsoft Windows Server 2008 and Vista are the successors to Windows Server 2003 and Windows XP. Windows Server 2008 and Vista arise out of the Longhorn project, and formerly Windows Server 2008 is Longhorn Server and Vista is the Longhorn client. Both products share a lot of common code in their engines, so in a sense both are joined at the hip. Although this book focuses on how Windows Server 2008 is different from Windows Server 2003 and how you can get the most out of that difference, we can't ignore this intimate connection between server and its intended client—and I won't. This isn't the first time that Microsoft has co-developed a client and a server; the Whistler project delivered Windows Server 2003 and XP as server and client, respectively. So perhaps this is Microsoft's pattern going forward.

Microsoft has learned a lot about servers and networking over time and has incorporated what it learned into each new version. Your first view of Windows Server 2008 may be the Server Manager application shown in Figure I.1. The Server Manager was a feature of Windows Server 2003, and so its look and feel might seem familiar to you. A close examination of this application reveals that it contains a number of new features: the incorporation of a Microsoft Management Console (MMC) tree into the left-hand pane, and a number of new sections such as the Roles Summary. Roles are a much more refined feature in Windows Server 2008 than it has been before, and while they have long been a central part of other operating systems such as Unix, they haven't been fully developed in Windows.

At first glance the Server Manager doesn't look all that different from the version that appeared in Windows Server 2003. And indeed, the Server Manager is derived from an application called Manage My Server that appeared in an earlier version of Microsoft Small Business Server. The progression doesn't appear all that different, although the underlying capabilities have been greatly expanded and enhanced. Thus most people will feel right at home with Windows Server 2008 once they spend some time with Vista, but there is a lot that's new and different in Windows Server 2008 that's under the hood.

To improve security Windows Server 2008 rewrote the TCP/IP stack completely (with IPv6 now a native service), a new server core, new web and terminal services, and Active Directory roles. To aid in hardening the operating system, Microsoft has added new features called identities, strengthened the function of certificates, and added a completely new scripting and command environment called PowerShell that exposes the operating system along with .NET objects to programmatic control.

It's not that these new features aren't powerful and useful—many of them are. Some features are future facing, such as the incorporation of IPv6, while other features such as Digital Rights Management (which is more of a concern in Vista) are nothing more than the swan song of the technology of yesteryear. So much of Windows Server 2008 is squirreled away into simple-looking dialog boxes that it can be hard to appreciate the power and complexity that the server offers. Much of this book explores these hidden features and attempts to separate the ones that you might want to use from the ones that are best left untouched.

FIGURE 1
The Server Manager application may be the first window you see in a fully installed copy of Windows Server 2008.

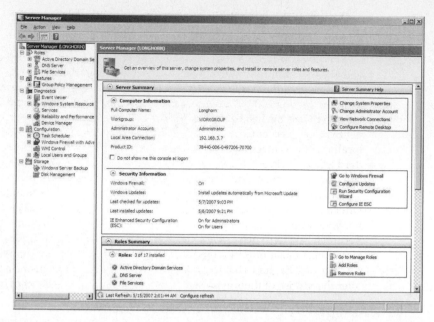

That's one of the primary goals of this book: to save you time. You don't need to learn about things that you already know, and you want to learn about the features in Windows Server 2008 that are new and different. With a shorter read than you'll find in many other competing titles, we hope that you'll be up and running these new technologies quickly and efficiently.

Shipping Editions

Ever since Windows 2000 Server replaced Windows NT Server, Microsoft has been slicing and dicing their server products into custom versions that different market segments would adopt. Windows 2000 split first into a "standard edition" and an "enterprise edition." A little later a version for the small-medium business (SMB) market called Microsoft Small Business Server emerged, and that product eventually split into one that contained SQL Server and one that did not.

Therefore, you shouldn't be surprised to learn that the Windows Server 2008 family of server network operating system (NOS) products contains all of the same versions of Windows Server that appeared in Windows Server 2003.

There's support for three different processor families:

- Intel x86 32-bit architecture

- Intel x64 architecture

- The Itanium version called IA-64

From the least feature filled and cheapest version of Windows Server 2008 the following versions of this NOS are offered for sale:

- Web Edition, which comes in x86 and x64 versions

- Standard Edition, which comes in x86 and x64 versions

◆ Enterprise Edition, available in x86, x64, and IA-64 versions

◆ Datacenter Edition, available in x86, x64, and IA-64 versions

You likely will run across a "version" of Windows Server 2008 that is called "Server Core" but you will have trouble locating a product SKU (stock keeping unit) for it. That's because Server Core isn't a product, but a role that's available in the Standard, Enterprise, and Datacenter editions of Windows Server 2008. The Server Core role isn't available in either the Web or Datacenter editions. In Server Core the installation of Windows Server 2008 has stripped out the graphics shell of Internet Explorer. Server Core is strictly configured and managed through the command-line interface locally, or by connecting to the system over a network and modifying the Server Core through standard MMCs. Server Core significantly limits the number of distributed network services that are run from the server. You'll find the .NET Framework doesn't run on this type of server.

A list of services that you might want to run on Server Core includes domain controller or Active Directory services; Active Directory Lightweight Directory Services (ADLDS), DHCP, and DNS network addressing; and file and print services. Other services for which Server Core has a use are Terminal Services such as Easy Print, Remote Programs, and Gateway, as well as in a Windows Server virtualization setup. You'll find much more on this in Chapter 14, "Server Core."

Microsoft has had a habit of releasing its Windows Small Business Server versions about 90 days after the release of their main server version releases. So this list of editions isn't complete. There are four more editions of Windows Server 2008 you may see:

◆ The Cougar project, which is expected to be a Windows Small Business Server system

◆ The Centro project, a version for the SMB market that might include Exchange

◆ Windows Home Server

◆ Windows Storage Server

You'll find a much more complete description of the different editions of Windows Server 2008 in Chapter 2, where we'll describe the features that all these editions include and omit.

March of the Chapters

Let's step through the chapters in the book and say a bit about what's in each chapter that might interest you (with my apologies to penguins). There are 14 chapters in this book. Although the material might make more sense to you if you read all of these chapters sequentially, it isn't necessary to read the chapters sequentially. Since all the chapters are cross-referenced and each chapter is a stand-alone topic or a couple of related topics, you can start where you like and read this book one chapter at a time as your interests dictate.

Chapter 1, "Windows Server 2008 Architecture," is an important chapter on system architecture. Windows Server 2008 has a lot of new plumbing, and even if you know where the plumbing was in Windows Server 2003 you'll want to read or at least skim Chapter 1 because Microsoft has moved many of the pipes around. There are two major additions to Windows Server 2008 that are introduced in Chapter 1: multiprocessor support and processor virtualization. Multiprocessor support influences how servers can scale, while virtualization describes how to run processes in protected space. The related concept of the hypervisor and low-level access to I/O is also put into context. Microsoft has taken one of the best hacker techniques available, the hypervisor, and adopted it to make Windows Server 2008 more secure.

Even if you decide to bypass Chapter 1's rather technical presentation of server subsystems, you may want to examine some of the system topology as shown in figures as it will help you better understand how Windows Server 2008 was built, its relation to Windows Server 2003, and how the new network stack and security features were designed. You can always refer back to this chapter if needed as you read additional chapters.

Chapter 2, "Deploying Windows Server 2008," describes in more detail server editions, from the small ones to the big ones, and all of the versions in between. Vista ships as a single DVD distribution from which you select the version that you want to install. Windows Server 2008 versions ship on individual DVDs, each with different choices available. Chapter 2 describes these differences, as well as the pricing model that Microsoft uses. That pricing will influence many purchases, so we'll also look at how Microsoft handles licensing, upgrade, client licenses, and other related issues in this chapter. Since pricing and licensing issues tend to be volatile, our discussion centers on Microsoft's philosophy and how that should influence your choices. We also look at license compliance tools in Windows Server 2008 used for license management.

With Vista's release Microsoft introduced a new system deployment scheme. A new image-based installation using a single container file called Windows Imaging Format (WIM) uses a single-instance system to capture all versions of Vista into a single compressed file. Imaging is a widely used technology for system deployment. Symantec (formerly Norton) Ghost is an example of a utility that creates and restores system images. A new boot environment called Preboot Execution Environment (PXE) 2.0 is used to install these system images. We'll look at Microsoft's automated deployment environment, the Microsoft Business Desktop Deployment Solution Accelerator, to see how it relates to the deployment of the Windows Server 2008 operating system itself. Chapter 2 will be important to you if you are in an administrative role where you are tasked with installing and certifying Windows servers in your organization.

Chapter 3, "Network Services," describes the changes in network services in Windows Server 2008. We'll briefly describe the state of network service administration, as there are new methods for starting and stopping services programmatically. Microsoft continues to develop distributed network services under the .NET Framework, and Windows Server 2008 ships with the latest version of the framework, version 3.0.

Security is a major focus of networking in Windows Server 2008, and just as Vista got locked down into administrator mode for a number of operations, Windows Server 2008 is built to limit system access. The main focus of Chapter 3 is the new TCP/IP stack and how it influences your network architecture. We'll discuss the potential impact of IPv6, see how it affects a developing quality of service (QoS) server capability, and see how the new network stack influences the web services networking protocol (HTTP).

Chapter 4, "Active Directory," is the first of two chapters on Active Directory. In this chapter you'll learn how Windows Server 2008 implements its security model, how network objects are managed in Active Directory, and the purpose of roles. With roles you can quickly assign a set of properties to a server, to systems, to users, and to groups that greatly speed up your NOS setup and can be valuable in maintaining a stricter and more rational set of security settings. The Add Roles Wizard (see Figure I.2) lets you quickly create new roles in your organization.

Roles have a long history in other operating systems, so one of the purposes of this chapter is to compare how Microsoft has implemented roles compared to Unix and see what kinds of interoperability are possible in a heterogeneous network.

FIGURE 2

The Add Roles Wizard lets you quickly create new roles, a feature that's been a major administration tool in Unix for years.

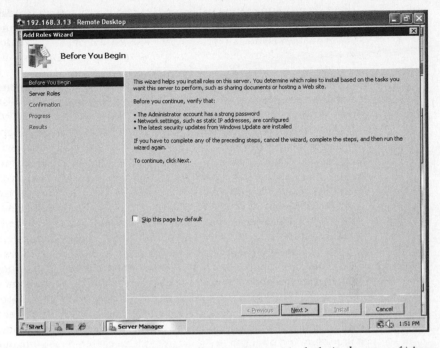

Active Directory got a major overhaul in Windows Server 2008, particularly in the area of identities and rights management services. In its role of managing policies and roles these services are now referred to as Active Directory Domain Services (AD DS). Other services such as Active Directory Federation Services (ADFS), Active Directory Lightweight Directory Services (ADLDS), (formerly Active Directory Application Mode), Active Directory Certificate Services (ADCS), and Active Directory Rights Management Services (ADRMS) have now been defined. The identity and certificate services are greatly enhanced, as will be described in more detail in Chapter 9. Windows Server 2008 now allows you to create trusted relationships with outside domains, and an Identity Integration Feature Pack is now part of the Active Directory Metadirectory Services. All of these services are essentially roles.

This chapter also covers the newly introduced read-only domain controller (RODC). RODCs allow you to deploy a configured domain server in a remote office. Perhaps you ship in the new server fully configured, or you install the software and required data from a DVD. In any event, the RODC is meant to be that: read-only. Since it cannot be altered, it does not participate in replication and subscription schemes, thus dramatically lowering the usage of network bandwidth over a WAN when throughput is limited. You'd use RODCs if the only connection is over a 56 kbps modem line, for example.

Chapter 5, "Policies and System Management," describes how to set and manage policies. The Windows Group Policy engine is refined in each version of the NOS. With Windows Server 2008 Microsoft has added some of the capabilities of several policy management tools that were add-ons for Windows Server 2003. There are many more policies in Windows Server 2008 that are available to you. Some of them affect logon properties across systems, domains, and applications—for example, single sign-on. Other policies can enforce security or control QoS issues.

Chapter 6, "File System Enhancements," describes how Windows Server 2008's file system has been improved. Microsoft continues to promise us a new object-oriented file system. The Cairo project that ran from 1991 through 1996, which is described at

```
http://en.wikipedia.org/wiki/Cairo_(operating_system)
```

was meant to deliver this grand concept. However, implementing a completely new distributed file system breaks many applications and systems, and so we've seen these improvements appear piecemeal. Cairo became part of the SQL Server—the Exchange, as well as the data store of the Active Directory; you'll also find elements of Cairo in Microsoft Internet Information Server (IIS), and in Windows Desktop Search.

What we didn't see was the Windows Future Storage (WinFS) object file system. That new file system was supposed to be part of Vista and by extension Windows Server 2008. However, it didn't make the cut into this version of the operating system. WinFS isn't dead—it's just on a slower development track. Pieces of WinFS are showing up in other technologies. The Entities feature in ADO.NET was part of the WinFS API. Some of the WinFS feature set shows up in the SQL Server database table editing tool called Orca (see `http://msdn2.microsoft.com/en-us/library/aa370557.aspx`), and it will be in the Katmai release (the SQL Server team loves to name projects after US national parks) of SQL Server, which is also at the core of the Microsoft System Center Operations Manager.

File system improvements continue to crawl along. Windows Server 2008 is no exception in this process of incremental file system upgrading. In Windows Server 2008, the major new features are volume encryption, a more fault-tolerant NTFS file system that monitors hardware status, and a new transactional feature. We know that Microsoft would eventually like to phase out the Registry as it is a major source of system errors and corruption, but Windows Server 2008 is not that operating system. This chapter also looks at the state of the Windows Registry, particularly changes in the Registry that support transactions, as well as changes that support the new features of Active Directory that were described in the previous two chapters.

Chapter 7, "Server Management," is the first of two chapters on administration and management. In this chapter we'll look at the graphical tools that are either upgraded or new in Windows Server 2008. We'll take a closer look at the Windows Server Management Console to see what functionality has been consolidated in that application. The Event Viewer, various utilities that access the provider information in the Windows Management Interface, and other related functions are also detailed here. One important topic in Windows of all types is service pack and patches, or what Microsoft calls "hot fixes." We'll look at Microsoft's Windows Update website as well as how to perform upgrades from local resources.

Chapter 8, "PowerShell," covers one of the more significant subjects in this book. PowerShell is Microsoft's new command shell environment and scripting language/tool (see Figure I.3). It borrows concepts from many languages, codifies several of Microsoft's scripting technologies into a unified set, and lets you command and control the many objects that are part of Windows, Office, and the distributed objects that are part of network services encompassed by the .NET Framework.

With PowerShell you can bring large parts of the Windows operating system, both local and remote, under programmatic control. If you ever wanted to tap the power that a C# (C sharp) programmer has under Windows, then PowerShell will make that possible—at least one line at a time. Under PowerShell you can run scripts in Visual Basic, VB Script, JavaScript, Perl, and other languages for which interpreters exist.

How powerful is PowerShell? Let's put it this way: the management of the latest version of Microsoft Exchange is built on PowerShell commands entirely, and the management GUI calls the PowerShell commands—albeit a smaller set of the commands than can be specified from the command line. Microsoft has hinted that future server applications will be built using PowerShell, and has stated that development of PowerShell will continue while the other scripting languages and tools that are part of current Windows technologies such as Windows Scripting Host won't be.

FIGURE 3
The Zen of Power-Shell—simplicity belying great power.

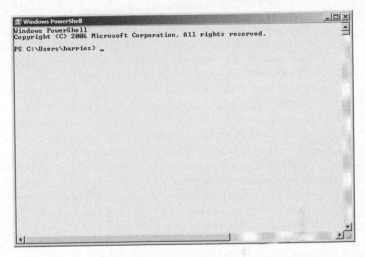

Chapter 9, "Security," describes one of the main project goals of both Vista and Windows Server 2008: improving security. Whereas for Vista security was important, for Windows Server 2008 security is essential. Microsoft can rely on patches and third-party applications to fix any of Vista woes, but given the nature of server operating systems, patches and hot fixes won't help secure Windows domains if there is an underlying weakness that can be exploited. In this chapter we look at some of the new security features in Windows Server 2008.

We've already mentioned the rewrite of the TCP/IP stack in Windows Server 2008. Several other network services have been either rewritten or enhanced. Security improvements fall into five broad areas of technology:

♦ Protocol enhancement with new authentication and cryptographic support

♦ Improvement to Windows Firewall

♦ Network share security enhancement

♦ NAP and network security enforcement refinements

♦ Server credentials and new authorization procedures

Was Microsoft successful in its security efforts? Only time will tell. However, applying these technologies will certainly make your servers more secure. As a general rule, crackers always go after the lowest hanging fruit that takes the least effort to compromise.

Chapter 10, "Clients, Interoperability, and Printing," speaks to Windows Servers' place in the world. In many corporations networks contain a mixture of servers and clients. Web servers often run Apache and people in the graphics department might run Macintoshes, so being able to inter-operate is a necessity these days. Windows Server 2008 offers new ways to manage mobile clients, new tools for Unix interoperability, a new network printing routine, as well as new methods for allowing client access to networking resources.

In this chapter we'll also look at how Windows Server 2008 interacts with older versions of the Windows server and client OS, and what you need to know about what is called "down-level" compatibility. Microsoft advertises Windows Server 2008 as working best with versions of Windows 2003, XP, and later, but the reality is that many people are still supporting versions of Windows 2000. So this is an important issue.

In **Chapter 11, "Performance Enhancements,"** you will learn about some of the performance enhancements in Windows Server 2008. The ability to use multiple processors and have access to large amounts of memory has been a feature of Windows Server for a while now. Microsoft has improved the tools you use to monitor and tune performance, which is the main focus of this chapter. We'll look at the Windows System Resource Manager, and explore how you can use that tool in your work. This chapter also reviews the progress made in virtualization, load balancing, and clustering.

Chapter 12, "Terminal Server," describes the changes to Terminal Server—a rather significant improvement over the previous version of the product.

This version removes one of the most confusing aspects of the terminal session: the window within a window. In the new version, Terminal Server looks like any other Windows window ("seamless windows"). The difference between local applications and remote applications has been blurred to the point where training users about the subtleties of using Terminal Server is a thing of the past.

There are also some new capabilities for remote users connecting to a Terminal Server. The Terminal Server Gateway allows users to connect to the Terminal Server using a new version of RDP (6.0) over an SSL-encrypted session and through corporate firewalls. Terminal Services Web Access provides users with a browser interface in which they can launch server-based applications. The Session Broker, a new management console, and other improvements make this version of Terminal Server easier than previous versions to work with. Just to keep you on your toes, there is also now a new licensing scheme for Terminal Server.

From the implementation of a single sign-on, to monitor spanning and large monitor support, to new management tools, you'll find new features everywhere. Terminal Server will also look different—the new version supports themes and what is called the Desktop Experience Pack.

Chapter 13, "Internet Information Services," describes the new version of Internet Information Server 7.0 (now called Internet Information Services). IIS 7.0 is a brand-new version built as a framework application with a set of installable modules for different security authentication, management options, and application development tools. The architecture of IIS has changed significantly, isolating one website from another, creating an application pool for each website, and isolating worker processes to each application pool. The process model and pipeline have been significantly improved.

IIS 7.0 can be lean and mean, or can be custom-fit to your particular application. The new web server is extensible through custom modules and the use of .NET Framework tools.

The management applications for IIS 7.0 have been greatly improved. The new IIS 7.0 Manager allows you to manage all web services as well as ASP.NET from the same console. Event logging, tracing, and the new command APPCMD.EXE provide the functionality of IIS Manager from the command line.

Chapter 14, "Server Core," concludes this book by discussing the Server Core role. Server Core is Windows Server without windows. The lack of a GUI means that Server Core is smaller, faster, and much less prone to attack. Server Core is a new paradigm and will require you to use new methods to manage this type of Windows Server role. Microsoft has high hopes for this type of server configuration, and indeed this kind of installation has been possible in other operating systems for a while.

So you see we've set ourselves an ambitious agenda here. This book will cover a lot of ground in a small amount of space, rewarding your time spent reading it with a lot of high-valued information.

So without further ado, let's get started.

Chapter 1

Windows Server 2008 Architecture

Any server operating system version upgrade involves changes to nearly every subsystem, and Windows Server 2008 is no exception. There have been kernel changes to allow for better processor virtualization, driver model changes to make drivers more stable and secure, a completely new TCP/IP protocol stack for better performance, a new graphics engine, and very significant changes to the Windows Class Libraries that give access to the Windows .NET Framework and Network Class Library. To a user learning Windows Server 2008, these changes underpin all of the new procedures that differentiate Windows Server 2008 and Vista Service Pack 1 (SP1) from the previous versions of Windows Server 2003 and Windows XP. So in order to provide a framework for our discussions in future chapters, this first chapter explains the Windows Server 2008 architectural model, along with the changes that they portend.

There have been enormous changes in the Windows Server architecture for this release of Microsoft's flagship product. As Microsoft's desktop OS and Microsoft Office slow down in revenue growth, Windows Server has become particularly important to Microsoft's fortunes. Microsoft Windows Server 2008 continues Microsoft's push to integrate web-based services into its server product. There are now strong links to the .NET Framework, both programmatically as well as in the look and feel of applications that will take advantage of the architecture that is described in this chapter. While Microsoft emphasizes the new modules that affect what the user can see, there are plenty of architecture changes to basic systems such as the kernel, memory, services, and many more. In this chapter, you will read about the most significant architectural goals of this release and how you can get even more value out of your investment in Windows Server.

Understanding the System's Roots

Writing an operating system for a new computer system has always been something of a heroic effort. In 1981 Tracy Kidder won a Pulitzer Prize and an American Book Award for his book *The Soul of a New Machine*, in which he describes the creation of the 32-bit Eclipse MV/8000 minicomputer at Data General. The company Data General was competing with at the time was Digital Equipment Corporation (DEC), their computers were the PDP-11 series, and that operating system was VAX (short for Virtual Address Extension).

The early history of Windows NT as documented in G. Pascal Zachary's *Showstopper! The Race to Create Windows NT and the Next Generation at Microsoft* (1994) was similarly chaotic. NT started as a co-development project between IBM and Microsoft; it was to be version 3.0 of OS/2, both companies having worked on versions 1 and 2. Windows 3.0's success led Microsoft to develop OS/2 API into an extended Windows API, at which point the joint project fell apart. IBM would go on to release OS/2 3.0 as their "Warp" version, which although something of a success in the business world never caught on with the general public. Microsoft chose another direction.

When DEC canceled the PRISM project in 1988, Microsoft was able to hire away many of the team members working in DEC West in Seattle. Systems architect David Cutler, who had experience with Virtual Memory System (VMS) and Reduced Instruction Set Computer (RISC) architecture, became the head of the development team that rewrote the Microsoft version of OS/2. The concepts of a microkernel, protective mode, an executive program, device drivers, and hardware abstraction all arise from the work of Cutler's group and the heritage that they brought to Microsoft. The basic idea behind Windows Server was that Microsoft (being a software company) should create an operating system that was portable from one hardware platform to another with a straightforward recompile.

The original NT project targeted development of IA-32 (Intel Architecture), MIPS (Microprocessor without Interlocked Pipeline Stages), Alpha, PowerPC, SPARC, and Intel i860 and i960. Microsoft released the first version of NT on July 27, 1993. Indeed, the multiplatform heritage of Windows Server is supposedly the origin of the NT name, as initial development of OS/2 3.0 was for the i860 processor code named N10, or "N-Ten." It is speculated, but not confirmed, that Microsoft replaced the NT name (which they marketed under "New Technology") with the year designations because of a trademark issue with Nortel Networks, whose Northern Telecom owns the NT trademark.

Today the Windows operating systems in general, and the Windows Server systems specifically, owe much of their success and many of their shortcomings to the design decisions made by the original NT team for Windows NT. There isn't space here to expound on why many of the technical features in Windows are a little goofy (you can take the Windows Registry as an example), but any reader interested in software history from a technical viewpoint should take a look at Raymond Chen's *The Old New Thing: Practical Development Throughout the Evolution of Windows* (2006).

System Overview

Windows Server is an example of a preemptive, multitasked, multithreaded operating system. The term *preemptive* means that the Windows operating system can switch the order of tasks held in memory based on a set of scheduling policies and priorities, a process commonly referred to as context switching. Windows can perform a context switch because it recognizes that a process has ended, that a process is blocked by a shared resource, or that the process has been switched to another processor. This behavior (which is a software version of a system interrupt) is performed by the kernel, and is different from a system in which tasks are scheduled through time sharing or through a system of hardware interrupts. There are many advantages to preemption, but the most important are that preemption uses resources more efficiently and that it can remove many instances of processes that are either CPU bound or input/output (I/O) bound, waiting for other processes to finish.

A process or task is the execution of program or service. You can see processes executing in Windows Server 2008 or Vista in the Task Manager, where the consumption of memory and CPU is given for each. Figure 1.1 shows the Process page of the Task Manager.

Although the Task Manager got an upgrade in Vista so that it shows more information and actually describes what each process is, it does not offer the most complete description you can get on your system. That honor belongs to the service- and process-related commands you can enter into PowerShell, which is discussed in Chapter 8, "PowerShell."

You can get to the Task Manager by doing any of the following:

◆ Right click the Taskbar and select the Task Manager from the context menu.

◆ Click an empty area of the desktop and press Ctrl+Shift+Esc.

◆ Click the Start menu, enter **TASKMGR** into the Search text box, then press the Enter key.

◆ Press Windows+R to open the Run dialog box, then enter **TASKMGR** and press Enter.

◆ Press Ctrl+Alt+Del and select Start Task Manager from the menu on the Login/Logoff screen.

FIGURE 1.1
The Task Manager has been upgraded to give more detailed information.

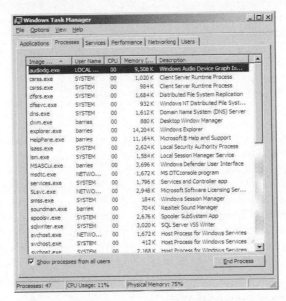

Windows gives you so many different ways to get to the Task Manager because the Task Manager allows you to kill errant processes and bring a server back to life. The information that the Task Manager presents to you is one of the best tools you have in improving the performance of Windows Server.

The Windows operating system examines processes, and decomposes them into the fundamental units of execution, which are called threads. Threads are assigned priorities and then added to the scheduling of the execution queue. Through context switching, all processes get access to the processor according to their priority, something that is often referred to as time slicing. When a process allows it, Windows can decompose the process into multiple threads, optimizing the processing and improving the process's performance (known as multithreading). Windows is capable of managing the event queue for a single process or to multiple processors through a Symmetric Multi-Processor (SMP) scheme. With time slicing, it appears that the system is doing multiple tasks at the same time, or multitasking, but that is only the net result of individual steps that are executing too quickly to be differentiated. The effect a user sees is akin to viewing a movie.

Windows 2000/NT Architecture

In its original conception, Windows NT was built as a modular system with two distinct layers. What the user sees and works with was called the user mode, and all hardware I/O was contained in modules that are part of the kernel mode. The kernel mode isolates programmatic control of hardware from the user mode, thus making the system both more stable and more secure. These two different layers were designed to execute in separate memory addresses, further isolating the User mode from direct hardware control. Figure 1.2 shows a schematic of the Windows 2000 operating system.

FIGURE 1.2
The heritage of the Windows operating system architecture is evident in this diagram of Windows 2000/XP.

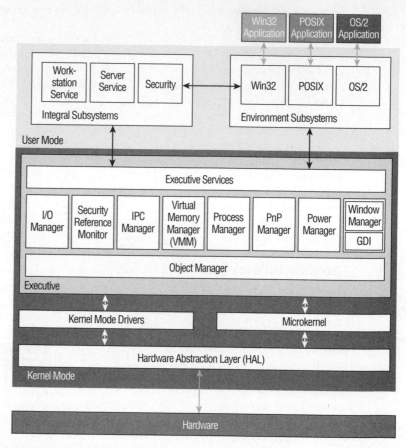

The kernel mode contains several major subsystems that are fundamental to its operation. The Hardware Abstraction Layer (HAL) is software that is specifically compiled for the hardware platform that Windows runs on, and is designed to make the operating system portable. When Windows is ported to a different type of computer, the HAL can be recompiled for that platform's instruction set. The HAL thus preserves the code, command set, and APIs of the remaining kernel mode components. The HAL's hardware code controls I/O interfaces, interrupts, and processor access.

The microkernel contains a minimal operating system: upon startup, it loads essential services for address space management, thread management services, and Inter-Process Communication (IPC). IPC is a set of methods for exchanging data between threads in one or more processes. In an operating system with a true microkernel, the size of that microkernel is very small. Real-time operating systems (RTOSs) that are used in embedded systems, such as vending machines or in cars, contain a microkernel. The Windows operating system is more appropriately referred to as a hybrid kernel.

Executive Services communicate with the user mode subsystems, converting program commands into object code in the Object Manager. Executive Services is where you find low-level security routines, interface and process management, graphics display routines, power management, and other vital services that make Windows Windows. These subsystems are organized into a set of "Managers," examples of which are the I/O Manager, Memory Manager, Cache Manager, Object Manager, and so forth.

In Windows 2000 (and Windows NT before that), the user mode contained two subsystems: those with integral services and an environmental subsystem. The environmental subsystem is a set of operating system routines that allow Windows to run different operating systems. The Win32 subsystem can run 32-bit Windows applications, and through Virtual DOS Machines (VDMs), it could also run 16-bit applications such as MS-DOS and Windows 3.1 in emulation. Environmental modules are extensible, as you can see with the module that supports OS/2 and another that supports the POSIX standard of Unix.

The integral subsystem in the user mode provides services to the environmental subsystem. High-level security such as resource access and the Active Directory is implemented in this security subsystem. The other two subsystems are networking services. Workstation is an API that communicates with the network redirector and communicates with other systems. Server is the API to a service that allows that local computer to provide services to other systems on the network.

With this brief overview of the Windows 2000 architecture, let's turn our attention to the changes that Windows Server 2008 and Vista SP1 have ushered in.

Architecture for Windows Server 2008

Microsoft first unveiled Windows Server 2008's architecture at the Microsoft Professional Developers Conference in 2003. Figure 1.3 shows the original system block diagram that detailed the major projects under the Windows Server 2008 umbrella.

FIGURE 1.3
Microsoft's original plans for their Windows Server 2008 project included reworking all of the higher-level system functions.

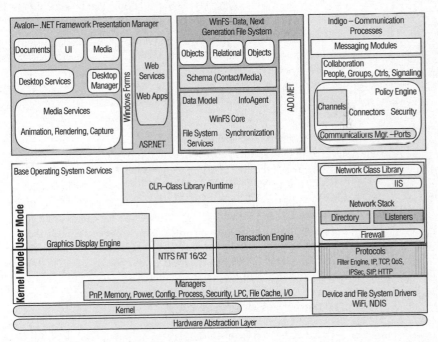

For an image map with a description of each of these separate modules, go to

http://www.ftponline.com/resources/longhorn/baseos.asp

Nearly all of the user mode modules were to be replaced in the new operating system. Among the changes were:

Avalon   Avalon was Microsoft's new presentation layer and next-generation user interface. Avalon became the Windows Presentation Foundation (WPF), and is the graphical front end to Microsoft .NET Framework 3.0 (once called WinFX).

Avalon introduces multiple new graphics standards. The API supported Extensible Application Markup Language (XAML) vector graphics (a form of XML), as well as extending 3D graphics with Direct3D. With the introduction of Direct3D version 10, Microsoft has a new video standard for rendering that introduces advanced shading and rendering technologies. Windows Server 2008 dropped support for the competing industry standard OpenGL, which now requires third-party support. Microsoft Silverlight is an XAML/JavaScript implementation of WPF that enables Flash-type vector animation based on .NET programming code.

Aero   Aero was the user experience module that brought the 3D graphics envisioned in the Windows Palladium project to commercialization. Aero overlies the presentation module. While Aero is much more important in the Vista Client, you can enable Aero on Windows Server 2008 as well.

Indigo   Indigo was the first network communication API. Indigo became the Windows Communication Foundation (WCF), and is a message service that allows programs to operate either locally or remotely. With WCF a program written in any language can be targeted to operate in a .NET virtual machine at runtime, and can run both locally and remotely as needed. WCF creates a service, a host environment to contain the service, a contract that defines the service methods, and the endpoints to which clients can communicate. It's rather similar in concept to how web services are supposed to operate.

WinFS   Windows Future Storage (WinFS) is a new relational database storage subsystem containing the next version of the Windows file system. WinFS didn't make the first release of Windows Server 2008, although some of the technologies were to be integrated into the next generation of Microsoft SQL Server (Katmai) and ADO.NET Entity Framework. According to Steve Balmer, CEO at Microsoft, this project is still alive and will be released at some unspecified later date.

CLR   Common Language Runtime (CLR) is the virtual machine module of Microsoft .NET. CLR is the Microsoft implementation of the Common Language Infrastructure (CLI) standard, which allows code written in high-level languages such as C# or Visual Basic .NET to be compiled using the Microsoft Intermediate Language (MSIL) as needed for runtime. MSIL is Microsoft's implementation of the Common Intermediate Language.

Network Class Libraries   Network Class Libraries are a set of objects that provide simple access to network services. You can set object properties, events, and methods, and use these objects in code to access the features of network protocols. The work in new network services in Windows Server 2008 has resulted in an entirely new TCP/IP stack (among other changes) for both Vista and Windows Server 2008.

WinFS and the Road beyond Cairo

WinFS is the latest incarnation of the Object File System that Microsoft has been talking about for nearly eight years now. So its failure to be included in Windows Server 2008 is certainly a major disappointment to many of us who follow the Windows platform professionally. WinFS, as you can clearly see in Figure 1.3, was at the center of Microsoft's plans for their new operating system. You can take WinFS's deletion as a measure of how extraordinarily difficult it is to switch the hierarchical file structure found in FAT and NTFS to an object-oriented relational database structure, where data is interwoven by tags and metadata.

Step back in time (if you would) to 1998 when the concept of an object-oriented file system was part of the Cairo project (circa 1991–1995). Cairo was the Twilight Zone of Windows Server, and the road to Cairo had many potholes. Cairo was abandoned, the object-oriented file system was put on hold, and a less ambitious project called Windows NT 5.0 came into being. According to legend, Windows NT 5.0 was the last major version of the Windows operating system that didn't bear a code name. NT 5.0 was branded as Windows 2000 Server.

The object-oriented file system was also a natural tool for the Component Object Model (COM) (begun in 1993), as COM supports object-oriented distributed IPC. A new file system called Storage+ was described (but never shipped) that supported COM. COM is the direct ancestor of a slew of technologies, including Object Linking and Embedding (OLE), OLE Automation, ActiveX, COM+, and Distributed COM. COM laid the groundwork for the current era's technologies: Microsoft .NET Framework and Web Services supported by the Windows Communication Foundation (WCF).

Given this long history of development, it's worth noting exactly why this technology has garnered so much interest at Microsoft. As it stands now, data stored by applications running on Windows can be "rich" in the sense that they contain complex data, but they aren't easily integrated with the data from other applications. This is a long-standing computer industry problem. A hospital might have a database that stores text fields, memo fields (large text fields), number fields, picture fields, even things commonly called BLOBs (Binary Large Objects) in a unified data store. That database might know that one field stores phone numbers, another field stores the X-ray images of its patients, and so on, but another application wouldn't be able to have knowledge of this metadata without a lot of additional programming.

Here's where the object-oriented file system comes into play. Suppose the hospital wanted to do a search for people of a certain age, who lived in a certain location, and whose X-ray indicated that they had a condition of concern in common so that they could contact those people with a letter. You can certainly do many, if not most of those things, in a database, but you couldn't do all of that from your operating system because the data is stored in proprietary or different formats, and stored without the metadata necessary to tie it all together. But if the file system could do this, you would achieve the following:

◆ Data independence of any application

◆ Integrated storage with a single data model

◆ Single instance storage where only one instance of the same object is stored

◆ Advanced search and data collection

◆ Expert systems and advanced data mining

So it's clear why Microsoft continues to develop technology in this area, and why what they learn becomes part of every major new data store such as Exchange, SQL Server, or Active Directory, that we see—just not, for the time being, the Windows Server file system.

THE CHILD OF .NET

Every version of the Windows operating system has at least one major initiative that it becomes known for. With Windows 95 and Windows NT 3.5 and 4.0, the major advances were made in networking and internetworking. Windows 95 gave us Internet Explorer integrated into the operating system (for good and ill, mostly ill), while NT provided the necessary wide area network (WAN) protocols that made the Internet accessible. With Windows Server 2000, the big advance was the incorporation of Active Directory, domains, and security structures.

Windows Server 2008 will most likely become best known for the APIs that managed the code necessary to integrate the .NET Framework into the operating systems. .NET 3.0 isolates the user interface aspects of an application on the client, while allowing the services themselves to be abstracted. Services become truly distributed so that they can run seamlessly on a local server or remote server.

Windows .NET 3.0 communicates with Windows Server 2008 through the four server APIs shown in Figure 1.4.

FIGURE 1.4
The .NET 3.0 stack
in Vista and now
Windows Server 08

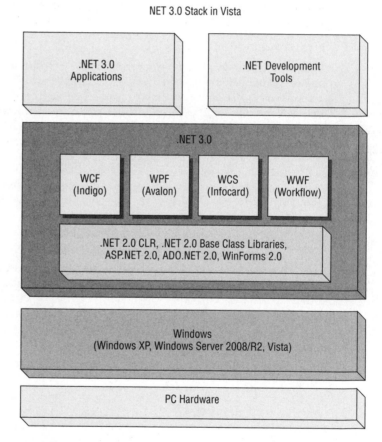

NET 3.0 Stack in Vista

Windows Workflow Foundation (WWF)   WWF is an API that allows an application to schedule and manage tasks, as well as sequences of tasks as integrated processes that are called workflows. WWF provides the system calls to apply business logic to objects, and the necessary mechanics to ensure that transaction integrity is maintained.

WWF manages objects in the .NET namespace, has a workflow engine, and supports program code created by Visual Studio 2005. The Microsoft website for WWF is at

`http://msdn2.microsoft.com/en-us/netframework/aa663328.aspx`

Windows CardSpace (WCS)   Formerly InfoCard, WCS is a software framework that provides access to secure digital identity stores, and access to authentication mechanisms for verifying logins on the Internet. CardSpace is part of the Microsoft Identity Metasystem initiative, whose goal is to unify identities across vendors and applications.

CardSpace applications demand virtual identification cards from users, and then create a secure token that is passed to the authentication authority users to define virtual information cards that can be passed to applications as user queries. When the user successfully answers the questions, the service transmits a digitally signed XML token that provides access to the application. Card-Space resources can be found at

`http://msdn2.microsoft.com/en-us/netframework/aa663320.aspx`

Windows Communication Foundation (WCF)   WCF is the new IPC communication stack and was described previously under the Indigo project. WCF is a service-oriented model that accesses the .NET namespace and that can span multiple network transport protocols, security systems, and messaging formats. Since WCF can span different services and protocols, it can also communicate across different topologies and architectures. Microsoft hopes to unify many of its older web services with WCF. For more information about WCF, refer to the MSDN site at

`http://msdn2.microsoft.com/en-us/netframework/aa663324.aspx`

Windows Presentation Foundation (WPF)   WPF is the user interface portion of the service and was described in detail under the Avalon project. More technical information about WPF may be found on MSDN at

`http://msdn2.microsoft.com/en-us/netframework/aa663326.aspx`

While all of these subsystems are APIs, they will be expressed by applications as a set of common features and functions that is enabled by Windows Server 2008 in the same sense that Active Directory was expressed in domain and application logons and in the common management routines used for diverse hardware and software. The .NET footprint will give Windows Server 2008 and Vista a certain look and feel that is unique to this particular server and client.

KERNEL MODIFICATIONS

From a hardware perspective (Figure 1.5) the kernel serves the same function that a conductor in an orchestra does. From a software perspective, the kernel is the program that interprets program commands to determine what operations are possible and what operations are allowed. The kernel doesn't directly communicate with the microprocessor. Instead, the kernel passes its commands in through to an assembler, which translates the commands into assembly or machine language, which is the actual microcode that the microprocessor understands. Modern assemblers create object code from assembly instructions.

Hardware I/O is made a kernel function for good reason. The kernel runs in what is called *protected mode*, isolating software from hardware. Figure 1.5 shows the basic topology of the kernel. The kernel isolates hardware from bad programs and bad programmers, and isolates good programs and good programmers from bad hardware. When a device fails, the kernel provides a graceful recovery from catastrophic failure.

FIGURE 1.5
An operating system's kernel isolates hardware from software.

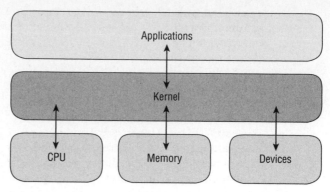

In Figure 1.6, the kernel stack is shown as a program stack, in contrast to the more hardware-centric illustration shown in Figure 1.5. The central features of the kernel are:

◆ Processor scheduling and threading

◆ Memory access and management

◆ Device I/O, often using device drivers

◆ Synchronization and communications

◆ Interprocess communication (IPC), or the timed management of events

FIGURE 1.6
The kernel communicates with hardware through the assembler.

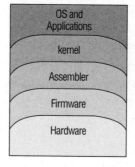

Changes to an operating system's kernel have a fundamental impact on all application and services. Although Microsoft doesn't advertise kernel changes to the general public, in part because they are more often used by developers rather than end users, Windows Server 2008 has several kernel enhancements that will significantly improve the system. Changes were made in Windows Server 2008 to the following system kernel functions:

◆ Memory and heap management. Memory is allocated from a large pool of available and unused memory that is called the *heap*. The heap is managed by indirect reference using a set of algorithms that organize the memory, allocate memory, and release the memory when it is no longer needed. Changes to the heap management routines can result in faster performance and better reliability. Every so often, Microsoft changes these routines, as is the case for the Windows Server 2008 and Vista core.

◆ Registry management; new features include performance optimizations, transactional support for Registry reads and writes, Registry filtering, and a Registry virtualization feature that can run legacy applications in isolated nonadministrator accounts.

◆ A new service model; a new type of service called Delayed Auto-Start decreases your server's apparent boot time by waiting until after your system boots to start these additional unattended started services. Other changes to services included a change in the Service Control Manager to isolate services by running them at the lowest level of privilege that they can allow, thus reducing their security vulnerabilities.

◆ Improvements to the Hardware Abstraction Layer (HAL) mechanism that support the new EFI and BCD boot environments (see the upcoming section "The New Boot Environment").

◆ The new Windows Hardware Error Architecture (WHEA). WHEA continues Microsoft's long, hard road down the path to meaningful system error diagnostics. It builds on the PCI Express Advanced Reporting to provide more detailed information about system errors and a common reporting structure.

◆ Kernel patch protection, code signing to ensure code integrity, and support for a more restricted version of protected processes—all of which are security features. These features are not new, but have been upgraded.

◆ A new dynamic link library (DLL) loader and improved thread pool.

◆ Hardware features such as dynamic partitioning, improvements to PCI/PCI Express interface, and the new boot environment.

◆ Power management and the ACPI 2.0 (Advanced Configuration and Power Interface) power-saving feature.

◆ Support for improved Plug and Play (PnP).

◆ Kernel-based digital signature security for drivers that can prevent unauthorized streamed content, for system patches, and for kernel-mode software installation.

Windows Server 2008 and Vista SP1 share the same kernel. That means that the first refresh of Vista to SP1 will bring many of these enhancements not only to the Windows Server platform but to the Vista client as well. It also means that Vista SP1 was in fact a major upgrade for Vista, as it is very rare for Microsoft to do a full kernel swap of a client as part of a point release. Vista SP1 is essentially a "new" operating system, and a full partner of Windows Server 2008.

Memory Support

The Windows operating system has a sophisticated memory manager, but in order to establish new capabilities in memory hardware and software access memory addressing is often changed. Microsoft made several changes to memory to support enterprise-class server systems, dynamic hardware partitioning, the new video architecture, and Terminal Services. They also modified their caching algorithms. One particular area that was completely reworked was the heap manager. The heap manager is a reference structure that points to the free store of unallocated memory. Since memory is used and released, this indirect system optimizes how memory is accessed and by whom. Memory access affects performance as well as the basic security of a system.

Non-Uniform Memory Architecture (NUMA) systems are large, multiprocessor, high-performance server systems that provide shared memory access. NUMA systems are particularly valuable to large enterprise operations because a NUMA system virtualizes hardware. In a multiprocessor system, you can have some processors running Unix and others running Windows, with each instance of an operating system running independently of the others. As the organization requires more computational power for one operating system, additional processors can be taken from one OS and given to the other. For NUMA to run effectively, it must be able to manage both CPUs and memory as a dynamic pool. The Memory Manager in Windows Server 2008 was rewritten to allow better handling of the allocation of virtual addresses, kernel page tables, and for the support for very large Registries, all features that make NUMA more robust.

If you've been running Vista, you know that the video subsystem was substantially upgraded from previous Windows versions. Part of the new graphics subsystem in Windows Server 2008 and Vista offloads more graphics routines from the CPU onto the video card's graphics processing unit (GPU), which calls for considerably more video memory. The Aero Glass interface requires a minimum of 256MB of video RAM. Simply maintaining the Windows+Alt CoolSwitch, Flip, or Task Switcher application requires something on the order of 56MB of video RAM.

Terminal Server received a big enhancement in Windows Server 2008, and that is the subject of Chapter 12. The main operational difference from a user prospective is the Terminal Services RemoteApp feature. A RemoteApp is a program that you can run in a Terminal Server session that behaves as if it was running locally on the user's computer. RemoteApp removes the problems users had with managing Terminal Server sessions and moving between the local desktop and the remote desktop. When two or more RemoteApps run, they can do so within the same Terminal Server session. To support RemoteApps the Memory Manager introduces a new type of memory construct called Terminal Services session objects. RemoteApps makes the experience of using the virtual desktop of Terminal Server equivalent (also known as transparent) in terms of user experience to local applications, something that will make it much easier for users to learn and use.

THE NEW BOOT ENVIRONMENT

Microsoft has created a completely new boot environment for Windows Vista and Windows Server 2008 that greatly improves the installation of the operating system, handling of backups and restores from images, and direct system startup into a mini-OS that is capable of network installations, system diagnostics, and repairs. The most important part of this new feature is the Boot Configuration Data (BCD) store. BCD is Windows Server 2008 itself, albeit a stripped-down version of Windows.

The BCD can boot from the PC BIOS or from the newer Extensible Firmware Interface (EFI). EFI is the renamed version of the Intel Boot Initiative, which is now supported by an industry group called the Unified Extensible Firmware Interface (UEFI) Forum (http://www.uefi.org). EFI is a software interface between the operating system and your computer's firmware that maintains a current table of platform information; boot services such as console, bus, and file system services; and runtime services such as Date/Time and the information contained in nonvolatile RAM. One of the nicest features of EFI's boot manager is the ability to abstract device drivers, a bootable shell (EFI Shell), and an extensible architecture.

NOTE   Sixty-four-bit Windows Server 2008 will not boot from a system with PC BIOS, or by using an abstraction layer. EFI is a requirement for any Intel Itanium system loading 64-bit Windows Server; Vista makes no such requirement on 64-bit chips such as AMD Opteron and others.

BCD is available during and after system boot, and while it was meant to support Vista and Windows Server 2008 it is a great general-purpose boot environment that can support numerous third-party tools. Indeed, many utilities will appear based on BCD in the future. There is some backward compatibility to Windows 2003 and XP; BCD will correctly launch NTLDR.EXE, which then draws its configurational data from the BOOT.INI file. Since BCD is so central to Microsoft's automated Windows deployment system, you'll find a more complete discussion of the BCD and deployment in the next chapter.

Windows Server 2008 SP1 and the 64-Bit Architecture

Microsoft has said on several occasions that Windows Server 2008 is the last version of the Windows operating system that would be designed in a 32-bit version. Therefore, if you aren't supporting an older application or some specialized hardware, installing the 64-bit version of Windows Server 2008 is a more forward-looking decision. Rumor is that Microsoft will release some service packs for its 32-bit server, but how long that version will continue to be supported is somewhat vague.

You can run 32-bit programs on 64-bit Windows Server 2008 in emulation. An emulator called WoW64 (Windows-on-Windows 64-bit) that runs in user mode interfaces between the 32-bit version of NTDLL.DLL and the kernel, intercepting kernel calls and redirecting them. WoW64 provides core emulation for NTOSKRNL.EXE. The WOW64.WIN.DLL performs memory management for 32-bit Windows programs, "thunking" data. Thunking data means that there is either a delayed computation or a mapping of machine data from one system form to another for compatibility. In this case, it is the latter. WoW64 maps 32-bit calls to 64-bit addresses, analyzes the returned data, and maps the data back to the 32-bit application running on Windows Server 2008. Support for 32-bit programs on Vista or Windows Server 2008 is good but not perfect, and with all emulations performance suffers. Native 64-bit programs almost always run faster because the code is optimized for higher throughput.

Virtualization and the Hypervisor

Most studies of network computing have consistently shown that the majority of servers operate with very low CPU utilization rates. If nearly 80 percent to 90 percent of your processing power is idle, you have not gotten your money's worth and there's an opportunity to realize considerable value. That's why virtualization is a hot topic; virtualization saves you money across the board with machines, plant costs, software, and personnel costs.

One of Microsoft's major project goals for Windows Server 2008 was to deliver a virtual machine technology that was bulletproof, highly compatible with the array of Windows software, and robust. The theme of virtualization is a common one, and is applied to the concept of dynamic allocation of resources. Virtualization abstracts physical hardware through a programmed reference system that dynamically points to and manages available assets. Physical memory is always virtualized with swap files on disk, and storage can be virtualized through RAID and across systems with a volume-based namespace.

Microsoft's goals were to virtualize CPU, memory, storage, and even network interfaces, and thus to be able to hot-swap virtual machines across hardware even as they are running. (The ability to hot-swap an entire operating system instance is something that is called Live Migration, but that is one feature that didn't make the first release of Microsoft's Windows Server 2008 virtualization package and will ship in a later version.) Imagine being able to run several operating systems or instances of an operating system, all isolated in their own virtual machine. You simply assign processors from a pool to an application instance upon demand. Virtualization is very powerful.

Windows Server virtualization is the result of a project that was code-named Viridian, and is an ongoing project at Microsoft. The group formed shortly after Microsoft acquired Connectrix and their Virtual PC program. Windows Server virtualization achieved some of these goals, and surely there is more to come. Microsoft System Center Virtual Machine Manager 2007, part of the Microsoft System Center family of system management products, permits you to define policies about resources and performance and lets you control all these features from a single console.

Virtualization is achieved using a program called a hypervisor. A hypervisor acts as an I/O redirector. Depending on the type of hypervisor you have, it is possible to run virtual machines that are compatible with any operating system that is compatible with the platform. For the x86 architecture, that would mean any or all of the following: different versions of Windows or DOS, Linux, NetWare, Solaris for x86, and maybe one day Macintosh. The Macintosh's Boot Camp utility allows you to run Windows on a Macintosh in a virtual machine on x86 today; an even better solution exists with Parallels (http://www.parallels.com/). You can find a rather extensive table comparing different virtual machine technologies at

http://en.wikipedia.org/wiki/Comparison_of_virtual_machines

Be forewarned that this is an area of great activity, so the list is volatile and subject to change.

A hypervisor controls an entire computer system. Hypervisors have been around for quite some time in various forms, and they are one of the favorite methods hackers use to take full control over systems. Indeed, Microsoft's hypervisor technology (which is now called Microsoft Hyper-V and is available as an option for Windows Server 2008) will probably make it impossible for competitors to gain this type of access in the future. A hypervisor can run two or more operating systems on:

◆ The same processor

◆ Different cores of a multicore processor

◆ Different cores on different single or multicore processors

There are actually two types of hypervisors, and each has some limits on its capabilities:

Type 1 Hypervisor This is a lightweight operating system that runs in a layer that loads over hardware and below the operating system that the hypervisor "hosts." The hypervisor boots the system and receives privileged access to Ring 0 and other low-level services. The first Type 1 hypervisor was probably IBM's CP/CMS system; IBM still uses the technology with their z/VM OS product. Other Type 1 hypervisors are VMware's ESX Server and Sun Microsystems' Logical Domains hypervisor, which was introduced in 2005. Figure 1.7 shows a Type 1 hypervisor.

FIGURE 1.7
Type 1 Hypervisor

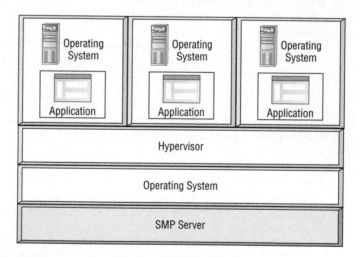

Type 2 Hypervisor Windows Server 2008 virtualization programs use a different type of hypervisor, referred to as a Type 2 hypervisor or Type 2 virtual machine, as shown in Figure 1.8. This type of program runs after the operating system has been loaded, and the guest operating system runs "on top of" or using the services of the hypervisor. The two most popular virtualization products in the world are probably VMware (http://www.vmware.com), which is now owned by EMC, and Virtual PC, which was acquired by Microsoft from Connectix. VMware is

the market leader. Both VMware and Virtual PC are Type 2 virtual machines. Figure 1.8 shows a Type 2 hypervisor.

FIGURE 1.8
Type 2 operating system

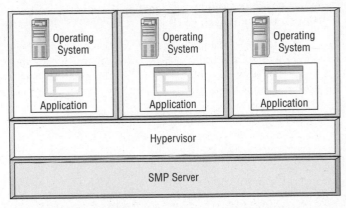

Virtual machines are often used to test applications and system configurations, to set up systems for performance testing (such as web clients used for loading), and to sandbox applications that might be unstable (such as beta software) or unsafe (testing viruses and malware). Sandboxing isolates applications from other programs on your system, and is used both for security and compatibility reasons.

Hyper-V adds virtualization capabilities directly into Windows Server 2008 (Figure 1.9), and creates a thin-layer Type 1 hypervisor that will co-exist with their type 2 Virtual Server product. You can run both or either of these two products individually, or migrate from the Virtual PC to the more powerful hypervisor product. The advantages of such a system is that it will allow finer control over hardware than a Type 2 system, easier dynamic allocations, and subsocket partitioning.

When Windows Server 2008 ships, Windows Server virtualization will allow systems to run up to 16 cores or logical processors at a time. The original plan was to allow for 64 processor instances. Other features that were scaled back to allow Windows Server 2008 to ship at the beginning of 2008 were some of the hot-add capabilities for both storage and memory. Hot swap, hot add, and Live Migration, as well as 64-processor limits, are features that competing products already have.

This version finally adds support for 64-bit programs running in 64-bit guest sessions, something that the earlier version couldn't do. Eventually Microsoft virtualization will permit users to migrate live systems entirely from one virtual system to another, and support the hot swap and hot additions of processors, memory, networking interfaces, and storage—but these features did not ship with the first release of Windows Server 2008 and were delayed until later. A Type 1 hypervisor should enable features like the hot edition of a network card or processor without reboot. The current plans are to have Windows running up to eight processors, and from 4GB to 32GB per each virtual machine.

Virtualization is an important feature, and is now part of competitive server platforms such as SUSE and Red Hat Linux, both of which have incorporated VMware into their systems. These systems use the Xen open source virtual machine, which is currently at version 3.0. This version will run Windows as a guest, and XenSource is expected to release a compatibility layer for the Windows Server 2008 hypervisor. Systems that run Xen guests can use this compatibility layer to move their sessions to Windows Server 2008. Xen is a Type 1 hypervisor; it runs in Ring 0 while its guest OSs run in Ring 1.

FIGURE 1.9
Windows Server
2008's virtualization
architecture

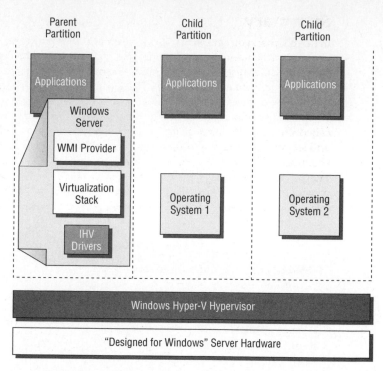

Hardware vendors have also incorporated virtualization instructions directly into their processors over the last couple of years. Intel calls their technology for the x86 architecture Intel VT (for Virtualization Technology); while their virtualization technology for the 64-bit Itanium series is called VT-i. To be enabled, Intel's VT requires that both the chip set and the software support these features. AMD's hardware extensions are called AMD Virtualization, or AMD-V. All K8 processors with F stepping support AMD-V. Stepping is similar to the version number in software, in that it increases as the process gets older and more optimized; hopefully, making the processor faster and more stable. The Standard Performance Evaluation Corporation (SPEC) has a working group developing methods to test virtualization technologies using their developed benchmarks.

As you consider virtualization as an option, consider also that virtualization will probably change Microsoft's licensing model. Currently, servers are sold with a base license for which you purchase additional packages of licenses on a per-processor basis. With virtualization, Microsoft can change their model to a per-instance license. The pricing scheme at launch includes eight versions of Windows Server 2008, with Windows Server 2008 Standard, Enterprise, and Datacenter editions offered both with and without the Hyper-V virtualization technology. Virtualization will appear on both 32- and 64-bit versions of Server, with the exception of the Itanium version of Server, which comes only in the 64-bit version. On average, Hyper-V adds around $30 to the cost of a server license, per processor, for all of these versions.

Summary

In this chapter, you saw how Windows Server 2008 has advanced architecturally. Higher user-level services, presentation, and graphics got a major boost in this version. Some base modules in the kernel module were also reworked and improved. Virtualization is a work in progress, but one that will eventually be quite powerful. There were also advances in systems such as Terminal Server that will be discussed later in the book.

One of the changes in Windows Server technology is the creation of a new boot environment called Windows Preinstallation Environment (PE). Windows PE is a light version of Windows that will let you boot to a working instance of Windows Server 2008 for both installation and troubleshooting. With Windows PE, you can initiate network installations; create, modify, and use system images; and automate your deployment of multiple systems with fine control. The next chapter considers what Windows PE can do for you, and how all of this new technology will impact your installation and deployment of Windows Server 2008 and Vista.

Chapter 2

Deploying Windows Server 2008

If you install Windows Server 2008 from a DVD locally, you might not notice that the installation routine for the Windows operating system hasn't changed much from previous versions. You'll see a set of dialog boxes similar to the ones that appeared in Windows Server 2003 and XP. You also might not notice that the installation proceeds a little faster than before. When you perform a network installation from a share point, those installations don't seem operationally different than in past versions either.

These similarities are deceptive. In almost all aspects, Windows Server 2008 installation rewrites the book on how Microsoft performs installations, how they package their products, and how people will deploy their operating systems going forward. The underlying philosophy becomes dramatically obvious when you perform automated installations, gear up to deploy installations on multiple systems, and perform medium- and large-scale deployments. Microsoft has made more advances in the deployment area than in any other area of Windows Server 2008 technology with the exception of the work that's been done on the .NET Framework and the underlying presentation services.

In this chapter, Microsoft's grand strategy for reducing the amount of pain administrators feel during Windows deployments and upgrades is unveiled. Several prominent research analysis companies have estimated that simply deploying Windows on a system in the enterprise can cost as much as $1,000 per computer. So the cost savings of implementing an efficient deployment strategy can be considerable. After looking at the installation of an individual server in brief, this chapter builds toward larger and larger methods for automated deployment.

Central to the new deployment technology is the creation and management of system images. Images are contained inside a new type of container file, the Windows image file (WIM), which replaces cabinet (CAB) files. New or improved tools from Microsoft support the migration of user settings when required, and allow a much finer control over the unattended installation answer file than was possible in previous versions. In medium-sized deployments, a partially automated deployment scenario called a "Lite Touch Installation" is described. Microsoft's scenario for large-sized deployments that are fully automated, called the "Zero Touch Installation," can be integrated with Systems Management Server (SMS), Microsoft Operations Manager (MOM), and the other large network management packages.

If you have deployed Windows 2003 using Microsoft's tools, you will find that all of those tools have been upgraded. There are also some new tools that this chapter introduces. The Windows Automated Installation Kit (WAIK), which includes Windows PE 2.0, the User State Migration Toolkit (USMT), and the System Image Management Utility, are all more powerful. The Application Compatibility Toolkit (ACT), an inventory system for software and hardware, can be used to create compatibility and remediation reports, and integrates with online resources such as vendor and user forums to provide even more information. For larger deployments, Microsoft offers the Business Desktop Deployment (BDD) Solution Accelerator, which collects all of these resources (along with a set of best-practice guides based on Microsoft's consulting practice) under one unified application called the BDD 2007 Workbench. With BDD 2007's team-based approach, a large-scale deployment is organized into functional teams for phased deployment. Both Lite Touch and Zero Touch deployments, as well as integration with network system management packages such as SMS, are supported by this solution.

All of these technologies come together to form a Windows installation system for the enterprise. Building on tools such as Windows PE and the USMT, Microsoft's BDD is a framework in which these tools, along with the Windows System Image Manager, WAIK, and other applications are integrated. Taken together, these technologies substantially improve the efficiency, control, and accuracy of any deployment of Windows systems, greatly amplifying what one administrator can accomplish and lowering any company's total cost of ownership for their Windows-based systems.

Stand-alone Server Installation

Most users who have installed Windows Server directly from distribution media will feel comfortable installing Windows Server 2008. The installation is both faster and requires fewer steps to complete. When Setup loads, a screen appears offering information about the system requirements. Table 2.1 shows the current system requirements for running Windows Server 2008.

TABLE 2.1: Microsoft's Recommended Requirements for Windows Server 2008

COMPONENT	REQUIREMENT
Processor	Minimum: 1GHz Recommended: 2GHz Optimal: 3GHz or faster **Note:** An Intel Itanium 2 processor is required for Windows Server 2008 for Itanium-based systems.
Memory	Minimum 512MB of RAM Recommended: 1GB of RAM Optimal: 2GB of RAM (Full installation) or 1GB of RAM (Server Core installation) or more Maximum (32-bit systems): 4GB (Standard) or 64GB (Enterprise and Datacenter) Maximum (64-bit systems): 32GB (Standard) or 2TB (Enterprise, Datacenter, and Itanium-based systems)
Available Disk Space	Minimum: 8GB Recommended: 40GB (Full installation) or 10GB (Server Core installation) Optimal: 80GB (Full installation) or 40GB (Server Core installation) or more **Note:** Computers with more than 16GB of RAM will require more disk space for paging, hibernation, and dump files.
Drive	DVD-ROM drive
Display and Peripherals	Super VGA (800 x 600) or higher-resolution monitor Keyboard Microsoft Mouse or compatible pointing device

Source: http://technet.microsoft.com/en-us/windowsserver/2008/bb414778.aspx

You will be asked about updating the installation with the latest components in the second screen, as shown in Figure 2.1.

FIGURE 2.1
The second Setup screen asks if you want to upgrade components during installation. For a stand-alone installation, it's a good idea to do so.

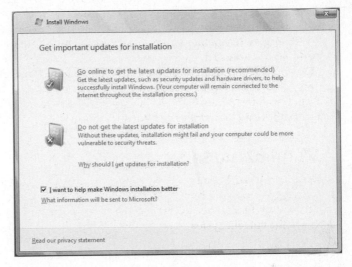

The one critical step in the installation appears as the next decision point. That step asks you to choose your version of the Windows Server 2008 operating system. The Windows Server 2008's installation media, just like Vista's, bundles all versions of the operating system into a single installation disc. If you examine the installation media, you will find that there is only one installation configuration—an example of the utility of the single-instance image container WIM files. Figure 2.7 later in this chapter shows the contents of that WIM file from within the Windows System Image Manager (Windows SIM). Table 2.2 describes these editions.

TABLE 2.2: A Comparison Matrix for Windows Server 2008 Editions

EDITION	PURPOSE	KEY FEATURES
Web	Building and hosting websites and services	No Client Access Licenses (CALs) required Terminal Server mode Cannot act as a domain controller Up to four processors (sockets) 10 client connection limit **Note:** This edition is planned but not implemented yet.
Standard	Small to medium businesses, general-purpose server	Support for file, print, secure Internet, and centralized desktop deployment
Enterprise	Medium to large businesses	Up to eight processors Clustering Non-uniform Memory Architecture (NUMA) and large memory access
Datacenter	High-security and -reliability applications	Minimum of eight processors, maximum of 64 Dynamic allocation of processors and memory

TABLE 2.2:   A Comparison Matrix for Windows Server 2008 Editions *(CONTINUED)*

EDITION	PURPOSE	KEY FEATURES
Standard Core	Single-purpose server for small to medium businesses	Low attack surface Similar performance characteristics to Standard
Enterprise Core	Single-purpose server for medium to large businesses	Similar performance characteristics to Enterprise
Datacenter Core	Single-purpose server for high-security and -reliability applications	Similar performance characteristics to Datacenter

After accepting the End-User License Agreement (EULA), you will be prompted to either upgrade or perform a custom (advanced) installation. The choices are enabled by what Setup detects on your boot drive. Custom is the fresh install option. Figure 2.2 shows the installation type screen.

FIGURE 2.2
Select the type of installation in this step.

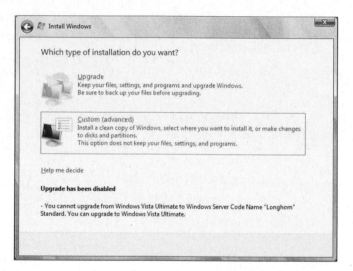

DISKPART, the new disk partition and formatting utility, runs and the last significant selection step in Setup appears. Here you can load device drives, select the boot partition, and if necessary, create and format a partition (not shown in Figure 2.3). With the completion of this screen the remainder of the first phase of Setup completes, and after files are installed, the system reboots and you are asked to supply information such as time zone, network settings, and more that will be familiar to you from previous versions of Windows Server setups of the past.

FIGURE 2.3
DISKPART lets you select and create a boot partition, while the Load Driver link uses DRVLOAD to allow you to load drivers.

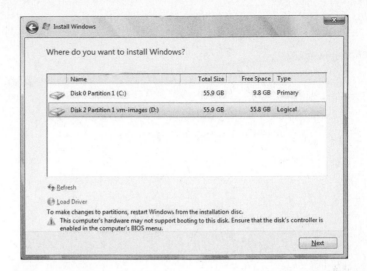

Server Deployments

A server-based deployment of systems is different from a stand-alone installation. In an installation, media is used to create a usable system one system at a time. Deployments create model systems, sometimes called master systems, where the compatibility of the configuration is tested and known prior to the installation on multiple systems. Deployments automate the process of installation, and thus require what is essentially a script that controls the deployment. For unattended installations, these scripts are called answer files. In Windows Server 2008 (and Vista) deployment uses an UNATTEND.XML file for a similar purpose.

Think of a deployment as akin to creating a recipe that can be rolled out to multiple systems of the same type. The bigger the deployment, the greater the need to use servers as the deployment engines—and Windows Server 2008 offers many advantages for Windows deployments. Deployments can be made fully automated, partially automated, or initiated and managed locally. There are three basic types of deployment scenarios, as illustrated in Figure 2.4:

Bare Metal, Fresh, or New System Deployment   Bare metal deployment formats a boot partition and installs the OS onto that drive. All prior data on the drive is lost.

System Upgrade   In a system upgrade, the new OS is installed *over* the old operating system. This type of deployment often retains your applications in an operable state. Your files, the file system of your boot drive, and many system settings are also retained.

Side-by-Side   A side-by-side deployment is a migration of applications and data from the older system to a system that has had Vista newly installed.

FIGURE 2.4
Microsoft's deployment technologies support three distinctly different types of system deployment: bare metal, upgrade, and a side-by-side scenario.

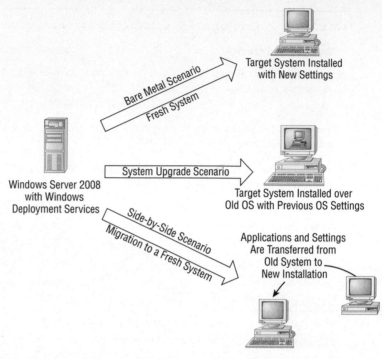

For large deployments, organizations may find that they are supporting all three types of deployments. Table 2.3 shows some of the advantages and disadvantages of the three basic deployment scenarios.

TABLE 2.3:   Comparing OS Deployment Scenarios

DESIRED PROPERTY	BEST SCENARIO
Prepare new computer systems for use by a user.	Bare metal or wipe-and-load scenario followed by user account migration.
Preserve the user's environment with the least amount of work.	System upgrade scenario.
Preserve the user's environment to create the most stable Vista system.	Side-by-side scenario followed by careful migration of compatible applications, settings, and user account.
Create the most stable Vista system.	Bare metal scenario followed by individual installation of certified applications and drivers.
Recycle old systems while migrating to new systems.	Use the side-by-side scenario; perform a migration of user accounts, applications, and settings. Then reformat old system and install an OS.

TABLE 2.3:   Comparing OS Deployment Scenarios *(CONTINUED)*

DESIRED PROPERTY	BEST SCENARIO
Create the system with the maximum compatibility to older applications.	Perform a side-by-side scenario followed by careful migration of compatible applications, settings, and user accounts.
Perform the lowest cost upgrade in terms of IT staff time and equipment.	Use the upgrade scenario.
Perform a deployment that allows you to migrate users from older legacy Windows OS (pre-Windows XP, etc.).	Perform a side-by-side scenario followed by careful migration of compatible applications, settings, and user accounts.
Create the best user experience for Windows Vista.	Start with new hardware and perform a fresh system or bare metal installation.
Extend the useful duty cycle of the organization's current set of computers.	Perform a side-by-side scenario followed by careful migration of compatible applications, settings, and user account.

Windows Preinstallation Environment

The Windows Preinstallation Environment (WinPE) 2.0 is a lightweight bootable version of the Windows Server 2008 core, also known as a microkernel. The original version of WinPE was developed by Microsoft for use by their large original equipment manufacturers (OEMs) like Dell and HP to make their PC manufacturing process more streamlined. Version 1.0 was based on Windows XP and version 1.1 on XP SP1.

Microsoft has taken what they've learned from their partners, borrowed some of the lessons from Windows Embedded, and created a highly practical boot environment. When a computer's BIOS passes off control of the system, WinPE loads to a command line. Think of WinPE as MS-DOS with networking support on steroids. WinPE 2.0 is now the boot environment of the Windows operating system installer, and ships with a small set of incredibly useful admin tools such as DISKPART, IMAGEX, DISKPART, DRVLOAD, NET, and NETCFG.

You can find Windows PE 2.0 and its supporting files in several locations:

◆ In the Vista or on the Windows Server 2008 installation disc

◆ In the Automated Installation Kit (discussed later)

◆ As part of the Microsoft Business Desktop Development (BDD) solution accelerator

◆ As part of various commercial utility packages

NOTE   The home page for the Microsoft Windows Preinstallation Environment is http:// www.microsoft.com/Licensing/sa/benefits/winpe.mspx.

It is also possible to download and use Windows PE separately if you have a partner or developer relationship with Microsoft. Windows PE 2.0 is not for widespread use, nor is it meant to be available to the average user. You won't find WinPE available for sale, nor can it be downloaded without registering the download. A license to install Windows Server 2008 or Vista, for that matter, does not give users the right to use Windows PE 2.0 in their own work. You have to have a system builder, OEM, or developer relationship with Microsoft to have that license. That is a shame, because Windows PE, along with the applications it provides such as IMAGEX, is a great way to back up your systems as images and provides a great solution for disaster recovery. Figure 2.5 compares Windows PE 2.0 to XP Pro and Server 2003.

NOTE Anyone interested in an open-source alternative to Windows PE should investigate BartPE, Bart Lagerweij's builder for a bootable live Windows CD or DVD. To obtain the BartPE builder, go to: www.nu.nu/pebuilder.

FIGURE 2.5
Windows PE 2.0 is a lightweight version operating system, and is operating system specific, as shown in this comparison between Vista/ Windows Server 2008 and XP/ Windows Server 2003.

Windows PE is valuable in not only deploying Windows Server 2008 and Vista, but in troubleshooting and repairing these operating systems. As Windows PE gets into wider use, I expect to see additional tools built on this technology specifically for diagnostic and remediation. For example, with Windows PE you replace damaged system files directly from a validated installation or WIM file so that you can then regain access to your system. Although Windows Server 2008 requires NTFS, it still supports FAT and FAT32 access, so Windows PE also provides access to these two different file types. Therefore, you can use WinPE to copy files to non-NTFS partitions for backup and restore. The same isn't true of Encrypting File System (EFS) partitions, which aren't accessible with WinPE.

An examination of the Windows Server 2008 installation disc shows you how the WinPE environment is structured. Figure 2.6 shows that the WinPE components are installed into the Boot folder.

FIGURE 2.6
WinPE files may be found in the Boot folder on the installation disc.

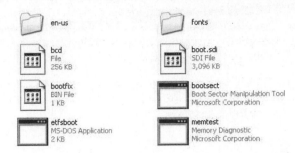

The files you see in Figure 2.6 have the following purposes:

Boot Configuration Data (BCD)   This file contains instructions and settings for boot applications, and replaces the BOOT.INI file used in Windows XP, Windows Server 2003, and prior versions.

The command-line tool BCDEDIT is used to modify the BCD. BCDEDIT is installed into Windows Server 2008 in the %WINDIR%\SYSTEM32 directory.

BOOTSECT   This tool modifies a hard drive boot sector so that BOOTMGR or NTLDR can access the drive.

BOOT.SDI   This file is a script that allows you to boot to images.

BOOTFIX   This is a boot sector testing and restore tool.

MEMTEST   A utility for testing a system's RAM prior to creating a RAM disk for the WinPE environment.

NOTE   To read "Walkthrough: Deploy an Image by Using PXE," go to http://technet2 .microsoft.com/WindowsVista/en/library/b001a736-91db-4f91-bd92- 278e267e06d91033.mspx?mfr=true.

One of WinPE's features is that it can be loaded into memory from removable media and run from a virtual RAM disk. The boot loader copies a compressed version of WinPE to the RAM disk. Once that is done, the boot loader mounts the RAM disk as the boot drive and starts the WinPE environment. With WinPE started, you can then remove the disc and put another disc in the drive that contains your utilities, needed drivers, and so on.

A Windows PE boot disc comes with the following command-line tools:

DISKPART   Creates and modifies disk partitions and volumes, replacing the FORMAT command.

DRVLOAD   Adds device drivers to an installation.

IMAGEX   Captures and modifies system images as WIM.

OSCDIMG.EXE   Creates an ISO file for a custom Windows PE build.

PEIMG.EXE   Creates and modifies WinPE images offline.

WINPESHL.INI   The Windows PE Shell is the initialization file for the WinPE command prompt.

WPEINIT.EXE   Initializes WinPE at boot time.

Most applications such as games and anything that requires the .NET Framework won't run, but many programs will. Windows PE excludes a number of I/O subsystems and some of the W32 networking APIs to limit its functionality. You will find that the following services aren't included in WinPE 2.0: access control, multimedia services, NetShow Theater Administration, OpenGL graphics rendering, power settings modification, print services, still image, tape backup services, terminal services and sessions, the Windows shell, user profile modification, and Windows station and desktop services. Note that OpenGL was removed from Vista and isn't in Windows Server 2008 either.

Windows PE 2.0 will run for 72 hours after it boots, and then shuts down. Prior versions would only run for 24 hours.

The Windows Imaging Format

Anyone who has suffered through rebuilding a Windows XP workstation from scratch knows how painful that process can be. If you are vigilant, backups can save you, provided your backup technology takes timely snapshots. A restore can be almost as painful as a rebuild, as you hope your software works well enough to apply the appropriate differential snapshots to your base copy. As the operating systems have gotten more complex, system imaging has become the preferred method of system backup. Images don't need to work at the file level, and indeed most don't. Most image programs work by copying data at the sector level without regard to the files they contain.

Symantec Ghost (formerly Norton Ghost), Paragon Technologies' Drive Backup, Acronis True Image, and Drive Snapshot, are examples of disk image backup utilities. ISO files are examples of sector-based image files. Sometimes this category of software is referred to as disk "cloning" software. A program such as Drive Snapshot or Ghost copies data on a sector-by-sector basis without regard for the data that the sector contains. Some system imaging programs are file based and maintain a directory of files that are part of an image; in that regard, file-based system imaging programs are similar to backup software.

When you move up to the large network management packages that are used to deploy systems en masse such as Altaris, LANDesk, Unicenter TNG, and IBM Tivoli, you'll find that those packages typically employ sector-based system images for their deployment. Sector-based images support a wider variety of file systems, different levels of RAID, and importantly for those packages, heterogeneous clients.

Windows Vista began and Windows Server 2008 extends Microsoft's new image-based installation technology. Using images to deploy systems isn't new; products like Norton Ghost have been doing it for years. However, Microsoft has extended the concept of images to single-instance container files called Windows imaging (WIM) files. At the operating system level, WIM is supported by the Windows Imaging API, `WIMGAPI`, which allows WIM files to be accessed and used by software. You can view the contents of a WIM file offline in software tools, as well as edit and manage the contents of the one or more system images that the file contains.

WIM files are the reason you can buy all of the versions of Vista on a single DVD as well as all the language support, and unlock your upgrade at a later date. You can view the contents of a WIM file in the Windows System Image Manager (SIM), where the single instancing becomes obvious when you go to open the Windows Server 2008 installation WIM file. As you can see in Figure 2.7, the utility asks you to specify the version of Windows Server 2008 that you want to install.

You can create WIM files from the command-line tool `IMAGEX` for storage and later deployment, viewing, adding to, and subtracting from the WIM image as needed.

Since WIM files support a specific operating system and a particular file system (NTFS), Microsoft's imaging technology is file based rather than sector based. While sector-based imaging has the advantages noted earlier, file-based imaging has its own set of advantages.

FIGURE 2.7
To see the contents of the Windows Server 2008 installation disc's WIM file, open it in the Windows System Image Manager; the dialog box prompts you for a selection of the version type.

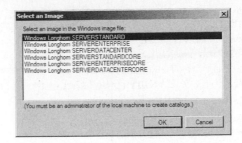

Because WIM files are sector based, those highly compressed files (about one-third of their original size) employ what is referred to as a Single Instance Storage (SIS) technology. In an SIS file, there is a single copy of any file kept in the WIM container. For example, if a certain DLL has the same file size, creation date, and modification date, only a single copy of that file would be kept even if it were used in all of the system images (Vista or Windows Server 2008) that are contained in the WIM file. Should a file be required in more than one location, a reference to that file is used in its place. Another nice feature of WIM files is that they don't require you to delete the original system directory or system partition prior to an installation. That is, it is possible to install from a WIM file without changing the contents of a disk, as the installation doesn't overwrite the files that already are on the disk.

WIM files are what made it possible to ship all of the versions of Windows Vista and Windows Server 2008, along with all their supported languages, on a unified DVD. Starting with a core component called MinWin, about 95 percent of the base code is installed. To include server roles and components, you then add modules to this core installation.

For Windows Server 2008, the modules change a standard server into an enterprise server, and so on. For Windows Vista, the additional modules are what transform Windows Vista Basic into Windows Vista Business, Premium, or Ultimate—or what alters any version into a localized version such as British English or another language such as German, French, Spanish, Chinese, or Russian. WIM files have unified Microsoft's software installation into a form that is both highly convenient for the customer and a great cost savings (and thus advantage) for Microsoft itself.

Keep in mind that the Windows Server 2008's distribution ships with WIM files that contain all of the hardware supported by that version of the operating system. For Windows Server 2008 on Intel x86, that distribution would contain all supported 32-bit chipsets and CPUs. The contents of a WIM file are limited only by disk size. When you install Windows Server 2008 from WIM files, you are only required to have a disk that is at least large enough to contain the uncompressed files that are installed. If you were installing the 64-bit or IA-64 versions of Windows Server 2008, each of those installations would start with a different DVD and a different set of WIM files.

WIM files are editable and are meant to evolve over time. As new device drivers, service packs, and applications are released, you update or install them into the WIM file. You add them directly to the image(s); it is not necessary to rebuild the master system and re-create an image to replace the one you already have. WIM files can be used to install not only Vista and Windows Server 2008, but also Windows XP, Windows Server 2003, and future versions. Older operating systems such as Windows 98SE, Windows 2000 (server and client), Windows Me, and others are not supported by this technology. Figure 2.8 shows the process for creating a WIM file.

FIGURE 2.8

The system imaging process depends on the IMAGEX command-line utility to capture a system image, PEIMG to install drivers and components, and the creation of a boot image with IMAGEX for deployment.

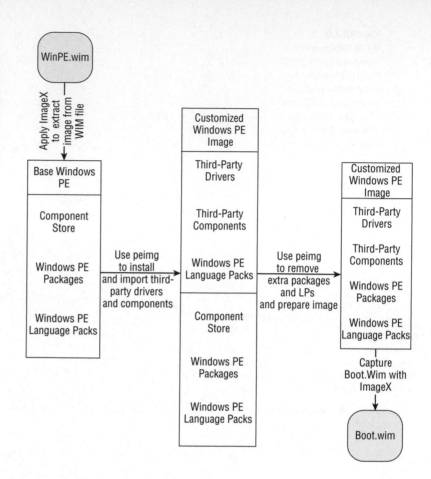

Windows Automated Installation Kit 3.01

Windows Automated Installation Kit (WAIK) is a set of central tools in system deployments. It includes the following:

- IMAGEX, the system image creation tool

- Windows System Installation Manager (SIM), which allows you to manage a library of images, modify those images, and create the UNATTEND.XML answer file for installations

- A documentation set for both of these tools

You can get WAIK from the Microsoft download center at:

```
http://www.microsoft.com/downloads/details.aspx?familyid=C7D4BC6D-15F3-4284-9123-
679830D629F2&displaylang=en
```

The Business Desktop Deployment package installs and requires WAIK to operate. Figure 2.9 shows how WAIK plays a central role in an operating system rollout. The program is installed on the imaging or technician computer, where it is used to image the master computer systems that are created in the test lab.

FIGURE 2.9

WAIK deployed on Windows Server 2008 images a model system (the master computer), stores and manages the image, and then deploys that image.

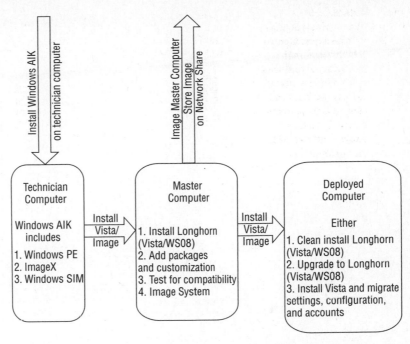

When you install WAIK, the tools needed to create a WinPE system are part of that package. To create a WinPE 2.0 disk:

1. With WAIK installed, click Start ➤ Program ➤ Microsoft AIK, then choose the Windows PE Tools Command Prompt command.

2. In the command prompt window, enter the command

```
COPYPE.CMD x86 C:\BOOTPE20\x86_PE
```

An x64 version of this tool exists for 64-bit systems. This command (see Figure 2.10) creates the x86_PE folder, expands the files required, and creates the correct directory tree.

The folder you create contains the WIMPE.WIM file; a MOUNT point (folder) where the WIM file created with IMAGEX is placed; an ISO folder, which has all of the files required to create a WinPE ISO image that can be burned to disk; and a BIN file that allows a disk with the ISO to be bootable. WAIK contains another command line tool OSCDIMG that creates ISO images.

To create an ISO to boot with, use the following command:

```
OSCDIMG -bc:bootpe20\x6_pe\etfsboot.com -n -o
c:\bootpe20\x86_pe\iso c:\bootpe20\x86_pe.iso
```

The switch -b specifies where the boot file is located; -n enables long filenames; and -o optimizes storage by enforcing single instancing of files inside the WIM files. There are many more switches to OSCDIMG, and you can read about them using the OSCDIMG /? command. When the process is complete, an ISO image file that you can burn to disk appears in the directory you specified. Figure 2.11 shows the output of the OSCDIMG command. The ISO file created on Windows Server 2008 with the process described here is 180 KB.

FIGURE 2.10
You can create a
WinPE environment
from within WAIK.

FIGURE 2.11
Using OSCDIMG to
create an ISO file

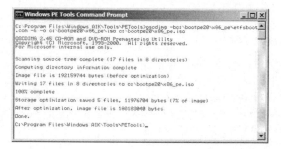

When you boot to the WinPE environment, you see a command window in place of the Windows Server 2008 logon screen. That window gives you access to the NTFS file system, a set of 32- and 64-bit hardware drivers, the ability to access the network, and the ability to run both 32- and 64-bit programs. You can also launch the program from within a command window when your WinPE disc is in your DVD drive (or from a network share). As a drive, WinPE mounts as the X: drive with the following two lines displayed:

```
X:\WINDOWS\SYSTEM32>WPEINT
X:\WINDOWS\SYSTEM32>
```

Of course, this is only the beginning of what is possible with Windows PE 2.0. You can modify the UNATTEND.XML file to modify Windows PE's startup settings.

Managing Images and Libraries

There are two utilities that you can use to create WIM files and system images. The first is the command-line utility `IMAGEX`, which is deployed as part of Windows PE. The second application that creates images is Windows SIM, which can collect, edit, and manage WIM files, as well as create an answer file (`UNATTEND.XML`) that can control the different steps of an operating system's installation.

Typically, companies support many models of computers, as well as multiple versions of the operating system. With the Windows imaging technology, careful selection of the range of hardware that is supported, and some scripting, you can develop image libraries to reduce the number of system images that has to be created from hundreds down to a handful. While the ideal goal of reducing all images down to a single master image is difficult in large deployments, it is entirely possible to reduce many systems down to just a handful of WIM files. With fewer images you can reduce disk and network bandwidth consumption, as well as the number of required distribution points.

To create an image:

1. Create the master system in the test lab with the operating system and applications to be rolled out and any customizations that are required.

2. Boot the system to a command prompt and then run the SYSPREP command to generalize the computer:

   ```
   C:\WINDOWS\SYSTEM32\SYSPREP\SYSPREP.EXE /OOBE /GENERALIZE /SHUTDOWN
   ```

   This command removes all user identification so that the system registered.

3. Reboot to a Windows PE prompt.

4. Run `IMAGEX` to create an image and save it in your image data store.

IMAGE TYPES

You can categorize WIM files into three distinct kinds of images, each of which has advantages and disadvantages:

Thick Images A thick image contains not only the operating system, but all core applications, as well as any other additional files that you want to install. Thick images are easy to build and don't require much scripting to deploy. However, thick images are not only costly in terms of their size, but anytime any application changes, the entire image must be tested and revalidated. Thick images present both network bandwidth and storage challenges, and create postimage creation problems.

Thin Images To narrow the number of images that you are required to create and support, you may want to consider a thin image. Thin images minimize the number of core applications that they contain. Applications are installed after the operating system has been deployed. Thin image deployment requires more operations and takes more administrative time, but also lowers the needed network bandwidth.

Thin images are tricky to create and require some planning to get right. However, they tend to be more stable than thick images and require less quality assurance testing to ensure that they work properly. Since the files are smaller, there's an initial savings involved in the infrastructure required to implement a deployment.

However, the initial deployment savings are offset by the extra effort that you have to go to later to install application. Those extra steps result in costs and added complexity in installing the applications after imaging. Also, since security is usually built into thick images, later stages in the deployment may lead to compromised security due to the additional step. The application installations must be scripted, and the infrastructure that pushes applications down to the desktops must be in place. Thin images are therefore best deployed by companies with enterprise network management applications (SMS, LANDesk, Altaris, ZenWare, etc.) and the in-house expertise to make this all work.

Hybrid Images When you mix thin and thick images together, you get a hybrid image. Hybrid images contain the operating system files as well as the installation files for supported applications as part of the image. The files that application installers need are stored on a network share.

Hybrid images support a variety of approaches to later application deployment. When users need an application, they can install it manually. Alternatively, a centralized system can be created that rolls out application installations at the time the system image is deployed, or that automatically rolls them out at a later date.

The advantage of a hybrid image is that it is relatively easy to create. Provided that an organization has a software distribution system, a hybrid approach can work well, but it also requires additional installation steps that add to system preparation time and costs.

Another way to approach a hybrid image is to create a thin image and then create versions of the thin image with additional applications. Since the thick image changes infrequently, it doesn't need to be tested. This approach only works well when the applications added are image friendly.

Figure 2.12 shows a set of images in the Windows SIM application.

FIGURE 2.12
The Windows SIM is part of the WAIK. It allows you to manage your library of system images.

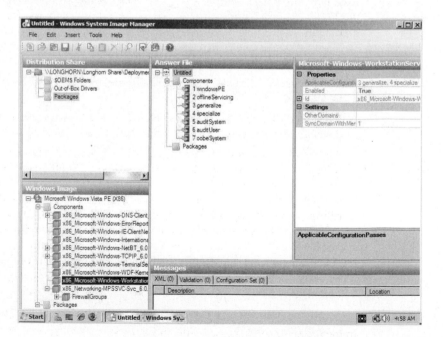

ANSWER FILES

To automate the installation of system images, you need to create an answer file that tells the installer what settings to apply at each step of the installation. That was true in prior versions of Windows Setup when installations copied over CAB files, extracted all the files, and then selected the files needed to configure the system. It is still true in Windows Server 2008's installation technology, where system files are contained in the WIM file and, through the use of the catalog, the appropriate files are extracted and copied directly.

What has changed is that the answer file is no longer a collection of text files that includes UNATTEND.TXT, SYSPREP.INF, WIMBOM.INI, and CMD.TXT. These files have been replaced by the UNATTEND.XML file. UNATTEND.XML contains the following tagged settings used by Windows Setup during installation:

- Boot partition information
- Image location, either local or in network deployment share
- The product key
- User account information
- Display settings
- Internet Explorer default home page and favorites
- and more . . .

Each UNATTEND.XML file is associated with a single installation, but any UNATTEND file can be used with any image. Setup is designed to bypass any component whose setting is specified in UNATTEND.XML but for which the component can't be found. Installation goes to completion based on default settings that replace the missing component's settings.

The tool used to create UNATTEND.XML files is the Windows System Image Manager shown in the previous sections. To build the UNATTEND.XML file, you need to populate two different sections:

Components Components are the settings that are entered or selected in the operating system installation.

Packages Packages are container files in which service packs, updates, and language packs are distributed. Packages are applied in the offlineServicing configuration pass.

An MSI file is one example of a package. When the UNATTEND.XML file specifies that a package be used, that software is added to the installation, along with any settings specified. If a package isn't specified, it is ignored. One package central to Vista is the Windows Foundation Package, which contains Media Player, Windows Backup, Games, and other key Windows features. You can choose to disable the Foundation Package, but if you do, Windows Media Player will not be available. The package is retained in your Windows image, but it isn't applied during the installation.

NOTE Keep in mind that Windows system deployments from a Windows Server 2008 system are meant to support Vista, and to a more limited extent Windows Server 2003 and Windows XP Professional.

Windows Setup runs through seven configuration routines during which settings are applied. In the order in which they execute, those passes are:

1. windowsPE: During this phase data entry is performed for Setup selections, DISKPART runs, the image is applied, and boot data is prepared.

2. `offlineServicing`: Here packages are added, security is applied, and drivers are configured.

3. `generalize` (On-Line Configuration): This phase configures components that allow the system to boot to the basic OS. It is in this phase that the license files are added, which will require you to register either during installation or at some point later in the future.

4. `specialize` (On-Line Configuration): Here UNATTEND.XML settings are applied to common and optional components.

5. `auditSystem` (FirstBoot): At the start of FirstBoot, Setup creates the unique system IDs.

6. `auditUser` (FirstBoot): SYSPREP runs and specialization is added so that the installation may be applied to the user who registers the system.

7. `oobeSystem`: The Out-of-Box Experience (OOBE) phase is the phase in which the EULA is accepted, and the Registration, Machine Name, Users, Connectivity, and Regional settings are applied.

You see these settings applied in Windows SIM to the UNATTEND.XML answer files that it creates. The UNATTEND.XML installation process has the following steps:

1. Launch SIM and then open the image that you want to create the answer file for.

2. Create a new answer file in SIM.

3. Add packages or components such as drivers for the specific setup that the deployment will support.

4. Step through each configuration step in the answer file settings and indicate the settings you desire.

5. Validate that the XML is syntactically correct.

6. Save the answer file.

The Application Compatibility Toolkit 5.0

Testing application compatibility is a necessary step in deploying an operating system. Although server operating systems run fewer applications than desktop systems, the stability of those applications is more critical than applications that run on desktops. Therefore, testing applications that run on Windows Server 2008 should be part of any deployment.

The Microsoft tool you can use to test compatibility on Windows Server 2008 is the Application Compatibility Toolkit (ACT). The latest version of ACT released as part of BDD 2.5 was ACT 5.0. When ACT is installed on a Windows Server 2008 system, the utility starts whenever you launch an application—that is, whenever an executable file is detected to be starting up. ACT then compares the application to a stored set of applications in a set of database files found at \%SYSTEMROOT%\ APPPATH to determine if this program has known incompatibilities with the current operating system. ACT's database can store entries not only for Windows Server 2008, but for Vista, Windows XP, and Windows Server 2003 as well. The entries also contain information about remediation of the issues, and the whole system undergoes periodic updates over the Internet from Microsoft.

ACT does three things for you. First, it produces a report and action plan for known issues. This report is input by the ACT community of IT users and the software Independent Software Vendors (ISVs). Second, an online forum called the Microsoft Compatibility Exchange provides more up-to-date discussion by users. Third, ACT can be used to push patches and upgrades from the server to clients as they become available. Figure 2.13 illustrates this process.

FIGURE 2.13

The Windows ACT deploys a set of agents that inventory network systems, store the data, and then compare the applications and hardware found to a compatibility database. ACT may turn into a long-term health monitoring solution as Microsoft develops this technology further.

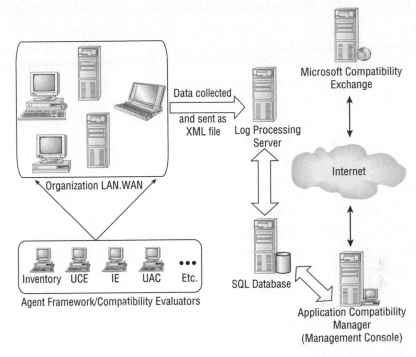

ACT comes with agent technologies that collect information about the systems on your network and report that information to your network framework application. Inventory agents in ACT include:

◆ Inventory Collector, which collects information about the software that is installed on your systems

◆ Internet Explorer Compatibility Evaluator (IECE), which polls for compatibility and security issues related to web and intranet sites

◆ Update Impact Analyzer (UIA), which reports issues with the Windows Update site

◆ User Account Control Compatibility Evaluator (UACCE), which tests user rights and access permissions for any known issues

If you have SMS deployed, you can use the SMS Software Inventory module to collect application data from the agents that ACT deployed on your network systems. SMS itself doesn't provide guidance for application compatibility, so in this sense ACT is complementary to the SMS inventory function. However, you can use SMS to roll out ACT.

The SMS Software Inventory module will also collect application data, but SMS stores that data in its own database. ACT's inventory data is separate from SMS, which for SMS is a SQL Server database file, and in the case of ACT either a SQL Server database file or a SQL Server Desktop Engine (MSDE) database file. SMS Software Inventory must run on existing systems, and is usually performed when a large sample or complete inventory is desired. Since SMS doesn't specifically offer application compatibility information for Vista, ACT doesn't overlap with SMS in this regard. ACT is also updated from the Internet so that it is current. You can use SMS to deploy the ACT inventory agents.

It's wrong to think of ACT as simply a deployment tool. Microsoft describes the application and associated forum and web services as an "operating system lifecycle tool." Whether this is truly so depends on how much effort Microsoft is willing to commit to developing ACT in future versions. However, it does bear watching.

Migrating User Data

It is unusual for user-based settings on a server system itself to be preserved during an installation. However, if you are using Windows Server 2008 to deploy other systems, you will be faced with the problem of migrating user settings. If you deploy a Vista system from Windows Server 2008 without migrating user settings, their application settings, and their desktops, you are going to have a large number of unhappy campers on your network. Not only do users expect to see their data on new systems, but they also expect to see it in the same folders. Migrating user settings is one of the more odious tasks in an OS deployment because you need to make sure that all hardware, drivers, operating system settings, and applications are supported. You also want to eliminate all obsolete or duplicated profiles and perform additional housekeeping. The best way to perform this deployment is to create a standard operating environment (SOE), which is one of your goals in your testing.

The Microsoft tool used to capture and restore user settings is the User State Migration Tool (USMT), which is part of WAIK. USMT supports three migration scenarios:

Upgrade or In-place Installation User data is on the system and only needs to be captured as a backup. Upgrades typically aren't as stable as fresh installations.

Side-by-Side Computer Replacement A new system is prepared and the user data is then migrated from the old system to the new one.

Clean or Wipe-and-Load Installation This scenario captures user data to another system, and restores the settings after the new operating system has been installed.

USMT is a scriptable CLI utility that supports Windows Server 2008, Vista, Windows XP, Windows Server 2003, and even Windows 2000 clients and servers as its data source. Destination or target systems can be Windows Server 2003, Vista Windows Server 2003, or XP. USMT uses a command called SCANSTATE to collect user state data from a source, compress the data, and copy it to a specified location (which is usually a network share or another computer). USMT's LOADSTATE command takes user state data, copies it to the target computer, and expands the data back to its previous state.

The steps for a migration of user settings with USMT are shown in Figure 2.14. Follow these steps for a side-by-side migration:

1. Run SCANSTATE to collect user state data from the source system.

   User data is compressed and then copied to an intermediate data store on the network. The operating system is installed on the target system.

2. Load any applications on the target system prior to migrating settings (recommended).

   Doing so gives you the latest version of the applications and the most compatible system state.

3. Run the LOADSTATE command to restore the user state data to the target computer from the data on the intermediate data store.

Wipe-and-load migrations require these steps:

1. Run the SCANSTATE command to collect user state data from the source.

User data is compressed and then copied to an intermediate data store on the network. The boot drive is reformatted and the OS image is installed on the same system the data was collected from.

2. Run the LOADSTATE command to restore the user state data on the system from the data on the intermediate data store.

FIGURE 2.14

The central mechanism for user state migration is the SCANSTATE command-line utility, which captures user settings and stores them in a database, and the LOADSTATE command, which restores those settings to a target system.

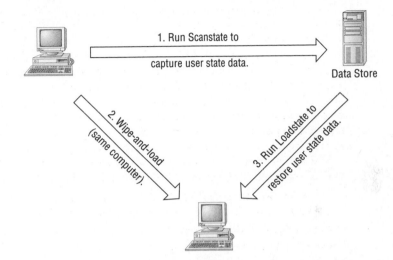

Among the settings that are retained are accessibility options, classic desktop, command prompt settings, desktop, dial-up connections, favorites, folder options, fonts, Microsoft Internet Explorer settings, the Microsoft Outlook Express store, mouse and keyboard settings, My Documents, My Music, My Pictures, My Received Files, My Videos, phone and modem options, Quick Launch settings, regional options, screen saver settings, sound settings, and taskbar settings, among others. What the USMT doesn't migrate includes: applications, DLLs, device drivers, Encrypting File System (EFS) data, certificates (in some instances), EXE files, hardware settings, passwords, and any synchronization files.

Settings are much more important in client systems than servers, but since Vista and Windows Server 2003 store user data in different folders, it is possible to migrate data into unexpected places. USMT can be controlled by settings in an XML file that allows you to customize the migration process.

Because Windows XP and Vista store user data in different folders—and indeed it is possible for users to have additional data in XP that is stored in folders outside of their profile in the Documents and Settings folder—USMT 3.0 lets you customize the XML files that it uses as its inputs to the migration process to let you customize the process. USMT lets you script the process and batch process it for any number of PCs. Without this capability, migration wouldn't be able to support a wide range of deployments.

During migration, USMT obtains its settings from several XML files. The configuration information is applied to the SCANSTATE and LOADSTATE commands. Modifying those text-based files is the first place to start when you want to customize a migration operation. The XML migration files include the following:

CONFIG.XML This file is created by the SCANSATE /GENCONFIG command to generate a custom configuration file. You create this file when all of the applications that are part of your master system are already installed. The command embeds the operating system identification, applications, and a list of the users that get migrated. The CONFIG.XML file is used to migrate either to or from Vista.

MFGAPP.XML This file is used for migration to and from Vista or XP, and it contains the application settings. You can edit this file to change which applications are installed or ignored.

MFGUSER.XML Inside this file is a list of the user folder, desktop settings, and files and file types to migrate to and from Vista or XP. Its name is a little misleading, as it doesn't migrate users.

MFGSYS.XML This file is mostly used to target XP systems and contains the operating system and browser settings. When a migration to Vista is performed, the information on these required settings is drawn from the Windows XP/2000 repositories. If the target is Windows XP, the MFGSYS.XML file must be included.

To create a custom script for migration, you first create and then edit the CONFIG.XML file. The format is easy to work with as each setting in the file has a conditional statement that contains a migrate = yes (or no) statement. To include a component, yes should appear in that statement; to exclude it, a no.

NOTE You can find the User State Migration Tool 3.0's home page at http://www.microsoft .com/technet/WindowsVista/library/usmt/91f62fc4-621f-4537-b311-1307df010561 .mspx?mfr=true.

Migration is your opportunity to eliminate obsolete profiles, application data, and other unnecessary settings. When used correctly, USMT can greatly improve a system's performance and stability. Therefore, you will want to give some thought to how you use USMT to deploy systems using Windows Server 2008.

Automated Deployment

Once an organization gets beyond about 100 desktops, deploying clients and servers becomes a large task. To minimize the effort involved in deploying the operating system, a set of master images are created based on the hardware that the organization supports. Images also reflect the operating system configuration, application suites such as Microsoft Office, and other custom user settings. Images are typically deployed from an image store, which is most commonly kept on a network share. For very large deployments, servers for controlling a deployment as well as supporting image deployment are often dedicated to the purpose.

Microsoft has developed a set of deployment technologies to help organizations roll out new operating systems. You've already seen elements of these technologies—the WIM file and WinPE—but there are a portfolio of tools that are offered, as shown in Table 2.4. The process begins when you create a master image from a system with all of the hardware, software, and settings to be deployed. The SYSPREP utility is then run on the master system to remove all identifying registration information from the image. With these steps completed, you can then use IMAGEX to create the system image and store that image on a network share. Essentially you are cloning that system onto target clients when you deploy them.

Table 2.4 summarizes the Microsoft tools used for image-based system deployments.

TABLE 2.4:   Microsoft Windows Deployment Tools

TOOL	DESCRIPTION
ACT	The Application Compatibility Toolkit 5.0 is used to determine what applications are compatible with Windows Server 2008, as well as monitoring the systems and pushing out applicable updates.
BCDEDIT	BCDEDIT is used to modify the Windows Server 2008 boot configuration.
BDD Workbench	A management tool that is part of the BDD framework solution for managing images used in a deployment.
BitLocker	Provides volume drive encryption in Windows Server 2008 and Vista.
IMAGEX	IMAGEX is the command-line utility that creates WIM system images, usually applied in the Windows PE environment.
OCSETUP	OCSETUP installs Windows components, and replaces SYSOCMGR used in its online mode.
PEIMG	PEIMG is used to modify Windows PE images.
PKMGR	This tool is used to modify the operating system. It replaces SYSOCMGR in its offline mode.
PNPUTIL	PNPUTIL is used to manage the driver store, allowing you to add or subtract drivers as required.
Setup	This is the installation tool, and replaces the previous installers WINNT and WINNT32.
SYSPREP	SYSPREP has been updated for Windows Server 2008 and Vista. This tool removes system identification prior to cloning.
USMT 3.0	User State Migration Tool 3.0 captures and restores user state data, including files, profiles, settings, and other information. This version migrates from Windows 2000 and XP to Windows XP, Windows Server 2003, Vista, and Windows Server 2008.
Windows Deployment Services	Replaces Remote Installation Services (RIS) and is used to deploy Windows Server 2008, Vista, Windows Server 2003, XP, and PE boot images.
Windows System Image Manager	Used to create and modify the UNATTEND.XML file that is used to control image installations. This system replaces the use of the Setup Manager and a text editor as the editor for answer files.

Business Desktop Deployment Solution

To facilitate the installation of complex enterprisewide solutions, Microsoft has developed a set of best practices bundled into an application framework that they collectively refer to as "solutions." These solutions utilize a structured team-based approach to deployment. Solutions are based on the resources created by Microsoft's consulting group. The Microsoft Solution Accelerator for Business Desktop Deployment or BDD is a downloadable collection of tools. It also installs informational and organizational resources, as well as a set of utilities for deploying Windows Vista and Microsoft Office 2007.

NOTE To read more about the BDD Solution Accelerator, go to that tool's home page at www.microsoft.com/desktopdeployment. With the solution installed, start by reading "Getting Started with Desktop Deployment," which you can access from the Deployment Overview section on the main page of the tool.

BDD Document Explorer is a team-based information and guidance framework, and BDD Workbench helps you manage images, distribution shares, and deployments. WAIK contains the Windows PE 2.0 environment, USMT, Windows SIM, and ACT 5.0, which are a collection of tools for analyzing existing applications that you want to deploy. Some of these tools are new to Vista, and all of the preexisting tools have been significantly reworked and upgraded. The download section of BDD is shown in Figure 2.15.

FIGURE 2.15
The Business Desktop Deployment serves as a central framework for automated deployment. You can even download Microsoft's deployment tools using this tool.

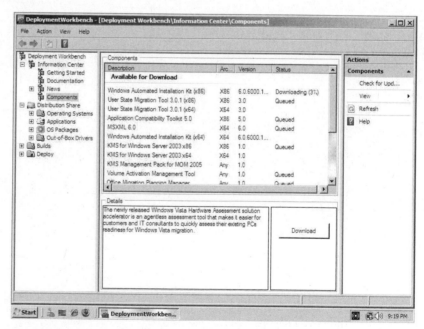

When you install the BDD solution, WAIK is installed as part of that solution if it isn't found on your system.

Figure 2.16 illustrates the various teams that are organized in a large-scale Windows operating system deployment. Table 2.5 shows the names of the different teams, the assigned resources, and their functions.

FIGURE 2.16
BDD breaks a deployment into a set of stages, each managed by teams.

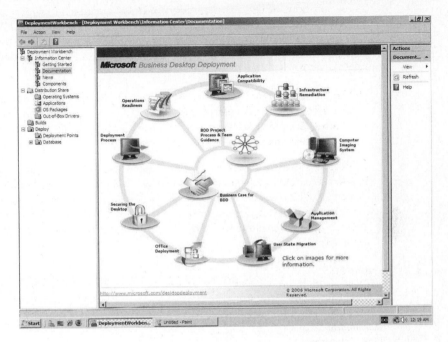

TABLE 2.5:   BDD Team Resources

TEAM	GUIDANCE	TEMPLATES
Core The design specification team	Plan, Build, and Deploy Guide Enterprise Learning Framework User Guide Woodgrove Enterprise IT Archetype	Inventory Template Communications Plan Functional Specification Migration Plan Risk Template Tool Training Plan Vision Scope Site Deployment Project Plan
Application Compatibility This team establishes an inventory, runs the application compatibility testing program, and sets up the test bed from which images will be created.	Application Compatibility Feature Team Guide	Use ACT 5.0 and other methods.

TABLE 2.5: BDD Team Resources *(CONTINUED)*

TEAM	GUIDANCE	TEMPLATES
Application Management The Application Management team is tasked with making sure the correct applications are delivered to the right desktops.	Application Management Feature Team Guide Office Deployment Guide	Application Knowledge Sheet Office Assessment Template Office Budget Plan Office Communications Plan Office Configuration Plan Office Current State Assessment Template Office Distribution Plan Office File Migration Plan Office Functional Specification Office Hardware Upgrades List Office Inventory Template Office Management Plan Office Pilot Plan Office Project Plan Office Risk Template Tool Office Test Plan Office Training Plan Office Vision Scope
Computer Imaging System This team is technically responsible for creating the image files used in deployment.	Computer Imaging System Feature Team Guide	Client Build Requirements
Deployment The deployment team creates and manages the network resources used to deploy OS images. They script and configure automated installations, using thick images for complete installations, thin images for minimal deployments followed up by application installations, or some hybrid approach.	Deployment Feature Team Guide Lite Touch Installation Guide Zero Touch Installation Guide Deployment Configuration Guide Deployment Configuration Samples Guide Zero Touch Installation Management Pack	Pilot Plan
Desired Configuration Monitoring. This team specifies the different image configurations.	Desired Configuration Monitoring Feature Team Guide	Sample manifests

TABLE 2.5:   BDD Team Resources *(CONTINUED)*

TEAM	GUIDANCE	TEMPLATES
Infrastructure Remediation. This team gets the infrastructure ready for deployment.	Infrastructure Remediation Feature Team Guide Volume Activation Guide	Assessment Template Current State Assessment Template Network and Workstation Hardware Upgrades
Operations Readiness. This team is tasked with making sure that the deployed systems run properly once deployment has been completed.	Operations Readiness Feature Team Guide	
Security This team hardens desktops and servers and lowers their attack surface.	Security Feature Team Guide	
Test This group's involvement runs throughout many of the phases of BDD, from creating and managing a test lab, to helping to specify image types, as well as testing to see that the deployment worked and created stable systems.	Test Feature Team Guide	Test Cases Workbook Test Plan Test Specification
User State Migration This team captures and stores user states, appropriately applying them to newly deployed systems.	User State Migration Feature Team Guide	

Source: Microsoft BDD *Getting Ready Guide*.

BDD Deployment Scenarios

For small deployments, you can use BDD to prepare a disc, USB key, or flash drive to create a WinPE boot disk that contains a WIM file, WAIK, and IMAGEX and away you go. When you boot WinPE, it opens a command prompt where you can start IMAGEX and apply the image to the system.

Deploying to a large number of computers is more problematical. If installing on an individual basis, the IT staff can become overwhelmed. An automated approach is required. BDD as a deployment platform starts to be useful with as few as 20 to 50 systems. For a deployment of that size (which is typically managed by a single individual), use BDD Document Explorer to set up and create images; capture, store, and install user states; and perform a manual or Lite Touch installation.

Once there are more than 50 systems per administrator, manual deployments become impractical. The next step up in size would be a medium-sized deployment, and Microsoft considers these deployments to start with organizations that have outgrown the Microsoft Small Business Server—usually around 100 clients. Medium-sized deployments typically don't have a management framework application such as SMS installed, or they make poor use of the one that they do have installed.

The installation of network management frameworks such as SMS depends in part on the nature of the business and the sophistication of the IT staff. As a general rule, Microsoft classifies medium-sized organizations as ones that start at 50 to 100 clients and top out at between 500 and 1,000 clients. In an organization of this type there are typically several IT staff who are involved in a deployment, but generally not enough staff to form teams.

Medium-sized deployments require support for a wider range of hardware platforms and applications than small deployments. The tools for determining compatibility become significantly more important, and the number of images being managed rises. The current recommendation for medium-sized deployments is that they employ manual and Lite Touch deployments, or some combination of both. The availability in the network infrastructure may be one of the gating factors before deployments can be fully automated in the organization.

BDD scales to very large enterprises. Large organizations are ones that have, as a minimum, between 1,000 and 2,000 desktops; organized deployment teams with specialized skills for each aspect of deployment; and the necessary network services required to run fully automated deployments. Microsoft has supported automated deployments for their operating systems in organizations with tens of thousands of desktops and servers. For large organizations, the full range of deployment types are available, including manual, automated, Lite Touch, and even Zero Touch deployment. The "Windows Deployment Services" section later in this chapter describes more fully how Lite Touch and Zero Touch deployments work.

OFFICE DEPLOYMENT

BDD supports and encourages organizations to install Microsoft Office as part of their master images. Applications that are part of the master are referred to as "core applications." Many companies prefer to upgrade their systems so that not only the operating system is newly installed, but also their version of Office is current. The BDD feature page for the installation of Office is called the Upgrading Office page, and the solution provides for the creation of an Office Upgrade Feature Team.

The recommended steps in an Office deployment with BDD are:

1. Form an Office Deployment team and create a project plan based on installing Office on test systems.

2. Create an Office Installation Point or share.

3. Have the Application Compatibility team test Office's compatibility; determine settings for system types and installation types.

4. Have the Application Compatibility team test the installation to check compatibility on the master systems.

   If you are installing Office 2007, the installation converts documents that are opened to the Microsoft Office Open XML format, so this step in the process needs to be considered. You can use the Microsoft Office File Conversion utility to use the Office Planning Manager inventory's output to perform batch file conversion. The process creates new XML files, but retains the older Microsoft Office file format just in case any incompatibilities are noted.

5. Have the Deployment team deploy Office to production systems.

6. Hand off the process to support staff once the operating system and Microsoft Office are installed.

Deployments of operating systems using BDD can use a single Office configuration or version, or they can use different versions of Office customized for a group of users. Office settings can be contained in either a patch file (MSP) or an Office Open XML configuration file. If a group policy allows users to modify their Office installations, then the users can make changes after deployment.

Just as Microsoft supports OS deployments, there are similar tools for Office deployments. The Microsoft Office Migration Planning Manager scans systems and inventories the various versions of Office on them. Additional tools for Office deployment include:

◆ Office Customization Tool

◆ Microsoft Office Setup Controller

◆ Microsoft Office File Conversion Tool

◆ Microsoft Office Local Installation Source

These tools are either included as part of the Microsoft Office 2007 Resource Kit (ORK), or can be downloaded from the ORK page on TechNet's Microsoft Office Desktop Applications TechCenter, which you can find at `http://www.microsoft.com/technet/prodtechnol/office/ork/default.mspx`.

During deployment, Office 2007 Setup is launched in quiet mode so that it will complete the installation without requiring an answer file. Previous versions of Office are removed, so you want to keep that in mind for system upgrades. If you need to retain the older versions of Office, modify the default installation. You can use the Office Setup Controller to add components to an Office installation.

One nice feature of the Office 2007 Setup is that you can roll out Office and its applications and components on a deployment schedule that you define so that you don't overburden your network or staff. The Office Customization Tool (OCT) lets you define the nature of the Office Setup deployment. OCT is a command-line tool that runs when you specify a switch for Office's SETUP.EXE. OCT for the Office 2007 system is described in detail at:

```
http://technet2.microsoft.com/Office/en-us/library/8faae8a0-a12c-4f7b-839c-
24a66a531bb51033.mspx?mfr=true
```

The Microsoft Solutions Framework

The Microsoft Solutions Framework (MSF) arises out of the work done by Microsoft's consulting group. MSF is a collected set of best practices organized within a framework to deliver a business solution. One of those business solutions is Windows operating system deployments, and the BDD Solution Accelerator uses the methodology of the MSF to achieve the deployment goals. MSF breaks down a large project such as an OS deployment into a collection of separate steps. Each step is assigned to a team populated with people with the requisite knowledge, skills, and abilities—what Microsoft refers to as KSAs—and each team has a project goal and a set of deliverables. Teams are expected to have a shared vision, open communications, accountability and responsibility, empowerment, an eye on delivering business value, the desire to invest in quality, the ability to manage risk and learn from experience, and agility.

NOTE The MSF site at www.microsoft.com/technet/itsolutions/msf/default.mspx contains white papers, links to newsgroups, templates, and some case studies. Microsoft also offers a three-day course called MSF Essentials (MS 1846A) for practitioners in solution delivery. The course teaches three disciplines: project management, risk management, and readiness management.

Solutions come with an organizational framework of principles, models, concept, guidelines, and organizational design; recommended practices; informational resources; planning guides; and software tools required to implement the solution. BDD has all of these features and is designed to be rolled out to customers and consulting groups. BDD is but one example of a solution from this Microsoft program; the Visual Studio 2005 Team System is another example. Solution frameworks exist for Exchange rollouts, mobile deployments, web and e-commerce system rollouts, web services, ERP, n-tier transaction systems, operations management system deployments, and even mainframe projects. Not all MSF solutions use the Team Model approach; some of the solutions are organized around a process model.

Figure 2.17 shows a conceptual drawing for the phases in an MSF solution, and more specifically in the BDD solution. The first step is in the specification of the deployment. Subsequent steps form the teams required to establish a test bed, inventory hardware and software, test applications for compatibility, create and manage the deployment infrastructure, and then perform the deployment itself. Each team and each phase in the project has both deadlines and milestones. Although teams are meant to function as a group, it is the team leader that is ultimately responsible for decisions and accountable.

FIGURE 2.17
Utilizing a team-based approach to deployment, the BDD Solution Accelerator is built on the structured approach of the MSF.

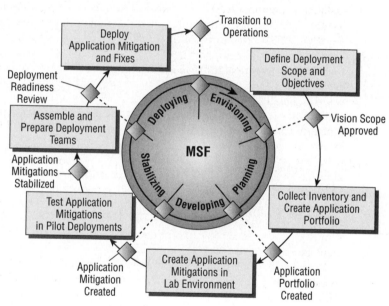

An MSF solution project isn't considered complete until the deployment is handed off to the IT staff that is tasked with supporting the system and its users. MSF is meant to dovetail with the Microsoft Operations Framework (MOF), which is another set of practices and methodologies that are meant to support ongoing operations such as IT. MOF solutions contain operational guides, templates, assessment and support tools, white papers, courseware, and case studies. MOF tends to give more emphasis to how people and processes interoperate in complex networking environments. So if you are working in a distributed and heterogeneous network, you may want to look more closely at this set of framework solutions.

NOTE To learn more about the Microsoft Operations Framework, go to www.microsoft.com/mof.

MFS is a solution delivery framework, while MOF is a service management framework. Whereas BDD is functionally organized around groups executing projects with known ends and deliverables, an MOF for Windows Server 2008 and client system management would be open-ended and process oriented. Microsoft's slogan for the two frameworks pretty much sums it up:

◆ MSF = "Build IT Right"

◆ MOF = "Run IT Right"

Consider MOF implementations for systems that are mission critical, that require high reliability and availability, and that can be centrally managed and supported. MOF is a standards-oriented effort, drawing on the work of a set of best practices called the IT Infrastructure Library (ITIL), which was developed in the United Kingdom by the Office of Government Commerce (OGC). Microsoft describes MOF as a superset of the ITIL.

Windows Deployment Services

Windows Deployment Services (WDS) is the replacement for the venerable Microsoft Remote Installation Services (RIS). It can be installed as one of the roles of Windows Server 2008. You can use WDS as a replacement for RIS, or you can work with RIS images in WDS in what is called "legacy" mode. As an organization migrates to Windows Server 2008 and WDS, you can even use a "mixed" mode, with a domain having both RIS and WDS servers. WDS requires Active Directory, and is most compatible with Windows Server 2008. Pure WDS-based deployments (when RIS isn't used) is considered to be a native mode. In native mode with Windows Server 2008, only WIM file-based installations are supported.

WDS has some advantages over RIS, particularly for Vista deployments (in which RIS doesn't function correctly and has limited options). You'll find that with RIS accessibility, language and localization features aren't supported. From the standpoint of automated deployments, RIS doesn't work with PXE boot scenarios, and WDS does. WDS supports both PXE boot and remote installations for systems booted using other methods.

WDS is your best bet if you want to perform remote boots since it can use a client-server protocol to push installation down to a client that has booted into the PXE Server extension. WDS lets you run an enhanced MMC, which you can use to install your systems with a WIM container file. In Windows Server 2008, WDS is a role migration tool and is installed as part of the Server Management console.

When a computer boots into the PXE Boot environment and is assigned a DHCP address, it sends out a message using the Trivial File Transfer Protocol (TFTP) to a PXE Server requesting additional instructions on how to proceed. For remote deployments, the PXE Server tasks the client to go to the WDS Server and download the WDS Client Installation program. That program then completes the initial boot sequence, and begins the OOBE phase of the installation. Setup locates the UNATTEND.XML answer file and proceeds through the installation using the appropriate image file.

You turn on the PXE Server as part of WDS, and you modify that server inside the WDS Properties dialog box. You can set options that do any of the following things:

◆ Provide no response to broadcasts

◆ Respond only to known client computer broadcasts as a matter of Group Policy

◆ Respond to all (known or unknown) client computer broadcast requests, again as part of Group Policy

You can also require clients to first notify the administrator before deployment proceeds. Essentially, you are enabling or disabling remote and unattended setups using these settings. Additional control over timing is also possible. The phases in the PXE boot process are:

1. The client loads PXE, gets a dynamic network address (DHCP), and broadcasts for a PXE Server.

   If the client doesn't get a response, it will continue to try to boot from other devices.

2. The PXE Server sends the PXEBOOT.COM file to the client, which then loads the BOOTMGR.EXE (Windows Boot Loader) and the BCD (Boot Configuration Data) file into memory.

3. A RAM disk is created and WinPE is copied to that X drive.

4. The WIM file is copied over the network to the client, where it is expanded sequentially and copied to the target system.

5. Windows Setup runs and the UNATTEND.XML file is used to control the installation.

Lite Touch Installations

A Lite Touch installation (LTI) is one in which an administrator must specifically initiate an installation. LTIs work best when a new operating system is being rolled out a few systems at a time. LTIs are differentiated from Zero Touch installations (ZTIs; described in the next section) in that ZTIs are policy based. With a ZTI a user can request an upgrade and then if the policy allows it the installation will either proceed or be scheduled for a convenient time.

To create an LTI deployment solution:

1. Use BDD to create your images and store them in your deployment point.

2. Deploy Windows Deployment Server in your domain, and ensure that DNS, DHCP, WINS (optional), and the Remote Access service are running and accessible by clients.

3. Configure WDS to boot Windows PE using PXE over the network.

4. Run the LTI wizard in BDD.

   You will need to specify whether LTI refreshes, upgrades, or replaces the OS, and provide the image location and a product key. If you use the Key Management Service (KMS), you will need to enter a Multiple Activation Key (MAK).

5. Enter the credentials required by clients to connect to the network share containing the image and UNATTEND.XML file.

6. Once you enter the information, the Begin button on the Ready to Begin page of the LTI wizard initiates the LTI.

Zero Touch Installations

Zero Touch installations (ZTIs) are policy-based automated deployments, where physical access to the systems being targeted or individual attention isn't practical. Often ZTIs are managed by network management packages such as SMS. Since it is policy based, ZTI has the following prerequisites:

◆ Active Directory

◆ Windows Deployment Server

◆ SMS ODD Feature Pack or another network management deployment package

ZTI runs as an unattended installation:

1. The target system boots and launches the PXE client.

2. A DHCP address is assigned.

3. The system is authenticated by Group Policy by its domain as a system that will have the new operating system deployed to it.

4. WDS Server loads the Windows PE OS into the client's RAM.

5. The configuration script starts, hardware is scanned, and the hard drive status is determined.

6. DISKPART creates a new partition if a new installation is required.

7. Setup runs using UNATTEND.XML, and the deployment is executed.

If you are trying to decide between an LTI and a ZTI deployment, consider the comparison chart shown in Table 2.6.

TABLE 2.6: LTI vs. ZTI Deployments

CHARACTERISTIC	LTI	ZTI
Best Used By	Small deployments of 25 clients or fewer and with low network bandwidth available.	Deployments where SMS is used
Deployment Method	New computer, Upgrade computer, Refresh computer, and Replace computer scenarios with network deployment. Or a stand-alone installation installed using a DVD driver or USB flash media-based image installation.	New Computer, Refresh Computer, and Replace Computer scenarios implemented within Microsoft SMS
Server Requirements	Windows Server in a domain with Active Directory, network share, and network	SMS, Windows Server, domain and Active Directory, and WDS installed
Microsoft Tools Required	Microsoft .NET Framework Microsoft Application Compatibility Toolkit Microsoft Core XML Services (MSXML) Microsoft Management Console User Settings Migration Toolkit Windows Automated Installation Kit	Microsoft .NET Framework Microsoft Application Compatibility Toolkit Microsoft Core XML Services (MSXML) Microsoft Management Console SMS 2003 SP 2 or later SMS 2003 Operating System Deployment Feature Pack or later User Settings Migration Toolkit Windows Automated Installation Kit

Summary

In this chapter you learned about aspects of both the installation of Windows Server 2008 and the use of Windows Server 2008 as a platform for Windows system deployment. Windows Server 2008 continues Microsoft's refinement of their deployment technology with many substantial improvements.

Microsoft has made the transition away from generalized CAB file installations, where all files are copied to the boot drive during installation, to an image-based technology. The new single-instance image container WIM file presents installers with a catalog of possible system configurations, copying over only those files that a particular installation requires. It is not only quicker but also more efficient, much less resource dependent, and probably more accurate.

The new microkernel Windows PE 2.0 boot environment offers a powerful tool for system deployment, modification, and troubleshooting. With WinPE, Windows users (administrators in particular) will have a boot OS that finally rivals what has been available to the Linux platform for some time now. Many of the utilities on Windows PE are new or have been substantially upgraded from their predecessors. IMAGEX captures and creates images, DISKPART is a new disk partition utility, and DRVLOAD, NET, and NETCFG upgrade previous utilities for adding drivers, connecting to networks, and troubleshooting networks.

Microsoft has introduced a new version of the Windows Automated Installation Kit (WAIK). The new version of the Application Compatibility Test tool is now both a diagnostic and trouble-shooting tool for analyzing systems prior to installations as well as into a platform for continuing to monitor system health. Microsoft has also released an enhanced version of the Business Desktop Deployment Solution Accelerator with significant new capabilities. The new information resources related to all of these improvements are impressive.

Network services are one area in which there have been continual changes in Windows Server technology. This version of Windows Server 2008 comes with some significant improvements such as a completely new TCP/IP stack, better IPv6 support, a new SMB protocol and other network drivers, as well as a bevy of network policies, including the new Network Access Protection (NAP) system. The next chapter discusses these improvements.

Chapter 3

Network Services

There are many new networking features in Windows Server 2008. Some are obvious because they show up in the management interface; others are transparent and even more significant. To support the transition from IPv4 to IPv6 as well as to improve security and performance, Microsoft rewrote the TCP/IP stack that shipped with both Vista and Windows Server 2008. The Next Generation TCP/IP Stack features many improvements in packet handling that are described in this chapter. Enhancements of the HTTP.SYS kernel-mode driver have added a new API for Internet transport, a new authentication scheme, improved auditing, and performance monitoring, as well as NETSH commands.

The Domain Name System (DNS) also got upgraded in Windows Server 2008 to support IPv6, as well as to add support for the new read-only domain controllers meant for branch offices. The performance of DNS has been improved for large zones, and a new GlobalNames zone allows you to store single-label names for an entire forest, no matter how large. IPv6 still remains a developing area.

Many other protocols have been improved or entirely rewritten. The Small Message Block (SMB) protocol used for Microsoft Networking and for storage access got a rewrite and a very significant performance boost. Also rewritten is the Network Driver Interface Specification (NDIS) 5.0, which is the interface between the kernel-mode network drivers and the Windows operating system. NDIS 6.0 provides the abstraction of low-level drivers that communicate with hardware to the drivers that provide network transport. True, this is all plumbing—but as we all know, tubes are important and these improvements add not only to performance but also to reliability and security.

Next Generation TCP/IP Stack

Microsoft rewrote the TCP/IP stack as part of the Windows Server 2008 core and dubbed the new design as the Next Generation TCP/IP Stack. The previous version of the stack was written in the mid-1990s when Windows NT shipped. Although it's been enhanced over the years, the stack needed a redesign to seamlessly accommodate IPv6, as well as to make the stack more secure and perform better. This new stack, in addition to appearing on Vista and Windows Server 2008, is more easily ported to other operating systems and is being rolled out to Windows CE, the Xbox, and Windows Embedded in future versions.

The TCP/IP stack is an essential piece of plumbing for Windows networking. That wasn't the case when the stack was originally designed, but over the years competing transport protocols and addressing schemes such as NetWare IPX and AppleTalk have been abandoned in favor of Ethernet and TCP/IP.

The Next Generation TCP/IP Stack is responsible for all the traffic Vista and Windows Server 2008 process that flows over the Internet, on intranets, and at this point, for almost all LANs, the traffic that is responsible for node-to-node communications. Therefore, this redesign has a fundamental influence on the performance of your network in a variety of ways. It's not obvious from the design, but this new stack has better support for hot-swapping components as well as allowing the TCP/IP stack to be configured dynamically without having to be restarted.

Architecture

Figure 3.1 shows a topological schematic of the new TCP/IP stack. Of particular note is the Network layer, which contains a single protocol that supports dual IP layer architecture that separates the IPv4 and IPv6 traffic. By default, both IPv4 and IPv6 are enabled. In Windows Server 2003 and XP, the stack was a dual-stack architecture with separate protocol components for IPv4 and IPv6, each with its own Transport layer.

FIGURE 3.1

The Next Generation TCP/IP Stack has separate channels for IPv4 and IPv6 so that they can both operate optimally at the same time.

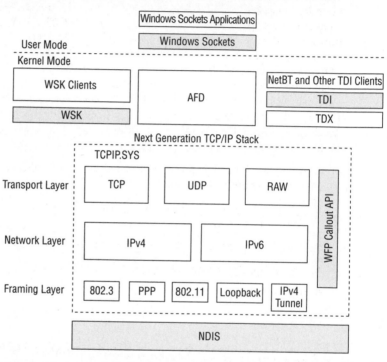

The IPv4 tunnel is a framing layer module that is used by some transitional IPv6 technologies. The Network layer adds the additional information necessary for IPv4 and IPv6 traffic. The Transport layer is where packets are created, either TCP or UDP, or as raw IP packets that don't required either of the other headers.

The Next Generation TCP/IP Stack is contained in the dashed rectangle that contains the Framing, Network, and Transport layers. There are two different system drivers that allow the API to access the stack: TCPIP.SYS for IPv4 and TCPIP6.SYS for IPv6.

The Callout API is part of the Windows Filtering Platform (WFP), which is new to Windows Server 2008. The WFP is an interface that allows applications to examine, filter, and alter packets through the whole TCP/IP stack. The API provides the mechanisms for Windows Firewall with Advanced Security to filter traffic by file type, but the same API is available to third-party developers to use to create firewalls of their own, or to enable other applications deep access to manipulate packets. Chapter 9, "Security," describes this feature of the Windows Firewall from an operational standpoint.

NDIS

Starting from the bottom of the stack, the NDIS 6.0 kernel-mode driver is new in this version of TCP/IP. It sits just below the framing layer where frames are created and the framing instructions are added. NDIS 5.1 could only have TCP receive protocol packets processed on a single CPU, or for a multicore processor on one core of the processor. NDS 6.0, which ships with Vista and Windows Server 2008, has what Microsoft is calling "receive-side scaling" and can task multiple processors with a balanced load of traffic from a network adapter.

WINDOWS SOCKETS 2

The TCP/IP stack communicates to user-mode applications through a set of APIs. You see the boundary between kernel mode and user mode at the top of Figure 3.1. Kernel modes run in protected memory space; user mode applications do not. There are two primary interfaces: the Windows Socket Kernel (WSK) and the Transport Driver Interface (TDI). Of the two, Winsock offers the better performance and uses the Windows Sockets 2 API, which is new in Windows Server 2008. TDI clients should use Winsock when possible, but the TDI interface is in Windows Server 2008 and Vista to provide support for older applications.

You can use Event Tracing for Windows (ETW) to view Winsock events in the Windows Event log. Events that you can monitor include Socket Creation, Bind, Connect, Accept, Send, Recv, and Abort. Tracing is performed from the command line using either the LOGMAN.EXE or the TRACERPT.EXE command. To use the Event Viewer for Winsock tracing, do the following:

1. Open the Event Viewer tool either from the Administrative Tools folder or from the MMC snap-in of the Server Manager.

2. Click on the Application Logs, and then navigate to the node Microsoft, Windows, Winsock, Operational Event.

3. Highlight Winsock/AFD, and in the Action pane click the Log Properties link.

4. In the Log Properties dialog box, click Enable Logging.

5. Click OK to start logging Winsock events.

Figure 3.2 shows the Winsock Operational Event application event log.

FIGURE 3.2

It is possible to monitor new network services in Windows Server 2008 in the Windows Event log. Shown here are events for the Winsock connections to the API.

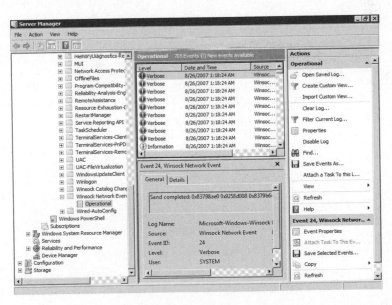

SECURE SOCKET TUNNELING PROTOCOL

The Secure Socket Tunneling Protocol (SSTP) is a new feature in Windows Server 2008 and Vista SP1 that allows you to create a virtual private networking (VPN) connection from a remote access client. SSTP clients tunnel through Network Address Translation (NAT) routers, firewalls, and proxies to a remote access server client and a Routing and Remote Access Service (RRAS) server. SSTP uses HTTPS as a transport layer so that traffic appears to these intervening services as if it is regular secure web traffic over the well-known HTTP and HTTPS ports 80 and 443. When you enable RRAS on Windows Server 2008, you turn on an SSTP listener that is essentially a VPN server.

Figure 3.3 shows the structure of an encapsulated packet that is used by a SSTP VPN connection. The IPv4 or IPv6 packet is encapsulated first with a Point-to-Point Protocol (PPT) and then with the SSTP header. The SSTP header is encrypted in the SSL session using public and private certificate keys. The TCP header and the IPv4 (or IPv6 if that is what is being used) are then added to provide the targeting information for the packet from client to server.

FIGURE 3.3

The SSTP packet architecture. The wavy lines indicate that the packet is much longer than the figure shows.

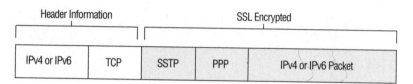

To operate correctly, the SSTP server must have a certificate for Server Authentication Enhanced Key Usage (EKU) to authenticate the SSTP server to the client when the SSL session is connected. The SSTP client then validates the server certificate with the certificate authority, and must have the root certificate of the certificate authority (CA) installed to do so.

The SSTP connection is a VPN tunnel and behaves as if it is a peer-to-Layer 2 Tunneling Protocol (L2TP) and PPTP VPN tunnel. Point-to-Point Protocol (PPP) traffic is encapsulated by SSTP, and framed to be compatible with HTTPS traffic. The encapsulation ensures that the HTTPS traffic can still be treated like a VPN tunnel and have a Network Access Protection (NAP) policy applied to it, run as IPv6 traffic (if necessary), and be compatible with the various authentication mechanisms required by VPN clients such as smart cards, logons, and connection managers not only for SSTP but for PPTP and L2TP as well. This new protocol therefore provides a logical migration away from remote access clients over PPTP and L2TP to SSTP in the future.

The SSTP protocol uses the following communications mechanism:

1. The SSTP client connects to the SSTP server using a dynamically assigned port on the client and port 443 on the SSTP server.

2. An SSL message is sent from the client to the server to create the session and the SSTP server sends the client its certificate.

3. The SSTP client validates the certificate, sets an encryption method, creates a session key, and then encrypts the session key with the public key of the SSTP server (part of the certificate).

4. The SSTP client senses the encrypted session key to the SSTP server where it is decrypted with the private key of the server certificate. This establishes the SSL session key and encryption method for the tunnel.

5. The SSTP client sends an SSL request method over HTTP to the SSTP server.

6. The SSTP client first negotiates an SSTP tunnel with the SSTP server, and then negotiates a PPT connection. The process authenticates the user with PPP and then sets the parameters for either IPv4 or IPv6 packets.

7. The SSTP client sends packets over the PPP link.

TCP/IP Offload Support

One of the newer mechanisms for improving the performance of servers is to perform what is called TCP/IP Offload Using an Offload Engine (TPCOE). You add a special application-specific integrated circuit (ASIC) either on the motherboard or, more likely, on an add-in card that has specialized hardware support for TCP/IP processing. The substitution can greatly lower the amount of CPU utilization on a server and speed up network performance.

The Next Generation TCP/IP stack supports TPCOE through the Network Driver Interface Specification (NDIS) miniport driver, as well for network interface cards. Any server that is I/O bandwidth limited benefits greatly from this approach. In modern servers, processing is so fast that most servers are in fact limited by their communication to the network or to peripheral devices. You see dramatic improvements due to TPCOE in web server applications (and server farms), cluster interconnects (such as Virtual Interface Architecture [VIA]), and in streaming applications.

TCP/IP Configuration

The mechanisms for changing network addressing; adding and removing network protocols, clients, and services; enabling and disabling components; and many other tasks are very similar in Windows Server 2008 and should be familiar to most people with Windows Server administration experience. To perform the operations in this system, you will need to be a member of the local Administrators group, or be delegated as having those levels of privileges.

To configure a connection:

1. Click Start ➤ Control Panel, and select the Network and Sharing Center command.

2. Click the Manage Network Connections link in the Tasks list of the Network and Sharing Center.

3. Right-click on the connection and then select Properties from the context menu.

4. To confirm the action in the User Account Control dialog box, click the Continue button.

   The Local Area Connection Properties dialog box appears, as shown in Figure 3.4.

5. Select Internet Protocol Version 4 (TCP/IPv4); then click Properties.

6. Either select Obtain the IP Address Automatically for DHCP or enable the Use the Following IP Address radio button and fill in the IP address, subnet mask, and default gateway.

7. Set either Obtain DNS Server Address Automatically, or enable the Use the Following DNS Server Addresses radio button and enter the Preferred DNS server address along with the Alternative DNS server address (optional).

8. Click OK to set the address; you do not need to reboot to have the address applied.

FIGURE 3.4

The Networking tab of the Local Area Connection Properties dialog box

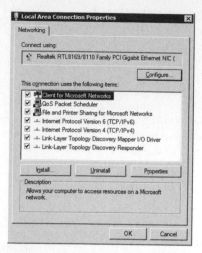

The Internet Protocol Version 4 (TCP/IPv4) Properties dialog box and the associated Advanced TCP/IP Settings dialog box both contain few new changes from previous versions of Windows. If you enable DHCP, the Alternate Configuration tab appears, allowing you to configure a secondary address, a feature that is more likely to be used on a laptop or other portable computer.

The procedure for setting the IPv6 address is similar, although the dialog boxes look a little different and require some different settings. An IPv6 address can be static or use a DHCPv6 server for its addressing. If you are specifying a static IPv6 address, you will be asked to supply the subnet prefix length and default gateway. The subnet prefix length is set to 64 by default and is standard, but can be changed.

NOTE For a primer on IPv6 addressing you can go to http://www.microsoft.com/technet/community/columns/cableguy/cg0206.mspx and read the article "Source and Destination Address Selection for IPv6."

You install services and protocols using the Install button found in the Local Area Connection Properties dialog box (Figure 3.4). The dialog box and mechanism for installing and uninstalling protocols and components hasn't changed from previous versions of Windows, although there are some different items that you can now select. Installation of new network protocols or components may require that you have the Windows Server 2008 installation disc or your third-party disc available to supply the source files.

WARNING Don't assume that network protocols and components that were designed to work with previous versions of the Windows operating system will work with Windows Server 2008. Go to the vendor's website to see if there are any updates available before you attempt the installation.

You don't necessarily need to remove a feature from the Network Connection Properties dialog box, particularly if you think that you might need the feature again at some later point. You can disable the feature and, when you need it again, enable it.

To disable a network service, protocol, or client, disable the checkbox to the left of the feature name that you want to disable, as shown earlier in Figure 3.4. To enable a network service, protocol, or client, enable the checkbox to the left of the feature name that you want to enable.

PROTOCOL BINDING ORDER

The order in which network protocols are listed in the advanced settings for a network connection determines the order in which communications using those protocols are tried in order to establish a connection with a networked computer. The goal of changing the protocol binding order is to move the protocol that you use the most or the one that is the most efficient to the top of the list so that it is tried first.

Changing the binding order can greatly speed up your connection times if you move the correct binding to the top of the list, or it can greatly impair your connection if you put the wrong protocol at the top—so be careful and test your new settings as required.

To change the protocol binding order:

1. Open the Network Connections Folder and select the Advanced Settings command from the Advanced menu.

   The Advanced Settings dialog box appears, as shown in Figure 3.5.

FIGURE 3.5

The Adapters and Bindings tab of the Advanced Settings dialog box

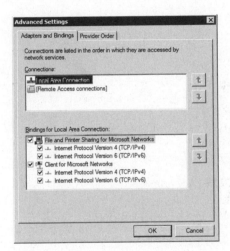

2. Click the binding you wish to modify in the Bindings for Local Area Connection list box and use the arrows to move the bindings up or down in the list.

3. Click OK to enforce your new settings.

NETWORK PROVIDER ORDER

The network provider order is the order in which Windows Server 2008 accesses other systems on the network. Consider making the following changes based on the role your Windows Server 2008 server plays on your network:

◆ For a general-purpose computer, move the Microsoft Windows Network to the top of the list.

◆ If the server is a Terminal Server, then it might make more sense to move the Microsoft Terminal Server Network Provider to the top of the list.

◆ For a Windows Server 2008 Web Server, the Web Client Network would be your choice.

◆ For a Windows File and Print Server or for a Storage Server, consider moving the NFS Network higher on the list.

The procedure for changing the network provider order is similar to the protocol binding order described earlier. Change the binding order by following that procedure with the following changes:

1. Click the Provider Order tab.

2. Highlight the Network Provider you wish to modify and click the up or down arrow to change its position on the list.

Figure 3.6 shows you the Provider Order tab.

FIGURE 3.6

The Provider Order tab of the Advanced Settings dialog box

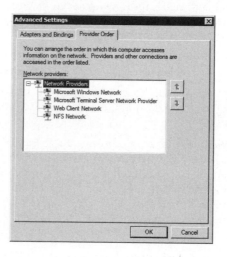

Why Use IPv6?

I believe that eventually all IP addressing will migrate from IPv4 to IPv6. IPv4, even with its limited address space, has proved remarkably resilient. Through the use of Dynamic Host Configuration Protocol (DHCP), private network addresses, and subnetting, it's been possible to have many more addresses served on the Internet than were ever thought possible by the designers of IPv4. However, one day the addresses will run out and the security enhancements available in IPv6 will prove compelling. If everything you want to control requires an IP address—your refrigerator, sensors in your car, the pacemaker in your chest, or the Radio Frequency Identification (RFID) tags on products in the store—then there will be no alternative but to move to the next-generation addressing namespace.

IPv6 doesn't just come with a larger namespace than IPv4, it has a *much, much, much larger* namespace.

For IPv4, you have 256^4, or 2^{32}, or 4,294,967,296, or a little over 4 billion addresses. That number might have seemed large once, but with Windows having shipped its billionth copy recently it is not out of reach. By contrast, IPv6 has an address space that is 2^{128}, or 3.40×10^{38}. By comparison, the number of stars in the universe is thought to be on the order of 10^{21}—more than the number of grains of sand on earth. According to my physics friends, 10^{38} is about the same order of magnitude as the possibility that I can quantum tunnel from my desk here in one room through a wall into another room. Thus the odds of running out of IPv6 numbers can be considered fairly small.

IPv6 also offers three other essential characteristics:

Enhanced routing   The IPv6 header is more efficiently packaged and supports a hierarchical routing scheme that makes routing IPv6 traffic much more efficient than IPv4.

Improved security   IPv6 requires IPsec, which cryptographically encrypts packets, as well as making it much harder to do port scanning against IPv6 addresses. For one thing, there are so many more possible IPv6 addresses that brute force and ignorance approaches to surmounting security are much more resource intensive.

Random scans are defeated by a system in Windows Server 2008 and Vista that generates random interface IDs for IPv6 addresses instead of using addresses assigned by NIC manufacturers. You can use the command `netsh interface ipv6 set global randomizeidentifiers= disabled` to disable this feature.

Self-configuring   IPv6 can be configured either by using a DHCPv6 server or a local router, or through the Neighbor Discovery Protocol (NDP).

NDP replaces the Address Resolution Protocol for IPv6 and allows for address assignment using stateless address autoconfiguration. NDP is only available for hosts and cannot be applied to routers.

IPv6 can have an address assigned by DHCPv6 using two different modes. In the DHCPv6 stateless mode, the host uses another method to obtain the IPv6 address and then uses the DHCPv6 service to accept the assignment of all other configuration details. The IPv6 prefix part of the address is usually autoconfigured by the router based on advertisement. By contrast, the DHCPv6 stateful mode assigns the IPv6 address along with all other supporting parameters from the DHCPv6 service only. Windows Server 2008 DHCPv6 supports both of these modes, and this service allows you to:

- Create IPv6 address scopes using a subnet prefix.

- Automatically create sparse IPv6 address from the large address space. Widely different addresses are harder to guess and more secure.

Other advantages are:

- Dynamic addresses can be nontemporary or temporary; the latter are used for a specific communications while the former are akin to IPv4 DHCP licenses.

- The DHCPv6 service supports server authentication in Active Directory.

- DHCPv6 can be audit logged, and the DHCP server configuration and state information can be imported and exported.

The Road to Teredo

Microsoft's Teredo technology allows organizations to transition from IPv4 to IPv6 by allowing nodes of either type to communicate with one another through a NAT using global IPv6 addresses. NAT (sometimes called network or IP masquerading) is an address remapping system usually found in a router or firewall that hides LAN addresses from the outside and makes it possible for private addresses to access the Internet through another system while retaining their anonymity. With Teredo, IPv6 traffic can communicate through a NAT without having to modify any application protocols, and since they are global addresses they are unique on the Internet.

Teredo first appeared in the Advanced Network Pack for Windows XP with Service Pack 1, and as part of the XP SP2 and Windows Server 2003 SP1 distributions. The technology is also part of Vista and Windows Server 2008, but with a few new enhancements:

◆ Domain member computers can now be manually configured.

◆ Teredo clients can now operate behind one or more symmetric NATs. A symmetric NAT maps the private address and port number to another public address and port depending on the destination system. For Windows Server 2008 or Vista, the system works when the destination computer is behind a cone or restricted NAT.

◆ Teredo now supports Universal Plug and Play (UPnP) for symmetric NATs.

The new Windows Firewall with Advanced Security supports Teredo for both IPv4 and IPv6 traffic. To have Teredo work with Windows Firewall, you define an exception, and that exception is more restrictive and therefore more secure than one a NAT applies. Also, the Windows Filtering Platform (WFP) that is used by security application developers supports secure IPv6 Teredo traffic.

HTTP Driver Enhancements

The HTTP.SYS kernel-mode driver for HTTP was rewritten as part of the release of the Windows Server 2008 core. While many of these enhancements are included with Vista, Windows Server 2008 exposes the server-side improvements for this very important communications protocol. HTTP, the communications protocol for all browsers, is a request/response mechanism for publishing and retrieving HTLM pages. Although we tend to associate HTTP with TCP/IP because HTTP is most often transported over TCP using IP addressing, there is no requirement that HTTP use TCP.

The following features have been enhanced for HTTP:

HTTP Server API 2.0   The HTTP.SYS kernel-mode driver is accessed through a user-mode API that is part of the HTTPAPI.DLL library. Applications written for Vista and Windows Server 2008 route HTTP URL requests, receive requests, and service responses through this API. Applications that use the HTTP Server API can share TCP ports with other HTTP Server API applications, allowing ports 80 and 443 to service multiple applications at once.

HTTP Server API 2.0 is backward compatible with HTTP 1.1 and supports features in IIS 6.0 such as authentication, bandwidth throttling, logging, connection limits, server state, 503 responses, request queues, response caching, and SSL certificate binding.

Server-side authentication   Support for server-side authentication is part of the API. This allows Kerberos authentication to occur on the server and without application support. Moving the mechanism for authentication to the operating system allows the process to run at a lower privilege level than it would if the application were forced to participate in the process.

Logging   The API will log requests and responses in W3C standard formats (**World Wide Web Consortium**), NCSA compliment browsers (National Computer Security Association), IIS, or the centralized binary log file.

NETSH commands   The NETSH HTTP command allows you to display the state of the HTTP.SYS service and cache, clear or log the HTTP buffers, change SSL certificate bindings, modify IP listen lists, alter timeouts, and change URL reservations.

ETW tracing of HTTP events   Event Tracing for Windows (ETW) can diagnose problems by logging the activity of the API calls into a log file. Events that are recorded include requests and responses, SSL and other authentication transactions, events, connections, cache object storage, service or application setup, and other activities.

Start an ETW trace from the command line using the following command: `logman start "http trace" -pf httptrace.txt -o httptrace.etl -ets`. You can stop the trace using `logman stop "http trace" -ets`. Data is stored in the `HTTPTRACE.TXT` file, with the first line `"Microsoft-Windows-HttpService" 0xFFFF`.

New performance counters   The HTTP counters that you can monitor display data about the URLs processed and cached, data send and receive rates, bytes sent and received, connections, GET and HEAD requests, and the state of the service request queue. Over 21 counters are now available for you to monitor the HTTP API.

Storage Networking

Storage networks have tended to use their own network protocols, transports, and media in order to attain higher performance to and from storage that would be possible over Ethernet and LANs. Technologies such as Fibre Channel were tuned for larger-sized packet transmission and for more reliable transmission, because unlike Ethernet on WANs you could count on a Fibre Channel network being reliable. In the late 1980s and 1990s, Fibre Channel would run as its own separate network to large storage devices, often controlled by and supporting hosts (servers mostly, but computers generally) that were connected to one another over Ethernet. In storage network parlance, Fibre Channel is "in-band" communications and Ethernet is "out-of-band" communications.

Two factors that have changed storage networking dramatically since the late 1990s and beyond have been the development of high-speed Ethernet networks and the massive capacity commodity storage. In an era of Gigabit Ethernet (GigE) and terabyte hard drives, the performance advantages that Fibre Channel and storage arrays have over Ethernet and server-based storage RAID have been disappearing and the cost advantages of the latter combination have become compelling.

Fast Ethernet has led to a proliferation of storage networking technologies that bridge Ethernet to Fibre Channel, Ethernet to SCSI; and to various IP storage technologies, of which iSCSI (SCSI over IP) is probably preeminent at the moment. Large-capacity disks, and particularly Serial Advanced Technology Attachment (SATA), has led SATA RAID to become increasingly popular. Both of these technologies have had additional support added in Windows Server 2008 to support them. Chapter 6, "File System Enhancements," describes the file server role, the new Volume Manager, and the new SMB 2.0 file access protocol, so for the moment let's skip these topics.

Storage Explorer

Windows Server 2008 introduces Storage Explorer, which is the storage networking equivalent of the Windows Explorer. Storage Explorer is a companion tool for the Storage Manager for SANs (SMfS) that appeared in the Windows Server 2003 R2 release. Storage Explorer allows you to:

- View your Fibre Channel (FC) and iSCSI fabrics (a multi-connected network architecture)
- Create and manage LUNs
- Create and manage iSCSI targets
- View your storage devices and servers
- Gain access to the TCP/IP management tools of devices

You can view Storage Explorer by selecting the Storage Explorer command from the Administrative Tools folder on the Start menu. Figure 3.7 shows the Storage Explorer MMC.

FIGURE 3.7
Storage Explorer allows you to view your storage networks, just as Windows Explorer lets you view your directory structure.

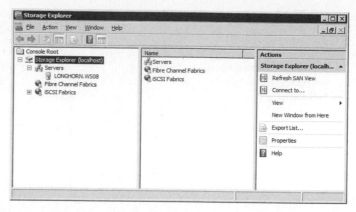

When taken as a combination, Storage Explorer and Storage Manager for SANs provide an all-in-two SAN management system. That's an important addition to Windows networking because SAN management packages are often very expensive and hard to implement. In storage networking, when it comes to the management console for a SAN, Windows Server is one of the only two server platforms that matter. The other platform is Sun Solaris. Of the two, Microsoft probably has a significantly larger market share when it comes to the storage management console.

iSCSI

The iSCSI interface takes SCSI communications and encapsulates it in TCP/IP packets so that the data can be sent over Ethernet from one iSCSI adapter to another. The "i" in iSCSI stands for Internet, although "e" for Ethernet would probably be more appropriate. iSCSI consists of an add-in card that connects to SCSI devices and a set of software routines and drivers that do the translation from SCSI to iSCSI and back to SCSI again. Although the technology was developed to connect to SCSI devices, the popularity of SATA RAID has led to the development of iSCSI connected to those types of devices as well. iSCSI may be seen as a lower-cost alternative to Fibre Channel.

The system has an initiator that sends out the iSCSI signal and a target that receives it. Figure 3.8 shows the iSCSI protocol stack. Traffic is protected by access control lists (ACLs) on the server(s), while communication is protected by Internet Protocol security (IPsec) and CHAP (Challenge Handshake Authentication Protocol). Access to LUNs is limited by the Windows host, a process referred to as LUN masking. A feature called iSCSI remote boot allows you to start a Windows Server 2008 (or Windows Server 2003) server over IP from a remote disk on a SAN.

What Windows Server 2008 adds to the picture is the Microsoft iSCSI Initiator. This was an optional download for Windows Server 2003, but is now part of the Windows Server 2008 distribution. The built-in initiator makes it very easy to create an iSCSI system.

To create an IP-based storage system, you need only configure an iSCSI device with the Microsoft iSCSI Initiator (similar to configuring a device driver), and then plug your device into a GigE switch. From the standpoint of a server operator, the iSCSI device shows up in Storage Explorer in the iSCSI node, or better yet appears in the Volume Manager, as if it is Direct Attached Storage (DAS). You can also perform these operations from the command line using the iSCSI command-line interface (CLI). After that, you can use the storage wizards to provision the storage and create the volumes you desire.

Among the Microsoft enterprise applications that benefit from multipath I/O are SharePoint Server, Exchange, SQL Server, and Microsoft Cluster Server (MSCS).

FIGURE 3.8
The iSCSI protocol stack with a request coming from a computer and going to a storage server through the Internet

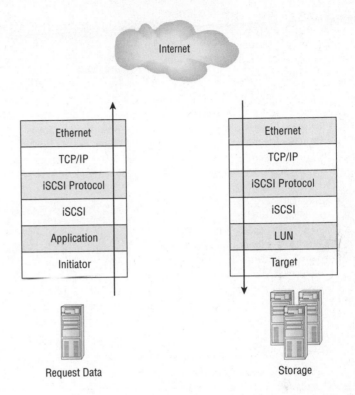

Request Data

Storage

Multipath I/O

Many server applications require a feature called multipath I/O, commonly referred to as multipathing. Multipathing supports network traffic flow through multiple network adapters or when applied to storage through the host bus adapters (HBAs)—usually, but not always, with a load-balancing feature. Multipath I/O is to network connections what a hard drive is to RAID—a means of ensuring dramatically improved performance and fault tolerance. Storage applications are one area that uses multipath I/O to improve performance to disk arrays, but usually the multipath portion of these applications is an expensive add-on to the main application.

Multipath I/O has been added to Windows Server 2008 as a set of drivers that you can install using the following procedure:

1. Open the Server Manager and click on the Features node of the tree control.

2. In the Roles Summary pane, locate the Roles section (it's usually the top section) and click the Add Features link.

3. In the Select Features step of the Add Features Wizard, enable the Multipath I/O feature; then click the Next button.

4. Confirm the selection and click the Install button to install the Multipath I/O drivers and support utilities.

Once the Multipath I/O drivers are installed, they can be configured in any of the following three ways:

◆ From the MPIO Properties dialog box

◆ Using the MPIO command in the Administrative Tools folder of the Start menu

◆ From the command line

In the first two instances, you see the same configuration dialog box, shown in Figure 3.9. Multipath applications connect to storage arrays that are managed using different industry standards. They can be Active/Active (both nodes accepting traffic at the same time) or SPC3 (Software Process Control) standards and work with the Microsoft device-specific modules (DSM). You use the DSM Install tab of the MPIO Properties dialog box to install third-party solutions for multipathing. Sometimes storage vendors use the Microsoft drivers and the MPIO architecture to create proprietary solutions, and then use the MPIO Properties dialog box for installation.

FIGURE 3.9

To install a multipath I/O application using the Microsoft drivers, open the MPIO Properties dialog box and select the DSM Install tab.

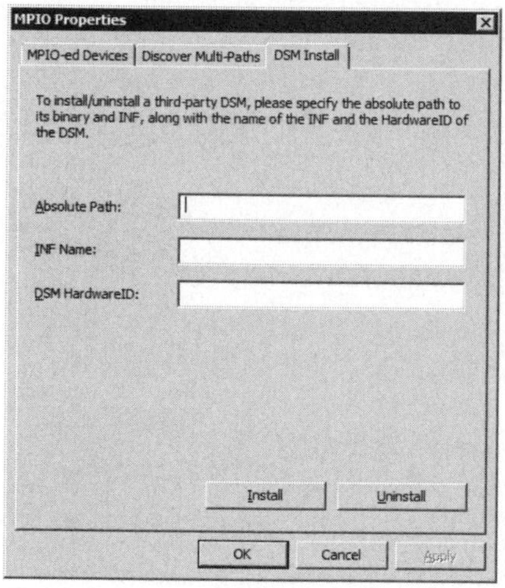

Multipath I/O supports high availability solutions with redundant multiple hardware paths. Here are some important considerations when using MPIO with enterprise applications:

Prioritized paths   One path is the primary path used for device requests. Additional paths are used for other traffic. If the primary path fails, failover is to the next path in order of their listing.

No load balancing   If you need load balancing you should install Network Load Balancing (NLB), which is another feature in Windows Server 2008.

Round-robin   DSMs can use the paths in a round-robin fashion, either in part (a subset) or in whole (all paths).

Dynamic least queue depth   While the load isn't balanced with **Memory Mapped Input/Output** (MMIO), the system can route requests to the path with the fewest outstanding requests in their request queue.

Weighted paths   Applications can assign a weight to a path, and the DSM will prioritize traffic based on those priorities.

Failback   A path can be assigned to a particular communications. Should that path fail, then MMIO reassigns that task to another path. When the primary path becomes active again, the system fails back to the primary path that was originally specified.

Summary

In this chapter we looked at the network architecture for Windows Server 2008 and the Windows Server 2008 core. Windows networking was rewritten at a basic level with Vista and Windows Server 2008, all the way down to the fundamental modules. The highlight of the new networking services is the Next Generation TCP/IP Stack, something that isn't obvious from a user's standpoint but that plays a fundamental role in improving all IP communications. The improvements in the new stack help support a more streamlined dual path for IPv4 and IPv6, and Microsoft continues to build on their transition tools from the former to the latter.

Storage networking is another area in which there have been improvements. Windows Server 2008 comes with a new Storage Explorer, multipathing options, and a built-in iSCSI initiator. It has never been so easy to implement large storage solutions as with this version of Windows Server.

In the next chapter, we'll explore changes to Active Directory. Active Directory modifications include improvement in its capability to support better security through more proactive identification security mechanisms. A read-only domain controller and a restartable Active Directory, along with the many changes that hundreds of Vista supporting group policies require, make the improvements interesting and valuable.

Chapter 4

Active Directory

Active Directory (AD) is so central to Windows networking it is hard to make any significant changes to Windows servers and clients without modifying it. Since AD was first introduced in Windows 2000, there have been changes with every version. Depending on how you look at it, Active Directory in Windows Server 2008 is the third major version and a rather mature system.

The changes in AD for this version are modest. From a topology standpoint, the introduction of read-only domain controllers should make it easier to deploy Windows in remote offices, delegate authority to users, and keep sensitive security information secure. A new security PKI security scheme as well as improvements in replication and auditing are also part of the changes.

One operational improvement, the introduction of the restartable Active Domain service, will make it easier to service domain controllers without having to go through the pain of reestablishing the service upon reboot. To support hundreds of new policies, AD contains hundreds of new entries, but the policy engine provides the only interface for these changes that you need to concern yourself with.

Introducing Active Directory

AD is what makes Windows networking network. It is both a system service and a database repository. AD authenticates users, stores vital system and application information, and plays the gatekeeper to domain resources. Windows Server 2008 brings us the concept of *roles* and *features*. A role is a collection of services that a server can perform, and its features are the individual capabilities available within a role. Directory Services is one of the roles you can define; it's a central role. If you first create a directory server, then this role creates and maintains your entire domain structure. Additional domain servers add fault tolerance, higher capacity, and better access.

Most of what's new with Active Directory in Windows Server 2008 falls into two main categories: better management and enterprise versions of AD for specialized purposes. Windows Server 2008 introduces a new type of domain server called a *read-only domain controller (RODC)* that contains only the AD database and that is much more resistant to hacking. RODC is meant for branch offices where a low level of security exists but where access to domain information suffers from low connectivity. The new management interface, new domain Group Policies for password management and auditing, and a new data-mining tool that creates point-in-time views all make AD easier to use. Directory Services can be restarted in Windows Server 2008 without having to resort to Directory Services Restore Mode to bring AD back online, as was the case previously.

Enterprise improvements to AD include the consolidation of a set of directory services for managing what Microsoft calls *Identity and Access (IDA)*. These services include AD Certificate Services, AD Federation Services, and AD Rights Management Services. All of these services were available in earlier versions, but it is Microsoft's vision to merge identity management into a single IDA platform based on Active Directory. Further development will lead past Windows Server 2008's release to the Identity Lifecycle Manager, which is a platform for managing user identities in the enterprise.

Fundamentally, Active Directory is one of those areas in Windows Server 2008 that benefits from general platform improvements while leaving the core functionality largely unchanged. After a brief overview of AD, we'll take a look at how the improvements in AD impact network architecture and how some of these improvements might show up as features in other applications. We will also take a general look at the concept of roles and features, and explore how these elements have been used to support Active Directory in particular.

Originally called the NT Directory Services (NTDS), Directory Services started development just after the release of Windows 95. NTDS became "Active" when Microsoft marketing decided to "Activate the Internet" with ActiveX. Active Directory first appeared as the child of Windows 2000, where at its initial release it was clearly a work in progress. A point upgrade from 1.0 to 1.1 followed quickly. The Active Directory that shipped with Windows 2003/XP was the version that brought major new functionality and made fundamental improvements to this network service. Forests, trees, organizational units, and many more features were part of that second major release.

NOTE Traces of NTDS remain, even in Windows Server 2008. The %WINDIR%\NTDS directory stores a log file for changes made to Active Directory.

Many people at Microsoft have worked on AD over the years, but the person who was most associated with its development was Jim Allchin. At Banyan, Allchin was the principle architect of Banyan VINES, a distributed network operating system that included the StreetTalk directory protocol. At Microsoft, Allchin worked on Cairo before heading NT development from version 3.5 until Vista shipped on January 30, 2007. Allchin's vision of creating "an architecture for reliable decentralized systems" is what Active Directory was meant to be—and has become.

Objects and Schema

AD is based on a standard, and thus can interoperate with other directory services. AD is Microsoft's version of the Lightweight Directory Access Protocol (LDAP); the term *lightweight* was meant to differentiate it from the X.500 Directory Access Protocol (DAP). DAP was a telecom standard and required the full seven layers (hardware/software) of the Open Systems Interconnection (OSI) protocol stack for communications. LDAP was lightweight in the sense that it narrowed the service to simply using the TCP/IP transport protocol.

All LDAP directories have the following features:

Directory Tree   A tree with entries at each node.

Nodes   Entries (or objects) that are containers for a set of attributes and that are extensible.

Attributes   Each attribute has a name (sometimes called its type or description), and each attribute can be multivalued.

Unique Entries   Each entry may be identified by its Distinguished Name (DN), to which is added the Relative Distinguished Name (RDN) of the entry's parent node's DN.

In Active Directory the DN consists of the following components:

- DC (Domain Component)
- O (Organization)
- OU (Organizational Unit)
- CN (Common Name)

When combined into a complete object identifier, an AD DN takes this form:

```
/DC=<OrganizationName>/OU=<DepartmentName>/CN=<ServerName>
```

Taken as a whole, an LDAP defines a *namespace*, and items in that namespace are *dynamic*, which means that the DNs are dynamic. When you take a user account in Active Directory and move it from one department to another, you are also changing the user object's DN. To identify an object in LDAP, you must assign a Universally Unique Identifier (UUID) to it. Microsoft's version of the UUID is the Microsoft Globally Unique Identifier (GUID). The GUID is a nearly unique number taken out of a namespace with 2^{122}, or 5.3×10^{36}, possibilities.

AD is implemented as an object-oriented database and stores metadata about network characteristics. *Metadata* is data that describes how a data set is organized. Metadata plays the same role as a schema does in a database or that an XML schema file plays in an XML data file. The directory services perform the role of an abstraction layer between clients and servers, users and resources, access of one namespace to another namespace, and so forth.

In AD, objects can be resources such as computers, printers, or an online volume; they can be services such as authentication (logon), e-mail, or messaging; and they can be user accounts, group accounts, and machine accounts—which are sometimes called computer or system accounts. You can categorize objects into groups, and the relationship between the objects in the directory tree is referred to as its schema. A *schema* is a little like an architectural blueprint.

The Landscape

Active Directory can have one directory tree in it, or two, or many. A collection of trees is called a *forest*, and in order for the forest to be constructed it must have one or more two-way (transitive) trust-related trees. In the AD hierarchy, each tree can have one or more domains and domain trees, which are organized into trust hierarchy linked by transitive relationships. Each domain is identified by a single namespace stored in a single database identified in the tree of domains by a DNS name that can be accessed by a DNS service. As you learned in the previous chapter, the Domain Name Service (DNS) translates IP addresses to friendly names; for example, it translates my publisher Sybex's friendly name, www.sybex.com, to and from the IP address 208.215.179.220.

There is a further grouping with a domain into which related objects can be grouped, called the organizational unit (OU). OUs exist in a hierarchy in the domain, which is valuable in structuring an organization's AD into logical units formed around functions (departments) or geographical locations. You can also define sites in AD. Whereas domains and OUs are logical groupings, a site is usually defined by a physical characteristic of the network, such as an IP subnet. Sites are useful when the hardware they define differs, such as a backbone subnet versus a dial-up connection. You can see how valuable knowing a site's properties could be in setting the policy a router uses to route packets.

Microsoft recommends that organizations minimize the number of domains and apply most Group Policies at the level of either the OU or a site. The reason for this recommendation is that it is more common to find resource delegation at the OU level, with very granular delegation occurring at site.

Distribution and Replication

The Active Directory Security Accounts Manager (SAM) database provides authentication for access to network resources. When AD first appeared in Windows 2000, directory servers were organized around a single primary domain controller (PDC) and one or more backup domain controllers

(BDCs). That version of the SAM database used a multimaster scheme to replicate changes between domain controllers. You create a PDC by using the PCPROMO command. In Windows 2000, if your PDC went down you could promote a BDC to a PDC, or you could migrate a PDC status to a BDC, downgrading the status of the original PDC. The method for replication and distribution of domain controllers changed dramatically with Windows Server 2003.

Windows Server 2003 and now Windows Server 2008 do away with BDCs, changing all domain controllers into peers. Changes in the databases use multimaster replication to propagate. Any server that isn't a DC is a member server, be it an application server, mail server, identity server, or any other specialized server.

The AD database is split into three naming contexts or partitions:

Schema Partition   This partition contains the definition of objects and attributes.

Configuration Partition   This partition stores the physical structure and topology of a forest.

Domain Partition   This partition domain contains the information about the topology and configuration of the forest.

In the replication process, the schema and configuration databases are replicated to all domain controllers in the forest. The domain partition is only replicated to other domain controllers that are in the same domain.

Directory Auditing

Since Active Directory is the gatekeeper to all of your network resources (and the Key Distribution Server [KDS] is the key master) having an audit trail that allows you to determine who has accessed what and when is a very valuable management feature. Auditing Active Directory has been a policy setting that you could put in place with Windows Server 2003 R2 as the global audit policy Audit Directory Services Access. As with any policies, you can turn them on and off with the Group Policy Object Editor.

Past editions of Window Server allowed directory access events to be recorded in the Security log but didn't offer any further granularity. Windows Server 2008 has four categories of directory service auditing:

- Directory Services Access

- Directory Services Changes

- Directory Services Replication

- Detailed Directory Services Replication

These four categories are part of the audit policy Directory Service Changes. Events are generated when an object in the directory is created, moved, altered, or undeleted. The new capabilities record attributes of these events, such as before and after values, previous and new locations, value at the time of creation, and so forth. You must have the Group Policy Management feature installed before you can audit Active Directory.

To enable directory auditing:

1. Click Start ➢ Administrative Tools ➢ Group Policy Management.

2. In the tree, open the forest (if there is one), then Domains, and then double-click on your domain. Double-click on the domain controllers to open the template.

3. Right-click on Domain Controllers Policy and select the Edit command.

4. Open Computer Configuration: double-click first on Windows Settings, Security Settings, Local Policies, and finally on Audit Policy.

5. Right-click on Audit Directory Service Access and then select Properties.

6. Enable the Define These Policy Settings checkbox.

7. Under Audit These Attempts, enable the Success checkbox and click OK.

As an alternate, with administrator credentials you can enter the following at the command prompt:

```
auditpol /set /subcategory:"directory service changes" /success:enable
```

With auditing turned on, you can specify which object security access control lists (ACLs) (or system ACLs, or SACLs) are monitored using the following procedure:

1. Click Start ➤ Administrative Tools ➤ Active Directory Users and Computers.

2. Right-click on the object you want to audit and select Properties.

   Most of the time, the object you want to audit is an OU for your domain.

3. Select the Security tab, click the Advanced button, and then select the Auditing tab.

4. Click Add and in the Enter the Object Name to Select section, enter **Authenticated Users** and click the OK button.

   You can audit other security principals, such as groups or systems, but users are the most common choice.

5. Click Descendant User objects in the Apply onto section.

6. Enable the Successful checkbox in the Write All properties in the Access section.

7. Apply your changes by clicking OK.

To view directory access events, open the Event Viewer and examine the Security log. In previous versions of Windows Server, this type of event was given an ID number of 566. In Windows Server 2008, the directory access audit ID is now 4662. You can filter the log to see just those event IDs. To view directory access audit events:

1. Open the Server Manager and expand the Diagnostics section, Windows Logs, and finally click on Security, as shown in Figure 4.1.

2. Click on the Filter Current Log link in the Actions panel, and in the Filter Current Log dialog box shown in Figure 4.2, enter the Event ID you want to examine and click OK.

   Event 4662 was for the general category, Event ID 5136 is for modifications, 5137 is for create, 5138 is for undelete, and 5139 is for moving an object.

FIGURE 4.1
The Security log
viewed in the new
Event Manager

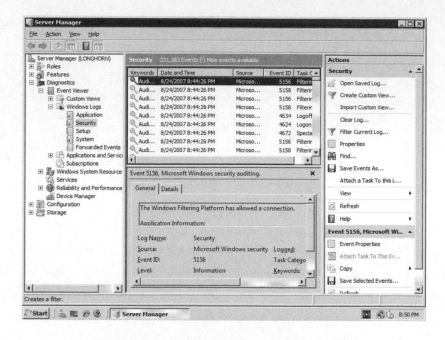

FIGURE 4.2
My Security log had
213,536 events—
which would be a
nightmare without a
filter. Filtering for
5136 yielded 15
events.

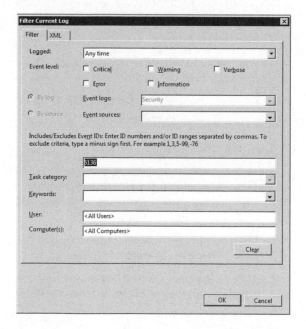

3. Double-click on the event of interest; the Event Properties dialog box appears as shown in Figure 4.3.

FIGURE 4.3

A modified object Directory Access event

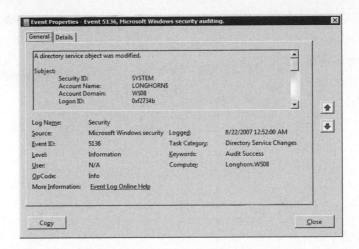

4. Use the up and down arrows to move between events, the scrollbar to view the remainder of the description, or the Copy button to copy the description of the event as text.

5. Close the dialog box to return to the Event Viewer.

The Event log contains detailed auditing data about the event. The following is an edited version of the event. This is where you get to use the Distinguished Name to figure out what's been changed. What's interesting about the following event data (and the reason that I've shown it) is to give you an idea of how Active Directory brings order to all the various objects found on a network:

```
Log Name:        Security
Source:          Microsoft-Windows-Security-Auditing
Date:            8/22/2007 12:52:00 AM
Event ID:        5136
Task Category:   Directory Service Changes
Level:           Information
Keywords:        Audit Success
User:            N/A
Computer:        Longhorn.WS08
Description:
A directory service object was modified.

Subject:
    Security ID:     SYSTEM
    Account Name:     LONGHORN$
    Account Domain:     WS08
    Logon ID:      0xf2734b

Directory Service:
    Name:  WS08
    Type:  Active Directory Domain Services

Object:
```

```
DN:    CN=RouterIdentity,CN=LONGHORN,OU=Domain Controllers,DC=WS08
GUID:   CN=RouterIdentity,CN=LONGHORN,OU=Domain Controllers,DC=WS08
Class:   rRASAdministrationConnectionPoint

Attribute:
LDAP Display Name:   msRRASAttribute
Syntax (OID):   2.5.5.12
Value:   311:6:501

Operation:
   Type:   Value Added
   Correlation ID:   {758118b4-42cc-48ba-a646-28598f346413}
   Application Correlation ID:   -
Event Xml:
<Event xmlns="http://schemas.microsoft.com/win/2004/08/events/event">
  <System>
    <Provider Name="Microsoft-Windows-Security-Auditing" Guid="{54849625-5478-
4994-a5ba-3e3b0328c30d}" />
    <EventID>5136</EventID>
…
    <Channel>Security</Channel>
    <Computer>Longhorn.WS08</Computer>
    <Security />
  </System>
  <EventData>
    <Data Name=
…
  </EventData>
</Event>
```

Creating a Domain Controller

There are two basic steps to creating a domain controller: selecting and installing the type of Active Directory role(s) you wish to operate in, and applying the DCPROMO command to the system. To install the Active Directory Domain Services (AD DS) server role, you can click on the Add Roles link in the server manager to launch the Add Roles wizard, and enable the Active Directory Domain Services check box. There are several different Active Directory role services, and the section "Active Directory Roles" describes these services in more detail.

With the role service(s) installed you must launch the Active Directory Domain Services Installation wizard. You can do this from the link in the AD DS section of the Server Manager, or you can enter DCPROMO at a Command Prompt window. In past versions of Windows server, the DCPROMO command would run without intervention to completion, and then ask you to restart your system to complete the installation. DCPROMO does have command switches (see http://technet2.microsoft .com/windowsserver2008/en/library/d660e761-9ee7-4382-822a-06fc2365a1d21033.mspx? mfr=true; or use the /? switch), but in most cases the command is executed without any options. In Windows Server 2008 the AD DS Installation wizard does present several options that you need to consider. Let's take a closer look at what's involved.

The wizard begins by displaying the informational screen about Operating System Compatibility shown in Figure 4.4. If you experience difficulty connecting to Windows Server 2008 from clients and other servers using the SMB file server protocol then you should consult the Knowledge Base article mentioned in the dialog box. Vista SP1 clients have the necessary algorithm and are not impacted by this issue.

FIGURE 4.4

New security protocols in Windows Server 2008 can impact connections to any system prior to Vista SP1 for SMB and domain joins.

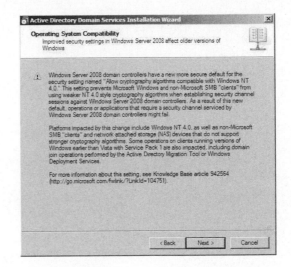

To install a domain controller, do the following:

1. Click the link in the AD DS section of the Server Manager for the AD DS wizard.

2. After reading the informational dialog box shown in Figure 4.4, click Next.

3. On the Name the Forest Root Domain enter the FQDN (Fully Qualified Domain Name) of the forest root domain for your domain controller into the text box; then click Next.

4. Select the Windows Server forest functional level, then click Next.

NOTE There are three different levels of domain services in a forest: Windows Server 2000 forests, Windows Server 2003 forests, and native Windows Server 2008 forests. When you run with earlier forest functional levels the DC runs with some of the later domain services turned off. For example, Windows Server 2003 forests add the following services to what was in a Windows Server 2003 forest: trust between forests, improved replication configuration, and linked value replication.

5. On the Additional Domain Controller Options screen, select the options you desire for this controller: installation of a DNS server, Global Catalog server, or Read Only Domain Controller (RODC); then click Next.

   For the first domain controller in a forest, only DNS Server is an available option. The RODC is described in more detail in the section "Read-Only Domain Controllers" at the end of this chapter.

6. Enter the location for the Database, Log files, and SYSVOL folders into their respective spots, as shown in Figure 4.5, then click the Next button.

FIGURE 4.5

The location of database, log, and SYSVOL files on different volumes can improve both performance and the ability to restore the Active Directory.

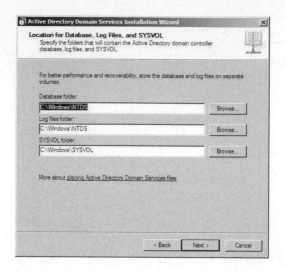

7. Enter the administrator password on the Directory Services Restore Mode Administrator Password screen; then click Next.

8. On the Summary screen shown in Figure 4.6 is a list of your chosen settings. You can export these settings in the XML answer file format for use in unattended installations. Click Next to begin the installation.

Depending upon a number of factors, domain controller installation takes several minutes to complete. As individual services such as DNS, the Group Policy Management Console, and others are installed, the wizard lists its current activity.

FIGURE 4.6

The Summary screen of the AD DS Installation wizard.

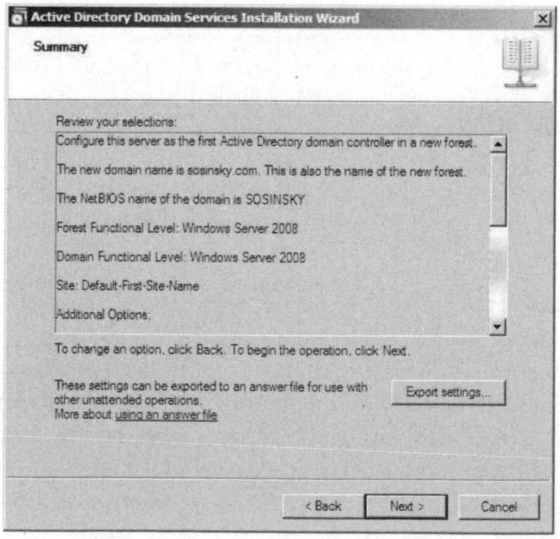

9. Upon completion you should see the final screen of the wizard shown in Figure 4.7. Click Finish, and restart your system.

FIGURE 4.7
The Completion screen of the AD DS Installation wizard.

Once the domain controller has been installed, you will be able to manage objects in the domain using the Active Directory Users and Computers, Active Directory Domains and Trusts, and the Active Directory Sites and Services MMC snap-ins. Each of these three tools is available from commands in the Administrative Tools folder on the Start menu, or can be accessed from the AD DS page in the Server Manager.

A fourth domain tool, the Active Directory Schema snap-in, is not installed by default and must be added manually. Working with AD schema is considered an advanced operation, and is protected by requiring additional steps to install. An administrator must first register the DLL by entering REVSVR32 SCHMMGMT.DLL at the command prompt. Once registered, the Active Directory Schema snap-in can then be added in the MMC from the list of snap-ins.

Active Directory Roles

One of AD's main tasks is to authenticate resource access. The AD first has to establish the identity of the machine and user, and then determine that the request is reliably originating from that source. Some requests are generated by systems (other computers), and many times the requests are generated by users. The desire to allow secure transactions over what are inherently insecure wide area networks such as the Internet makes the problem daunting.

Public Key Infrastructures

Many of the basic mechanisms for identity and authentication were already part of the original Windows 2000 Server release, albeit scattered about in separate applications. In Windows Server 2000 Microsoft already had a Public Key Infrastructure (PKI) based on the Kerberos protocol in place. Kerberos uses a certificate authority (CA), or trusted third party, to issue signed digital certificates that authenticate users, systems, applications, web services, and even smart cards. Authentication in Kerberos is on a per-transaction basis, with each request along with the appropriate digital certificate going to the CA and a session ticket issued that validates the transaction.

NOTE For a detailed discussion of how Microsoft Kerberos operates, read "Kerberos Technical Supplement for Windows" found at `http://msdn2.microsoft.com/en-us/library/aa480609.aspx`.

Figure 4.8 shows you the Microsoft Kerberos implementation over Security Support Provider Interface (SSPI). SSPI lets applications plug into security systems without having to change the network interface to the security system, and abstracts authentication from the actual communication transport. The details of how tickets are generated, what's in a ticket, and the mechanism by which the different systems validate the transaction are interesting but would take too long to explain here. Suffice it to say that Kerberos is reliable, having had its security tested by many people for many years.

FIGURE 4.8

The basic mechanism for a PKI transaction using the Kerberos protocol

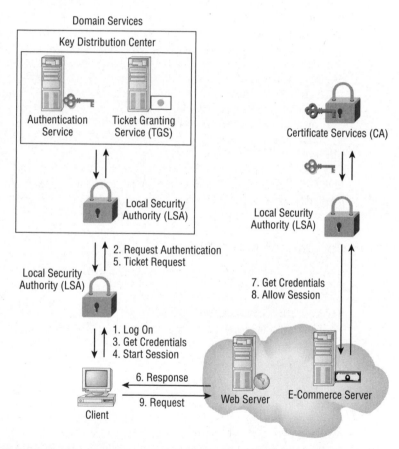

On Windows Server 2000 you installed and managed Certificate Services to handle the Windows network portion of the PKI exchange separately from Active Directory. AD and Certificate Services were two separate applications, although as you can see in the figure they are both "directory services" and relied on each other to provide the means to identify and authenticate users in what is essentially a three-way exchange: request, authentication, response. Windows Server 2008 integrates the Certificate Services into the Active Directory Domain Services role, allowing you to manage both together.

Metadirectories

Microsoft based its Active Directory on an industry-standard LDAP implementation for good reason. In order to rule the networking world, Windows must be able to interoperate with other directory services. In the enterprise world everyone has a directory. There's Novell eDirectory (once known as Novell Directory Services, or NDS), Sun Java System Directory Server, IBM Tivoli Directory Server, Fedora Directory Server, ApacheDS, OpenDS, Apple Open Directory (OS X Server), and so on. These directory services can exchange information because they are based on LDAP and LDAP is based on the X.500 standard. Exchanging information is basically a mapping exercise.

In Windows Server 2000, the product that did the mapping was an add-on application called Microsoft Metadirectory Services (MMS). MMS consolidated the information found in all the various directories that an organization might have into one consolidated repository that synchronized with the others. One directory to bind them all, one directory to rule them...

With MMS 2.2 on a server, management agents scattered about, and LDAP, Active Directory could provide information contained on another directory service such as Lotus Notes (Lotus Domino actually). That made it easier for Microsoft to displace products like Exchange and Novell NDS, although since the implementation of unifying metadirectories is primarily a large enterprise exercise it is unclear just how successful Microsoft has been in this area.

The Microsoft Identity Integration Server (MIIS) was rolled out with Windows Server 2003 to replace MMS 2.2. MIIS improved on MMS by providing not only a repository but also a unified view of directory data in the enterprise. Microsoft differentiated MIIS into two products. The first was Microsoft Identity Integration Server 2003 SP1 Enterprise Edition for directory consolidation and synchronization, account provisioning, and password management; it could be used between directories of all types. The second product (released around Windows Server 2003 R2) was the freely distributed Identity Integration Feature Pack 1a, and it offered the same features but only worked between the AD Directory Service, Active Directory Application Mode (ADAM; described in a moment), and Microsoft Exchange.

Customized Active Directory Versions

Microsoft began to customize the Active Directory after the release of Windows Server 2003 by introducing more authentication services. Active Directory Application Mode (ADAM) was probably the most widely used of these new services. You can think of ADAM as an application-specific directory service that can be deployed with applications that are designed to use directory services. With ADAM in place, you can deploy an applications server without it having to be dependent on a domain controller to operate. ADAM stored its own application specific data and supported the one (and only one) application that it was installed and configured for. Each instance of ADAM had its own directory, its own SSL and LDAP ports, and even its own set of events in the application log. ADAM was a component of Windows Server 2003 R2, but could be installed as an add-on to Windows Server 2003 and Windows XP.

Windows Server 2003 also added to the AD and Certificate Services the Authorization Manager. Authorization Manager featured role-based access control (RBAC), which assigns permissions for resource access to users based on their business needs. Windows Server already had object access control in the access control list (ACL) security scheme. RBAC enables users in a line-of-business application to obtain access to a specific resource based on the role they play in their business, not just from their Windows networking privileges. Authorization Manager was something that you could add to application—a set of COM interfaces expressed as an MMC snap-in that allow an application to verify users.

Two other policy-based services arrived with Windows Server 2003 R2: Windows Rights Management Services (RMS) and Active Directory Federation Services (ADFS). RMS allowed only an authorized RMS client to have access to confidential information such as Sarbanes-Oxley and **Health Insurance Portability and Accountability Act of 1996** (HIPAA). RMS used the services of Active Directory, PKI, Internet Information Server, and SQL Server (at the server end) and Microsoft Office 2003 and Internet Explorer (at the client end) to create the system needed.

ADFS provides a Single Sign-On (SSO) for Internet users based on a profile that is defined by the WS-Federation Passive Requestor Profile (WS-F PRP) protocol. ADFS is another service that extended AD to authenticate users on a session basis (rather than a transaction) across the Web by establishing trust relationships between ADFS and other parties.

Integrated Authorization

Windows Server 2008 had as a design goal the intent to consolidate all of these various services and products into a single solution for identity and access services. To summarize the previous sections, here are the services that identify and authorize after Windows Server 2003 Release 2:

◆ Active Directory

◆ Certificate Services

◆ Authorization Manager

◆ Active Directory Application Mode

◆ Rights Management Services

◆ Active Directory Federation Services

◆ Microsoft Identity Information Server 2003

In Windows Server 2008, the first five of these services have been consolidated into the Domain Services role. Figure 4.9 shows how these services relate to one another. You no longer see ADAM because it is now called the Active Directory Lightweight Directory Services (LDS).

FIGURE 4.9
Windows Server 2008 has turned many of the identity and access services into AD role services.

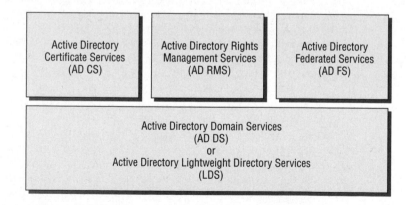

You can still add the Authorization Manager to the MMC, although some of the functionality of setting role-based security is now part of the way you set ACLs in the Active Directory.

To add Authorization Manager to the MMC, do the following:

1. Click Start ➢ Run, enter **MMC** in the Run dialog box, and press the Enter key.

2. Select the Add/Remove command from the File menu.

3. In the Available snap-ins list, select the Authorization Manager, click the Add button, and then click OK, as shown in Figure 4.10.

FIGURE 4.10
You can add the Authorization Manager as well as other MMC snap-ins using the Add or Remove Snap-ins dialog box.

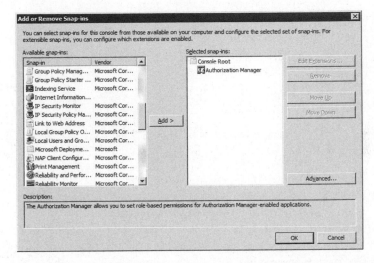

Note that the new naming convention has AD followed by the service name in all cases except for LDS. The Active Directory Domain Service (AD DS) is the role, and the new Certificate Services, Rights Management Services, and Federated Services are role services run off of the AD DS. When Active Directory is put into the application mode (previously called ADAM), the Active Directory Lightweight Directory Services (LDS) is run in place of AD DS.

You can add LDS as you can the other AD services by using the Add Roles wizard of the Server Manager, as shown in Figure 4.11. You can still use the DCPROMO command to create AD DS, but these other services are more conveniently added with the wizard.

In this new management context, the roles of each of these components haven't changed much. The Authorization Manager's function seems to have disappeared as a separate entity, and ADAM and ADFS have been renamed to LDS and AD FS, respectively.

The major changes in identity and access management are expected to be in the next version of MIIS 2003, to be called the Identity Lifecycle Manager (ILM). ILM will improve on MIIS's credential mechanism by enabling users to enable their smart cards, reset their own passwords, set up security groups and distribution lists, get access to other groups from the group members, and perform many of these functions from within their desktop and within Microsoft Office applications. From a user standpoint, a request for access from within Outlook would be accompanied by an Approve or Reject button in the recipients' message. ILM will also be made available through components that can be part of a SharePoint portal.

FIGURE 4.11
The new directory services can be added directly from the Server Manager's Add Roles wizard.

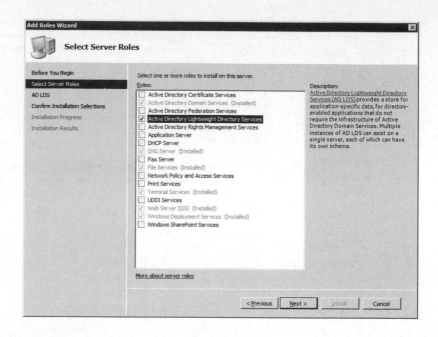

Read-Only Domain Controllers

The read-only domain controller (RODC) is a new domain controller that is being introduced with Windows Server 2008. The RODC is meant to solve the problem of domain services for branch offices or remote sites being hampered by a poor bandwidth connection, low security, and/or lack of IT staff. The RODC has the following features:

Read-Only AD Database   The RODC contains the entire AD DS database, but is missing account passwords. Read-only means that no changes can be written to the RODC, either from local clients or from applications.

Read-Only Domain Name System   When a DNS server is installed on an RODC, the data contained in the DNS partitions on your writable hub DNS servers can be replicated to the RODC. The system doesn't update clients DNS records—instead, they are sent to another referral DNS server. The DNS service on the RODC will then look at the update of DNS records and request that their writable domain server counterparts replicate back that one DNS record. In this manner, the risk of having a DNS request point to a bogus address is diminished and is limited to one request only.

Administrative Role Removal   RODC allows a domain user or a security group to perform the operations that would normally be a local administrator's right. The delegated administrator can then perform many of the maintenance tasks required to support the RODC and its users.

RODC Filtered Attribute Set   In order to support applications that require credentials to operate, you can store those credentials on an RODC but in a unique way. A feature called a *filtered attribute set* allows you to configure settings on the schema master so that the attributes defined by an attribute set cannot be replicated from the RODC elsewhere.

Some credentials cannot be added to a filter set, specifically features that support Microsoft security services. The list includes AD DS, Local Security Authorities, the Security Accounts Manager (SAM) database, and security providers like the Kerberos authentication protocol. If you add one of these credentials to a filter set, the RODC is programmed to return an LDAP error "unwillingToPerform."

NOTE Windows Server 2003 doesn't support filtered attribute sets. This means that if you plan to deploy RODCs in your organization you should keep in mind that the server is meant to connect to a forest with a Windows Server 2008 server.

Credential Caching The RODC is configured to support a small number of users. When initially configured, the RODC contains only the local machine account and a Kerberos ticketing (krbtgt) account. The domain administrator adds all other user accounts, machine accounts, and server accounts for the small number of people that the RODC is meant to service.

Upon deployment in the branch, it appears as if the RODC is a Key Distribution Center (KDC), but in reality the RODC relies on the writable domain controller to sign or encrypt all ticket requests. If an RODC were to be compromised, it would not be able to grant a ticket to any other network site because the cryptographic engines are isolated from the authenticating server.

A user requesting access to the RODC is authenticated at the writable domain server, and the account credentials are then sent back to the RODC from the hub. Password replication policy may be set so that a changed password registered at the writable domain server can be replicated back to the RODC and that password is then cached on the RODC. Thereafter, the RODC services local requests for logon by going to the credential cache. The risk to the organization is limited to only those accounts cached in the RODC.

Unidirectional Replication In order that the RODC stay current but not be modified by local clients, replication proceeds in only one direction: from the writable domain controllers to the RODC. Any changes that were made on an RODC should it be compromised aren't replicated to the replication partners. As replication proceeds, any changes would be replicated away. Unidirectional replication will use the AD DS and the Distributed File System Replication (DFSR) service for inbound replication.

Microsoft has high hopes for RODCs, envisioning a time when all WAN connections to domain servers in branch offices are RODCs, as shown in Figure 4.12. Only time will tell.

Domain Topologies

In the original domain implementation that shipped with Windows Server 2000 a primary domain controller (PDC) was supported by any number of backup domain controllers (BDC). When a PDC failed or was taken offline, a BDC was promoted to a PDC. To update domain controllers, this system featured the undesirable characteristic of having a significant amount of domain replication traffic. Windows domains also developed inconsistencies in domain data when the PDC was switched to another system or corrupted.

To lessen the dependency of the domain infrastructure on the PDC as a single point of failure, Microsoft moved to a domain model where BDCs were eliminated in favor of a distributed system of equal domain controllers. A scheme called *multimaster replication* was introduced to synchronize data across the group of domain controllers, replacing the older scheme, which was called single-master or master-slave replication.

FIGURE 4.12
The RODC offers a new domain topology for organizations that maintain branch offices across WAN connections.

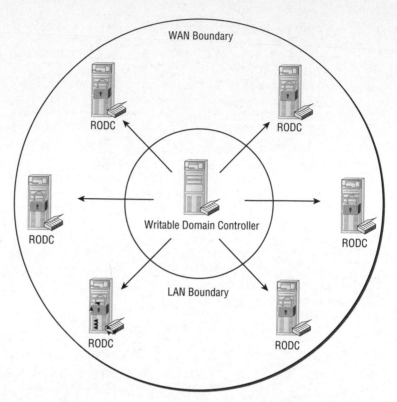

The benefits of multimaster replication are that the loss of a master doesn't impact the updating of the database and that domain controllers can be distributed across a network and in different locations. However, multimaster replication is difficult to implement, always leads to some inconsistencies due to communication latency, is asynchronous, and therefore doesn't always obey the principle of ACID transactions—which is why AD has taken a long time to develop.

Active Directory uses a system that isn't a pure a multimaster scheme but instead has an update pattern that updates all servers, but only over a certain amount of time. This replication pattern balances minimizing replication traffic against loss of data consistency. AD's replication scheme isn't quite as fault tolerant and error free as a completely implemented multi-master replication scheme where replication would involve all servers at the same time. Therefore, the scheme Microsoft uses, sometimes called a Floating Single Master Operations replication, or more generally an Operations Masters topology, is sufficient to accommodate large domains and realistic network bandwidths.

Domain topologies have largely followed along with the replication schemes, locating domain controllers as was appropriate to the business structures that existed. Domain schemes have included the following:

- Central master domain and a domain hierarchy

- Multiple master domains

- Resource domains

- Remote domains

- Various combinations of these approaches

Designing a domain topology is more of an art than a science, with each different domain structure offering its own strengths and weaknesses. Given the nature of trust relationships, deciding between one type of topology and another can be a complex and difficult decision, one that often requires system architects who are expert at this kind of project.

To this level of complexity you can add the extra capabilities of a RODC and the impact that deploying this type of controller could have on your infrastructure. RODCs could help an organization centralize their domain structure so that remote offices need not have a writable domain controller. But beware—the applications that are used may need to be able to operate with a read-only functionality. Thus, take careful consideration before you deploy an RODC when a full domain controller is required.

Restartable Active Directory

The last of the additions to the AD that this chapter discusses is the restartable Active Directory Domain Service (AD DS). You can start and stop AD DS either from the Server Manager or by using a command-line command. The ability to stop and start the AD DS without rebooting the system requires less time for a domain server to be offline while undergoing routine maintenance. All Windows Server 2008 domain controllers have the restartable AD DS feature, regardless of any other services that they are performing.

To stop and start an AD DS:

1. Open the Server Manager and click Active Directory Domain Services in the Services (Local) tree control.

2. In the System Services portion of the Details pane, click Active Directory Domain Services.

3. To stop the server, click the Stop button that is circled in Figure 4.13.

4. To start the server, click the Start button.

FIGURE 4.13
To stop and restart AD DS without rebooting, use the buttons in the Server Manager.

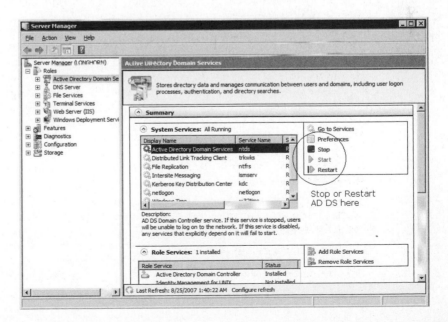

The ability to start and stop AD DS means that there are now three different states that the service can be in: started, stopped, and restore mode. In the stopped mode, which is new in Windows Server 2008, the server appears to other servers as if it is both in the restore mode state as well as a member server of the domain. The NTDS.DIT Active Directory database is unavailable, which routes requests for directory services to other domain controllers. If a domain controller cannot be contacted, the logon occurs under the Directory Services restore mode on the stopped server. Figure 4.14 summarizes how the three different modes of the restartable AD DS relate to one another.

FIGURE 4.14
When you stop and restart AD, it cycles through three separate states. This diagram shows how they relate to one another.

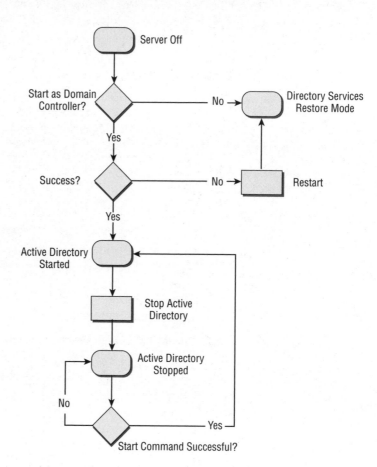

Summary

Active Directory has been simplified through the use of the Windows Server 2008 management interface. Microsoft has consolidated a number of directory-related identity and access services under that same management interface, making a set of confusing servers more manageable. You'll find new ways to audit access to directory services in Windows Server 2008, as well as a new kind of secure domain controller for branch offices called the read-only domain controller. Previous versions of Windows Server forced you to restart AD whenever you needed to perform certain tasks such as defragmentation or backup. With this new version of AD, you can stop and restart domain services without needing to reboot.

In the next chapter you will learn about the changes that have been made to the Windows Group Policy model. One change, the ability to control domain server passwords through policy, is new, but there are hundreds of new policy settings. You will learn about many of these new capabilities in Chapter 5.

Chapter 5

Policies and System Management

Each new version of Windows Server since Windows 2000 Server has shipped with Active Directory (AD). Active Directory, as you learned in the previous chapter, serves the same function for a domain as the Registry does for a computer. AD stores settings that can be applied to resources, and those settings affect the operation of software, hardware, network connections, access of security objects to these resources, and much more. AD is also an object-oriented database. When you want to manage and configure systems and users, you can apply a set of rules, called policies; when applied to groups, they are called Group Policies. Although Group Policies aren't applied to security objects directly, security group filtering policies can be applied to security settings and to Windows and application deployments as well.

The last major revision of the Windows Group Policy engine was for the Windows Server 2003 and Windows XP operating system release. Windows Server 2008 doesn't change the fundamental way in which Group Policies are defined and implemented, but there are numerous minor changes that this chapter will describe. Windows Server 2003 and Windows XP have nearly 1,700 Group Policy settings, to which Windows Server 2008 adds nearly 700 more. Some of the Windows Server 2008 settings manage new features such as Aero and the Desktop Experience; other settings improve, consolidate, or fix existing policy settings. Among the new categories of policy settings of note in Windows Server 2008 are the ones found in these areas:

- ◆ Automated device installation and configuration
- ◆ Hybrid hard disk management
- ◆ Network access protection
- ◆ Power management routines
- ◆ Printer driver installation
- ◆ Removable storage policies
- ◆ System diagnostics and remediation
- ◆ User Account Control

Significant reworking of the Vista user interface, printing, and other modules have led to considerable changes to certain areas of Group Policy, including:

- ◆ Firewall policies
- ◆ Help system
- ◆ IPsec

♦ Printer management

♦ Shell visualization

♦ Start menu and Taskbar policies

♦ Synchronization and scheduling

After a short review of how the Windows Group Policy engine works, this chapter then describes the tools that ship with Windows Server 2008 for Group Policy management and the changes in those tools. After looking at the Group Policy Management Console (GPMC), the Group Policy Object Editor (GPOE), and Group Policy templates, we explore the new policy types. Policies work hand in hand with the user and group accounts in Active Directory, so this chapter will put your knowledge about these security objects and profiles to work. Quality of Service (QoS) is another network-based policy that is described at the end of this chapter.

Group Policies and Active Directory

Policies are the "business logic" of Windows domains. Each domain contains its own instance of Active Directory. AD is a hierarchical object-oriented database for machines, users, and named collections of objects, such as software. To create and enforce policies, Windows has an infrastructure that consists of a Group Policy engine, a set of client-side extensions (CSEs), and tools, such as templates, for writing policies.

Policy settings are managed as a set of virtual objects collectively referred to as Group Policy Objects (GPOs). Each GPO is stored in the Active Directory Group Policy container along with all of the policy attributes. There are default attributes, some that users can modify as part of their profile, and a rather larger set of attributes that comes under administrative control. GPOs are stored in Group Policy templates in a hierarchical folder structure stored in the file system at SYSVOL\ POLICIES. Ready-made administrative templates control security settings, available applications and allowed settings, script usage, and other policies that are available for installation, making the administrator's job a little easier. The actual implementations of policy settings are stored in the Registry for applications and aspects of Windows that are policy enabled.

NOTE To learn more about Windows Group Policies, visit the Microsoft Windows Server TechCenter at http://technet.microsoft.com/en-us/windowsserver/grouppolicy/default.aspx.

The following settings are managed by Group Policies:

Registry policies These settings are managed in the Administrative Templates node of the Group Policy Object Editor.

Security policies Security policies control aspects of access for the local computer, domain, and network resources. GPOs do not directly modify security groups. Instead, you assign Group Policies to users and groups and, through security filtering, apply policy options to security groups.

Internet Explorer settings Policies can alter the way Internet Explorer appears to clients, allow options such as executing scripts and certain downloads, and more.

Software deployment policies With a policy an administrator can control when and to whom an application is published. There are additional policies that let you update or uninstall applications. The control of Remote Installation Services (RIS) for Windows deployment is also under policy control.

Automation   Scripts come under policy control, allowing changes to startup and shutdown, logon and logoff, and application behavior through scripts.

Redirection   With policies you can map volumes, folders (directories), and other resources. You can also redirect the special shell folders such as My Documents to other locations on a per-user and per-group basis.

These policies are part of the Windows Server operating system, which for Windows Server 2008 consists of 2,400 different sets of controls. An administrator can set the control for all managed objects in a domain from a single location. However, the Group Policy infrastructure is also available to third-party applications. Indeed, not only can applications set policies for the existing Windows policies, they can also define policies specific to their own application. Third-party management applications can set both their own Group Policies, as well as the policies used by other applications.

Other than available disk space, there is no limit to the number of Group Policies that you can create and enforce in a Windows domain. Microsoft recommends that organizations use more GPOs with fewer settings (say 5 to 20), rather than a small number of GPOs with a large number of settings.

Administrative Template Files

Windows Vista and Windows Server 2008 use the GPOE and GPMC to get Registry-based settings that are stored in administrative template files. The file format for Windows Server 2003 and XP policies is the ADM (AD Management) file. Windows Server 2008 introduces a new XML-based ADMX file format, which allows for the following new behavior:

Central data store   All new and converted policies are still stored in SYSVOL, but this new format consolidates the information so that it can be read by Windows Server 2008 servers and Vista clients as a single data store.

In Windows Server 2008, you can optionally store your ADMX files in %SYSTEMROOT%\SYSVOL\ DOMAIN\POLICIES\POLICYDEFINITIONS instead of inside each GPO. Fewer files means lower replication traffic as well.

Lower storage requirement   On average, each GPO stored in an ADMX file is 4MB smaller than the same version of the policy stored in an ADM file.

For a domain with multiple GPOs, the savings in storage size can have a major impact on the amount of replication traffic, which can significantly improve network performance when you make a domain-wide change in the GPO.

ADMX Schema   ADMX files follow a schema in Windows Server 2008 that is part of the .NET Framework 3.0 specification.

Dynamic loading of policies   Policies are loaded into memory as needed.

Multilingual support   ADMX files define language-neutral template policies stored in the Registry. Related ADML files provide language-specific resources that are applied to ADMX files, as required by the language that an administrator sets for the systems under policy control. This new feature lets an administrator create a policy in one language and apply it elsewhere in a different language. The policy can be changed in the second language and the change is seen by the administrator in the first language.

NOTE   It's best to think of the policies contained in ADMX files as supersets of the policy sets found in the older ADM file.

For the most part, the use of ADMX files will be transparent in domains composed of Windows Server 2008 and earlier versions of Windows—which for economic reasons usually are referred to as "legacy systems." While Windows Server 2008 servers and Vista clients read ADMX files, older ADM policy-setting files that don't have an ADMX replacement will continue to be displayed using the policy Microsoft Management Console (MMC) so that legacy systems can be managed without interruption. For the purposes of Windows Server 2008 domains, ADM policies can be managed for Windows Server 2003, Windows XP Pro, Windows Server 2000, and Windows 2000 Pro clients.

Anything older than the systems mentioned here—for example, Windows NT Server or Workstation 4.0, Windows Me, and Windows 98SE—are not supported. All these systems are security risks, and shouldn't be left on your network in any case. When you open the GPOE in these earlier supported versions of Windows, you will not see the template policy settings stored in ADMX files, although you will see these settings displayed in the reporting module of the GPMC.

If you make a change to the older settings that are found in ADM files such as SYSTEM.ADM, INETRES.ADM, CONF.ADM, WMPLAYER.ADM, or WUAU.ADM, those changes will not be recognized or read by Windows Server 2008 or Vista, and they will not appear in policy tools on those systems. GPOE reads administrative template ADMX settings from either the local system or the central ADMX policy store. After those policies are loaded, the GPOE then reads ADM files that appear on Windows Server 2003, Windows XP, and Windows 2000 servers and clients that are part of the domain, and loads the policies that haven't been migrated to the new ADMX files.

Older Windows systems such as Windows Server 2003 do not load the new template policy settings that have been created in Windows Server 2008's ADMX files. Changes made in ADM files that don't have ADMX replacements will be applied to all supported versions of Windows.

The Group Policy Engine

The Group Policy engine that shipped with Windows Server 2003 and Windows XP Group Policy was part of the Winlogon service, and the USERENV.DLL was used to log policy events to the %WINDIR%\Debug\UserMode folder along with other logon functions.

This new version of the Group Policy engine that ships with Windows Server 2008 and Vista is built differently. Group Policy now runs as its own service; Figure 5.1 shows the Group Policy Client service running in the Services MMC. If this service is disabled, Group Policies are not applied to the system. As a unified service, the new Group Policy architecture requires fewer services to start up to support the policy engine and therefore uses less memory and system resources in most instances. That should lead to improved policy performance. With a policy service, it is also now possible to update Group Policy files by starting and stopping the service, and without the need to reboot your server.

The service runs as a Svchost process so that Group Policy events are now logged in the Event Viewer in the System log as an event message under the category of Microsoft ➤ Windows ➤ GroupPolicy. Therefore, in the Group Policy Operational log, this version of the Group Policy engine makes it much easier to trace the policy events that have taken place and to troubleshoot policy issues than in previous versions of Windows.

FIGURE 5.1

The Group Policy
Client service

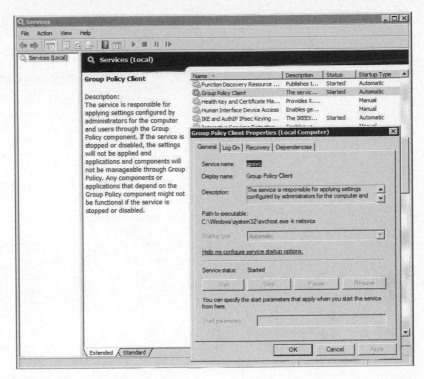

To view a policy event in the Operational log:

1. Open the Group Policy Management Console.

2. Scroll down the control tree in the left pane and select the local system GPO in the Group Policy Results section.

3. Click the Policy Events tab in the Results pane (on the right).

4. Double-click on the event you're interested in.

The Event Properties dialog box appears, revealing the policy event details, as shown in Figure 5.2. Group Policy settings apply to the file system and to Active Directory, so when a GPO is invoked it is up to the client to decide which settings to apply based on the hierarchy contained in the GPO. Selection is also based on computer versus user settings so that there are four specific classes of settings in a GPO:

◆ Computer file system path

◆ User file system path

◆ Computer directory service path

◆ User directory service path

Computer policies include system configuration, security, application configuration, and startup and shutdown scripts. The user policies include many of the same policy settings, as well as a few extra ones, such as folder redirection, allowed and published applications, and others. The general rule is that computer policies take precedence over user policies.

FIGURE 5.2
The Group Policy
Management service

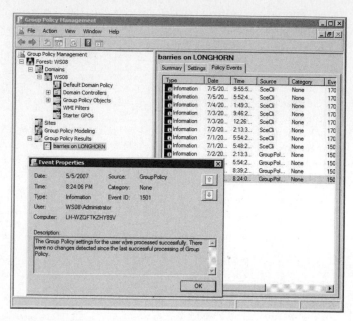

GPOs are applied to the different AD containers such as a site, domain, or organizational unit (OU). A GPO can apply to (or be linked from) multiple containers, and a container can reference (or contain the link to) multiple GPOs. Active Directory is organized in a hierarchy that enforces precedence in the settings that are applied for users and groups, as you can see in Figure 5.3.

FIGURE 5.3
Active Directory
policy precedence

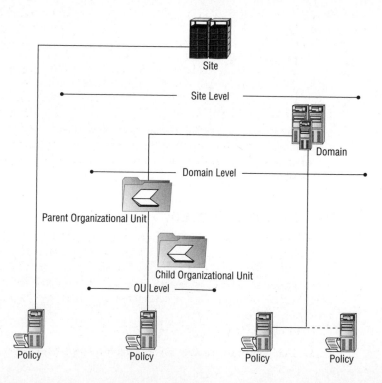

The vast majority of policies are placed in the domain container because performance can be significantly affected by policies that span sites or that are part of another trusted domain. GPOs are stored at the domain level in either the Group Policy Container (GPC) or in the Group Policy Template (GPT). AD replicates GPC policies between domain controllers using the AD replication service. GPTs are replicated using the Distributed File System (DFS) Replication, which replaces the File Replication Service (FRS) that was used in the Windows Server 2003 and XP versions of the Group Policy engine. A GPO can only be applied when the versioning in the GPC and GPT for the object is synchronized.

A new replication algorithm called Remote Differential Compression (RDC) lowers the amount of network traffic by only replicating changes between domain controllers. Additional compression of the data also helps to lower the amount of bandwidth that replication traffic consumes. The following rules apply:

1. Any GPO that is assigned at the site level applies to every computer and user in all of the OUs and domains in that site.

2. Any GPO linked to a domain is applied to all OUs, and to all users and groups in the domain.

3. Any GPO linked to an OU applies to the users and groups of that OU and to any OU that is a child OU. If multiple domains have members in an OU, the policy settings do not apply outside of the assigned domain.

To enforce the precedence described in this list, Group Policies are applied locally first, then sites, then domains, and finally, at the OU level, parents followed by children at the time the system starts up and when the user logs on. The user's profile is loaded and then the system applies Group Policies. The RefreshPolicy function controls how often a user's policies are updated; by default the setting is every 90 minutes. It is possible to manually force an update using the GPUDATE.EXE command.

NOTE   The one exception to updates is application deployment, which only occurs during startup or logon.

Group Policy is inherited and cumulative. If you wish to enforce a specific GPO, you can set an attribute called No Override. In that instance, the policy can't be altered by any container lower in the AD hierarchy. You can also set another option called Block Inheritance if you wish to have that policy apply only at the level you specified and no level lower. No Override will be applied in preference to Block Inheritance, and neither attribute can be applied in local GPOs.

An administrator can limit the application of a GPO to a user or group with a filter. You filter the scope of a GPO by adding or removing users and groups from the access control list (ACL) within the security settings for that particular object. Doing so changes the ACL for the objects that the policy affects.

Policy Management Tools

The primary Microsoft tools for managing Group Policies are the GPMC and the GPOE. Both of these tools are MMC snap-ins. The GPMC is a scriptable interface for different policy classes, while the GPOE is integrated into the GPMC and is where you edit each GPO's settings.

To work with the GPMC, you need to install the Group Policy Management feature first. In Windows Server 2003 and Windows XP, these tools were separate downloads and were not part of the operating system distribution.

To install the Group Policy Management feature:

1. Click Start; then select the Server Manager command.

2. In the Server Manager detail pane (on the left), click the Features item, then click the Add Features link in the right pane.

3. In the Add Features wizard, click the Group Policy Management checkbox, then click the Next button and complete the steps of the wizard.

The Group Policy Management Console

To launch the Group Policy Management Console (GPMC), do any of the following:

◆ Click Start ➢ All Programs ➢ Administrative Tools, and select the Group Policy Management command.

◆ Press Windows+R; then enter **GPMC.MSC** in the Run dialog box and press Enter.

◆ Open a command prompt window, enter **GPMC**, and then press Enter.

The GPMC then appears, as shown in Figure 5.4. Table 5.1 lists the basic operations of the GPMC.

FIGURE 5.4

The Group Policy Management Console

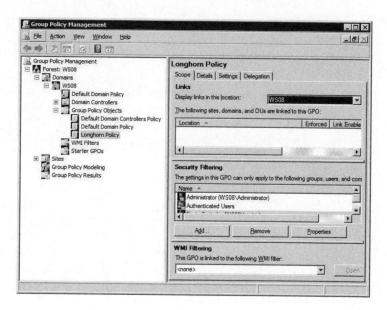

TABLE 5.1: Group Policy Management Console Operations

ACTION	PROCEDURE
To create a new GPO	Right-click the Group Policy Objects in the forest or domain, select New, and enter a name in the New GPO dialog box.
To edit a GPO	Locate the GPO, right-click on it, and then select the Edit command and make changes in the Group Policy Object Editor (described below).

TABLE 5.1:   Group Policy Management Console Operations *(CONTINUED)*

ACTION	PROCEDURE
To find a GPO	Right-click on the forest or domain, select the Search command, and enter a search string in the Search for Group Policy Objects dialog box. Filter your search accordingly.
To delete a GPO	Locate the GPO, right-click on it, and then select the Delete command.
To copy a GPO	Drag and drop the GPO of interest, or right-click on that GPO and select the Copy command.
To link a GPO	Right-click on the GPO and select the Link an Existing GPO command. In the Select GPO dialog box, select the GPO and click OK.
To filter using security groups	Click on the GPO and in the results pane, click the Scope tab; then click Add. In the Enter the Object Name to Select box, add the group, user, or computer and click OK. Refer to Figure 5.4 for this feature.
To import settings from a GPO	Right-click on the GPO you wish to import into, then click the Import Settings command to open the Import Settings wizard.
To add a domain	Open the forest, right-click on Domains; then select the Show Domains command. Check each domain you wish to add; then click OK.
To specify a domain controller	Right-click on the domain; then select the Change Domain Controller command. Select the Domain Controller option; then click OK. The domain controller you specify will be the source of the domain's group policies. (You can perform the same action at the forest level.)
To add a forest	Right click on Group Policy Management, and then select Add Forest. In the Add Forest dialog box, enter the DNS or NetBIOS name of any domain contained in the forest you wish to add; then click OK.
To add a site	Right-click on Sites, and then select the Show Sites command. Enable the checkbox for the site(s) you wish to add; then click OK. Sites only appear in the console when you explicitly add them.
To block inheritance of a domain or OU	Right-click on the domain and select the Block Inheritance command. Any blocked object will have a blue exclamation mark in the console tree.
To create, print, or save a report of GPO settings	Double-click on the GPO; then click the Settings tab to view a report. Right-click in the Settings pane; then select the Save Report or Print command to perform those actions.

TABLE 5.1: Group Policy Management Console Operations *(CONTINUED)*

ACTION	PROCEDURE
To back up GPOs	Right-click on the Group Policy Objects and select the Backup All command. In the Backup Group Policy dialog box, enter a location and description of the backup. You can also back up individual GPOs.
To restore GPOs	To restore from a backup, right-click on Group Policy Objects and select the Manage Backups command. Select the backup in the Backed Up GPOs list, then click Restore.

Keep in mind that, if you copy or import a GPO across domains and forests, references may no longer be correct or features that were enabled in one might not be enabled in the other. To aid in migration, administrators often create a migration table using the Migration Table Editor. The editor scans GPOs or the backups you have made and can then populate the table automatically. To view the Migration Table Editor, right-click on Domains or on the Group Policy Objects, and then select the Open Migration Table Editor. With the editor open, specify the source, then Browse, and save the settings into a file. Figure 5.5 shows an example of the Migration Table Editor.

FIGURE 5.5
The Migration Table Editor can scan and store GPO settings so that they can be examined and changed when the GPO is moved or copied.

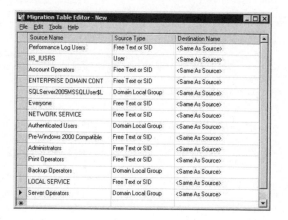

The Group Policy Object Editor

The second major tool used to modify GPOs is the Group Policy Object Editor (GPOE). This tool is installed as part of the Group Policy Management feature, and you access it from the GPMC using the Edit command for a GPO.

To open the GPOE, do one of the following:

◆ Right-click on the GPO you wish to modify and select the Edit command from the context menu.

◆ Right-click on the GPO inside any container that has a link to that GPO and select the Edit command from that location.

In Figure 5.6, we are using the GPOE to modify the properties of passwords at the machine level.

FIGURE 5.6

Use the GPOE to modify policies for computers and users.

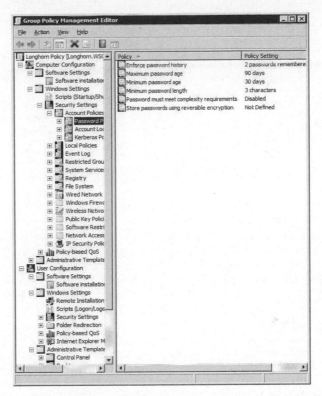

As you edit policies, keep in mind that the level of the GPO you modify affects whether your setting is enforced. Only Administrators, Domain Administrators, or a Group Policy Creator Owners group can modify a specific policy. Be especially careful when you modify a default domain policy or a default domain controller policy. When you set a policy, it doesn't get applied until the user's policies are refreshed. If you need immediate enforcement, you will have to manually force a refresh.

Policy Scopes

In linked GPOs, you have the options of enforcing a GPO, disabling users or computers, and disabling a GPO entirely. You set these options at the link level by right-clicking on the GPO link and enabling or disabling the Enforced, GPO Status, or Link Enabled commands, respectively. All of these commands have the effect of controlling the scope of a group policy.

Policies are an important area of network system behavior, and it's only natural to conclude that they would come under programmatic control of the WMI interface. Indeed, you can use WMI filters to control the scope of a GPO as it is applied to computers on the network. A GPO can be linked to a WMI filter, which is a container that appears in the GPMC. When the GPO is evaluated, the WMI filter acts as a Boolean and either enables (1, or True) or disables (0, or False) the policy. Keep in mind that WMI doesn't apply to Windows 2000 Server and clients and is ignored by those systems. Figure 5.7 shows a WMI query within the GPOE.

FIGURE 5.7
The WMI interface is another container in the GPMC that lets you link to and control GPOs.

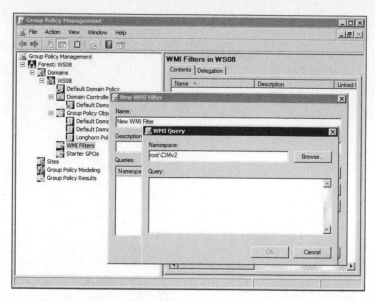

After you add the new WMI filter and name it, you need to select a namespace containing the objects you wish to control and then perform a query against those objects to select (filter) the objects you want the WMI filter to apply to. You can add more queries and then save them when you are done. By default, only Domain Administrators, Enterprise Administrators, and Group Policy Creator Owners groups are allowed to create WMI filters. You can import, export, or copy WMI filters by using the Import WMI Filter, Export WMI Filter, and Copy (and Paste) commands on the GPO's context menu.

To set a link for a GPO from a WMI filter:

1. Click the GPO of interest. Only groups or users with GPO Edit permissions can set the link.

2. On the Scope tab in the Results pane under WMI Filtering, select the WMI filter from the drop-down list.

3. Confirm your selection by clicking the Yes button.

Only one WMI filter can link to a GPO, and a WMI filter can only link to a GPO in the same domains. WMI filtering only appears on Windows Servers 2008 and 2003.

At some point you will need to determine whether or not a policy will be applied to a specific object, and under what conditions. The analysis that gives this information is called the Resultant Set of Policy (RSOP), and it performs the same function as a report. The RSOP tool is located in the GPMC and can be assembled from a wizard.

To determine the Resultant Set of Policy:

1. In the GPMC console tree, double-click the forest you want to query.

2. Right-click on Group Policy Results.

3. Assign the computer and user that you want to analyze.

4. Complete the Resultant Set of Policy wizard. When you get to the results pane, either select Save Report to save the report, or select Print to print it. You can print the results as text or as a web page (HTML) that is compatible with Internet Explorer 6 or later.

The Group Policy Results appears as a summary in the results pane, as Figure 5.8 shows.

FIGURE 5.8
A report of the Resultant Set of Policies is useful when you are trying to scope the behavior of interacting policies.

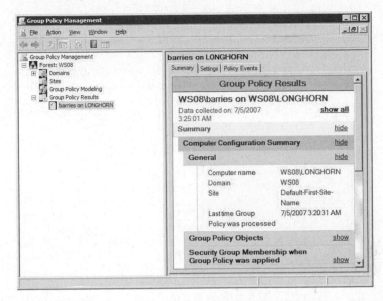

A tool related to RSOP allows you to model Group Policy interactions and create an analysis of the expected impact of policy settings. This tool, called the Group Policy Modeling Wizard, works by allowing you to query the appropriate objects. To simulate RSOP with Group Policy Modeling:

1. Double-click the forest you wish to model.

2. Right-click on Group Policy Modeling, select Group Policy Modeling Wizard, click Next, and follow the instructions in the wizard.

3. You can print or save the report to analyze the model at your leisure.

NOTE Both the Group Policy Results and the Group Policy Modeling Results can be saved in XML format. If you want to do this at a later time, simply rerun these two operations a second time.

Local Group Policy Objects

A Local Group Policy Object (LGPO) contains the policy settings that are applied when a system or user logs on to the domain. In the Group Policy engine of Windows Server 2003 and Vista, each system could have just one LGPO, which limited the use of local policies on a per-user and a situational basis. Windows Server 2008 and Vista both support multiple LPGOs stored on a system, thus offering new policy configurations and greater flexibility.

When you use a system as a shared computer in a domain, you can store an LPGO for each local user or for each built-in group. For workgroups in which each system stores its own LPGO, you can apply multiple LPGOs on a per-user basis. Typical instances where multiple LPGOs are valuable are computer labs, kiosks, libraries, dedicated single-purpose multiuser workstations, and other shared systems.

With multiple LPGOs to work with, it is much easier to create a highly restricted policy setting for user access while retaining a full set of capabilities for an administrator. Administrators can also disable Group Policy settings locally without having to alter the domain policies.

Group Policy Preferences

Starting with Windows Server 2008 RC1, Microsoft integrated a set of policy tools that were obtained in the acquisition of DesktopStandard into their base Windows Server 2008 installations. The feature, now called Group Policy Preferences, was part of the PolicyMaker Standard Edition and PolicyMaker Share Manage products that DesktopStandard sold as domain policy add-ons. Preferences are part of the Group Policy Management Console (GPMC) for Windows Server 2008 and can also be enforced by the Remote Administration Tools (RSAT) that can be installed on Windows Vista SP1. To have Group Policy Preferences run on client systems, you will need to install the client-side extension for your particular Windows version. CSE is available as a download for Windows XP SP2, Windows Vista, and Windows Server 2003 SP1. Both Windows Vista SP1 and Windows Server 2008 ship with CSE.

NOTE   Microsoft continues to sell DesktopStandard's GPOVault product, which tracks changes made to GPOs. GPOVault is a GPMC plug-in. The DesktopStandard policy-based security product was spun off into a company called BeyondTrust, which offers it as their Privilege Manager (www.beyondtrust.com).

Group Policy Preferences create a mechanism that administrators can use to allow users to select their own particular settings. Whereas Group Policy is strictly enforced by the Policy section of the Registry or by Access Control Lists (ACLs), Preferences are not. Group Policy also works by disabling elements of the user interface. Preferences are stored with the applications that they apply to, and therefore don't require an application to be "policy aware" to operate. Group Policy is applied based to an entire GPOs based on WMI filters.

Preferences are applied using a more granular item-level targeting scheme where individual items can be changed within a GPO. As an example of how this might be useful, a policy could set the power management scheme settings for your systems, while a preference could inact a single setting for a specific computer type such as a laptop. Policy filtering can require the support for complex WMI queries, while Preferences are set within the GPMC.

Policy settings are enforced based on the hierarchy shown in the image below. When a Group Policy applies to an operation it can be applied so that it enforces the setting it applies to or it can allow the setting to be user selectable as a Preference. User-selectable Preferences can be applied once, or applied every time policy settings are refreshed. In the instance where user preference is allowed the Preference can be for a once-only application of the Preference or every time the policy settings are refreshed. Take special note of any circumstance where Group Policy is to be enforced, but upon searching the application or feature's policy settings in the Registry, it is found not to be Group Policy aware. In this instance, Group Policy Preferences take over and the apply-once option for the preference is disabled.

To set a Group Policy Preference, do the following:

1. Click Start ➤ Administrative tools, and then select the Group Policy Management command.

2. Expand the Preferences node for either the Computer Configuration or for the User Configuration, depending upon which object you wish to modify.

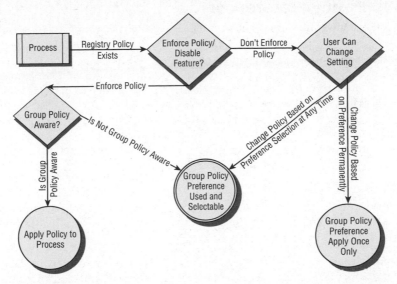

3. Right click on the setting of interest and select the New command from the context menu; then select the Preference item of interest. The policy object properties dialog box appears as shown in the image below.

For example, when you select New for the Folder Shares preference you only see the New Share preference. Other Preferences such as Control Panel Settings Folder Options may offer multiple Preferences such as Folder Options (Windows XP), Folder Options (Windows Vista), and Open With.

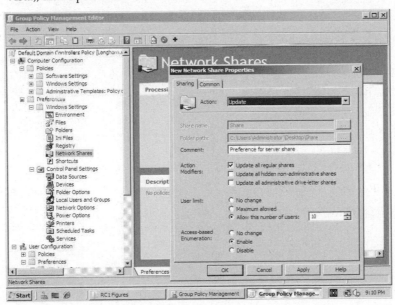

4. Double click on the setting of interest and make your selections on the Preference tab.

5. Click on the Common tab and set the Group Policy Preference properties you desire.

6. If you want to set a scope for this Preference, click on the Item-level targeting check box, as shown in the image below, and then click on the Targeting button. This tab also allows you to set the run-once option.

Targeting is done through a set of rules that you build from within the Targeting Editor.

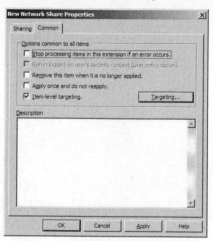

7. To create a Targeting rule click on the New Item button and select the object that the rule operates on, as shown in the image below.

8. Click on the Add Collection button to enter the rule that is used (line two in the image below).

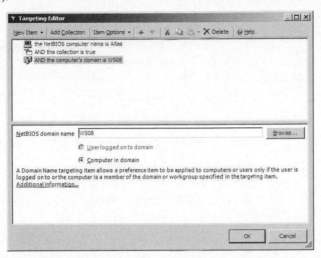

9. Click on the Item Options to set the condition that the item has to satisfy; then click OK twice to create the Preference.

Not every Preference is found in both the Computer Configuration node and the User Configuration node. The Computer Configuration node is the only one that has the Network Shares and Services Preferences that you saw above. The User Configuration Applications, Drive Maps, Internet Settings, Regional Options, and the Start Menu Preferences are only User Configuration Preferences and aren't found in the Computer Settings node. Table 5.2 lists some of the Preferences that are available and their major options.

TABLE 5.2:   Group Policy Preference Settings.

PREFERENCE TYPE	DESCRIPTION
Windows Preferences	
Drive Maps	Drive Maps can create, update, replace, and delete network drive mappings. This is a much more convenient and reliable method for working with drive mappings than logon scripts are. Multiple items can be mapped by policy, supporting different organizational groups or locations.
Environment	You can set the system environmental variables and path in this Preference.
Files	With Files Preferences you can create, update, replace, and delete files on a computer. File can be specified by paths and wildcards. You might use this Preference to copy configuration files to user profile folders.

TABLE 5.2: Group Policy Preference Settings. *(CONTINUED)*

PREFERENCE TYPE	DESCRIPTION
Folders	With Folder Preferences you can create, update, replace, and delete folders on a computer. File can be specified by paths, but this feature doesn't support wildcards. This Preference could be used to delete temporary folders, or perform maintenance.
INI Files	Create, replace, update, and delete individual properties from INI files.
Network Shares	Manage network shares on multiple or targeted systems.
Registry	In Registry Preferences you can create, update, replace, and delete registry settings on one or more systems. Three different Preferences allow you to configure a Registry Item, Collection Item, or Registry Wizard. A Registry Item is an individual registry setting (e.g., REG_DWORD). Collection Items are Registry folders. The Registry Wizard imports Registry setting(s) from the local or from a remote system; either a single setting or entire branches.
Shortcuts	Shortcuts provide a means to create, update, replace, or delete shortcuts for file system objects, URLs, and items that appear in the shell. Shell objects include the Control Panel folder, Recycle Bin, and so forth.
Control Panel Preferences	
Data Sources	The Data Sources Preferences can specify Open Database Connectivity (ODBC) data sources for users and computers. Although you can use Group Policy to distribute applications, there are no settings in Group Policy for configuring ODBC.
Devices	Use the Device Preferences to allow or restrict specific device classes for users or computers. Removable media, floppy drives, USB ports, and more are controlled by Preferences. Note that Devices do not prevent these devices from being installed, but enables or disables the device once installed. Use Group Policy to prevent users from installing devices.
Folder Options	Folder options are Preferences that you can set from within the Folder Options dialog box on the Windows desktop. Common settings are for showing hidden folders, displaying file extensions, and so on. The Open With Preference is a file association between the file extension and the application that is used to open that file.
Internet Settings	You can use Internet Settings to control the options that are found in the Internet Options control panel. These settings are also exposed in the Options dialog box within Internet Explorer. Options can be set for IE versions 7, 6, and 5. Preferences can be set for security levels, home page, connections, and more.
Local Users and Groups	Use the Local Users and Groups Preferences to configure local user accounts and groups on one or more systems. You can create, modify, and delete these accounts.

TABLE 5.2: Group Policy Preference Settings. *(CONTINUED)*

PREFERENCE TYPE	DESCRIPTION
Network Options	The Network Options Preferences allow you to configure Virtual Private Network (VPN) or Dial-Up Network connections.
Power Options	The Power Options Preferences provide a means to configure the settings in the Power control panel. Policies you can configure include behaviors and schemes.
Printers	The Printers Preference can create, modify, or delete shared printers, TCP/IP connections and local printers. Through targeting you can specify which computer, location, or organization is affected.
Regional Options	Specify date, time, currency, and number formats based on locale.
Scheduled Tasks	The Schedule Tasks Preferences allow targeting users and computers for scheduled tasks that are specified in this Task Scheduler. Scheduled tasks can be programs that run, scripts, and other automated tasks.
Services	Services Preferences offer a method for setting the behavior of system services. You can set the startup behavior (automatic, manual, or disabled), service action (start, stop, or restart), logon, and recovery behavior.
Start Menu	The Start Menu Preferences allow you to configure the Start Menu so that different items are displayed: recent items, desktop items, and so forth. Targeting can customize the Start menu by user, or for specific computer types such as laptops.

New Policy Settings

With over 700 new policies in Vista and Windows Server 2008, it can be hard to determine which are the most important of these new settings. In the sections that follow, I'll highlight some of the most important. Refer to Table 5.3 for a summary of new Group Policies.

TABLE 5.3: New and Updated Windows Server 2008 Group Policy Settings

SETTING TYPE	DESCRIPTION	LOCATION
Antivirus	Controls access to e-mail attachments by file type.	`User Configuration\ Administrative Templates\ Windows Components\ Attachment Manager`
Background Intelligent Transfer Service (BITS)	Allows peer-to-peer file transfer within a domain. It uses BITS Neighbor Casting introduced with Vista/ Windows Server 2008.	`Computer Configuration\ Administrative Templates\ Network\Background Intelligent Transfer Service`

TABLE 5.3:   New and Updated Windows Server 2008 Group Policy Settings *(CONTINUED)*

SETTING TYPE	DESCRIPTION	LOCATION
Client Help	Allows users to access different help systems: local, offline, trusted, and/or untrusted.	`Computer Configuration\ Administrative Templates\ Online Assistance` and `User Configuration\Administrative Templates\Online Assistance`
Deployed Printer Connections	Allows a printer to automatically be deployed, even for shared systems or locked-down systems. Supports roaming users' printer access. This setting is helpful because it allows printers to be assigned based on a mobile user's location. This policy lets you assign printers based on geographical location.	`Computer Configuration\ Windows Settings\ Deployed Printers` and `User Configuration\Windows Settings\ Deployed Printers`
Device Installation	Devices can be installed or blocked based on the type of device or a device ID. The new policy settings here can control USB drives, optical drives, and removable media, something that can make your network's data more secure.	`Computer Configuration\ Administrative Templates\ System\Device Installation`
Disk Failure Diagnostic	Displays of information from disk failure diagnostic routines run on Windows Server 2008 and Vista.	`Computer Configuration\ Administrative Templates\ System\Troubleshooting` and `Diagnostics\Disk Diagnostic`
DVD Video Burning	Alters the options available to users when recording to optical media.	`Computer Configuration\ Administrative Templates\ Windows Components\Import Video` and `User Configuration\ Administrative Templates\ Windows Components\Import Video`
Enterprise Quality of Service (QoS)	Allows central management of network traffic for Vista clients. The Differentiated Services Code Point (DSCP) can apply a marking and throttle rate to applications without those applications having specific QoS support.	`Computer Configuration\Windows Settings\Policy-based QoS`

TABLE 5.3: New and Updated Windows Server 2008 Group Policy Settings *(CONTINUED)*

SETTING TYPE	DESCRIPTION	LOCATION
Hybrid Hard Disk	Hybrid hard disks contain flash-based cache systems that improve disk performance. This policy setting manages the use of the cache, startup and resume optimization routines, the solid state mode, and how the disk behaves in power save mode.	`Computer Configuration\ Administrative Templates\ System\Disk NV Cache`
Networking: Quarantine	Sets policies for the Health Registration Authority (HRA), Internet Authentication Service, and the Network Access Protocol (NAP).	`Computer Configuration\Windows Settings\Security Settings\ Network Access Protection`
Internet Explorer	An expanded policy for Internet Explorer Group Policy settings lets you alter the policy setting without propagating settings of the administrative workstation used to alter IE's settings.	`Computer Configuration\ Administrative Templates\ Windows Components\Internet Explorer` and `User Configuration\ Administrative Templates\Windows Components\Internet Explorer` in the Group Policy Object Editor
Networking: Wired and Wireless	A policy for centrally managed networks and media.	`Computer Configuration\Windows Settings\Security Settings\ Wired Network (IEEE 802.11) Policies` and `Computer Configuration\Windows Settings\Security Settings\ Wireless Network (IEEE 802.11) Policies`
Power Management	Sets a policy that enforces all power management settings found in the Control Panel. This new policy allows you to set individual or group power settings, which could result in cost savings. Microsoft has estimated that it might be possible to save as much as $50 per year per desktop if this policy is properly applied.	`Computer Configuration\ Administrative Templates\ System\Power Management`
Printer Driver Installation Delegation	Allows nonadministrators to install drivers for printers and other devices without being assigned administrative privileges.	`Configuration\Administrative Templates\System\Driver Installation`

TABLE 5.3: New and Updated Windows Server 2008 Group Policy Settings *(CONTINUED)*

SETTING TYPE	DESCRIPTION	LOCATION
Removable Storage	Set policies that restricts READs and WRITEs to removable storage.	`Computer Configuration\ Administrative Templates\System\ Removable Storage Access` and `User Configuration\ Administrative Templates\ System\Removable Storage Access`
Security Protection	New rules can be set for opening (or denying) ports, connections, and resources. These rules can be applied to IPsec and Windows Firewall. This new policy allows you to set one or the other type of security or both.	`Computer Configuration\Windows Settings\Security Settings\ Windows Firewall with Advanced Security`
Shell Application Management	This policy controls aspects to certain features of the UI: the Start menu, icons, the toolbar, and the Taskbar.	`User Configuration\ Administrative Templates\Start Menu and Taskbar`
Shell First, Experience, Logon, and Privileges	This expanded set of GPOs can control the way a user logs on to a system (logon dialog box) and how roaming profiles are used. Also can be used to redirect (mapped) folders such as Document, Pictures, etc.	`User Configuration\ Administrative Templates\ Windows Components\`
Shell Sharing, Sync, and Roaming	These policies turn Autorun on and off for specific devices and media; affect partnerships for mobile devices; control the synchronization schedule and settings for mobile devices; and create and alter workspaces.	`User Configuration\ Administrative Templates\ Windows Components\`
Shell Visuals	These policies apply to the Aero interface and screen saver, and control desktop search and window views.	`User Configuration\ Administrative Templates\ Windows Components\`
Tablet PC	Use the policy settings for tablet PCs to control Tablet Ink Watson and Personalization, tablet desktop features, input panel configuration, and touch. (Tablet Ink Watson is an error-reporting program for Tablet PCs.)	`Computer Configuration\ Administrative Templates\ Windows Components\<setting>` and Setting = `Input Personalization; Pen Training; TablePC\Table PC Input Panel;` and `TabletPC\Touch Input`

TABLE 5.3: New and Updated Windows Server 2008 Group Policy Settings *(CONTINUED)*

SETTING TYPE	DESCRIPTION	LOCATION

Terminal Services	Terminal Services policies can control different connection features. You can set redirection device access for remote systems, and which protocol or encryption method is used. You can enforce the use of Transport Layer Security 1.0 (TSL), RDP encryption, or a negotiated security method as well as the level of encryption.	`Computer Configuration\`
		`Administrative Templates\`
		`Windows Components\`
		`Terminal Services and`
		`User Configuration\`
		`Administrative Templates\`
		`Windows Components\Terminal`
		`Services`

Troubleshooting and Diagnostics	System-detected application issues, memory leakage, and resource allocation problem tracking can be turned on and off as well as the Windows assisted help for these services.	`Computer Configuration\`
		`Administrative Templates\`
		`System\Troubleshooting and`
		`Diagnostics`

User Account Protection	These policy settings control the way account elevation is performed, how elevation is applied to application installations, determining the least privileged user account, and how to virtualize file and registry WRITE failures to user specific folders.	`Computer Configuration\Windows`
		`Settings\Security Settings\`
		`Local Policies\Security Options`

Windows Error Reporting	Turns on (the default) or off Windows feedback.	`Computer Configuration\`
		`Administrative Templates\`
		`Windows Components\Windows`
		`Error Reporting and`
		`User Configuration\`
		`Administrative Templates\`
		`Windows Components\`
		`Administrative Templates\`
		`Windows Error Reporting`

NOTE These settings apply to Windows Server 2008 and Windows Vista (Business, Professional, and Ultimate).

Network Location Awareness

The Network Location Awareness feature is meant to bring the response to changing network conditions under policy control using Windows resource management technologies. Since a Windows domain can detect system state, connection and session states, and wireless network availability through a number of methods, those states are made available to Group Policy clients.

In the past, resource detection policy was dependent on the Internet Control Message Protocol (ICMP) or PING mechanism to determine if a resource was available. PING was the default method used in past versions of Windows for mobile users to connect to a domain controller when they connected via a slow connection. If PING failed, the Group Policy would fail. Now through Network Location Awareness if the mobile client establishes a VPN connection, then Group Policy initiates a refresh of both user and machine policies, and will do so automatically every cycle of the refresh time. Since many administrators turn off ICMP at the firewall, this issue has required the resolution that is now provided.

Network Location Awareness can be employed to assist in the following areas:

◆ Altering a system during boot-up by controlling options in the Preboot Execution Environment (PXE).

◆ Setting policy that determines the bandwidth available to a client without having to use PING. This policy allows you to block the ICMP protocol and makes a firewall more secure.

◆ The client can update Group Policy when it detects the connection to the domain controller. Connection events that refresh client Group Policy include laptop connection, successful negotiation of a VPN session, return of the client from standby or hibernation, and return from system quarantine.

◆ Assign resources to a client upon that client's startup based on resource detection. If a network adapter is unavailable, a Group Policy can be triggered that doesn't try to load the driver or create the connection. In some instances, this can result in much shorter boot times.

The Network Access Protection Policy

You can have all the security in the world protecting your network from outside threats, but if a system with a virus, Trojan, worm, Rootkit, or other malicious piece of naughtiness is brought inside your network firewall it may do you no good. Unhealthy clients can cause your network to catch cold. Windows Server 2008 introduces the Group Policy settings collectively referred to as Network Access Protection (NAP) to solve or at least alleviate this problem.

NOTE Network Access Protection is described in detail in Chapter 9 in the section "Network Access Protection."

NAP does several things to protect your network. It evaluates the health of Vista clients that log on to a domain with a Windows Server 2008 server using a set of health requirements so that those requirements must be satisfied before an authenticated connection can be made. If a laptop user disconnects from the network and while disconnected turns off Windows Firewall, NAP forces that user to turn the firewall back on before allowing the connection. One variation of the policy will automatically turn the firewall back on, forcing automatic remediation of the policy.

Security software vendors will eventually adopt NAP policies to ensure that spyware detection and antivirus software not only has the latest database or signatures, but performs a scan prior to connection.

You can view NAP settings by opening the GPMC and then opening the GPOE. Navigate to the following location:

```
Network GPO\Computer Configuration\Windows Settings\Security Settings\
➥Network Access Protection\NAP Client Configuration\Enforcement
```

Figure 5.9 shows the enforcement policies that are at the heart of NAP.

FIGURE 5.9

The Network Access Protection policy enforces a certain health level before a workstation or laptop can log back on to the network.

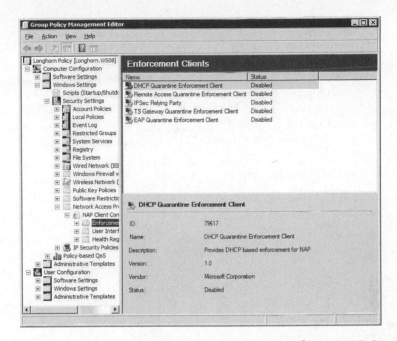

In the enforcement section, you can specify which enforcement clients run, how a NAP client is displayed in the Windows Server 2008 UI, and which health registration settings are used. During a NAP client's evaluation, settings are encrypted and sent to a server for validation. If your domain uses certificates, then that server is a Health Registration Authority server. Figure 5.10 shows a conceptual design of a NAP infrastructure.

The really clever part of NAP is what happens to clients that don't meet the health requirements specified by the set of policies that are applied—they are quarantined. Quarantine is the policy applied to unhealthy clients.

You can apply any of the following set of rules:

DHCP Quarantine Enforcement Client This policy enables health policies for DHCP addressing. An unhealthy client can be assigned to a special subnet or denied a DHCP address entirely.

Remote Access Quarantine Enforcement Client Access through a VPN is controlled by this policy.

IPSec Relaying Party Any IPsec computer-to-computer communication can be evaluated.

TS Gateway Quarantine Enforcement Client The health of a remote computer connecting to a network through a Terminal Server gateway can be controlled using this policy.

EAP Quarantine Enforcement Client The Extensible Authentication Protocol (EAP) enforces the health policy for 802.1x clients attempting a wireless connection or using an authenticating switch to connect.

Additional capabilities include the ability of an organization to add branding to the NAP policy so that the connecting user can see who is validating their connection, see an image or logo, and also see text with an explanation or description of which parts of the NAP User Interface Settings are being deployed. More complex are the set of policies that are part of the Health Registration Settings. Health registration may include Trusted Health Registration Authority Servers, the use of certificates, the application of different cryptographic services, as well as hash algorithms and more.

FIGURE 5.10
Network Access Protection infrastructure can involve many services and elements.

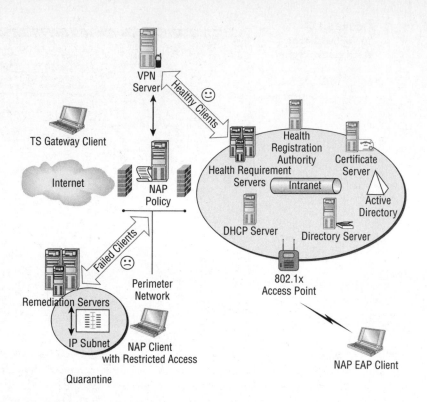

Device Management Policies

Device management is one of the thorniest issues that most administrators face today. The installation of certain devices represents a potential security threat, such as a USB or external drive. Even when devices such as printers are essential to users, there are issues with how these devices are installed, who can connect to them, and where users can connect to devices from. Windows Server 2008 continues Microsoft's evolution to bring a wide variety of devices under Group Policy control for both security and convenience reasons.

Windows Server 2008 brings several sets of device management policies to the table:

Device Installation Restrictions This policy allows an administrator to control which users and groups can use USB or flash drives, or other thumb drives by denying them the ability to install device drivers. Figure 5.11 shows this policy setting in the GPOE. You can find the Device Installation Restrictions policies at `Computer Configuration\Administrative Templates\System\Device Installation\Device Installation Restrictions`.

This policy doesn't prevent users from actually using those devices—that's what the Removable Storage Access policy does.

FIGURE 5.11
Device Installation
Restrictions policies

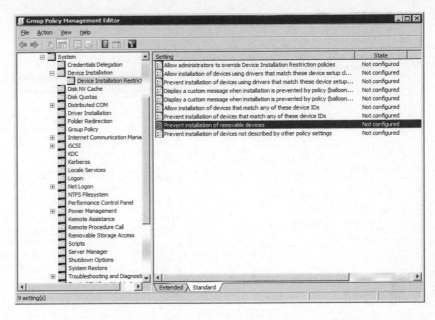

Removable Storage Access   This policy (see Figure 5.12) can allow or deny read and/or write access to floppy drives, CD and DVD discs, removable disks, tape drives, storage devices, and WPD devices. You can find the policy at Computer Configuration\Administrative Templates\System\Removable Storage Access.

The category of WPD devices include PDAs such as Windows Media, Pocket PC, and Palm devices; cell phones; and media players such as iPods and Zunes.

FIGURE 5.12
Removable Storage
Access policies

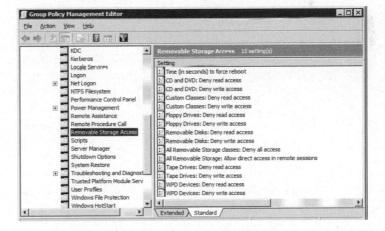

Printer Driver Installation Delegation   Printer driver installation is an administrative head-ache. From a support standpoint, installation requires a large amount of administrator time, and from a security standpoint, delegation to a user requires elevating that user's access rights. This new policy (see Figure 5.13) allows User group members to install printer and other device drivers as specified by the GUID for the device class, as well as allowing Windows Update to be the source of drivers. Drivers must be signed to be allowed under this policy, which is located at:

```
Computer Configuration\Administrative Templates\System\Driver Installation\
  ➡Allow non-administrators to install drivers for these device setup classes
```

FIGURE 5.13
Printer Driver Instal-
lation Delegation is a
single policy setting
but one that is a great
time-saver.

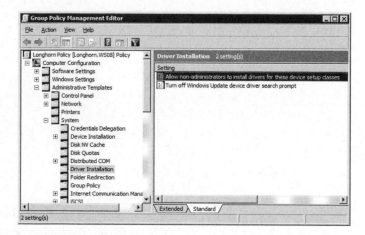

User Account Control Policies

One of the more noticeable changes to Vista was the User Account Control (UAC) system that is used to install installation, start services, and perform other actions requiring elevated privileges. Every time a user's screen darkens and the dialog box appears asking for your permission to proceed, that is UAC in action, as shown in Figure 5.14.

NOTE   User Account Controls are described in detail in Chapter 9 in the section "User Account Controls."

FIGURE 5.14
Actions that can lead
to significant system
changes, such as open-
ing an MMC like the
GPMC, trigger a UAC
event.

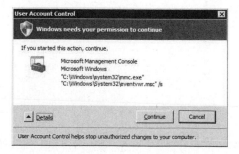

The system was designed to lower the Vista (and Windows Server 2008) attack surface to viruses, spyware, and other nasty boys by running Vista and Windows Server 2008 with lower privileges even when the user is logged on as an administrator. When you give your permission, the system elevates the process to the level required to perform the action—even to an administrator level if that was your logon level. If you were logged on as a standard user, you will be asked to provide administrator credentials in order to perform an action that requires this level. So finally it makes sense to log on to a Windows system as something other than an administrator, which Unix users (as root) have been doing for quite some time.

The range of control that you have over UAC under policy control spans the gamut:

◆ Allowing UAC

◆ Denying users or nonadministrators the right to supply credentials that elevate their rights

◆ Restricting which applications can be installed and/or if they must be signed

◆ Restricting UAC access to users who are in secure locations

◆ Altering the UAC behavior for the built-in Administrators group so that they aren't subject to UAC

◆ Turning off UAC completely

Frankly I don't find UAC all that intrusive. Nor am I bothered by the number of times it appears during an average session on a Vista system. When I'm administrator I appreciate having to actually think first before I do something that will modify my system at the administrator level. However, some users may not like these intrusions, and depending on the configuration of your network it might not be necessary in all instances. Through the User Account Control settings UAC comes under policy control. Figure 5.15 shows some of the settings that are exposed by this settings group; the policy is located at:

```
Computer Configuration\Windows Settings\Security Settings\Local Policies\
➥Security Options\User Account Control
```

FIGURE 5.15
User Account Control is a group of settings found in the Security Options policy.

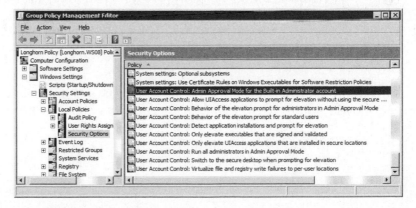

The 10 GPO settings for UAC are:

◆ Admin Approval Mode for the built-in Administrator account

◆ Behavior of the elevation prompt for administrators in Admin Approval Mode

◆ Behavior of the elevation prompt for standard users

◆ Only elevate executables that are signed and validated

◆ Only elevate UIAccess applications that are installed in secure locations

◆ Account Control: Run all administrators in Admin Approval Mode

◆ Switch to the secure desktop when prompting for elevation

◆ Account Control: Virtualize file and Registry write failures to per-user locations

◆ Use Certificate Rules on Windows Execcutables for Software Restriction Policies

◆ Optional subsystems

Since Chapter 9's section called "User Account Controls" has a complete description of this feature and the policy settings above are largely self-explanatory, see that chapter for a fuller description of these settings.

One setting isn't self-explanatory: *Account Control: Virtualize file and Registry write failures to per-user locations* refers to allowing legacy (pre-Vista) applications the right to write files to locations that are no longer supported in Vista. In the past, applications that ran under the administrator account could write data during runtime to %ProgramFiles%, %Windir%, %Windir%\system32, and the HKLM\Software\... key in the Registry. Enabling this setting allows UAC non-compliant applications to continue to follow this practice. Applications of this type are missing a required execution level (internally in the program) or an application compatibility database. This setting is enabled in Vista by default.

All of the 10 UAC settings found in Windows Server 2008 were shipped with the first version of Vista. Windows Server 2008 brings these settings under policy control at the server level and combines with Vista to make the Vista/Windows Server 2008 environment more secure than previous Windows server/client combinations.

Quality of Service

Quality of Service (QoS) refers to the control of network traffic so that an application, client, or user can expect a certain level of performance. It arises out of the telephone industry as part of the X.902 standard and has been applied to packet-switched networks such as TCP/IP.

A QoS network manager will measure:

◆ Available network bandwidth

◆ Application usage by examining packets and protocols used

◆ Traffic source and destination

◆ Port usage

and from these measurements allow the application of a set of policy rules that control network usage. QoS doesn't guarantee a high level of performance; what QoS refers to is the assurance of a certain level of guaranteed service. Applications that benefit from QoS policies include voice-over IP (VOIP), streaming media such as Real streams, videoconferencing, mission-critical applications requiring a stable network link, and other similar applications.

The process of applying QoS policy is sometimes referred to as *packet shaping* (when control is exercised over protocols and applications), *bandwidth throttling* (when the control is over the amount of the network pipe made available), or *provisioning*—but whatever you call it, the desired result is still the same: controlling network traffic to achieve desired results.

Sometimes QoS services run in an appliance such as Packeteer's PacketShaper (`http://www.packeteer.com/`), or the smaller-capacity iShaper. Cisco, the dominant company in the network router business, sells QoS as a core service in their Catalyst line, and those routers are widely used by ISPs to control network access based on traffic type. QoS services sometimes show up in firewalls and proxy servers; indeed, QoS can be any device that network traffic can flow through. QoS can be implemented in hardware and software, and is most often a combination of both.

At its heart, QoS is a policy-based service. Although QoS has been in Windows Servers for a while now, each new version of Windows Server continues to add support for this increasingly important network service. The development of QoS on network servers is in some ways the reverse of the way routers developed. Routing is a much simpler service that was part of some servers such as Sun's Solaris. Eventually the service was developed enough to be packaged as a commodity appliance, which is where Cisco came in. QoS has been on network appliances for a while. However, QoS is an ever-increasingly complex service and it now finds itself migrating onto servers systems.

In Windows, QoS policy can be applied to a user or machine account based on a login and session or on a policy applied at a group level. QoS leverages Active Directory to define the priority of traffic using a system called Differentiated Services Code Point (DSCP), which was defined in RFC 2474. DSCP puts an identifier into an IP header field that can be used by routers to prioritize packets. The second feature of Windows QoS is throttling, which is a policy-based assignment of bandwidth, usually outgoing bandwidth from server to clients. Figure 5.16 shows the general architecture of the QoS service in Windows Server 2008 and Windows Vista.

FIGURE 5.16

Windows Server 2008 QoS policy architecture

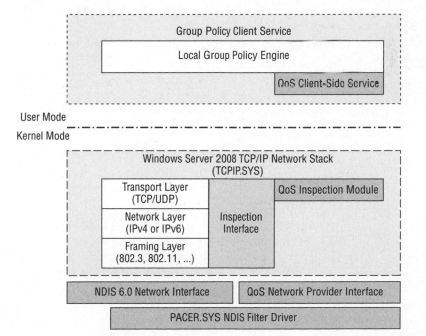

The key operations in applying QoS policy are:

1. Policies are sent to the client Group Policy engine from Active Directory, where they are forwarded on to the QoS client-side server and QoS Inspection module.

2. The Transport layer has a packet receive event and communicates with the QoS Inspection module. If the parameters of the packet transport match the policies that are stored, then a data flow is enabled with the corresponding QoS parameters for DSCP and throttling.

3. PACER.SYS receives the flow directions from the QoS Inspection module and sends the flow number to the Transport layer.

4. A packet that matches the receive event (called an endpoint) arrives and is marked with a flow number in the Transport layer.

5. The Network layer then gets the flow control data from PACER.SYS and sends the packet to the network Framing layer.

6. The Framing layer then sends the market packet to PACER.SYS, which then sends it to NDIS 6.0 on a schedule based on the flow number.

   The packet is sent immediately if no throttling is required, or with a delay if needs to be throttled.

I've said that QoS is a complex, policy-based service, and the previous steps are summarized from an 18-step description that you can read on the Cable Guy's column at

`http://www.microsoft.com/technet/community/columns/cableguy/cg0306.mspx`

The important point to grasp here is that if no policy exists for QoS relating to the packet in question, it is transported through the stack without any delay. QoS doesn't impact performance in that instance. The whole QoS policy mechanism is application independent, and can be applied to packets as they arrive. Additionally, since IPSec doesn't alter the way packets are framed, QoS policies can be applied to that type of traffic as well.

Figure 5.17 shows the Windows Server 2008 QoS policy settings (available at `Computer Configuration\Administrative Templates\QoS Packet Scheduler`), with the bandwidth-throttling feature highlighted. Policy settings under the control of the Windows Server 2008 administrator consist of the following:

◆ DSCP value of conforming packets. DSCP is a QoS service-type level such as Best effort, Controlled load, Guaranteed, Network control, or Qualitative service type.

◆ DSCP value of nonconforming packets. The same type values as above are offered for this setting.

   DSCP is a Layer 3 transport, and packets conform when they arrive with DSCP already assigned.

◆ Layer-2 priority value. This alternative means of controlling QoS uses an alternative link layer.

FIGURE 5.17
QoS Group Policy
Settings

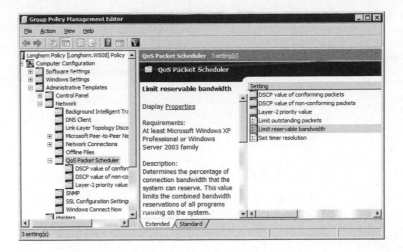

Summary

Group Policy brings powerful controls over networked systems under administrative control from a central management console. There are many policy settings, and you are required to understand how polices are assigned to users and machines at a local and global level, that knowledge gives you very fine control over system behaviors. Use Group Policy to make your systems run more efficiently, add or remove features, and touch nearly every feature that Windows Server 2008 supports.

There are some unique advantages to the Windows Server 2008/Vista Group Policy coupling that become apparent when you study all of the new policy settings that are found in Windows Server 2008. NAP, UAC, and some of the other policies described here require this new version of clients and servers. However, Windows Server 2008 continues to support networks containing Windows Server 2003 and XP and Windows Server 2000 clients and servers.

This chapter only touched on some of the more interesting new policies, and there are many more that are worthy of your attention. Continued advances in devices have led to new areas of policy. You will find support for hybrid hard drives, improved disk and system diagnostics, more advanced power management, and new wireless protocol support in Windows Server 2008. Some of these new features are described elsewhere in this book.

You can't know everything that there is to know about Group Policy settings, but you can dive in wherever you like. A study of the settings of interest that you find in the GPOE will reward you with many new capabilities. Group Policies can make your systems run more efficiently, can vastly improve your security, and can help you tailor your applications more closely to your needs.

In the next chapter, we examine the Windows file system, how it was originally meant to be developed for Windows Server 2008, and what it shipped as. Although we won't be seeing the next-generation Windows Future Storage file system (WinFS), there are many new wrinkles in using Windows as a file server, as well as in the Server Managers tools for file management. The self-healing and transactional file system routines, as well as the File Server Resource Manager, make it easier to manage large and distributed storage networking assets. You'll also find that file screens make it easier to block out unwanted content.

Microsoft has started to include tools for managing storage area networks (SANs) in Windows Server 2008 and greatly improved the creation and management of network shares. Storage quotas and a new file-sharing SMB protocol round out a list of changes that will make managing storage easier. While it isn't quite the revolutionary change that some of us were hoping for, the many new features are definitely valuable.

Chapter 6

File System Enhancements

When I first wrote the outline for this chapter, I had anticipated that Microsoft would finally deliver their fourth-generation file system, Windows Future Storage (WinFS). As I mentioned in the introduction, Microsoft has been working on the next-generation file system for nearly a decade, first in the Cairo project and through iterations into Windows Server 2008. The work has been rolled out in dribs and drabs, underpinning the object-oriented database architecture for new versions of SQL Server, Microsoft Exchange, and Active Directory in days gone by. However, that clean break of the operating system to an object-oriented, hyper-connected file system has proved to be elusive. One can speculate that Microsoft is being careful, not wishing to break the tens of thousands of applications that run successfully on the Windows platform.

Still, this is a chapter about what *is*—and not about what *could* have been. There have been improvements in the Windows NTFS file system, especially in the areas of improved reliability, distributed storage, encryption and security, data protection, and a new role for Windows Server 2008 called the file server role. These areas matter a great deal to server folk, so there's a lot in this chapter you should find of interest.

The Windows NT File System

The *Windows NT File System* (NTFS) is the file system used exclusively by Windows Server 2008, and it has been the file system shipped with all versions since Windows NT. The file system has undergone numerous improvements over the years, some internal and some external, in order to support improved performance, reliability, devices, and so forth. Although the full specification of NTFS is proprietary to Microsoft, much is known about the NTFS file system, and through various APIs, developers have access to the file system at a very low level.

The Windows NTFS file system has gone through five major versions: 1.0, 1.1, and 1.2, which appeared in Windows NT through Windows NT 4; version 3, which appeared in Windows 2000; and finally version 3.1, first introduced with Windows XP. Because versions 1.2, 3.0, and 3.1 were released with Windows NT 4, Windows 2000 (NT 5.0), and Windows 2003 (NT 6.0), you may see those file systems being referred to by the operating system numbers. Although versions of NTFS are largely compatible with one another, as newer options such as shadow copies and quotas were introduced, the previous versions of the operating system couldn't support these features.

NTFS imbues everything that is Windows, from the properties of files and their metadata to the extension of the file system's metadata to support Active Directory indexing. No wonder that it has been a decade-long pilgrimage (literally beginning with the "Road to Cairo," discussed in Chapter 1) to replace this third-generation file system with a new-generation file system that is both fully objectified as well as hyperlinked, fully indexed, and instantly searchable in the same way that business intelligence database tools perform data mining on databases. That file system was to be WinFS, and would have been a break with the current technology that will probably require another new operating system to be achieved.

NTFS uses UTF-16 (16-bit) code for filenames. For Unicode, 16 bits represents the 65,535 different characters. The limitation on the filename length is 255 characters.

NOTE   One of the most useful PowerToys that Microsoft offers to "Genuine Windows" users is SyncToy, currently at version 1.4. This backup utility lets you synchronize, echo, subscribe, contribute, or combine files from one folder to another. SyncToy analyzes the path of files from and to their source and destination and rejects any path that is more than 255 characters. Download this cool tool from `http://www.microsoft.com/windowsxp/using/digitalphotography/prophoto/synctoy.mspx`.

NTFS indexes the file system metadata in a B+ Tree structure, which is sometimes called a Quaternary Tree. B+ Trees are very efficient at providing block data access, and they are popular as file systems for Unix and Linux and in large SQL databases.

In a B+ Tree system, data (as illustrated in Figure 6.1) is referenced by index keys, which are sorted into a dynamic multilevel structure. The "tree," which is really an upside-down tree with the root at the top, has a set of keys in an index segment, and as data is inserted, appended, or deleted, the keys are restructured.

Only the index segments (which are also called *blocks* or *nodes*) at the bottom of the tree point to the records that contain data. All higher-level keys reference keys in lower nodes. The more keys in a node, the fewer steps there are in traversing the tree (the number of keys is called the *order*). Traversing *binary trees*, which are used to index file structures, is slower because the tree has more levels to sort through.

FIGURE 6.1

In a B+ Tree structure, nodes contain keys that point to keys in other nodes. Only the bottom nodes have keys that point to data. The tree shown here is a balanced B+ Tree; the plus refers to the links between nodes at the lowest level.

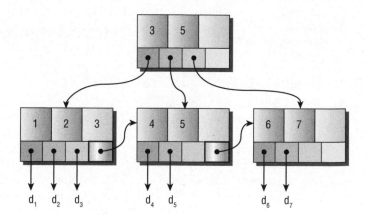

Disk Management

You can format disks using the Disk Management snap-in of the Server Manager (Figure 6.2). When Windows formats a raw disk using FDISK, it marks the first few blocks on the disk in a way that establishes ownership as part of the boot sector. Formatting also creates a master file table (MFT), which stores file and directory data at the start of the disk into a set of metafiles that are invisible to the operating system. Those invisible files are as follows:

◆ $MFT, the MFT file.

◆ $MFTmirr, the mirror copy of the first 16 MFT records that is written to the exact center of a drive. A third copy of the MFS can be located anywhere else on the disk where data can be written.

◆ $LogFile, the journaling file system log.

◆ $Volume, which contains data about the volume label, file system version, size, etc.

◆ $AttrDef, which is a list of file attributes that a volume contains.

◆ $., the root directory (note the period in the name).

◆ $Bitmap, the bitmap representation of free space in the volume.

◆ $Boot, the boot sector of the bootable partition.

◆ $Quota—in Windows 2003/XP, quotas list the amount of disk space users have access to.

◆ $Upcase, which correlates file and directory names from Unicode so that upper- and lower-case letters can be searched as one.

All the MFT data is stored in files that are contained in records. We tend to think of files as data stored sequentially on disk. Actually, data on NTFS is referenced in the MFS and stored on the data sections of a volume in "streams" (a sequential collection of data that contains the necessary instructions for reassembling the sequence even if the parts are separated in transport). We see the main stream of a file contribute to the amount of used space on disk, but streams can allow additional data to be assigned (invisibly) to a file. Streams don't find much use, but the abstraction exists in NTFS and can make the concept of a file a rich one indeed. Everything stored to disk in NTFS is a file. A directory is a file that stores the references to the other files and subdirectories that it contains in a binary tree.

FIGURE 6.2
Meet the new Disk Management—the same as the old Disk Management.

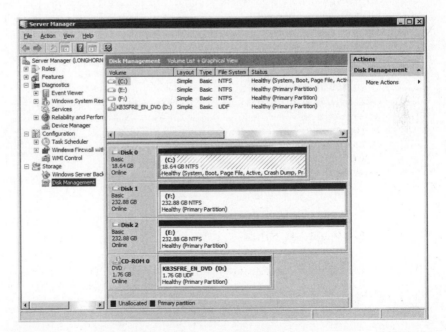

NTFS is meant to be fault tolerant, and one way to make a database system more fault tolerant is to use the concept of a transaction and a transaction log. If a write operation fails because there is a problem with the disk media, the operation is rolled back, the sector is marked as damaged and inaccessible, and the data is written somewhere else. Or if the power is lost during a write, when

NTFS reboots it checks the transaction log (`$LogFile`) and finds any transactions that are marked incomplete. Those transactions are also rolled back to their previous state and the sector written to is marked as free or available again. If the data damaged is the transaction log itself, then examining the disk will indicate that the data was written or hasn't been started. The completed data is left intact and the transaction is marked as successful, or in the case of data not yet written, the transaction is rolled back in the log.

This feature is called *journaling*, and it is the one feature that separates modern file systems from older, less capable ones. Journaling doesn't fix all errors, but it does make sure that the file system itself isn't corrupted. When you run CHKDSK, it doesn't repair damaged file data, but it does ensure that the files in the file system point to real data and that the data in those sectors are at least consistent with the error checking that the file system provides.

Full-Volume Encryption

The Windows Server 2008 core has as one of its major goals improved security at the file system level throughout the Windows platform. Through the introduction of a Trusted Platform Module (now at version 1.2) and with BitLocker software introduced with Vista, you can encrypt files, folders, and the boot volume, making important data impenetrable to hackers or to thieves, and making data deletion more secure. Even swap files and temp files are encrypted. The main impetus is to encrypt laptops, which are often lost in transit or stolen. BitLocker is included as part of Vista Enterprise and in Vista Ultimate. Microsoft has taken these features and combined them into a server-based feature on Windows Server 2008 called BitLocker Drive Encryption (BDE).

NOTE For more information about the Encrypting File System (EFS) and Windows Server 2008, refer to `http://technet2.microsoft.com/windowsserver2008/en/library/f843023b-bedd-40dd-9e5b-f1619eebf7821033.mspx?mfr=true`.

Windows Server 2008 offers full-volume encryption and extends encryption to volumes that aren't the boot volume. Volumes that can be encrypted are "data volumes," which are volumes on drives that are mounted by Windows Plug and Play. Server encryption supports Extensible Firmware Interface (EFI), a new BIOS specification, as well as a new multifactor authenticator module. The authenticator combines a startup key (SK) stored on a USB drive and a personal identification number (PIN), both of which are authenticated by the TPM (Trusted Platform Module). The industry working group Trusted Computing Group (TCG), which defined the TPM, also defined the EFI specification.

The Crypto Next Generation (CNG) CryptoAPI, which serves as the underpinning for SSL among other secure technologies, was upgraded with Vista, and has had a number of new features added for the Windows Server 2008 release. Most of these features are of more interest to developers than they are to users, but they impact third-party products that will be developed in the future. Improvements in the Next Generation Crypto API include:

- A new crypto configurator, better key storage

- Process isolation for operations using keys

- Extensible random number generators (important for creating secure keys), improved thread safety, and a kernel-mode cryptographic API

- Extended support for additional algorithms

According to Microsoft there has also been a lifting of the export signing restrictions that have accompanied past encryption technology.

Full-volume encryption and BitLocker technology are optional features incorporated into Bit-Locker Drive Encryption (BDE), which you install into the Server Manager.

Self-Healing NTFS

The so-called "Self-Healing NTFS" is a new feature in Windows Server 2008 that runs a low-level disk repair in the background, detects corruption in the file system, and repairs it on the fly. You can think of it as equivalent to CHKDSK but you don't have to reboot and take your server out of service to perform the operation. There are no settings for this feature; it runs by default, and the only way to know if it's working is if it posts an error telling you that a repair is under way, displays the repair progress, and tells you the condition of your file system upon completion.

Little has been written about Self-Healing NTFS, and the technology is based on changes made to the kernel so that CHKDSK can run in the background. Whereas to NTFS a file is a file, the Self-Healing NTFS technology will save data of critical system files so that your server is rebootable after a repair. According to Microsoft, it still may be necessary to run CHKDSK in "extreme conditions."

The algorithm is designed to save as much data as possible and to reduce failed file system mounting requests due to a corrupted volume. When Windows Server 2008 detects that a volume is marked "dirty," it accepts the mounting request and begins the repair immediately. A volume with catastrophic damage will still not mount even with Self-Healing NTFS running and will require an offline repair.

One of the features of Self-Healing NTFS is that it provides notification through the CHKDSK program about directories that it has repaired, as well as an update sequence number (USN) that is part of the OS journal entries. The USN change journal is a persistent log that contains all changes that are made to files, directories, and other NTFS objects on a volume. The database entry record contains the object that was modified as well as the particular change made, and it is in an historical order, with new records added to the end of the file. Among the programs that consult the USN change journal are the Indexing Service, File Replication Service (FRS), Remote Installation Service (RIS), and Remote Storage. With Windows Server 2008, that list probably includes Windows Deployment Services, as well.

As repairs are under way, messages are posted and authorized users can monitor and administer the repair operation. They can start a disk verification, disconnect users, and turn off current operations until the repair is completed. Self-Healing NTFS posts a progress status for users.

Personally, I'm not giving up my copy of SpinRite (which analyzes and repairs disks; see http:// www.grc.com) to find out if this technology is a solution to the large number of errors generated by the modern class of large hard drives. However, any time you can make something diagnose problems automatically you greatly improve the effectiveness of the technology. Time will tell.

Transactional NTFS

Transactional NTFS (TxF) applies a technique used in database technology to ensure that an operation is complete and recorded before it is committed; this is the concept of atomicity. A change to the file system either completely fails or completely succeeds. If the operation fails, then TxF uses data stored in an intermediate data store to roll back the state of the file system to its previous state. When the operation succeeds, the success is marked in the file journal as committed, and the intermediate data is either saved as a transaction log or released from memory.

The Kernel Transaction Manager (KTM) was introduced with the Windows Server 2008 core to support atomic NTFS transactions and was released with Vista. When an object is accessed, its previous state is recorded, the change is made, and then the change is compared to the data in the transaction log. TxF works in concert with the NTFS journaling file system, where many transactions are written by low-level routines and often transfer data as blocks and not files. Since many system errors such as Registry and file system corruption occur when multiple threads try to access the same system resource at the same time, TxF may have some impact on eliminating errors of this type.

TxF is of more interest to developers than it is to end users, as it enables a developer to write programs that can use this service to create file output code that is more reliable than previous versions of Windows could offer. For example, TxF ensures that a Save file operation succeeds or it reverts your file to the previous state. When a change is made to a set of files, TxF enables a developer to specify the changes as a single transaction and ensure that all changes succeed or are rolled back. In concert with the Distributed Transaction Coordinator, developers can use TxF to ensure that a transaction is reproduced over multiple systems. That's why TxF is so valuable to processes such as replication or system deployment.

File Services Role

Perhaps the widest installed role Windows servers perform is that of file servers—or what was once categorized as file and print servers. File servers are a very refined category, and one area that sees continual development in every server release. You can get a sense of just how important file servers are by considering the number of features or services that this role offers, as well as how much new development has taken place.

Most books on Windows Server technology tend to gloss over file services and generally make short shrift of the subject. It isn't considered as glamorous a topic as many others described in this book. Services such as the Distributed File System, File Replication Service, Shadow Copy, and indexing services don't get deployed nearly enough in small and medium-sized networks, and are only installed in larger organizations when the prohibitive cost of storage, security, and data recovery are more fully considered. Some organizations *never* get it regardless of their size (for which computer hardware, software, and consulting companies are forever grateful). File services are one of the most high-value services you can install.

File Server Resource Manager

To better help manage storage, Microsoft has collected a suite of tools called the File Server Resource Manager (FSRM) that makes its first appearance in Windows Server 2008. Some of what's in the FSRM are older tools that have been repackaged under the Server Manager framework in this new role, along with a number of new tools for reporting and analysis. The tools in this suite address issues such as the enforcement of storage policies (quotas, for example), determine the types of files that exist in your storage devices, create and maintain shares, and generate storage reports. With these tools in place, you can recover lost storage and do capacity planning for future acquisitions and reassignment. Given that most organizations spend 50 percent or more of their hardware resources on storage, the FSRM is a powerful tool that will be a welcomed addition to the toolkit. Figure 6.3 shows the main screen for the FSRM.

The FSRM is an example of a class of software known as storage resource management (SRM) packages. Some SRM packages go well beyond what the FSRM offers, performing feats of legerdemain such as live data migrations, hot backups of volumes and disks, disaster recovery, and integration into enterprise-class network management frameworks. Nearly all SRM packages include monitoring tools, as well as extensive reporting functions that provide a drill-down capability. HP OpenView, IBM Tivoli, CA Unicenter TNG, and others all have SRM packages that can integrate into them. SRM packages tend to be quite costly. Although SRM has a high return on investment and a fast payback, this category of software hasn't really gotten traction in the marketplace.

FIGURE 6.3
The FSRM is a capable storage resource manager but lacks some of the analytical and reporting features found in the more complete packages. It is a new role in Windows Server 2008.

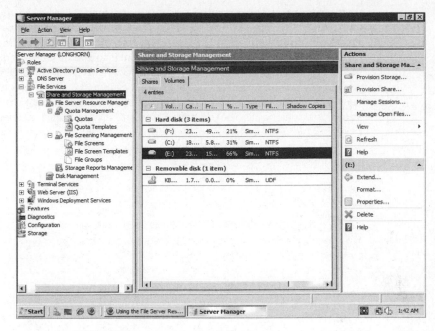

The Windows Server 2008 FSRM allows you to do the following:

◆ Enforce disk quotas by user or policy

◆ Create file screens that limit the types of files that users can save to disk and monitor those attempts

◆ Apply quota and file screen templates to new volumes or folders

◆ Run instant or recurring storage reports that measure disk usage

What's missing from the FSRM that's in the more fully developed SRM packages such as HP StorageWorks, Sun HighGround SRM, IBM Tivoli SRM, and others is the more complete analysis and reporting tools. However, considering how valuable SRM is, its inclusion in Windows Server 2008 represents real value for many companies.

To work with the FSRM, you must first install the file services role. That service installs a set of tools that allow you to manage storage and work with both administrative and network shares.

Volume Management

If you examine Figure 6.3, you will probably recognize that it contains the elements of the older Disk Management utility, which included a dumbed-down version of the Veritas Volume Manager and Microsoft's disk partitioning utility. The Volumes tab of the Share and Storage Management dialog box offers you a new Provisioning Storage Wizard, but there's been little new added to the capabilities of this area. You can do the following:

◆ Create and manage logical units numbers (LUNs), assigning them to servers or clusters

◆ Format, manage, and delete volumes

◆ Create RAID 0 stripes and RAID 1 mirrors, or a combination of both—but no levels with parity data such as RAID 5

When you select a drive, the commands associated with volume management appear in the bottom section of the Actions panel. These commands are also on the context menu for disks. The Properties command opens the same Properties dialog box you would see if you opened the Computer folder right-clicked on the drive and selected the Properties command from the context menu. The Properties dialog box in Windows Server 2008 adds a new tab, Shadow Copies (Figure 6.4), which was previously a menu command. NTFS Security settings, compression and indexing (General tab), CHKDSK (which you can now run without rebooting), defragmentation, and backup are still options on the Tools tab, and access to drivers (Hardware tab) is still largely unchanged.

FIGURE 6.4
The Properties dialog box for a drive in Windows Server 2008 now sports a Shadow Copies tab, but in most other ways it is identical to Windows Server 2003.

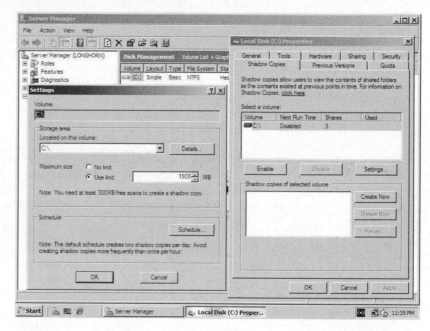

Shadow copies are snapshots that you take of a volume or share that allow users to view and access the contents of those objects as they were at a previous time (in other words, Windows Server 2008 rolls back to a previous file version). You can create shadow copies manually or schedule them to occur at regular instances.

NOTE One feature that had been expected to be part of Windows Server 2008 but has been dropped is the Single Instance Storage (SIS) feature. SIS examines the files in a volume or drive and stores only one copy of the same file. You saw SIS as a feature in the deployment technology for Windows Server 2008; it is used by the Windows System Image Manager (SIM). In a conference call, some of the product managers at Microsoft said that SIS will be in the next version of Microsoft's Storage Server. SIS has been previously released for Exchange and Microsoft's NAS operating system software.

SHARE MANAGEMENT

Whereas volume management is a repackaging exercise, Microsoft has finally given us a tool for managing shares in a central location on the Shares tab of Share and Storage Management. Figure 6.5

shows a selected share, and displays some (but not all) of the properties of the share. The column titles of the share are (from left to right): Share Name, Protocol (storage such as SMB), Location, Quota, Free Space, Shadow Copies, and File Screening. You can view or hide these column names and move them around, so what you see might be a little different from Figure 6.5. Simply having all of these tools for creating and managing shares in one place is the really important new feature in file management, but I don't want to leave out some other new features (which we will discuss in more detail shortly): the new SMB2 storage protocol and file screening.

FIGURE 6.5

The Share tab in Share and Storage Management provides Windows Servers with a convenient, powerful, and most importantly, centralized tool for managing both administrative (system) and network shares.

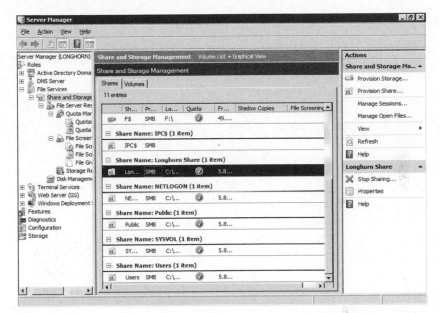

The major capabilities in share management are revealed in the Provision a Shared Folder wizard, so it's a worthwhile exercise to take a look at some of the steps of this wizard.

To create a share using the Provision a Shared Folder wizard:

1. Open the Server Manager, click on the File Services node in the tree control, click on the Share and Storage node, and then select the Shares tab (if necessary).

2. In the Actions panel, click the Provision Share link to launch the wizard.

   The Shared Folder Location screen appears, as shown in Figure 6.6.

3. Specify the share in the Location text box, or create a new share using first the Browse button and then the New Folder button in the Browse for Folder dialog box. Also, select the volume where it will be located.

4. If you need to create a new volume for your share, click the Provision Storage button.

5. Click the Next button to move on to the NTFS Permissions step (Figure 6.7), which displays a dialog box similar to what you see in the Share Properties dialog box's Security tab.

   Click the Advanced button to open a dialog box that allows you to specify permissions as well as ownership of the share.

FIGURE 6.6
On the NTFS Permissions screen, you can set user and group access to shares.

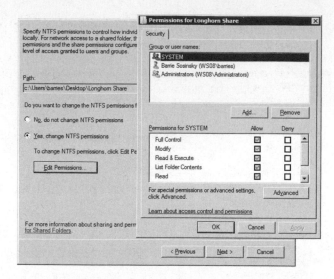

FIGURE 6.7
The Shared Folder Location screen lets you create a new folder to share or set the properties of a share you've already created.

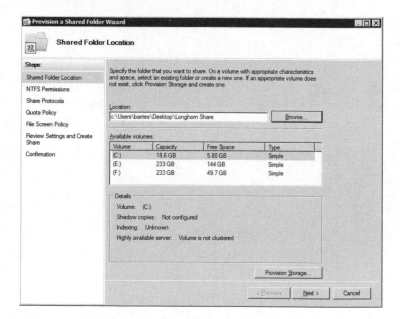

6. Click the Yes, Change NTFS Permissions radio button and then click the Edit button; set the permissions desired in the Permissions dialog box; and click first OK and then Next to proceed to the Share Protocols screen shown in Figure 6.8.

   Windows Server 2008 allows you to specify either the Small Message Block (version 2) protocol, or if installed, the NFS protocol used by many Unix clients and storage devices. The steps you see if you have NFS installed and select NFS as your protocol are slightly different. You can also allow clients to use both SMB and NFS to access a share.

FIGURE 6.8
If you have installed NFS, you are given a choice between accessing the share using NFS or NTFS. Use NFS for Unix clients or Linux NAS devices.

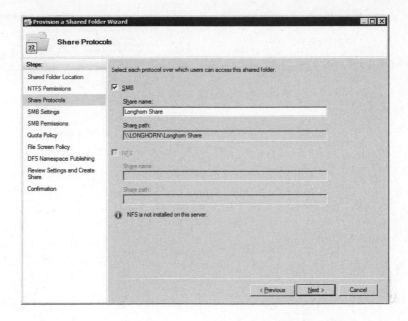

7. Specify the name of the share; then click Next to view the SMB Settings screen shown in Figure 6.9.

Using the Advanced dialog box of the SMB settings (or NFS settings), you can control the number of concurrent users who access your share. You can also allow or disallow whether users can cache share files for offline usage in the Advanced dialog box.

FIGURE 6.9
The SMB Settings dialog lets you define the number of user connections as well as enable offline caching.

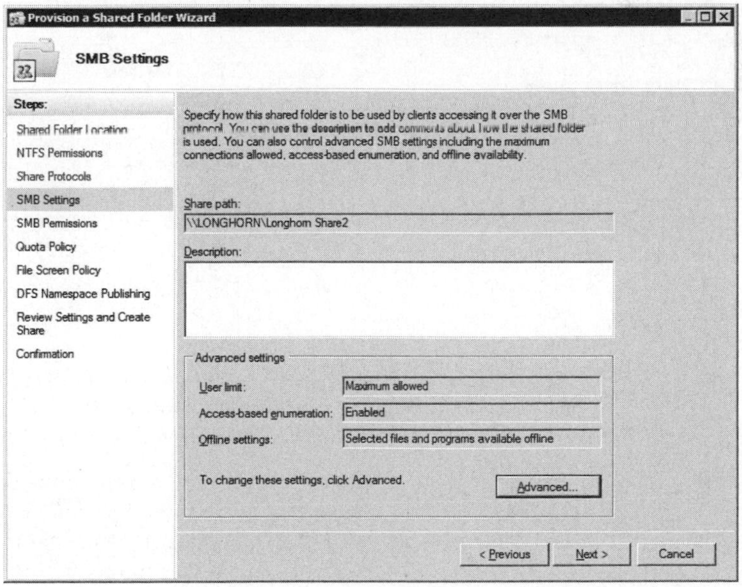

8. Click Next to view the SMB Permissions screen (Figure 6.10), which is similar in function to the NTFS Permissions screen you saw earlier in Figure 6.7.

The important thing to note is that Windows Server 2008 gives a user the least possible access allowed under NTFS or SMB (NFS), restricting access. For example, if you allow the Administrator full read-write access to a share under NTFS but only a User-level read-only access under SMB, then that user will have read-only access.

FIGURE 6.10
The SMB Permissions screen is a second layer of access that restricts NTFS access if possible.

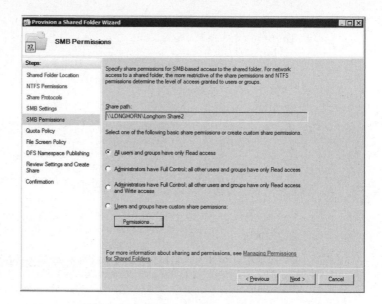

9. Click Next to view the Quota Policy screen shown in Figure 6.11.

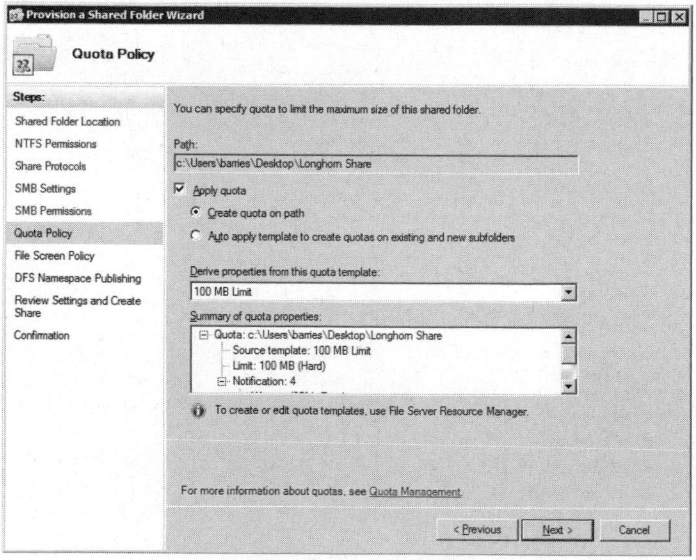

FIGURE 6.11
Quotas are policy-based settings that can be applied in this step of the Provision a Share Folder wizard.

NOTE   As you move through the wizard, previous steps become enabled as links that allow you to go back to a certain step and alter your settings.

10. Select the Apply Quota checkbox if you want to enforce a quota, and select either the Create Quota on Path or the Auto Apply Template to Create Quotas on Existing and New Subfolders; then use the Derive Properties from This Quota Template drop-down box to define your quota limit.

    The Derive Properties from This Quota Template box shows your current policy for storage. The template used by default has the following settings: 100 MB Limit, 200 MB Limit Reports to User; 200 MB Limit with 50 MB Extension, 250 MB Extended Limit, Monitor 200 GB Volume Usage, or Monitor 500 MB Share. The limits also change as a function of the size of the volume the share is on.

    See the "Quota Management" section later in this chapter for more information on this topic.

11. When you click the Next button in the Quota Policy screen, the File Screen Policy screen appears, as shown in Figure 6.12. A *file screen* is a setting that prohibits files of a certain type from being saved to a file share. To turn on a file screen, select the Apply File Screen checkbox, and then select the file screen type from the Derive Properties from This File Screen Template drop-down list.

    You can apply the following screens: Block Audio and Video Files, Block E-mail Files, Block Executable Files, Block Image Files, and Block Executable and System Files.

FIGURE 6.12
File screens restrict the file types that can be stored on a share, and offer a level of protection against user abuse.

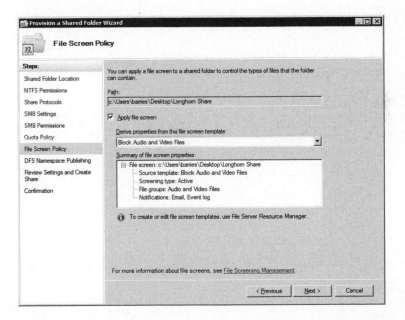

12. Click Next to view the final settings step in the wizard, DFS Namespace Publishing, as shown in Figure 6.13.

The Distributed File Service (DFS) is a method for creating copies of the content of a share in different physical locations. DFS is particularly useful when you have a large number of users who have to access the same content, or you have geographically separated users who need access to the same content. To use DFS you must create a namespace, enable DFS Replication in Active Directory, and install the Replicate Data to and from This Server feature of the file server role.

FIGURE 6.13
To replicate your folder to other locations, enable the DFS Namespace Publishing feature in this step.

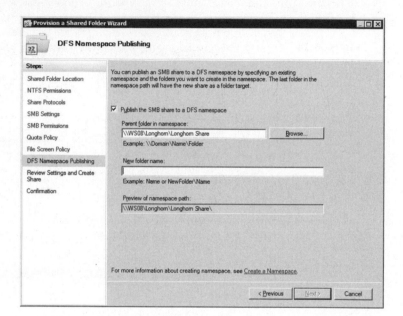

13. At this point you have completed all of the settings steps; click Next and then Finish to apply your settings.

The really nice thing about the Provision a Shared Folder wizard is that it gives you a look at nearly all of the features that you can apply to a share in the Server Manager. A number of tools have been consolidated into this role and feature, giving you all of the tools necessary for managing shares.

To unshare the folder and disable user connection, click the Stop Sharing link in the Actions panel. When you stop sharing, the share is removed from the list and you will need to re-create the share and set its properties if you wish to have users access it again. If you simply want to end a user's session, click the Manage Sessions link in the Actions panel; to block a user's access to files or folders, click the Manage Open Files link instead. The dialog boxes show you the current sessions or current files and allow you to select the ones you wish to close.

QUOTA MANAGEMENT

For file services a *quota* is the amount of disk space in which a user can store data before being denied additional storage space. You can set quota policy as a Group Policy Object in the Group Policy Management tool, but it's a lot more convenient to work with storage policies in a place where you can modify storage resources. When you install Windows Server 2008, it installs a set of default quota templates, and you can apply these templates to users and groups as required.

To view the quotas currently in effect, click on the Quotas item in the Server Manager tree control of the Quota Management feature. You can use that tool to create new quotas if you need to. If you select the Quota Templates tool, you'll see the screen shown in Figure 6.14. In the Quota Templates Actions panel, you can create a new quota based on another template or define one with custom properties. You can also edit templates by double-clicking the Edit Template Properties link in the Actions panel or by double-clicking the quota template that you want to alter.

FIGURE 6.14
You can create and alter quotas in the Quota Management section, as well as create and edit quota templates.

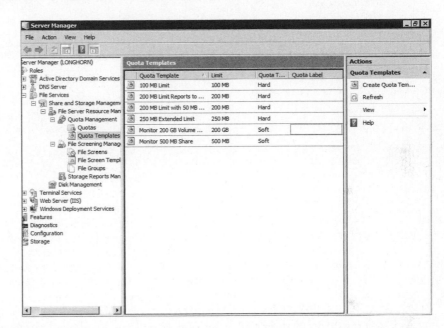

Aside from the Space Limit size, the most important setting is whether the quota has a hard limit or a soft limit. A *hard* limit is just that: users will be denied additional space once they have consumed their allocation. *Soft* quotas do not restrict users from exceeding the limit of the quota.

Quotas have a number of valuable options that you can set at different thresholds in the Threshold Properties dialog box shown in Figure 6.15. You can:

◆ Send e-mail messages

◆ Record events in the Event log

◆ Run scripts (commands)

◆ Create and store or e-mail reports on different storage aspects such as large files, duplicate files, and files by users or groups

As you will see in the next section, you can apply quotas as a policy to any action that is defined as a file filter (file screen).

FIGURE 6.15

Use the Quota
Template Properties
to edit an existing
quota template.

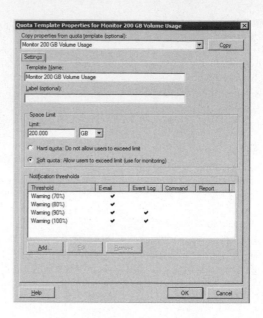

FILE SCREENS

As you saw in the Provision a Shared Folder wizard, you can block the ability of users to create files of a certain type on a share. In the wizard you can specify a single screen, but using the File Screening Manager gives you much greater control over not only setting multiple screens but modifying a file screen so that it can manage the file types you want to be part of a screen.

As with quotas, file screens are policy objects that you apply templates to. File screens can be active and physically block the creation of file types, or they can be passive and simply provide a warning when the file is created. Applying an existing policy is straightforward: you can use the Provision a Share wizard or you can go to the File Screens section of the File Screening Management section of the Server Manager.

To create or edit an existing template:

1. Click on File Screen Template in the File Screening Manager node of the Server Manager tree control.

2. Click the Create File Screen Template link in the Actions panel.

   The File Screen Template Properties dialog box appears as shown in Figure 6.16. This same dialog box appears if you double-click an existing template and edit the properties.

3. Fill in the template name and the screening type, and select files in the Select File Groups to Block list box.

   Of particular interest is the File Group Properties dialog box, which appears when you click the Create or Edit button under Maintain File Groups. This dialog box, shown in Figure 6.17, lets you filter files by file extension and also filter files containing any particular character pattern, along with appropriate wildcards.

4. Click OK to return to the File Screen Template Properties dialog box, and then click OK again to create your policy.

FIGURE 6.16
The File Screen
Template Properties
lets you either create a
new policy or edit an
existing one.

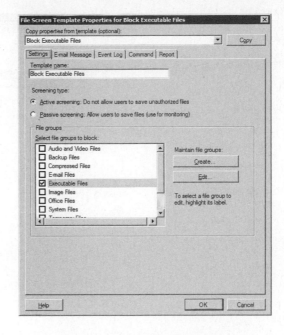

FIGURE 6.17
You can specify file
types by file extension
or files conforming to
a certain pattern of
characters.

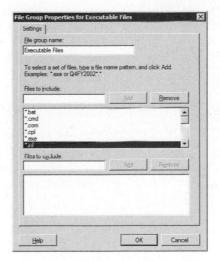

5. Click on the File Screens tool in the Server Manager tree node, and then use the Create File Screen link in the Actions panel to apply the filter(s) you want to enforce.

Space precludes a complete exposition of the properties that you can set for a file screen (also known as a file filter), but you have the same set of properties for this policy as you do for quotas. That is, you can elect to send e-mail messages to users and administrators when a screen is violated, record to the Event log, trigger a script as a command, and create and issue reports on this topic. If you want a quick overview of the files that are either included or excluded (you can do both) in a file type, click on the File Groups node of the tree control. The center panel of that control is shown in Figure 6.18.

FIGURE 6.18

In File Groups you can use not only the extension names themselves, but extension names formed by wildcards as part of your filter.

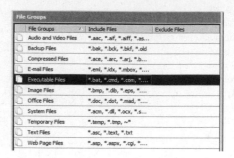

File Groups	Include Files	Exclude Files
Audio and Video Files	*.aac, *.aif, *.aiff, *.as...	
Backup Files	*.bak, *.bck, *.bkf, *.old	
Compressed Files	*.ace, *.arc, *.arj, *.b...	
E-mail Files	*.eml, *.idx, *.mbox, *....	
Executable Files	*.bat, *.cmd, *.com, *....	
Image Files	*.bmp, *.dib, *.eps, *....	
Office Files	*.doc, *.dot, *.mad, *....	
System Files	*.acm, *.dll, *.ocx, *.s...	
Temporary Files	*.temp, *.tmp, ~*	
Text Files	*.asc, *.text, *.txt	
Web Page Files	*.asp, *.aspx, *.cgi, *....	

WINDOWS SERVER 2003 FILE SERVICES

The Windows Server 2003 File Services are a set of file services that first appeared with Windows 2003 and are bundled as part of a package. The Windows Server 2003 File Services feature has two major components: the File Replication Service (FRS) and the Indexing Service. FRS describes the multimaster replication scheme that was used by Windows 2003 for domain servers as well as with many distributed application servers such as Exchange and SQL Server. FRS has been superseded by the DFS system, and if you are using Vista clients and Windows Server 2008 servers, you should move to DFS Replication instead.

The second part of the Windows 2008 server is the Indexing Service. Indexing Service catalogs the contents of local volumes as well as data on remote Windows Servers that the Indexing Server has access to. With the Indexing Service running on one system, you can use the Windows Search service to query the index from another system.

Distributed File System

The Distributed File System role, as noted earlier, is a system of replicated folders that support improved access to content. DFS is supported by two additional services: DFS Replication and the DFS Namespace. Replication requires Active Directory to have DFS Replication added to its schema. Replication has been referred to as "Diff over the wire." You can install DFS from the Manage Your Server MMC or by using the File Server Resource Manager and File Server Management. The latter approach uses Add or Remove Control Programs for the installation.

DFS Namespaces maps a list of folders to a list of target folders specified by their UNC path. Targets are given a priority that determines which folders are replicated in what order. If a client is not able to contact a folder in the namespace, it is possible to create a failback folder on another server. The DFS Management MMC is the one utility that gives you a centralized view of your DFS system. In it you can delegate the authority to manage DFS objects, as well as set permissions for users and groups to access DFS. You can also rename folders in the DFS and move them about in the namespace as conditions dictate.

To open the DFS Management tool:

◆ Select Start ➤ Administrative Tools ➤ DFS Management.

◆ Or, enter **DFS** in the Start Search text box of the Start menu.

The DFS Management MMC appears, as shown in Figure 6.19. The New Folder dialog box appears open in this figure.

Use the DFSCMD command to manage DFS from the command line.

FIGURE 6.19
The DFS Management utility lets you replicate folder to targets and organize your namespace. You have a virtual view of all of your DFS folders, just as if they were on the same drive.

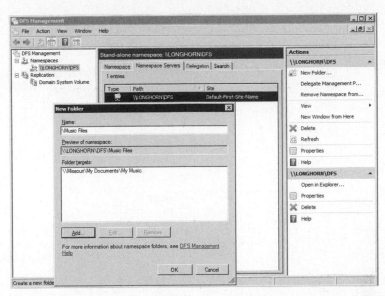

To best utilize DFS, you should create a DFS namespace. This namespace is a mapped view of all of the shared folders in the DFS system. DFS namespaces create a virtual file system that makes it appear as if the folders are on the same drive. You don't need to create a namespace to use DFS, but it does make DFS management much easier. Namespaces can be domain based or stand-alone. The domain-based approach offers fault tolerance with less scaling, while stand-alone namespaces aren't replicated and scale to many more folders. When you add the DFS role service to the File Services role, the process launches the Add Role Services wizard. Figure 6.20 shows you the Select Namespace Type page of this wizard, which is the second step in the process.

FIGURE 6.20
A DFS namespace can be replicated and limited in size, or it can be stand-alone on a Windows Server 2008 server and much larger. For very large DFS installations, it makes sense to have a stand-alone server as a management platform.

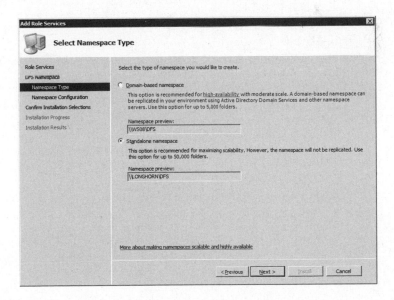

Namespaces have a hierarchy, as illustrated in Figure 6.21. Each object in the namespace is specified by a UNC path. Note that all of these servers can be in different geographical locations. Replication can be a bandwidth hog, so you want to pay particular attention to the replication performance over low-bandwidth connections. For this reason companies sometimes pre-stage new DFS servers when they are at the end of a low-bandwidth connection such as a branch office. It's also valuable to create replication groups so that most replication traffic communicates over high-bandwidth connections.

FIGURE 6.21
The topological elements of a DFS namespace

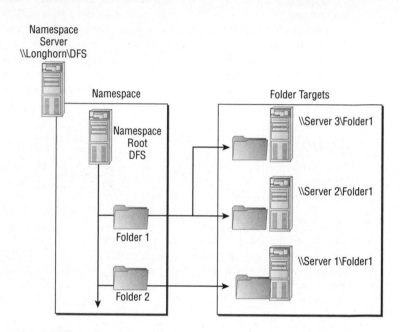

SMB 2.0

The Small Message Block (SMB) protocol is a network transport protocol that allows clients to access file services from servers. In the seven-layer ISO/OSI network model, SMB is an application-level network RPC protocol that uses named pipes and provides client authentication.

SMB is used for shared access not only to file services but to printers, serial port devices, and (of course) in Windows to other Windows computers. When you open the Network Properties dialog box and see the protocol Microsoft Windows Network, this means you are working with an implementation of SMB. Also, the open source file server system called Samba (used by many network-attached storage devices) is based on SMB and Common Internet File Services (CIFS) protocols.

SMB2 is the replacement for the industry file-sharing standard, and its main benefit is that it offers dramatically better throughput over the network. Version 2.0 appeared with Vista and uses packet compounding, better message signing, more efficient security mechanisms, and more persistent handles and links. In tests with media servers (large files), Microsoft has said that SMB 2.0 can deliver 30 to 40 times the performance of SMB 1.0. That is a 3,000–4,000 percent improvement, which is amazing. SMB 2.0 is used for Windows Server 2008–to–Windows Vista communications. Communications between these two Windows Server 2008 core systems and older versions of the Windows OS revert back to SMB 1.0.

Microsoft Services for Network File System

Microsoft Services for Network File System (MSNFS) defines communications between a client and a server for shared files using the NFS application-layer transport protocol. NFS is widely used in the industry by other operating systems, and its use by Windows Server 2008 allows Windows NFS shares to be mounted and accessed by heterogeneous clients such as Unix on the network.

To use NFS, you must install and configure user identity Windows-to-Unix mappings connecting the Active Directory Domain Services schema to the Identity Management for Unix service. The second requirement is that you configure Microsoft Services for NFS. The AD Domain Services Lookup or User Name Mapping requires that Microsoft Service for NFS be configured to query the appropriate source. Settings impact both NFS servers and clients. Finally, your Export NFS shares must have share access permissions. You need to select filename encoding (ANSI, BIG5, or others) for the filenames, and then set share access to clients on a user and group basis to make the system work correctly. Clients must configure identity mapping, configure service for NFS settings, and select "Mount NFS Shares to *drive letter* or to a UNC Path."

Summary

In this chapter you learned about the new disk, file, and volume management tools that are part of Windows Server 2008. On the surface it looks as if Windows Server 2008's new file tools are simply a repackaging exercise. However, Microsoft has greatly simplified the system administrator's job by consolidating the toolkit into just a few locations. The new Server Manager is a substantial improvement over previous management tools and will likely be the focus of nearly all of your operations in that area.

When you look under the hood, you find that there are numerous changes to many of the technologies involving storage. Some are almost invisible, such as the new SMB 2.0 (aka Microsoft Windows Network); others are operationally noticeable, such as file screens and full-volume encryption. There are numerous wizards in this new version of Server that make it much easier to set and edit the features that were described.

In the next chapter, we continue to explore the management tools that ship with Windows Server 2008.

Chapter 7

Server Management

Windows Server 2008 is more of an evolutionary release rather than a revolutionary advance. There are some great new features in this server version: virtualization at the operating system level and PowerShell are two that come to mind. Also, the significantly enhanced .NET Framework, a rewritten TCP/IP stack, and the image-based deployment tools you've read about offer important value to Windows Server 2008 adopters. Those features are also incremental improvements. However, there are so many incremental improvements that make Windows Server 2008, when taken as a body of work, significantly easier to manage and less prone to user error.

Server management is one area of technology that Microsoft "gets" and I think one that it has always gotten. Every version of Windows server from NT through 2000, 2003, and now Windows Server 2008 has had refinements of the tools used to manage increasingly complex networks of systems. Microsoft's forays into right-sizing their servers, which early on led them to release the Back-Office suite for the enterprise, Small Business Server, and Datacenter Server, has prepared them well. Microsoft has been slicing and dicing servers and server apps for about as long as they've been in this business.

Microsoft fans and server devotees will recognize that the management tools in this server release are the best versions yet. In the Server Manager, which is a third- or fourth-generation version of the Manage Your Server tool, is extensible and logically organized, and provides access to roles, features, diagnostics, configuration, the Storage Manager, and more. You'll find yourself reaching for the Start menu a lot less often in Windows Server 2008 than before.

Another new tool described in this chapter is an extension of what used to be part of the installation and deployment of the operating system. The Initial Configuration Tasks console replaces a few of the settings that you might select during Setup and moves them into a single location. This includes setting the Administrator password, setting the time zone, configuring networking, and updating and customizing the server.

To round out the chapter, a number of golden oldies have undergone updates, including the Task Manager, the Event Viewer and server logs, and all of the utilities that use the Microsoft Management Console (MMC) and the Windows Management Instrumentation (WMI) interface. When good servers go bad and Windows reports to Microsoft, this version of server returns troubleshooting help that's almost helpful (instead of useless). It's one more step down the road toward servers that heal themselves.

If you want to find out how to get things done in Windows Server 2008, then this chapter is the one to read.

Command-Line Tools

Microsoft has continually been beefing up command-line tools in their servers, and Windows Server 2008 is no exception. Since the bulk of this chapter describes the Server Manager console and its various snap-ins, you shouldn't be surprised to learn that there is a command-line version of the

Server Manager called SERVERMANAGERCMD.EXE that is found at %WinDir%\System32. You can get help for this utility (which has a lot of options) by executing the command SERVERMANAGERCMD /?. The output for this very useful command appears as follows:

```
C:\Windows\system32>servermanagercmd /?

Usage:
ServerManagerCmd.exe
Installs and removes roles, role services and features.
➥Also displays the list
of all roles, role services, and features available, and shows which are
installed on this computer.

        -query [<query.xml>] [-logPath <log.txt>]
        -install <name>
            [-setting <setting name>=<setting value>]* [-allSubFeatures]
            [-resultPath <result.xml> [-restart] | -whatIf]
➥[-logPath <log.txt>]
        -remove <name>
            [-resultPath <result.xml> [-restart] | -whatIf]
➥[-logPath <log.txt>]
        -inputPath <answer.xml>
            [-resultPath <result.xml> [-restart] | -whatIf]
➥[-logPath <log.txt>]
        -help | -?
        -version


Switch Parameters:
  -query [<query.xml>]
        Display a list of all roles, role services, and features available,
        and shows which are installed on this computer. (Short form: -q)
        If <query.xml> is specified, the information is also saved to a
        query.xml file, in XML format.
  -inputPath <answer.xml>
        Installs or removes the roles, role services, and
➥features specified
        in an XML answer file, the path and name of which is represent by
        <answer.xml>. (ShortForm: -ip)
  -install <name>
        Install the role, role service, or feature on the computer that is
        specified by the <name> parameter. (Short form: -i)
  -setting <setting name>=<setting value>
        Used with the -install parameter to specify required
➥settings for the
        installation. (Short form: -s)
  -allSubFeatures
        Used with the -install parameter to install all subordinate
        role services and features along with the role, role service, or
        feature named with the -install parameter. (Short form: -a)
```

```
 -remove <name>
        Removes the role, role service, or feature from the computer that
        is specified by the <name> parameter. (Short form: -r)
 -resultPath <result.xml>
        Saves the result of the ServerManagerCmd.exe operation
➡to a <result.xml>
        file, in XML format. (Short form: -rp)
 -restart
        Restarts the computer automatically, if restarting is necessary to
        complete the operation.
 -whatIf
        Display the operations to be performed on the current computer
        that are specified in the answer.xml file. (Short form: -w)
 -logPath <log.txt>
        Specify the non-default location for the log file. (Short form: -l)
 -help
        Display help information. (Short form: -?)
 -version
        Display the version of the Server Manager command that is running,
        Microsoft trademark information, and the operating system.
        (Short form: -v)
```

Possibly the most useful version of the SERVERMANAGERCMD.EXE command is the –QUERY option. It takes a while for this executable to build its list and display it, but the results you get are similar to what you see in Figure 7.1 and can run three or four screens long. You can use the MORE (|) pipe to see output a screen at a time, or redirect output to a printer or a text file with the > pipe.

FIGURE 7.1

Manage Your Server from Windows Server was a launchpad for different management utilities.

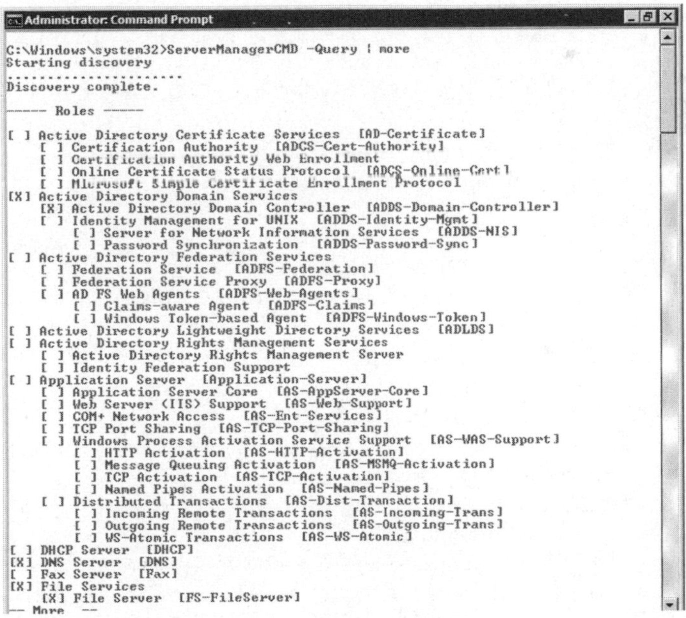

SERVERMANAGERCMD.EXE displays at a glance the roles and features that are installed on the server as well as their command-line names. You can use the names to add and remove roles and features as required.

Among the useful things you can do from the command line with SERVERMANAGERCMD.EXE are:

◆ Build an inventory of roles and features on a local or remote system.

◆ Add and remove roles and features, one or more at a time. For multiple additions and deletions, you will need to supply an XML answer file.

◆ Change default settings.

◆ Manage a Windows Server Core system. Since Windows Server Core doesn't have a GUI, this command is an essential management feature for Server Core.

◆ Manage certain applications such as Exchange or SQL Server 2008.

Space precludes the full exposition of all of the commands that you can use in Windows Server 2008 for system administration. Command-line tools got a significant boost with Vista, and as is tradition at Microsoft, commands that were part of the Windows Resource Kit were moved into the standard distribution. Windows Server 2008 has this same set of tools, listed in brief in Table 7.1.

TABLE 7.1:   Key Command-Line Administrative Tools

COMMAND	DESCRIPTION
AUDITPOL	View and change audit policies.
BCDEDIT	Boot loader editor.
BITSADMIN	Background Intelligent Transfer utility manager.
CHGLOGON	Enable or disable session logins.
CHGPORT	Assign COM ports.
CHGUSR	Change install mode.
CHOICE	Select an item from a list and return the index.
CLIP	Send selection to the Clipboard.
CMDKEY	Modify user names and passwords in the Credentials Manager.
DISKPART	Create and modify disk partitions.
DISKRAID	Create a RAID set.
DISPDIAG	Display diagnostics.
EXPAND	Extract .MSU files (Microsoft Update Standalone Installer).
FORFILES	Select a file(s) and execute a command against a selection. This is valuable in batch jobs.

TABLE 7.1: Key Command-Line Administrative Tools *(CONTINUED)*

COMMAND	DESCRIPTION
ICACLS	Formally the CACLS command, ICACLS allows you to view and change access control list (ACL) files.
ISCSICLI	Microsoft iSCSI Initiator.
MKLINK	The Make Link command can be used to create and edit shortcuts, hard and symbolic links, and junctions.
MUIUNATTEND	Used to install language packages (Multilingual User Interface) during unattended installations.
NETCFG	The WinPE network stack.
OCSETUP	The Windows Optional Component Setup command lets you modify the packages used during an installation.
PKGMGR	Windows package manager.
PNPUNATTEND	Audit system during an unattended online driver install.
PNPUTIL	Microsoft PnP manager.
QUERY	Query {Process|Session|TermServer|User} builds a list of processes that are running and the person running them.
QUSER	Display logged on users
ROBOCOPY	An update XCOPY command.
RPCPING	PINGs a system over RPC (Remote Procedure Call).
SETX	View, create, and edit system and environmental variables. The SETX command can use arguments, Registry keys, and even text files for the value of the variable.
SXSTRACE	A system tracing utility.
TAKEOWN	Take ownership of a file. You must have administrator rights to do so.
TIMEOUT	Set a timeout period for accepting or ignoring keyboard entry.
TRACERPT	Microsoft TraceRpt builds a report from the Event Trace logs.
WAITFOR	Sends, or waits for, a signal on a system. When /S is not specified, the signal will be broadcasted to all the systems in a domain. If /S is specified, the signal will be sent only to the specified system.
WBADMIN	Server Backup command.
WCEUTIL	Windows Event Collector command lets you create and modify Event Collections.

TABLE 7.1: Key Command-Line Administrative Tools *(CONTINUED)*

COMMAND	DESCRIPTION
WEVTUTIL	Windows Event command line utility.
WHERE	Find and display the path to files that match the search criteria. WHERE searches the current directory and any directories listed as part of the PATH environmental variable.
WHOAMI	Can be used to get user name and group information along with the respective Security Identifiers (SID), privileges, logon identifier (logon ID) for the current user (access token) on the local system, i.e., the currently logged-on user. If no switch is specified, the tool displays the username in NTLM format (domain\username).
WINRM.CMD	Windows Remote Management command.
WINRS	Windows Remote Shell.
WINSAT	The Windows System Assessment Tool command accesses the Windows Experience Index (WEI) and measures a system's performance potential in different hardware areas.

The Initial Configuration Tasks Console

The Initial Configuration Tasks (ICT) console replaces the Manage Your Server tool that was part of Windows Server 2003. The latter is shown in Figure 7.2, while the former is shown in Figure 7.3. Although they look similar, they are actually quite different both in design and in function. Whereas Manage Your Server was the start and the end of this console, the Initial Configuration Tasks console is meant to be used a few times and then dismissed. When you click any of the command links in ICT, a wizard is launched that guides you through the setup process. In Manage Your Server the links led you directly to management utilities where you performed the tasks shown.

Manage Your Server was always available as a menu command, even when you dismissed it using the Don't Display This Page at Logon checkbox. When you are finished with ICT and you dismiss it using the Do Not Show This Window at Logon checkbox, you'll have a hard time finding it again. The replacement is the Server Manager, which is a more complete and refined management tool. In this chapter we'll have an in-depth look at the Server Manager and some of its components.

NOTE If you close ICT, you can reopen it from %WinDir%/System32/OOBE.EXE. OOBE stands for "Out of Box Experience," and is the application that manages part of Windows installation routine, the parts that ICT replaces in Windows Server 2008.

When Windows Server 2008 first boots after an installation, it does so to a minimum of system roles. You need to add all of the roles you want on the server one at a time, and ICT's wizards help walk you through this process. Since many roles have associated dependencies (such as services that must run correctly to have the role function), the process for role installation in ICT is easier for inexperienced administrators because they will make fewer mistakes in setup. The Server Manager is meant to pick up where ICT ends, displaying any errors or warnings about services and roles that aren't functioning correctly. So I recommend that you complete ICT, dismiss the utility, and make the Server Manager your central management console.

FIGURE 7.2
Manage Your Server from Windows Server was a launchpad for different management utilities.

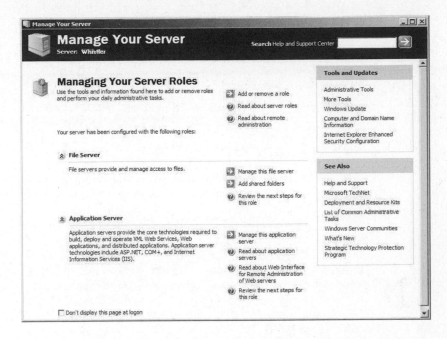

FIGURE 7.3
The Initial Configuration Tasks console is a list of all of those steps that used to be part of the installation process. Think of it as a "to-do" list after installation, because once you perform these tasks you won't be coming back here again.

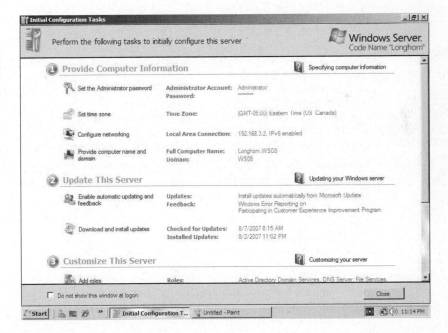

The following settings are exposed in ICT:

◆ Administrator password

◆ Time zone settings

◆ Networking settings

◆ Microsoft Update settings

◆ Add Roles

◆ Add Features

◆ Enable Remote Desktop

◆ Configure Windows Firewall

ICT has a Print, E-Mail, or Save link at the bottom left of the window that provides a report (see Figure 7.4) on your server's status that you can view, print, or store. Near that link is the Do Not Show This Window at Login checkbox, which you should enable once you've set up your initial configuration because it shortens Windows startup times. There are more capable places to go to perform all of the functions of ICT once you have these settings to your liking—each is an MMC snap-in that exists as a tool in the Administrative Tools folder. This report is stored by default at %SYSTEMROOT%\USERS\<*USERNAME*>\APPDATA\ROAMING\MICROSOFT\WINDOWS\SERVERMANAGER\ INITIALCONFIGURATION.HTML.

FIGURE 7.4

The Print, E-Mail, or Save Link opens a report of your settings inside your browser. You can choose to save the information about the current status of your computer's initial configuration.

```
------------------------------------------------------------
     Provide Computer Information
     ------------------------------------------------------
     Administrator Account: Administrator
     Password: ********
     Time Zone: (GMT-05:00) Eastern Time (US & Canada)
     Local Area Connection: 192.168.3.2, IPv6 enabled
     Full Computer Name: Longhorn.WS08|
     Domain: WS08


     ------------------------------------------------------
     Update This Server
     ------------------------------------------------------
     Updates: Install updates automatically from Microsoft Update
     Feedback: Windows Error Reporting on Participating in Customer
Experience Improvement Program
        Checked for Updates: 8/7/2007 8:15 AM
        Installed Updates: 8/2/2007 11:02 PM


     ------------------------------------------------------
     Customize This Server
     ------------------------------------------------------
        Roles: Active Directory Domain Services, DNS Server, File Services,
Terminal Services, Web Server (IIS), Windows Deployment Services
        Features: .NET Framework 3.0, Desktop Experience, Group Policy
Management, Remote Assistance, Remote Server Administration Tools, Removable
Storage Manager, Simple TCP/IP Services, Windows Internal Database, ...
        Remote Desktop: Enabled
        Firewall: Off
```

Microsoft Management Console

Many of the utilities that you see in Windows are built on top of the Microsoft Management Console (MMC). MMC is a component framework that adds functionality by loading a set of "snap-ins," or MMC-compliant components. Third-party applications can use the MMC API and show up inside the framework, but nearly all Computer Management utilities that you find in the Administrative Tools folder are MMC applications. Among the utilities that are MMC snap-ins are Device Manager, Disk Defragmenter, Event Viewer, Performance Monitor, and Services. It's hard to launch one of the server utilities that doesn't make use of MMC. But the use of MMC goes well beyond just utilities. Exchange Server administration console, Terminal Server managers, Group Policy utilities, Active Directory, Shared Folders, Device Manager, and so many more enterprise applications use the MMC for their management framework. So if you know a little about MMC, you already know a lot about all of these applications.

MMC has had a long development cycle. Version 1.0 shipped as part of the Windows NT 4.0 option pack in 1997. After several point versions, version 2.0 of MMC was part of the Windows XP / Windows Server 2003 Whistler release. The current version of MMC is 3.0, and that version appeared with Windows Server 2003 R2 and with Windows Vista. Version 3.0 was released to support snap-ins that were based on the .NET Framework, as well as Windows Forms. Support for .NET and related technologies reduced the amount of code required by a snap-in and added debugging tools. MMC 3.0 snap-ins use an asynchronous user interface programming model. From the standpoint of a user, the MMC framework presents a consistent interface that separates "things" or objects in the tree control, attributes or properties in the middle detail pane, and methods or actions in the right action pane.

The 3.0 snap-ins must always be in compliance with Data Execution Prevention (DEP) guidelines. With DEP, Windows can intercept a program call intended to write code in a nonexecutable memory region and terminate the process. Certain exploits such as buffer overflows and structured exception handling (SEH) overwrites work by this mechanism. DEP has both a hardware component as well as a software component. Add on top of DEP the User Account Control (UAC) service, and MMC 3.0 has been additionally enhanced against unauthorized access. You should expect to see a UAC dialog box appear, as shown in Figure 7.5, whenever you open an MMC console. If you don't see a UAC dialog box you should find out the reason why and address it. Chapter 9 describes the UAC in more detail, but it's a useful form of insurance on a server.

FIGURE 7.5
The User Account Control opens whenever you load the Computer Manager's Snapin Launcher, asking for confirmation of the action so that the privileges can be temporarily elevated.

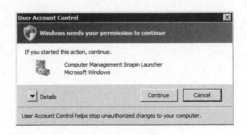

NOTE For more detailed information about MMC, refer to http://msdn2.microsoft.com/en-us/library/ms950376.aspx.

Server Manager

Windows Server 2008 continues the trend of consolidating utilities on the Start menu into multi-functioned interfaces. Server Manager incorporates nearly all of the Windows Server 2008 management utilities into a single console, giving you a single place from which you can perform almost all of your important configuration tasks. Windows Server 2008's Server Manager (now at version 6.0) is more complete, more logically organized, and easier to use than previous versions of this utility. As Microsoft adds the organizational concept of "roles" and "features," you'll find that when a role or feature isn't working properly it is marked as not functioning in the Server Manager. In many instances when something isn't working this version of the Server Manager tells you what you need to do to get it fixed, even if it doesn't always tell you exactly how to go about it step by step. The Server Manager is the single best tool for determining your system's health and for gaining access to the tools needed to get problems fixed.

The Server Manager's overview screen, shown in Figure 7.6, displays the identity of your server, its network properties, IP address, Product ID, and the login account. Below the Computer Information panel in the Server Summary are these panels:

Security Information   This panel links to the Windows Firewall, sets Windows Update policy, and links to the Security Configuration wizard. These features are described in more detail in Chapter 9, "Security."

Roles Summary   Roles are services that a server can perform. Roles were discussed in more detail in Chapter 4.

Features Summary   A feature is a component that you install to provide a service or support a role. When a role isn't performing correctly, it is typically because a feature is missing or improperly applied. This panel lets you see what feature is installed.

Resources and Support   Here, you can turn on Windows Error Reporting, participate in Microsoft's Customer Experience Improvement Program (CEIO), and link to the Windows Server Tech Center.

FIGURE 7.6
The Server Manager is the central management utility in Windows Server 2008, bringing together in an MMC a disparate set of snap-ins. You can have this tool launch at startup, or open it from the top of the Start menu.

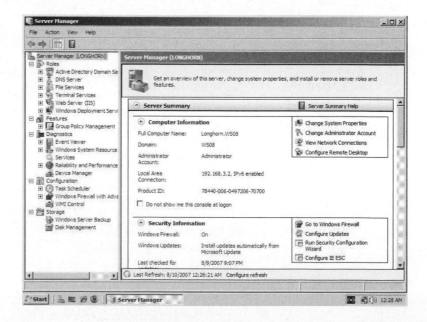

You have control over which features appear in the Server Manager window by making modifications in the Customize View dialog box, shown in Figure 7.7. The Action menu has a Customize View command, and when you use that command to close the Action panel, the Server Manager puts an Action menu on the menu bar with the same command.

FIGURE 7.7

Use the Customize View dialog box to control what you see in the Server Manager window.

In order to make your server fully functional, the Roles node of the Server Manager is the very first place you should look after you've completed the installation—that is, once you've performed all of the tasks and enforced all of ICT settings. Click the Roles node in the component tree (left panel) to see a Role Summary section at the top of the detail pane. From here you can add and remove roles, and determine what Windows Server 2008 is capable of doing.

Each node can be opened or collapsed by double-clicking on the section bar. In the default setup shown in Figure 7.8, Windows Server 2008 flags problems in three areas: Active Directory Domain Services, File Services, and Terminal Services. The red "railroad crossing" icon indicates that either the role's service didn't start up or that error events were detected in one of Windows Server 2008's event logs. Since each of these roles is a hyperlink to each role's detail pane, you can click to drill down further to investigate. The Active Directory Domain Services pane loads, which shows more detail on the error.

FIGURE 7.8

Many of the listings in MMC are hyperlinks that you can click on to move about. The links in the Roles Summary section open the corresponding detail pane.

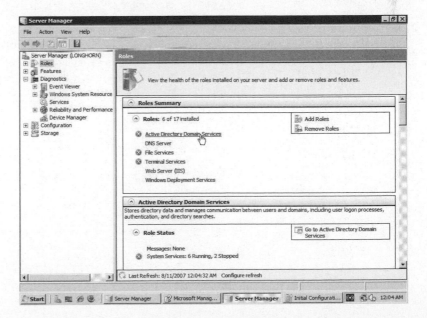

Figure 7.9 shows the Active Directory Domain Services detail panel. When this pane opened it showed that the Distributed Link Tracking Client service was stopped. When we clicked the Start button, the service started up and the issue went away. It's possible that an experienced person would look at the system log and realize that errors were generated relating to this service—but that fact would take a while to figure out, and probably would be missed by most people. The issue was resolved in the Server Manager in a fraction of the time. If the problem was an error event and not a service, you would see a link such as Go to Event Viewer in the detail pane that would provide you with the next level of drill-down. The Event Manager is described in more detail in the section "The Event Viewer."

FIGURE 7.9

You can often resolve issues directly from within the Server Manager, or from a snap-in or utility directly loaded into or accessible from this location.

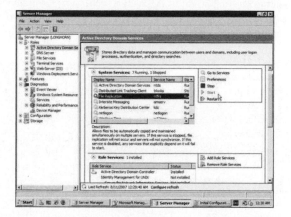

Many error conditions in Windows Server 2008 such as an errant Terminal Service client connection can be resolved quickly by examining the Terminal Services section. The listing shows an error condition due to missing client CALs, and since the functionality is right there in the Server Manager you can resolve it by launching Terminal Server Licensing (from within the Server Manager) and making the necessary changes. The Server Manager might not help you figure out exactly what you need to put into the Licensing wizard, but it will get you to the right place to take the next step.

The Server Manager indicates the overall health of your system and provides you with a recipe book for making your server and its network run better, or at least correctly. If you scroll down the detail pane you'll see the Resources and Support section (Figure 7.10), which provides a set of best practices and links to additional help. The Server Manager in Windows Server 2003 had much less support, was considerably less well interconnected, and wasn't nearly as useful as the one in Windows Server 2008. It's pretty clear that Microsoft spent a lot of time improving this most important of their centralized management tools.

FIGURE 7.10

Think of the Resources and Support section at the bottom of each role panel as what Microsoft's Clippy would have wanted to become when he (she or it?) grew up.

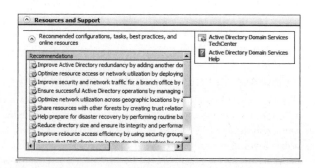

Device Manager

The Device Manager is one of those utilities that has been squirreled away in the Computer Properties dialog box for a long time. Previously you would right-click on Computer, select Properties, click the Hardware tab, and then click the Device Manager button to open the Device Manager. Of course, if you threw a pinch of salt over your shoulder and entered the command **DEVMGMT.MSC** into the Run dialog box, that would have worked too.

In Windows Server 2008 the Device Manager has been moved into the Server Manager (see Figure 7.11), where you can access it directly. There isn't anything particularly new in the Device Manager, but its inclusion in the Server Manager illustrates the principle behind this new version of the Server Manager. All of the MMC components that have been scattered about the Windows interface are consolidated into the Server Manager. You can still go into the Computer Properties dialog box and get to the Device Manager that way as well.

FIGURE 7.11
The Device Manager is no longer a right-click and a tab away buried in Computer Properties. It too may be found in the Server Manager in the Reliability and Performance Section.

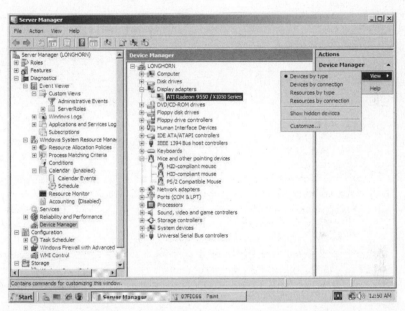

Services are another example of the centralization of MMC utilities into the Server Manager, as shown in Figure 7.12. If you click on Services you'll see the same familiar Services display that first showed up as a control panel, then as an Administrative tool, and now as a Server Manager snap-in. Typing **SERVICE.MMC** in the Run dialog box also gets you to the Services utility. Services no longer appear in Windows Server 2008 as a control panel, but the command is still there in the Administrative Tools folder of the Start menu, and you can bring it up in the Windows Server 2008 Find dialog box (Start ➤ Run, and click the Find button) by typing **SERVI**. When you access Services any other way than through the Server Manager, it opens in its own console with no other resources.

Windows System Resource Manager

The Windows System Resource Manager (WSRM) is Microsoft's answer to Solaris 10's Sun Management Center. With WSRM you can create policy-based settings that provide access to system resources such as CPU and memory. In an era of multiple CPUs and multiple cores, WSRM offers you a level of control to manage your applications, albeit in a very coarse manner. For example, WSRM only kicks in for CPU utilization when the processor loading climbs to over 70%. Figure 7.13 shows the WSRM main page.

FIGURE 7.12
Deemed too useful to
be buried in the con-
trol panels forever,
Services is another
one of the new snap-
ins that makes a wel-
come appearance in
the Server Manager.

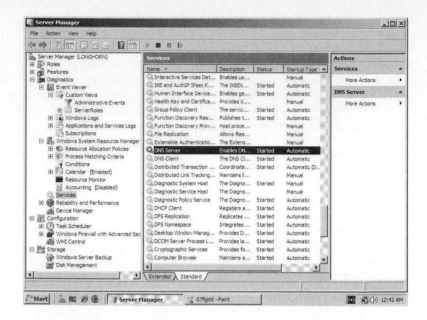

FIGURE 7.13
The Windows System
Resource Manager
provides QoS-like
access to system hard-
ware, monitoring, and
scheduling based on
policy settings.

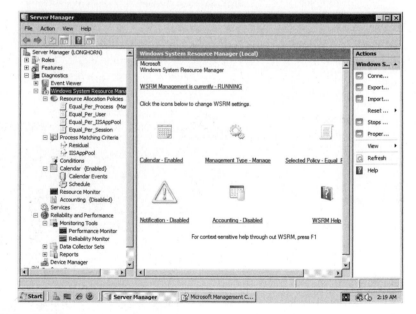

Use WSRM to do the following:

◆ Create policies that control access to system resources (primarily CPU and RAM) based on
policy settings

◆ Use a calendar to schedule access to resources

- Link resource access to events and conditions

- Store resource usage data into a log file for performance analysis

While these four capabilities are powerful, it's best to consider WSRM a work in progress—something you should keep an eye on, as future versions of this utility are likely to be more powerful and play a central role, particularly on larger server systems. As it stands now, there are four built-in resource allocation policies that you can apply in WSRM: Equal_Per_Process, Equal_Per_User; Equal_Per_Session, and Equal_Per_IISAppPool.

You can also create custom policies. The Resource Access Policy (RAP) allocates system resources using custom rules. Another custom policy, Process Match Criteria (PMC), allows you to link programs and services to a RAP, on a user or group basis. The inverse action to RAP is the creation of an Exclusion List that denies access to programs and service on a user or group basis. The custom version of the linkage of resources to events or conditions (such as a cluster node failure) is through a trigger-based conditional policy application. Finally, WSRM supports custom calendar-based policies that support different RAPs being enforced at different times and on different days. You'll want to check the Help system for more information on WSRM.

Reliability and Performance

The Reliability and Performance section of the Server Manager is a collection of familiar tools such as Performance Monitor; new tools such as the Reliability Monitor; and a central location to manage Data Collector sets and reports, which are based on data that you specify and collect in logs. Most of these tools are now supported by a set of wizards and templates that help you create and manage the associated log files. As with the newly reworked Event Viewer (see the section "The Event Viewer"), the Reliability and Performance section has a nice overview that you can use to drill down on the factors that you wish to examine. Figure 7.14 shows the Reliability and Performance utility's Resource Overview (new in Windows Server 2008), which combines several of the most commonly used counters displayed in Performance Monitor windows.

FIGURE 7.14
The Reliability and
Performance utility

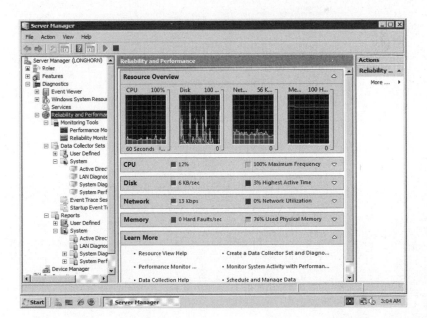

The Windows Reliability and Performance Monitor combines the functions found previously in the Performance Logs and Alerts (PLA), System Monitor, and the Server Performance Advisor (SPA) tools. The Reliability and Performance section of the Server Manager offers a new overview of your system's performance with the capability to drill down on the various factors to get more information. When you click the arrow at the right of a resource, you get a display of the components that are involved in the resource's utilization. For CPU, that listing is a list process type display, just what you would see on the Processor tab in the Task Manager, but without the integration into a system of related tools. Similarly, the Disk section details the processes that are accessing your disk(s) at the moment. The Learn More section is a set of help files, collection principles, and best practices that you can apply in the Reliability and Performance tools.

The Reliability Monitor and Performance Monitor can be accessed by the user groups, as can the log files. Users cannot create or change any of the Data Collector Sets, nor can they perform data collection in the Performance Monitor. Data Collector Sets are by definition not available to the Users group. To give a user complete access to reliability and performance data, you can add that user to the Performance Log Users group. If you are an administrator, you can view reliability data on remote systems.

To turn on the Remote Registry service on the remote system, do the following:

1. Click Start, right-click on Computer, and then select the Manage command to start the MMC on the remote system that you wish to monitor.

2. In the tree pane, click on Services and Applications, and then click on Service to highlight that function.

3. In the center console pane, right-click on Remote Registry and then select Start.

4. If you want to be able to examine the Reliability Index on that computer at future times, change the service startup state to Automatic.

5. Close the MMC on the remote computer.

The remote system must be running the RACAgent scheduled task for you to view reliability data remotely. This service is on by default but can be disabled.

To open the remote Reliability Monitor on the remote system, use this procedure:

1. Click Start, right-click on Computer, and then select the Manage command to start the MMC on the remote system that you wish to monitor.

2. In the tree pane, click on Computer Management (Local), and then click Connect to Another Computer.

3. Enter the name of the computer or browse to that computer, and click OK.

PERFORMANCE MONITOR

The Performance Monitor, or PerfMon (Figure 7.15), is a graphical display of real-time performance based on the data collected by a set of small programs called counters. You can add counters that measure total disk usage, rate of page faults, % CPU utilization, and more. There are literally hundreds of counters that you will find in Windows, and whenever you install a program such as Microsoft Exchange, it often adds even more counters. Counters (like events) are vital in the development process for an operating system or application, and you can use them for the same thing that developers use them for: to measure and improve performance, to gauge the impact of changes, and to troubleshoot your system.

FIGURE 7.15

The Performance Monitor, formerly the Resource Monitor, shows up in the Server Manager. While this view is in a convenient place, chances are that you will want to use the Performance Monitor by itself when doing serious benchmarking work.

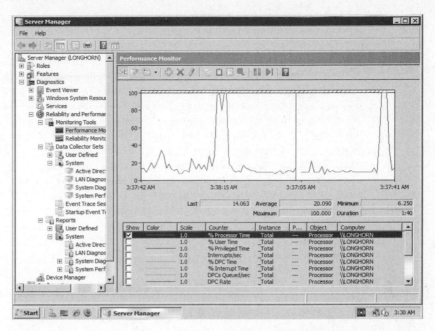

The Performance Monitor is a central tool in an administrator's collection for determining where problems exist and for optimizing systems. Some would argue that the Performance Monitor is *the* most important tool in diagnosing problems; however, I would rate the Performance Monitor and the Event Viewer as being equally important.

If you don't know how your systems perform at some state in time, you are hard-pressed to know whether you need to buy more equipment to support your work or utilize your equipment in a better way. It is considered good practice to store essential performance data in a set of log files, printouts, and reports that you can use to analyze your systems at a later date. Nothing will help you get that Gigabit Ethernet backbone you've wanted for your network from management quicker than having powerful historical trending data based on performance.

The Performance Monitor is easy to use and manage. If you've set up graphs in Excel, then you'll have no problems here. The most important part of working with PerfMon is selecting the right counters to get meaningful information, and you can add and remove counters using the Toolbar Add (+) button or by right-clicking on the Performance Monitor and selecting Add Counters from the context menu.

Typically Microsoft's resource kits offer a lot of in-depth information on PerfMon, counters—especially newly added counters—and additional operational resources. Many resource kits also provide additional counters for you to add to PerfMon.

THE RELIABILITY MONITOR

The second interesting tool you will find in the Performance and Diagnostics portfolio of utilities is the Reliability Monitor. With the Resource Monitor snap-in, you can get an overview of the events from a historical basis that alter system reliability. Reliability is a plotted result of an algorithm that is calculated by the events that the monitor detects as well as other factors. (In this regard the concept is a little like the Windows Experience Indicator that evaluates systems for Aero performance.)

The System Stability Index is a number from 1 to 10, with 10 being the most stable. The index is a weighted average that counts recent failures more heavily in the index than past failures, and displays changes in the system over time. If a system is sleeping or turned off, data isn't collected and the index isn't altered. Also, when there isn't a reasonable data set collected on the day(s) shown on the graph, then a dotted line appears in place of the graph line.

When Windows Server 2008 detects an installation failure or a program fault, it lowers the System Reliability Index. Figure 7.16 shows this combination bar and line plot chart. The Reliability Monitor can be quite helpful in determining when there are repeating patterns of events, as well as when there are related ones. When you click on a bar that represents a two-day period (in the System Stability Chart), you are shown the events that occurred that day. Days without events tend to trend the System Reliability Index up toward more positive numbers slowly over time, but the rise in the index for good days isn't as steep as the drop is for system problems. When you install new applications, the index drops until the observed impact on the system can be determined.

The Reliability offers a great amount of drill down information. You can click on the graph where you see events of interest and you can determine what the event was and get more detail. In Figure 7.16 the cursor at 8/2/2007 displays two events from that day, one informational and the other a critical event.

FIGURE 7.16
The Reliability Indicator is a graphical representation of the events that impact your system's stability boiled down to a single measurement.

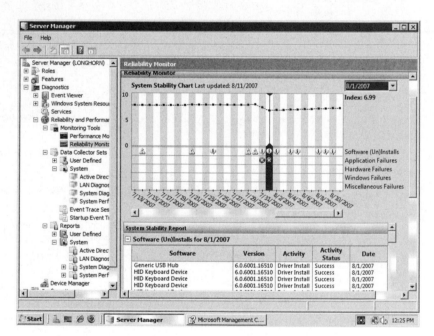

DATA COLLECTOR SETS

Data Collector Sets are logs that are established and stored for a single session, or as part of a regular analysis. This feature was once part of the Server Performance Advisor that shipped with Windows Server 2003, and has been upgraded in Windows Server 2008 and Vista. In the Data Collector Sets node, you can create, schedule, and edit data logs. You can also establish the collection parameters as a performance log template and schedule that collection to take place at some point in the future. Stored data collection logs are one of the best methods available to you to analyze performance difference over long periods of time.

You can log data in Data Collection Sets using the following data types:

◆ Performance counters

◆ Event Trace data

◆ System configuration data stored in the Registry

You can base a Data Collector Set on a template or on a Data Collectors set in Performance Monitor, or use individual collectors and alter the options for that collector(s) in the Data Collector.

Storage Manager

The Storage node of the Server Manager consolidates two important tools that manage data on disks: the Disk Management utility and Windows Server Backup. Figure 7.17 shows the Storage node opened to the Disk Management console.

FIGURE 7.17
The Storage Manager is Windows' graphical representation of DISKPART, the new partitioning utility that is part of the WinPE 2.0 boot utilities.

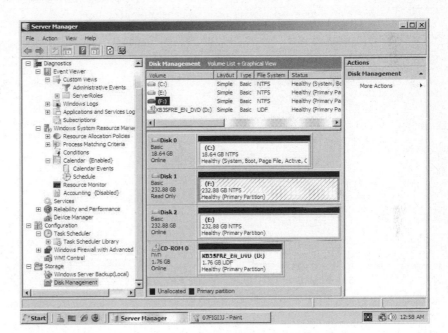

Disk Management allows you to:

◆ View disks on different storage subsystems.

◆ Create a logical unit number (LUN) for a recognized disk, set the size of each LUN, and assign a LUN to a server or as part of a server cluster.

◆ Create, edit, or delete a volume using DISKPART, as a partition of several different types (e.g., Basic, Dynamic, and so forth).

◆ Shrink or expand a volume on disk.

- Format the volume with the NTFS file system.

- Enable the Shadow Copies feature that saves snapshots of a drive over time.

- Create and enforce a disk quota policy based on users and groups.

- Set up a disk share.

- Run Check Disk (CHKDSK) and Defragmentation utilities. Defragmentation is a feature-limited version of Diskeeper's (previously Executive Software) Diskeeper utility.

- Create some basic RAID sets such as spanned disks, JBOD ("Just a Bunch of Disks"), RAID 0, RAID 1, and RAID 0+1.

These functions are either available by right-clicking on the disk object and selecting context menu commands, or by setting options from within the Properties dialog box of that object. There are no new features in the Storage Manager in Windows Server 2008 that didn't exist in Vista or Windows Server 2003.

The Storage Manager also integrates Windows Server Backup into the Server Manager for versions of Windows Server 2008 other than the Standard Edition. If you wish to use Backup on a Windows Server 2008 Standard Edition system, you have the option of running the MMC snap-in on a remote system or managing that utility remotely. On the surface it doesn't appear that anything significant has changed in Backup 2008, but Microsoft's website lists the following improvements:

- Faster backup using Volume Shadow Service (VSS) and block-level (or sector-based) transfers

- Simplified restoration of data, of the system volume, and even of applications that are VSS enabled like SQL Server

- Better scheduling with new wizards

- Automated disk management so that backup data is written to available disk space in a proportionate manner

- Remote administration

- Backup to DVD media, and the creation of backups for off-site storage and disaster recovery

Backup 2008 does not support backup to tape storage, although you can back up to tape using the tape drivers that are still included with Windows Server 2008. For tape backup you will need to use a third-party backup software solution.

The Event Viewer

Windows is an event-driven environment. The operating system acts on commands and performs operations based on those commands. Modern computers are so fast that you never get the sense that a "wait state" exists in which processing stops and new instructions are fetched from the event queue, but that is indeed what happens. The computer's clock ticks at high speed, and periodically (also at a high rate) your BIOS generates an interrupt signal that will pause in thread execution if just for an instant. The new instructions are examined and execution begins again based on a set of rules in the operating system.

Hardware and software vendors play a lot of tricks to make their systems more efficient. Programs are prioritized so that they have a certain execution order: essential system processes get the highest priority, foreground applications have a high priority, and background applications run when system resources become available. An errant program that hangs your system does so usually because there's an error. Each error event is stored as an entry in one of Windows event logs: the System, Application, or Security logs. You have the option to turn logging off, and that might make sense on a workstation, but not on a server. The event logs are the primary historical diagnostic tool you use to see what problems exist, get information on how to fix those problems, and analyze your system to improve its performance. The Event Viewer is Microsoft's GUI tool for event analysis. You can now view the Event Viewer from within the Diagnostics section of the Server Manager, as shown in Figure 7.18.

NOTE   The first tools that operating system programmers build into their operating systems are: events and event logs; and counters and a performance monitor to measure counter output. Operating system developers use those tools to test the health of the operating system as it is being built as a feedback loop. As they see the impact of the changes they make in their programs and hardware on performance (or on security) they make appropriate changes in their code and routines. The more you know about these two diagnostic systems therefore, the better able you are to optimize your server and avoid future problems.

FIGURE 7.18
The Overview and Summary section of the Event Viewer gives you the top-level view of all of the events recorded in your logs.

An examination of the Event Viewer will reveal two new logs: the Setup log, which appeared in Vista and can work hand in hand with installation tools such as Windows Automated Installation Kit and the Business Desktop Deployment Solution Accelerator, and the Forwarded Events log.

Setup Log   The Setup log records installation events, as well as any events that change the configuration of the system. When you run DCPROMO to upgrade a server to a domain server, or add a server role such as a DNS service, that change is recorded in the Setup log.

Forwarded Events Log   The Forwarded Events log stores event entries from another connected system(s) on a subscription basis. The purpose of the Forwarded Events log is to create a repository of events from systems that are involved in processes that you need to troubleshoot from a central location. Forwarded Events is similar in principle to the old SYSLOG system that was meant to aggregate events collected on Unix systems onto a Windows Server.

As you add new roles to Windows Server 2008, new logs will appear in the Event Viewer. When you expand the Diagnostics tree in addition to the five Windows logs, there are multiple role-related Application and Services logs, and an even larger number of service logs in the Microsoft node.

TROUBLESHOOTING WITH THE EVENT VIEWER

The Event Viewer got a substantial upgrade in Windows Server 2008's Server Manager. You will probably notice the Overview and Summary section, which presents the collected events in your logs as an aggregation. In previous versions the only way to find error events was to open the individual logs. This overview categorizes events into types and lets you drill down on critical events, errors, warnings, and so on. If you expand one of the sections (as shown in Figure 7.19), you will find that the log further categorizes events into those that took place in the Last Hour, 24 Hours, 7 Days, and stored in the logs overall in number and by event type. Second-level drill-down from the overview leads to event types, shown in Figure 7.19. In that figure, the two sections Critical and Audit Failure are expanded and the Critical Event stored in the Application log is highlighted. Just double-click on the area of interest, or click the Plus icon to open the Event Type in the detail pane.

FIGURE 7.19
Second-level drill-down from the Overview and Summary section identifies by category each stored event type in your logs.

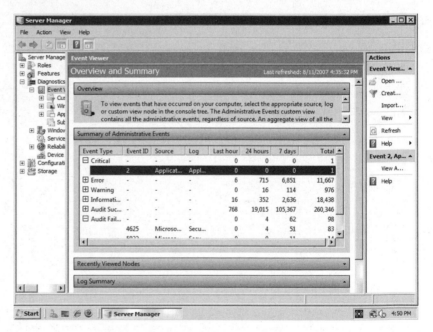

The third-level drill-down is to the actual event itself, as shown in Figure 7.20. The highlighted critical event on this system was due to an incompatibility of Windows Media 11 with Windows Server 2008 in the Beta 3 build. In this instance, launching Windows Media Player finished the installation and removed the error. Unfortunately, while it is much easier to find the problems in your system and isolate their cause, the remedies aren't always clearly offered. However, this is still much better than previous versions of the Event log, and you'll nearly always find a solution.

FIGURE 7.20
While the Event View-
er still exists, the ap-
pearance of that
utility within the
Server Manager is
most likely the first
place you will now
check to see what's
gone wrong (and
what's gone right).

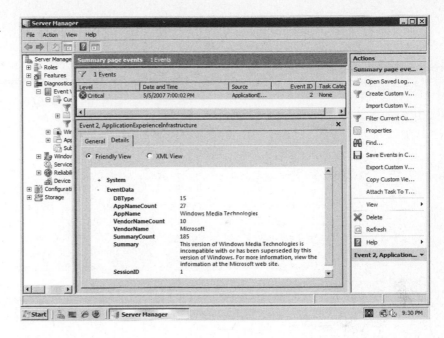

EVENT SUBSCRIPTIONS

Forwarded Events is a little more involved than the other logs and requires some thought and configuration, so let's consider its purpose in a little more detail. Forwarded Events creates an aggre-
gated log of events of the type(s) you filtered on from systems that are subscribed to this log. The
log can exist on the local server called the "collector computer," or since you can view remote
nodes, you can view this log stored at other locations. If you have a process such as distributed replication that involves two or more systems, the Event log is only useful in analyzing the problems
when the event data from all systems related to replication can be stored in a single location. The
subscribing systems are referred to as "forwarder computers." Since events are DateTime stamped,
the collected log events offer you a powerful tool in sequencing issues and relating them to the
different computers involved.

The subscription should be defined first at the subscriber computer in a Forwarded Events subscription. Because data in a subscription can be defined in either direction, you specify the source
systems (forwarder computer(s)) there.

To set up a subscription to the Forwarded Events log:

1. Right-click on the Subscriptions node name and select Create Subscription from the context menu.

   The same command appears on the Action menu when Subscriptions is highlighted. The
   Subscription Properties dialog box appears, as shown in Figure 7.21.

2. Enter a name in the Subscription Name text box and a description in the Description text box
   (optional).

3. Select Forwarded Events (if required) from the Destination Log drop-down menu.

   You may wish to examine the Destination Log menu, as subscriptions give you many
   choices of log file to select from.

FIGURE 7.21
Subscription Properties allow you to collect events of a specific type and from specific sources and direct those events to be recorded in the Destination log of your choice. You can use subscriptions to analyze distributed network system behavior.

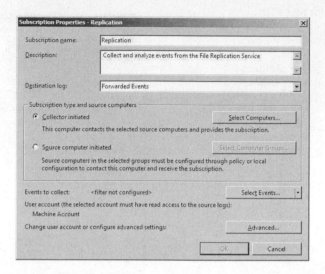

4. Click the Add button to add a system(s) to the subscription service. In the Select Computer dialog box that appears, specify the system and click OK to return to the Subscription Properties dialog box.

   Note that subscriptions can be based on Active Directory machine or user accounts, and can be organized into or use groups for convenience. In most instances you will base your selection on computer or machine accounts.

5. Click the Select Events button and select the Edit command to open the Query Filter dialog box, shown in Figure 7.22.

6. The Advanced button in the Subscription Properties dialog box (Figure 7.21) opens up a dialog box that lets you set the subscription speed. Make your selection from Normal Mode, Minimize Bandwidth, or Minimize Latency, and then click OK.

   Normal Mode sets the source to send five events every 15 minutes. Minimize Bandwidth changes the subscription to respond to requests from the destination, and applies both a batch timeout and a fetch interval of six hours. The Minimize Latency mode will gather events using requests from the destination system, but with a timeout of only 30 seconds.

7. Make your selections for when an event is logged, the Event Level setting, and so forth; then click OK. The subscription appears in the Subscription panel.

NOTE The Remote Server Administration Tools (RSAT) provides the services required to remotely manage roles, services, and features on Windows Server 2008 or Windows Server 2003 servers. RSAT is a feature that you add using the Add Features wizard. It is anticipated that more and more MMC tools will be made RSAT compatible over time, but that only a few tools will have this compatibility at the time of Windows Server 2008's first release.

FIGURE 7.22
Log files are database files, and the Event Viewer is an MMC component that is the front-end to a database. To create a filter for events that are part of a subscription, click the Select Events button to open this dialog box.

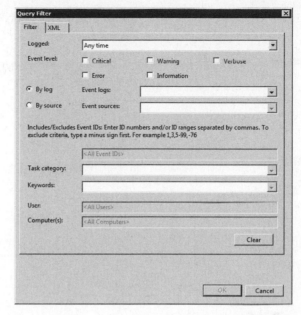

When you add a system to the subscription, you may be asked to start the Windows Event Collector Service and set that service to Automatic (which means it starts automatically after a delay). The Collector Service is a listener service that records the events from remote systems. For Forwarded Events to work properly, both the collector computer and the forwarder computer must be running the Windows Remote Management service (WinRM). You can issue the command WINRM QUICKCONFIG at the command prompt to start and configure WinRM. Configuration starts WinRM and tunnels through the Windows Firewall to create the WinRM listener at HTTP://<CollectorIP>, which then accepts the input from forwarded systems.

CUSTOM VIEWS

If you use the Event Viewer to examine your system, chances are that you will create a view in the Event Viewer that you will want to return to from time to time. Custom views are stored recipes that re-create a view at a later time. As with subscriptions, a custom view relies on the creation of a query. To create a custom view:

1. Right-click on the Custom View node (nodes are sometimes referred to as containers) and select the Create Custom View command from the context menu.

   Or with Custom View highlighted, you can select the Custom View command from the Action menu.

2. In the Create Custom View dialog box, shown in Figure 7.23, set these options: Logged, Event Level, By Log (and select from the Event Logs drop-down) or By Source (and select from the Event Sources drop-down), Task Category, Keywords, User, and Computer(s).

The Logged drop down box lets you filter the Event log for a time period of your choosing, such as Anytime, Last Hour, Last 24 Hours, and a custom time period that you set. The Event level is the label that the Event log gives to particular events, and most often you will be interested in the Critical Events. To a lesser extent you may want to look at Warnings and Errors. The By log filter allows you to select which event log you want to see, while Event Sources allows you to select different Windows modules (.NET Runtime, ADSI, Browser, and so forth).

The bottom text and drop down list boxes allow you to filter by a specific error type. You can set a filter for a specific Error ID, Task category, or Keyword.

FIGURE 7.23

The Create Custom View dialog box is another filter query selector, similar to what you saw in the Subscriptions selection.

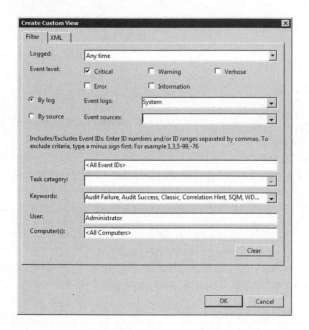

3. Click OK to create the custom view, which is then saved to a file and displayed in the Event Viewer.

There are so many potential applications for custom views that there isn't space here to fully describe this helpful feature. You could create a view that traps the events related to a specific user to see if security was violated, or filter on a service or event type to see if there are errors related to hardware or software.

There is one new interface feature that appears in this revised tool that hasn't been part of the Windows interface before: if you click on Event Log, you will see a multiselect list that replaces the grouped checkboxes or a nested dialog box, as shown in Figure 7.24. You'll probably see this feature show up in many more Microsoft applications, as it solves a complex selection process with an elegant solution.

Task Scheduler

Unix has its CRON; Microsoft has its Task Scheduler. The Task Scheduler allows you to runs different commands and executables based on specific dates and times, or to schedule tasks that run periodically. Figure 7.25 shows the Task Scheduler's overview page.

FIGURE 7.24
The new multiselect drop-down combo list box found in the Event Viewer

FIGURE 7.25
The Task Scheduler utility lets you schedule and control programs and scripts.

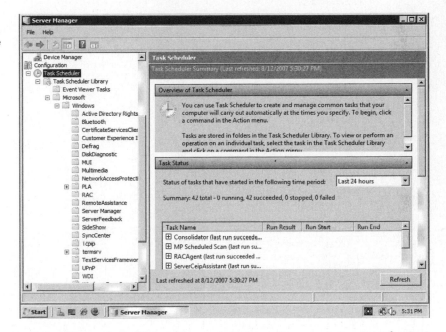

When you create a task, it is saved as a file within a task folder and you can view it in the Task Scheduler Library section of the Server Manager. You can also see whether a task has run by checking the Task Status section. An Active Task section shows you tasks that haven't yet run but are still scheduled. You can use the security features of Windows Server to limit access to tasks to appropriate users. Tasks can be hidden from view as well as secured.

Task execution can be tied to:

Triggers A trigger polls for the establishment of a condition and then executes the task. Among the settings are On a Schedule, At Logon, At Startup, On Idle, On an Event, At Task Creation/Modification, On Connection to User Session, On Disconnect from User Session, On Workstation

Lock, and On Workstation Unlock. You can also apply settings such as delays, repetitions, stop after a certain period, activate at, expires at, and enabled to tasks that a trigger executes in the Task Scheduler.

Actions Actions are work that is performed while a task is running. You can think of them as subtasks, and each schedule can have up to 32 actions associated with it. Among the actions you can apply in a schedule are starting a program or script (with or without arguments or switches), sending an e-mail, or displaying a message. Table 7.2 shows a list of program actions that you can use in the Task Scheduler.

Conditions A condition is a state; a task runs when the condition is detected. You can specify idle conditions, power conditions, and network conditions.

TABLE 7.2:   Programs That You Can Run as an Action in a Task

NAME	PROGRAM OR SCRIPT	ARGUMENTS
Run a script	CSCRIPT.EXE Note: To run a script, you can specify the name of the script file with no arguments instead of specifying cscript.exe, and the default script host is used to run the script.	`<script file>`
Copy a file	ROBOCOPY	`<source file> <destination file>`
Start a service	NET	start `<service name>`
Stop a service	NET	stop `<service name>`
Shut down	SHUTDOWN	-s
Restart	SHUTDOWN	-r
Log off	SHUTDOWN	-l
Disk cleanup	CLEANMGR	/sagerun
Defragment a disk	DEFRAG	`<drive letter>`
Check a disk	CHKDSK	`<drive letter>`
Map a drive	NET	`<drive letter> <network path>`
Connect to a dial-up network	RASDIAL	`<entry name>`
Disconnect from a dial-up network	RASDIAL	`<entry name> /disconnect`

TABLE 7.2:   Programs That You Can Run as an Action in a Task *(CONTINUED)*

NAME	PROGRAM OR SCRIPT	ARGUMENTS
Archive an event log	WEVTUTIL	al <log path> Note: This program is not available on operating systems prior to Windows Vista.
Display a web page	IEXPLORE	<URL> Note: This program should be started from the %ProgramFiles%\Internet Explorer directory.
Play something	WMPLAYER	<media file path> Note: This program should be started from the %ProgramFiles%\Windows Media Player directory.

Not all execution types are available on all client systems. Windows Vista will support all of the current execution specifications, but earlier clients such as Windows 2000 systems will be missing some of these settings in all of these categories.

WMI Control

WMI is a sophisticated and complete database of system functions and management data that can be accessed by network management applications such as System Management Server (SMS) or Microsoft Operations Manager (MOM), LANDesk, Altaris, ZenWorks, Unicenter, and Tivoli, among others. Scripts or applications in Windows Server 2008 and Vista can request WMI data using the Windows Remote Management service. WinRM is a Microsoft implementation of the WS-Management Protocol, which communicates between programs and WMI repositories using the Simple Object Access Protocol (SOAP). WMI is the Microsoft version of Web-based Enterprise Management WBEM, which is an industry-standard management protocol that accesses device data in the Common Information Model (CIM).

If all of these acronyms or fancy names make you dizzy, the ideas behind them are simple. Each compliant device stores data about the device, the device properties, current conditions, or any other information you want to store in a standard database file format whose contents are entirely customizable. The remaining standards tell programs how to request information from this database and how to write information back when required.

The Windows Management Instrumentation (WMI) Control tool lets you modify WMI settings on both your local system or on remote systems. In the Server Manager that ships with Windows Server 2008, the functions that you can actually control are limited. You can back up the WMI repository, change the default namespace (used when applied to scripts), and set the security access of users and groups to the WMI.

The following changes in WMI were made in Vista's release:

◆ User Account Control (UAC) was applied to WMI communications.

◆ Namespace security was improved and security auditing of WMI events was added.

◆ Security descriptors can now be retrieved and modified, as well as manipulated by scripts.

◆ The Event Tracing for Windows (ETW) module now logs and traces WMI events, taking the place of the older WMI log files.

No significant changes to WMI technology have been added to Windows Server 2008 since Vista. WMI is enabled for remote access. However, the addition of the security layer represented by the UAC complicates building scripts that can manipulate remote systems. UAC is enabled on Windows Server 2008 and Vista, so this requirement is more of an issue for older versions of the Windows operating system. A user on the remote machine who is also a member of the local Administrator group will be treated as a user and not as an administrator, since UAC filters by user and not by group. Therefore, it is still important to check how the remote system is accessed from a security standpoint to see if the correct credentials are presented.

Remote connections require that WMI RPC traffic be able to pass through firewalls and the appropriate port(s) need to be open. A user must have the right to make the remote call, a right referred to as Launch and Activate. To modify a user's Distributed Component Object Model (DCOM) rights, use the `DCOMCONFIG.EXE` command. An additional requirement is that the user must have a valid WMI namespace path as well as the Enable Remote and Enable Account rights for that namespace. Since these two rights are assigned to the local administrator, it may be necessary to add these rights in order to have a remote WMI script run. The WMI namespace security requirements must be met, and these rights can be viewed and updated using the `WMIMGMT.MSC` command. Finally, the WMI object must not only exist but must be viewable and, if necessary, editable. These requirements create a high bar for scripts to meet to succeed.

The remote access of WMI data is too complex to be convenient, and this is clearly an area in which better management tools are required. Undoubtedly, this will be further developed in future versions of Windows Server.

Eventually many network management functions will be migrated to a series of third-generation Microsoft enterprise frameworks that will comprise the Microsoft System Center. Microsoft MOM will be replaced by the next-generation System Center Operations Manager. SMS will become the System Center Configuration Manager, and several additional network management packages in different areas. The following components are available from Microsoft:

◆ Microsoft System Data Protection Manager `http://www.microsoft.com/systemcenter/dpm/default.mspx`.

◆ System Center Essentials 2007 (`http://www.microsoft.com/systemcenter/essentials/default.mspx`)

◆ System Center Virtual Machine Manager 2007 (http://technet.microsoft.com/en-us/scvmm/default.aspx).

◆ System Center Capacity Planner (2007) (http://www.microsoft.com/systemcenter/sccp/overview/default.mspx)

To keep your eye on this area of technology, go to the System Center home page at `http://www.microsoft.com/systemcenter`.

Summary

In this chapter you learned about some of the system management tools found in Windows Server 2008. Microsoft has considerably beefed up its offering in this area, adding a number of new command-line utilities, as well as a central server management framework, the Server Manager. The Server Manager consolidates MMC snap-ins that were a number of separate utilities in previous versions of the server operating system. Computer system identification, roles and features, Terminal Services and Web Server configuration, Event Viewer, Services, Device Manager, Task Scheduler, Server Backup, and Disk Management are all components in the Server Manager, along with a host of other tools.

The Server Manager also introduces many new tools. This chapter highlights some of these new tools, such as the Reliability and Performance indicator, monitoring tools, and Data Collector Sets. Reporting is stronger in this version of the management tools, and it has become easier through a set of consolidated overview screens to control and better manage your systems. The Server Manager is the best tool yet for determining system health, and will dramatically change and improve the management of Windows Servers. System management is one of the strongest areas of Microsoft Server technology, and the new Server Manager is proof of that statement. The Server Manager will reward the time spent on it with dramatically better administrative efficiencies.

In the next chapter you will be introduced to the Windows PowerShell, which is the next generation of the Windows command-line and scripting environment. PowerShell redefines your notion of the command-line, giving you access to the complete world of Windows programming objects. Think of PowerShell commands as one-line programs with the power of C# and you have some idea of the power that this command processor offers. It is one of the most significant new releases from Microsoft in this version of Windows.

Chapter 8

PowerShell

With the introduction of Vista and now Windows Server 2008, command-line administration has gained a powerful new tool: Windows PowerShell. PowerShell is a command-line shell coupled with a scripting language that administrators can use to manage and control systems across the network. PowerShell had been called the Microsoft Shell (MSH), and most recently the "Monad" Shell during development. PowerShell opens in a window showing a single command prompt, and so it appears to be no different than the command processor CMD.EXE that has shipped with Windows for many years now. However, PowerShell is anything but simple. Inside PowerShell Microsoft has created a powerful command-line environment with a standardized command language syntax that borrows from many command-line interfaces (CLI) in use today—distilled into a command set of about 60 verbs or actions.

PowerShell was built to be as backward compatible as possible. PowerShell doesn't require you to give up scripting or automation tools that you're already fluent in. You'll find PowerShell is compatible with C++ (C Sharp) code, scripts in JavaScript or VBScript—indeed, any language for which an interpreter has been written (and there are a few!). You can combine PowerShell verbs with the thousands of Windows, Office, .NET Framework, and Windows Management Instrumentation (WMI) objects, and more. These objects are the nouns that the PowerShell verbs act upon. With PowerShell commands, you can monitor and modify local or remote systems, their Registries, services, Active Directory, and more. Microsoft expects PowerShell to be the central tool used by administrators and power users going forward, so be forewarned.

With PowerShell you can perform most of the actions that experienced programmers program to accomplish, but as single-line code without event code. PowerShell commands execute code immediately. So if you know PowerShell and its capabilities well, you can perform any of the complex, multistep tasks that system management applications do, albeit one step at a time. Here are some of the many tasks that you can automate and control with PowerShell:

- Creating XML-based data or HTML files

- Working with system services, processes, and the Registry

- Using the Active Directory Services Interface (ADSI)

- Creating ActiveX Data Objects (ADOs), Component Object Model (COM) objects, and .NET Framework objects

- Creating WMI objects

- Configuring and managing Terminal Server

- Configuring and managing Internet Information Services (IIS) 7.0

◆ Managing local and remote systems

◆ Writing scripts in various scripting languages, or deploying scripts with the Windows Scripting Host

PowerShell is literally a Swiss Army Knife for system management.

Getting Familiar with PowerShell

Command-line administration and scripting is one area in which Windows has made slow but steady progress over the years. The advantage of the command-line interface (CLI) is that you get much faster access to system data since you don't need to populate a complete GUI with data. Windows Server has clearly lagged behind Unix and other network operating systems when it comes to CLI management. The earliest versions of Windows merely ported the 16-bit DOS command utilities, while later versions of CMD.EXE ran inside a 32-bit environment as a 16-bit emulator. All the while Microsoft continued to add additional commands that bolstered the new features that were being introduced but never really solved the problem of making CMD.EXE a central management tool.

It became clear after Windows NT Server's release that, in order for Microsoft's network operating systems to be relevant in the Internet age, the company needed to support the various higher-level scripting languages, such as JavaScript, Perl, VBScript, and Python, that execute server-side logic. Without broad script support, Windows servers were at a disadvantage compared to Linux (which had the added benefit of lower acquisition costs) and to Unix (particularly Sun Solaris). Open source applications like the Apache web server dominated the early Internet.

Microsoft's answer to the challenge of script language support was twofold. The Windows Scripting Host (WSH), which arrived with Windows 2000, added a command-line interpreter that could run scripts in multiple languages from a command prompt with output to either the command prompt or to a window. WSH was a major step in command-line administration for Windows, but WSH didn't quite close the gap other operating systems had with scripting languages. The second initiative developed the Microsoft Management Console (MMC) and snap-ins. Many more commands and settings could be brought under administrative control in the MMC.

Over time Windows has incrementally added CLI commands and add-on tools in resource kits and other distributions. For the knowledgeable Windows administrator, it has been estimated that command-line tools now available expose perhaps 98 percent of the directly addressable Windows APIs at the CLI. That means that if administrators are sophisticated enough, they can run complex programs and operations from the CLI, albeit one line of code at a time. The trick, of course, is that you must know where to look for the commands, and that before PowerShell you have to apply the commands from within multiple tools to use them. PowerShell exposes Windows and Office objects (through their API) to programmatic control.

Microsoft exposes Windows internals through an extensive structured object model accessed by published APIs. If you understand the Windows and Office object models, very powerful methods come under your programmatic command. That is why Microsoft has to be extra careful about security whenever it introduces any new version of Windows or Office—that along with the fact that Windows represents a richly populated target for evildoers. Scripts become a very powerful and potentially dangerous tool in the hands of relatively unsophisticated people wishing to do harm. The object model also makes Windows a programming platform of choice for many. From a system administration standpoint, programmatic system control lets you tap into this power and will make you much more effective. For the power user, PowerShell provides access to skills that allow for greater system customization. Strong scripting skills are worth their weight in gold; they are in great demand.

Distributed Services

Windows Server 2008 doesn't exist in a vacuum; it runs network services and applications used by other operating systems and clients. Windows is often the administration platform for a network—a central management console, but not always. Just as often, a Windows server is a service provider: an application server, a file or web server, an addressing (DNS or DHCP) service, a domain service such as LDAP or Active Directory, or something else. To order for these services to be useful, these services must be able to be programmatically administered, and therefore industry standards must be embraced. Windows interoperability often follows what has come to be called the "embrace and extend" model. The company embraces an emerging standard, and then often adds (extends) features that have the effect of making standards somewhat proprietary.

The WMI service is an example of an interoperability standard that you learned about in Chapter 6. WMI is based on the industry-standard Common Information Model (CIM). WMI lets you manage information obtained from systems and devices using standard data formats and communication protocols, and provides a control mechanism for these devices that will work on other systems. WMI is an example of Microsoft's version of a shared standard, and because CIM was meant to be extended by vendors, WMI is truly standards based. With WMI you can integrate Windows systems into a heterogeneous network fully of CIM-compliant devices, and get a detailed view of the working and interactions of all those devices. PowerShell exposes WMI to programmatic control.

For a proprietary Microsoft standard, you need look no further than the .NET Framework. This framework installs a set of addressable objects supporting distributed network and internetworking services, so-called "web services." A more technical description of Microsoft .NET would define it as a set of software modules that have discoverable methods and a compact function. These objects are accessible over the Internet using standard communications protocols such as XML and SOAP. Microsoft's .NET is now Windows system software, whereas it was an optional installation for older versions of Windows. PowerShell exposes .NET Framework objects to programmatic control.

Microsoft .NET was Microsoft's answer to Java Enterprise Edition—a set of program modules that can serve common language–independent functions. Microsoft .NET objects are executed in a runtime environment using the Common Language Runtime (CLR), which is just another name for the Microsoft .NET Framework. Just like Java, CLR appears to run an application inside a virtual machine, abstracting program execution from the details and constraints of the system that it runs on. When .NET applications and scripts run, they can be system independent (just as Java applets are), and you can run these programs on any version of Windows you choose. Open source implementations of Microsoft .NET exist for other platforms, but these programs are not as popular as Java.

With PowerShell, you can draw on the range of services that Microsoft provides both locally on the server as well as on remote systems. The power of PowerShell allows it to be the basis for the administration of the latest version of Exchange, and not only does command-line administration of Exchange rely on PowerShell commands, so too does the GUI used to manage this messaging platform. That is, commands in the Exchange GUI are translated into PowerShell commands and can be used to manage Exchange servers across the enterprise.

At the moment you can work with PowerShell using the Task Manager, the Performance Monitor, Task Scheduler, and Reliability Core in both Windows Server 2008 and Vista, as well as with the Server Core role for Windows Server 2008. You should expect to see PowerShell form the basis for many of the new Microsoft enterprise server application management tools going forward. MMC commands will probably form the basis of PowerShell scripts that you can save as templates, modify, and combine into more sophisticated scripts as MMC snap-ins are migrated to the PowerShell command language.

The list of Microsoft projects that use PowerShell at the time of this writing include (in addition to Windows Server 2008 and Exchange):

◆ System Center Operations Manager 2007 (formerly, MOM)

◆ System Center Virtual Machine Manager 2007 (VMM)

◆ Windows Compute Cluster Tool Pack

◆ System Center Data Protection Manager 2007 (DPM)

◆ Microsoft Transporter Suite for Lotus Domino

Installation

PowerShell did not ship with the first released versions of Vista, but started shipping with Windows Server 2008 in beta 3 of that product. All future distributions of Windows should include PowerShell as a Windows component. PowerShell also is available for download for the following operating systems:

◆ Windows XP SP2

◆ Windows Server 2003 SP1

◆ Windows Server 2003 R2

To find download instructions for the different versions of PowerShell, go to the "How to Get Windows PowerShell 1.0" web page, which you can find here:

`http://www.microsoft.com/technet/scriptcenter/topics/msh/download.mspx`

After PowerShell is released on all platforms you can go to the Microsoft Download Center at `http://www.microsoft.com/downloads/` and download from there. PowerShell will run on x86, x64, and IA64 processor architectures.

REQUIREMENTS

To use PowerShell, you must first install it on your system. PowerShell is a freely downloadable Windows component, and can be used as part of your current system license. PowerShell has the following requirements:

Operating System   Windows Servers 2008 and 2003 SP1 and R2, Windows Vista, and Windows XP SP2 or later

Processors Supported   Intel X86, X64, and IA64

Microsoft .NET Framework 2.0 or Greater   The .NET Framework home page is found on Microsoft's website at `http://msdn2.microsoft.com/en-us/netframework/default.aspx`. You can download the .NET Framework from `http://msdn2.microsoft.com/en-us/netframework/aa569263.aspx`.

Additionally, you may want to install the Windows Scripting Host as it provides backward compatibility to a large library of previously developed scripts that you can use in PowerShell.

NOTE   On 32-bit versions of Windows, Windows PowerShell is installed, by default, in the %SystemRoot%\System32\WindowsPowerShell\v1.0 directory. On 64-bit versions of Windows, a 32-bit version of Windows PowerShell is installed in the %SystemRoot%\SystemWow64 \WindowsPowerShell\v1.0 directory and a 64-bit version of Windows PowerShell is installed in the %SystemRoot%\System32\WindowsPowerShell\v1.0 directory.

GETTING STARTED

Once you have installed PowerShell and have satisfied the requirements for the installation of its supporting components such as the .NET Framework, you can start PowerShell from the Windows command prompt, or directly from its menu command or program icon.

To start PowerShell from the command prompt:

1. Click Start ➢ Run and enter **CMD** in the Run dialog box, or press Windows+R.

2. Press Enter to open a command prompt.

3. Change directories to the one that contains the PowerShell program, enter **%SystemRoot%\System32\WindowsPowerShell\v1.0**, and press Enter.

4. Enter **PowerShell.exe -NoProfile** to start PowerShell without a profile file that is used to modify the program.

Alternatively, you can start PowerShell from the Start menu command: Start ➢ All Programs ➢ Windows PowerShell 1.0 ➢ Windows PowerShell. In either case, PowerShell's prompt appears as shown in Figure 8.1.

To see PowerShell's startup options, enter **PowerShell.exe -Help** in the Run dialog box.

NOTE   PowerShell commands are not case sensitive. They are only shown here in this manner to make the commands easier to read.

FIGURE 8.1

The Zen of PowerShell

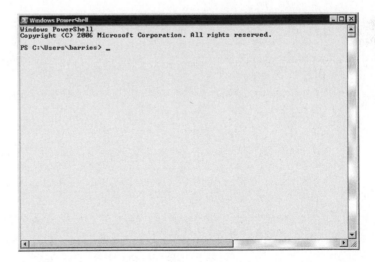

Among the startup options are Command, Help, InputFormat, NoExit, NoLogo, Noninteractive, NoProfile, OutputFormat, and PSConsoleFile.

When PowerShell runs, it loads the console and snap-ins (collections of cmdlets and providers); then profile files are processed. You can think of a *profile* as a script that customizes the PowerShell environment, adding aliases, changing the console configuration, and adding special functions. Profiles can apply to an administrator, all users, a single user, or a group of users.

If this is the first time you are using PowerShell, you may not be able to run scripts. PowerShell has a feature called the execution policy that limits users from running scripts without certain safeguards. This feature is described later in this chapter in the section "Execution Policies." If you want to get started right away, you can learn more about the execution policy by entering the following command at the PowerShell prompt:

```
get-help about_signing | more
```

Help will tell you how to configure the Set-ExecutionPolicy RemoteSigned cmdlet. If you want to enable scripts, enter the following:

```
set-executionpolicy -ExecutionPolicy "RemoteSigned"
```

To end your PowerShell session, type **EXIT** (typing **QUIT** doesn't work) at the command prompt and then press the Enter key.

SNAP-INS

PowerShell uses the concept of a snap-in, which is a collection of cmdlets or providers that are related in functionality. After you install PowerShell, you will find that there are several snap-ins already installed for you. Each snap-in runs in its own namespace. For example, the Core snap-in's namespace is Microsoft.PowerShell.Core. Core cmdlets alter the way the PowerShell engine operates. Other snap-ins are Host, Management, Security, and Utility. To see which snap-ins are part of your installation, enter the command **GET-PSSNAPIN**. Figure 8.2 shows you the result.

FIGURE 8.2
The extensibility of PowerShell is indicated by the use of snap-ins.

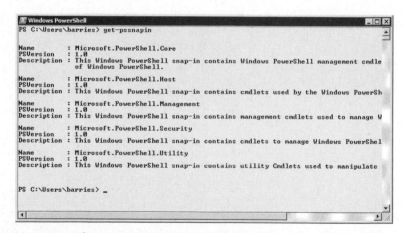

Snap-ins portend a future time when snap-ins for PowerShell are what you install into the MMC, or at least are the underlying engine for MMC snap-ins. If you want to see which cmdlets are part of any snap-in, use the following command:

```
GET-COMMAND -COMMANDTYPE CMDLET | WHERE-OBJECT {$_.PSSNAPIN -MATCH "<snapin_name>"}
```

To see which providers are included, use this command:

```
GET-PSPROVIDER | FORMAT-TABLE NAME, PSSNAPIN
```

Almost all providers are part of the PowerShell Core; the Certificate provider is contained within the Security snap-in. Providers are important because they can be added by third-party providers, they will be enhanced by Microsoft, and you can create your own snap-ins to support the different sets of management functions that you perform.

GETTING HELP

One great feature of Unix is its MAN (or manual) pages. When you work in Unix, the MAN command brings up extensive online help. MAN is highly configurable, so you can see a simple explanation of the command, or with a modifier such as VERBOSE, see a detailed description of a command that in some instances can run many pages. Man pages are online, and they are indexed by the major search engines. You only need enter the command name such as MAN PS to be taken to one or another version of the Unix man pages that have been posted. The man descriptions are somewhat limited in their effectiveness because one form of Unix, such as Sun's Solaris, has different options and switches than, say, Red Hat Linux, but usually you can figure out what you want from this exercise. Underlying PowerShell is a help system of similar depth and complexity to the Unix man pages.

The intent of PowerShell's developers was to create a help system that was online, discoverable, self-documented, and complete. PowerShell commands are simple action words—but as with all CLI languages, PowerShell commands can be modified by a variety of modifiers or switches that can greatly change the output or action's consequence. You can use the *alias* MAN as a substitute for the GET-HELP cmdlet.

To start learning about what the PowerShell help system can do, enter **HELP** by itself and all of the things you can get help for will be listed, including aliases, cmdlets, providers, and HelpFiles. To see how help works, enter **GET-HELP**. As Figure 8.3 indicates, chances are that your display is larger than your window. Pipe the MORE modifier and you can page through output one page at a time using the spacebar, or by pressing Enter one line at a time. The result of the GET-COMMAND | MORE command is the output shown in Figure 8.3.

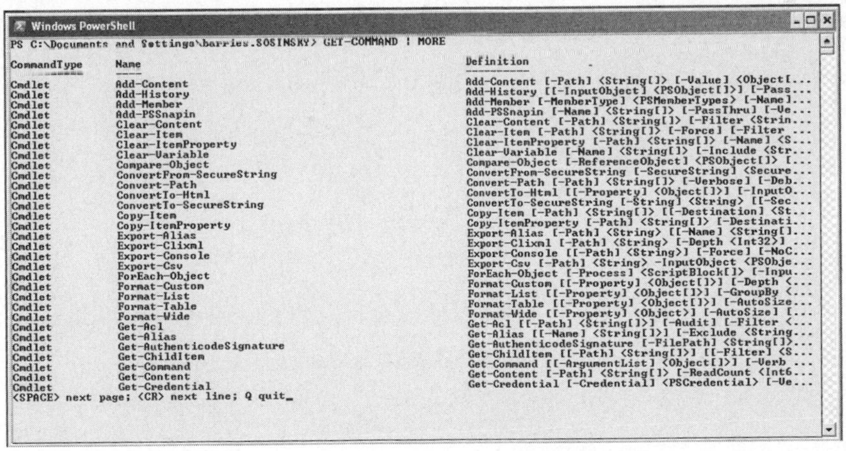

FIGURE 8.3
Use the GET-COMMAND at the ps command prompt to see what commands are available to you.

You also may want to learn about PowerShell's built-in commands (cmdlets) by entering the command GET-COMMAND | MORE, which lists all of the 129 (and counting) cmdlets. There are different levels of help, so that adding the property -DETAILED or -FULL displays more information. The property -EXAMPLES displays an examples section output. VERBOSE displays the entire contents of help for a command, modifier, or property. You can enter CLS (CLEAR SCREEN), which is an alias for PowerShell's CLEAR-HOST cmdlet and only the prompt will show.

For example, let's consider our old friend PROCESS, which in Unix is the PS command. Power-Shell's equivalent is the GET-PROCESS cmdlet. So if you enter GET-PROCESS by itself, the command executes and you see a list of your running processes. To get help for GET-PROCESS, you would enter GET-HELP GET-PROCESS, or more simply GET-HELP PS, since PS is an alias or substitute for the GET-PROCESS command. You can define your own aliases as described in this chapter. Let's say you remember the PS command but don't know PowerShell's equivalent. You can enter MAN PS as you would in Unix and PowerShell will return the help page for the GET-PROCESS command.

If you just used the GET-COMMAND, the list will scroll off the screen before you can get a good look at it. You may recognize the | symbol as a "pipe," or redirection, command. To discover more about any command, you use the GET-HELP <*command*>; and GET-HELP itself can be modified to be brief or VERBOSE, and so you certainly want to get help for HELP with the command GET-HELP HELP. That's about as friendly as a CLI can be, and it's probably enough to get you started.

Cmdlets

Windows PowerShell is both a Windows shell and command interpreter environment with a built-in scripting language. The PowerShell runtime engine contains its own command parser as well as automation for binding command parameters. PowerShell 1.0 initially shipped with 129 built-in command utilities called cmdlets (pronounced "command-lets") that can operate on objects, some of which can be used to format and display command results with the PowerShell CLI. Since Power-Shell is extensible, you should expect to see more cmdlets added by Microsoft to the base utility in future releases. Indeed, since you can add your own cmdlets to the environment, a robust library of PowerShell scripts should be available over time.

Cmdlets can:

- Perform system administration tasks
- Start, stop, and modify system services
- Mount file systems and work with the contents
- Identify, start, stop, and modify processes
- Read and write to event logs
- Create formatted reports for viewing
- Query and examine certificates stores
- Mount the Registry as if it was a file system and modify Registry keys
- Access, display, modify, and control WMI providers
- Manage Active Directory through the ADSI
- Access, control, and modify standard members of the COM objects.
- Command .NET objects to perform actions, passing them the appropriate data for them to act on

 ◆ Access, control, and modify ActiveX Data Objects

 ◆ Read and write to XML and HTML data files

So you can see that with PowerShell you can access nearly all the objects and technologies that you need to control Windows systems. The technology extends to any addressable object on a network, and isn't limited to a local system.

NOTE You'll find the Windows PowerShell home page in the Technology Centers section at `http://www.microsoft.com/windowsserver2003/technologies/management/PowerShell/default.mspx`.

Syntax

Windows PowerShell opens in a command prompt window, and thus it looks superficially identical to `CMD` or other text-based command-line interfaces. This similarity is deceiving because PowerShell is not a text processor like `CMD.EXE`. PowerShell doesn't call executable programs such as `FDISK`, `FORMAT`, or `XCOPY`. PowerShell parses commands that operate on objects, and with the `OUT` command you control where the results get displayed. The `FORMAT` command in PowerShell lets you modify the format of the output, and bears no relationship to MS-DOS's `FORMAT` command, which is a disk utility. If you don't specify parameters for the output or the format, then the result of any PowerShell command is displayed as plain text in the PowerShell window of your display.

Cmdlets are identified by "verb-noun" combinations, A PowerShell script's verb-noun command syntax attempts to unify what has been up to now a Babel of scripting commands. Each scripting language might retrieve data with a command such as `LOAD`, `OPEN`, `FETCH`—PowerShell uses only the verb `GET`. Similarly, the command that stores data might be `SAVE`, `PUT`, or `STORE`—PowerShell uses only the verb `SET` and combines these commands with standard naming conventions, common parameters and options such as `SORT`, `FILTER`, `GROUP`, and `FORMAT` that can alter the way objects are manipulated and data is returned. All of these PowerShell commands are cmdlets that are meant to be used with other cmdlets.

The point of this quest for syntactical precision is to reduce the overall number of commands that you need to remember in PowerShell to the absolute minimum. At this point, although PowerShell ships with 129 cmdlets, a working knowledge of about 60 of these verbs will make you a very capable scripter. Your goal in learning PowerShell is to remember the verb or action, and then know where to go to get the name of the object or "noun" that can be displayed or manipulated. Commands are relatively simple words that you use in everyday speech—`GET`, `FORMAT`, `SORT`, `SET`—that are easy to remember.

Pipelines are very powerful commands. A pipeline, or pipe, takes the output of the command on the left and passes it as input to the command on the right. You can have multiple pipes, and in effect each pipe adds a step in a multistep program. Pipes can redirect output to:

 ◆ A display

 ◆ A file

 ◆ Another program

 ◆ A printer or another device

and many other destinations as well.

PowerShell also makes extensive use of wildcard symbols. The question mark (?) symbol can be replaced by any single character, while the asterisk symbol (*) can be replaced by any possible set of symbols. You can get help on a topic in PowerShell by using the ABOUT_ command. To see a description of wildcards, enter the following:

    GET-HELP ABOUT_WILDCARD

or to see all conceptual help topics, enter this:

    GET-HELP ABOUT_*

When you work in PowerShell, you are working with instances of .NET objects. From the command line you can access not only command-line tools, but also COM objects and the .NET Framework Class Library (FCL). A .NET object describes data and the methods that you can use to manipulate that data. An object is therefore a data entity that has both properties and methods associated with it. You can equate properties to characteristics, and methods to actions. Thus in the object model the object BALL can have associated with it the property of Color which can be set to Red, and the method Throw, which is an action that takes the parameters of speed, direction, spin, and the like. A service is another example of an object.

Each cmdlet is an object that is discoverable by piping the name to the GET-MEMBER cmdlet. For example, GET-LOCATION | GET-MEMBER will return the output shown in Figure 8.4. Notice that each object returns the properties of its object class. If you enter the TypeName into MSDN, you will find further information about this object. Objects, as you have already seen, can pipe their output to other objects as a command input.

FIGURE 8.4

You can expose the properties of an object by piping the command to the GET-MEMBER cmdlet.

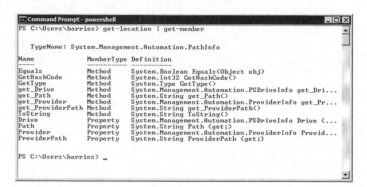

The FORMAT-LIST, FORMAT-TABLE, FORMAT-CUSTOM, and FORMAT-WIDE cmdlets offer powerful methods for creating displays and reports, and the topics bear further study in the topics list.

Since PowerShell is a command environment, commands and scripts are performed immediately. PowerShell does not provide event-oriented commands; instead, commands evaluate states or conditions prior to performing immediate actions. That doesn't mean that PowerShell ignores errors. It is good practice to build error-checking logic into scripts, and PowerShell supports this by allowing you to check for conditions before executing commands.

Let's say that you are an administrator working on an important project and from PowerShell you need to do some housecleaning and delete (using the REMOVE-ITEM cmdlet) a number of directories. It's late at night, and you're tired—you've made a mistake and entered a command that will delete the entire contents of your company's main database. Windows will ask you if you are sure that you want to delete the directory, and since you are a pro you just hit the Enter key. Poof, it's gone. PowerShell has a fail-safe mechanism, the -WHATIF option. If you get into the habit of adding -WHATIF to the end of your commands, not only will you get a warning, but PowerShell will show you the actions it will take if you confirm the action. You are much more likely to catch a mistake if you use this option.

Command-Line Services

Two of PowerShell's often-used capabilities are the enumeration of services and service management. You can see what services are running on a system by using the GET-SERVICE command by itself. Figure 8.5 shows the output of this command.

FIGURE 8.5

The GET-SERVICE command lists all services, tells you their status, and explains what the service's name means.

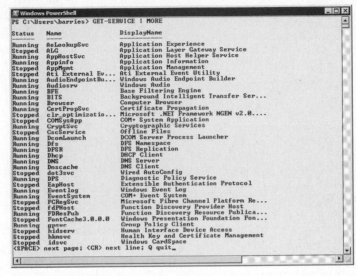

Services can be turned on and off using the following commands:

◆ RESTART-

◆ START-

◆ SUSPEND-

◆ STOP-

so that START-SERVICE <servicename> will start a service, and STOP-SERVICE <servicename> will stop that service. This capability is useful to examine a remote system using the following syntax:

```
GET-SERVICE -COMPUTERNAME <SYSTEMNAME>
```

Similarly you can use GET-PROCESS to display all running processes on your local system, or filter the list by using the -NAME <string>. As you experiment with the GET-PROCESS command, you will find that you can expose many more parameters about processes than are found in the Task Manager. PowerShell gives you much finer control over services and processes, as well as access to remote systems for which you have access privileges. Figure 8.6 shows the output of the GET-PROCESS cmdlet on a Windows Server 2008 domain server.

You can navigate file systems in PowerShell in much the same manner that you navigate file systems in MS-DOS. Aliases such as CD (for SET-LOCATION), DIR, and LS (GET-CHILDITEM), and directly entering a path all work in PowerShell. You can use the period symbol for the current directory, the asterisk for the contents of a directory, and access environmental variables such as $HOME and $PSHOME for the home and PowerShell installation directories, respectively. The cmdlets GET-ITEM, NEW-ITEM, REMOVE-ITEM, SET-ITEM, MOVE-ITEM, and COPY-ITEM serve the functions of change location, create, delete, move, and copy. You can use the aliases in Table 8.2 for these functions.

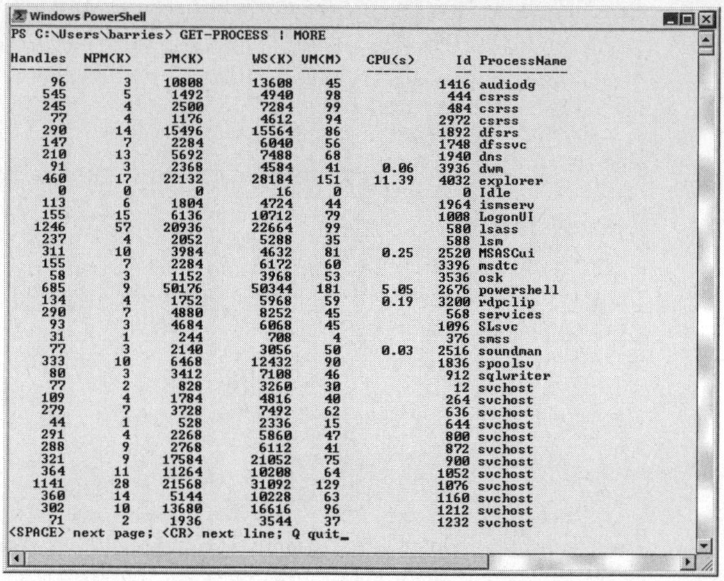

FIGURE 8.6

The GET-PROCESS | MORE command lists all processes running on a system, revealing much more information than the Task Manager does.

```
Windows PowerShell
PS C:\Users\barries> GET-PROCESS | MORE

Handles  NPM(K)    PM(K)     WS(K) UM(M)    CPU(s)     Id ProcessName
     96       3    10808     13608    45               1416 audiodg
    545       5     1492      4940    98                444 csrss
    245       4     2500      7284    99                484 csrss
     77       4     1176      4612    94               2972 csrss
    290      14    15496     15564    86               1892 dfsrs
    147       7     2284      6040    56               1748 dfssvc
    210      13     5692      7488    68               1940 dns
     91       3     2368      4584    41      0.06     3936 dwm
    460      17    22132     28184   151     11.39     4032 explorer
      0       0        0        16     0                  0 Idle
    113       6     1804      4724    44               1964 ismserv
    155      15     6136     10712    79               1008 LogonUI
   1246      57    20936     22664    99                580 lsass
    237       4     2052      5288    35                588 lsm
    311      10     3984      4632    81      0.25     2520 MSASCui
    155       7     2284      6172    60               3396 msdtc
     58       3     1152      3968    53               3536 osk
    685       9    50176     50344   181      5.05     2676 powershell
    134       4     1752      5968    59      0.19     3200 rdpclip
    290       7     4880      8252    45                568 services
     93       3     4684      6068    45               1096 SLsvc
     31       1      244       708     4                376 smss
     77       3     2140      3056    50      0.03     2516 soundman
    333      10     6468     12432    90               1836 spoolsv
     80       3     3412      7108    46                912 sqlwriter
     77       2      828      3260    30                 12 svchost
    109       4     1784      4816    40                264 svchost
    279       7     3728      7492    62                636 svchost
     44       1      528      2336    15                644 svchost
    291       4     2268      5860    47                800 svchost
    288       9     2768      6112    41                872 svchost
    321       9    17584     21052    75                900 svchost
    364      11    11264     10208    64               1052 svchost
   1141      28    21568     31092   129               1076 svchost
    360      14     5144     10228    63               1160 svchost
    302      10    13680     16616    96               1212 svchost
     71       2     1936      3544    37               1232 svchost
<SPACE> next page; <CR> next line; Q quit_
```

PowerShell creates an abstraction called a PowerShell drive that provides access to a data store. You are doubtless familiar with file systems that are mapped to drive letters in all programming and scripting languages. PowerShell extends this concept to allow you to map the Registry as drives, as well as the certificate store. The Registry maps to the HKCU: and HKLM: drives, which are the Hive Key Current User and Hive Key Local Machine, respectively. The certificate store mounts as the CERT: drive. In this regard, PowerShell is unique. You can access the Registry in either CMD.EXE or a program such as Windows Explorer, and this gives an administrator powerful access to system settings.

You can list your current drives with the GET-PSDRIVE cmdlet. A typical display for the GET-PSDRIVE command would return the following:

```
Name            Provider      Root
----            --------      ----
A  FileSystem   A:\
Alias           Alias
C  FileSystem   C:\
Cert            Certificate   \
D  FileSystem   D:\
E  FileSystem   E:\
Env             Environment
F  FileSystem   F:\
Function        Function
G  FileSystem   G:\
H  FileSystem   H:\
HKCU            Registry      HKEY_CURRENT_USER
HKLM            Registry      HKEY_LOCAL_MACHINE
I  FileSystem   I:\
Variable        Variable
Z  FileSystem   Z:\
```

This ability to access the Windows Registry is a very powerful feature. If you want to isolate the Registry hives only, then use the PSPROVIDER parameter as follows:

```
GET-PSDRIVE -PSPROVIDER REGISTRY
```

PSPROVIDER offers the ability to create new PowerShell drives, mapping the drives to the appropriate location and naming them.

Accessing WMI Providers

WMI is a powerful tool for system management. Many programs use these service providers to obtain information about devices that are published by the service, as well as providing a control mechanism for these devices. WMI provides information and services that .NET currently does not, so accessing WMI PowerShell greatly extends what the command environment is capable of. WMI is object oriented, and organizes objects into classes that have properties and methods.

To see a complete list of all WMI items, you can enter the following command:

```
GET-WMIOBJECT -LIST
```

PowerShell will return 200–300 WMI providers. If you want to get information about a specific service, you would enter it by name. The command GET-WMIOBJECT WIN32_PROCESS returns very detailed output. You may be surprised by the depth of information that WMI provides. PowerShell maintains a help topic on WMIOBJECT that you can access by entering GET-HELP WMIOBJECT. Here are a few examples to give you a sense of the services that you can access from WMI with PowerShell:

```
GET-WMIOBJECT WIN32_SERVICE -COMPUTERNAME <IP ADDRESS>
```

will return the services running on the system whose IP address you specify.

```
GET-WMIOBJECT WIN32_BIOS | FORMAT-LIST *
```

will display the BIOS information as a formatted list. Adding the -COMPUTERNAME parameter lets you get this information from a remote system.

Command Guide

Table 8.1 lists the cmdlets that were in PowerShell version 1.0 at the time it was released. If you peruse this list, you can see that PowerShell's cmdlet structure reduces the number of commands into command classes. If you learn the major categories—ADD, CLEAR, COPY, EXPORT, FORMAT, GET, NEW, OUT, REMOVE, SET, START, STOP, and WRITE— you have most of the command structure learned. Then all you will need to learn are the most common nouns, and then mix and match them appropriately. As you can see, this approach greatly lessens the amount of effort you need to put into learning PowerShell.

TABLE 8.1:   Built-in PowerShell 1.0 Cmdlets

NAME	DEFINITION
Add-Content	Add-Content [-Path] <String[]> [-Value] <Object[...
Add-History	Add-History [[-InputObject] <PSObject[]>] [-Pass...

TABLE 8.1: Built-in PowerShell 1.0 Cmdlets *(CONTINUED)*

NAME	DEFINITION
Add-Member	Add-Member [-MemberType] <PSMemberTypes> [-Name]...
Add-PSSnapin	Add-PSSnapin [-Name] <String[]> [-PassThru] [-Ve...
Clear-Content	Clear-Content [-Path] <String[]> [-Filter <Strin...
Clear-Item	Clear-Item [-Path] <String[]> [-Force] [-Filter ...
Clear-ItemProperty	Clear-ItemProperty [-Path] <String[]> [-Name] <S...
Clear-Variable	Clear-Variable [-Name] <String[]> [-Include <Str...
Compare-Object	Compare-Object [-ReferenceObject] <PSObject[]> [...
ConvertFrom-SecureString	ConvertFrom-SecureString [-SecureString] <Secure...
Convert-Path	Convert-Path [-Path] <String[]> [-Verbose] [-Deb...
ConvertTo-Html	ConvertTo-Html [[-Property] <Object[]>] [-InputO...
ConvertTo-SecureString	ConvertTo-SecureString [-String] <String> [[-Sec...
Copy-Item	Copy-Item [-Path] <String[]> [[-Destination] <St...
Copy-ItemProperty	Copy-ItemProperty [-Path] <String[]> [-Destinati...
Export-Alias	Export-Alias [-Path] <String> [[-Name] <String[]...
Export-Clixml	Export-Clixml [-Path] <String> [-Depth <Int32>] ...
Export-Console	Export-Console [[-Path] <String>] [-Force] [-NoC...
Export-Csv	Export-Csv [-Path] <String> -InputObject <PSObje...
ForEach-Object	ForEach-Object [-Process] <ScriptBlock[]> [-Inpu...
Format-Custom	Format-Custom [[-Property] <Object[]>] [-Depth <...
Format-List	Format-List [[-Property] <Object[]>] [-GroupBy <...
Format-Table	Format-Table [[-Property] <Object[]>] [-AutoSize...
Format-Wide	Format-Wide [[-Property] <Object>] [-AutoSize] [...
Get-Acl	Get-Acl [[-Path] <String[]>] [-Audit] [-Filter <...
Get-Alias	Get-Alias [[-Name] <String[]>] [-Exclude <String...
Get-AuthenticodeSignature	Get-AuthenticodeSignature [-FilePath] <String[]>...

TABLE 8.1:   Built-in PowerShell 1.0 Cmdlets *(CONTINUED)*

NAME	DEFINITION
Get-ChildItem	Get-ChildItem [[-Path] <String[]>] [[-Filter] <S...
Get-Command	Get-Command [[-ArgumentList] <Object[]>] [-Verb ...
Get-Content	Get-Content [-Path] <String[]> [-ReadCount <Int6...
Get-Credential	Get-Credential [-Credential] <PSCredential> [-Ve...
Get-Culture	Get-Culture [-Verbose] [-Debug] [-ErrorAction <A...
Get-Date	Get-Date [[-Date] <DateTime>] [-Year <Int32>] [-...
Get-EventLog	Get-EventLog [-LogName] <String> [-Newest <Int32...
Get-ExecutionPolicy	Get-ExecutionPolicy [-Verbose] [-Debug] [-ErrorA...
Get-Help	Get-Help [[-Name] <String>] [-Category <String[]...
Get-History	Get-History [[-Id] <Int64[]>] [[-Count] <Int32>]...
Get-Host	Get-Host [-Verbose] [-Debug] [-ErrorAction <Acti...
Get-Item	Get-Item [-Path] <String[]> [-Filter <String>] [...
Get-ItemProperty	Get-ItemProperty [-Path] <String[]> [[-Name] <St...
Get-Location	Get-Location [-PSProvider <String[]>] [-PSDrive ...
Get-Member	Get-Member [[-Name] <String[]>] [-InputObject <P...
Get-PfxCertificate	Get-PfxCertificate [-FilePath] <String[]> [-Verb...
Get-Process	Get-Process [[-Name] <String[]>] [-Verbose] [-De...
Get-PSDrive	Get-PSDrive [[-Name] <String[]>] [-Scope <String...
Get-PSProvider	Get-PSProvider [[-PSProvider] <String[]>] [-Verb...
Get-PSSnapin	Get-PSSnapin [[-Name] <String[]>] [-Registered] ...
Get-Service	Get-Service [[-Name] <String[]>] [-Include <Stri...
Get-TraceSource	Get-TraceSource [[-Name] <String[]>] [-Verbose] ...
Get-UICulture	Get-UICulture [-Verbose] [-Debug] [-ErrorAction ...
Get-Unique	Get-Unique [-InputObject <PSObject>] [-AsString]...
Get-Variable	Get-Variable [[-Name] <String[]>] [-ValueOnly] [...

TABLE 8.1: Built-in PowerShell 1.0 Cmdlets *(CONTINUED)*

NAME	DEFINITION
Get-WmiObject	Get-WmiObject [-Class] <String> [[-Property] <St...
Group-Object	Group-Object [[-Property] <Object[]>] [-NoElemen...
Import-Alias	Import-Alias [-Path] <String> [-Scope <String>] ...
Import-Clixml	Import-Clixml [-Path] <String[]> [-Verbose] [-De...
Import-Csv	Import-Csv [-Path] <String[]> [-Verbose] [-Debug...
Invoke-Expression	Invoke-Expression [-Command] <String> [-Verbose]...
Invoke-History	Invoke-History [[-Id] <String>] [-Verbose] [-Deb...
Invoke-Item	Invoke-Item [-Path] <String[]> [-Filter <String>...
Join-Path	Join-Path [-Path] <String[]> [-ChildPath] <Strin...
Measure-Command	Measure-Command [-Expression] <ScriptBlock> [-In...
Measure-Object	Measure-Object [[-Property] <String[]>] [-InputO...
Move-Item	Move-Item [-Path] <String[]> [[-Destination] <St...
Move-ItemProperty	Move-ItemProperty [-Path] <String[]> [-Destinati...
New-Alias	New-Alias [-Name] <String> [-Value] <String> [-D...
New-Item	New-Item [-Path] <String[]> [-ItemType <String>]...
New-ItemProperty	New-ItemProperty [-Path] <String[]> [-Name] <Str...
New-Object	New-Object [-TypeName] <String> [[-ArgumentList]...
New-PSDrive	New-PSDrive [-Name] <String> [-PSProvider] <Stri...
New-Service	New-Service [-Name] <String> [-BinaryPathName] <...
New-TimeSpan	New-TimeSpan [[-Start] <DateTime>] [[-End] <Date...
New-Variable	New-Variable [-Name] <String> [[-Value] <Object>...
Out-Default	Out-Default [-InputObject <PSObject>] [-Verbose]...
Out-File	Out-File [-FilePath] <String> [[-Encoding] <Stri...
Out-Host	Out-Host [-Paging] [-InputObject <PSObject>] [-V...
Out-Null	Out-Null [-InputObject <PSObject>] [-Verbose] [-...

TABLE 8.1: Built-in PowerShell 1.0 Cmdlets *(CONTINUED)*

NAME	DEFINITION
Out-Printer	Out-Printer [[-Name] <String>] [-InputObject <PS...
Out-String	Out-String [-Stream] [-Width <Int32>] [-InputObj...
Pop-Location	Pop-Location [-PassThru] [-StackName <String>] [...
Push-Location	Push-Location [[-Path] <String>] [-PassThru] [-S...
Read-Host	Read-Host [[-Prompt] <Object>] [-AsSecureString]...
Remove-Item	Remove-Item [-Path] <String[]> [-Filter <String>...
Remove-ItemProperty	Remove-ItemProperty [-Path] <String[]> [-Name] <...
Remove-PSDrive	Remove-PSDrive [-Name] <String[]> [-PSProvider <...
Remove-PSSnapin	Remove-PSSnapin [-Name] <String[]> [-PassThru] [...
Remove-Variable	Remove-Variable [-Name] <String[]> [-Include <St...
Rename-Item	Rename-Item [-Path] <String> [-NewName] <String>...
Rename-ItemProperty	Rename-ItemProperty [-Path] <String> [-Name] <St...
Resolve-Path	Resolve-Path [-Path] <String[]> [-Credential <PS...
Restart-Service	Restart-Service [-Name] <String[]> [-Force] [-Pa...
Resume-Service	Resume-Service [-Name] <String[]> [-PassThru] [-...
Select-Object	Select-Object [[-Property] <Object[]>] [-InputOb...
Select-String	Select-String [-Pattern] <String[]> -InputObject...
Set-Acl	Set-Acl [-Path] <String[]> [-AclObject] <ObjectS...
Set-Alias	Set-Alias [-Name] <String> [-Value] <String> [-D...
Set-AuthenticodeSignature	Set-AuthenticodeSignature [-FilePath] <String[]>...
Set-Content	Set-Content [-Path] <String[]> [-Value] <Object[...
Set-Date	Set-Date [-Date] <DateTime> [-DisplayHint <Displ...
Set-ExecutionPolicy	Set-ExecutionPolicy [-ExecutionPolicy] <Executio...
Set-Item	Set-Item [-Path] <String[]> [[-Value] <Object>] ...
Set-ItemProperty	Set-ItemProperty [-Path] <String[]> [-Name] <Str...

TABLE 8.1: Built-in PowerShell 1.0 Cmdlets *(CONTINUED)*

NAME	DEFINITION
Set-Location	Set-Location [[-Path] <String>] [-PassThru] [-Ve...
Set-PSDebug	Set-PSDebug [-Trace <Int32>] [-Step] [-Strict] [...
Set-Service	Set-Service [-Name] <String> [-DisplayName <Stri...
Set-TraceSource	Set-TraceSource [-Name] <String[]> [[-Option] <P...
Set-Variable	Set-Variable [-Name] <String[]> [[-Value] <Objec...
Sort-Object	Sort-Object [[-Property] <Object[]>] [-Descendin...
Split-Path	Split-Path [-Path] <String[]> [-LiteralPath <Str...
Start-Service	Start-Service [-Name] <String[]> [-PassThru] [-I...
Start-Sleep	Start-Sleep [-Seconds] <Int32> [-Verbose] [-Debu...
Start-Transcript	Start-Transcript [[-Path] <String>] [-Append] [-...
Stop-Process	Stop-Process [-Id] <Int32[]> [-PassThru] [-Verbo...
Stop-Service	Stop-Service [-Name] <String[]> [-Force] [-PassT...
Stop-Transcript	Stop-Transcript [-Verbose] [-Debug] [-ErrorActio...
Suspend-Service	Suspend-Service [-Name] <String[]> [-PassThru] [...
Tee-Object	Tee-Object [-FilePath] <String> [-InputObject <P...
Test-Path	Test-Path [-Path] <String[]> [-Filter <String>] ...
Trace-Command	Trace-Command [-Name] <String[]> [-Expression] <...
Update-FormatData	Update-FormatData [[-AppendPath] <String[]>] [-P...
Update-TypeData	Update-TypeData [[-AppendPath] <String[]>] [-Pre...
Where-Object	Where-Object [-FilterScript] <ScriptBlock> [-Inp...
Write-Debug	Write-Debug [-Message] <String> [-Verbose] [-Deb...
Write-Error	Write-Error [-Message] <String> [-Category <Erro...
Write-Host	Write-Host [[-Object] <Object>] [-NoNewline] [-S...
Write-Output	Write-Output [-InputObject] <PSObject[]> [-Verbo...
Write-Progress	Write-Progress [-Activity] <String> [-Status] <S...

TABLE 8.1:   Built-in PowerShell 1.0 Cmdlets *(CONTINUED)*

NAME	DEFINITION
Write-Verbose	Write-Verbose [-Message] <String> [-Verbose] [-D...
Write-Warning	Write-Warning [-Message] <String> [-Verbose] [-D...

NOTE   As you enter commands, you can use a feature called *tab expansion* that shows you the commands that are possible based on the partial command that you entered already. Simply press the Tab key and select the command desired from the list.

Aliases

To make PowerShell easier to learn, the developers have created aliases for commands that you may already know from CMD.EXE, external commands, and even Unix so that you can use them. So you will find that commands like CLS or CLEAR for Clear Screen work in PowerShell by being mapped to the CLEAR-HOST cmdlet. Table 8.2 shows some of the command equivalents that you can use in PowerShell. You can translate common equivalents by using the GET-ALIAS *<command-equivalent>*.

TABLE 8.2:   Commonly Used Command Equivalents

COMMAND EQUIVALENT	POWERSHELL COMMAND
Gc	GET-CONTENT
CD	SET-LOCATION
CHDIR	SET-LOCATION
CLEAR	CLEAR-HOST
CLS	CLEAR-HOST
COPY	COPY-ITEM
DEL	REMOVE-ITEM
DIFF	COMPARE-OBJECT
DIR	GET-CHILDREN
ECHO	WRITE-OUTPUT
ERASE	REMOVE-ITEM
ghy	GET-HISTORY

TABLE 8.2: Commonly Used Command Equivalents *(CONTINUED)*

COMMAND EQUIVALENT	POWERSHELL COMMAND
HISTORY	GET-HISTORY
KILL	STOP-PROCESS
LP	OUT-PRINTER
LS	GET-CHILDREN
MAN	GET-HELP
MOUNT	NEW-PSDRIVE
MOVE	MOVE-ITEM
POPD	POP-LOCATION
PS	GET-PROCESS
PUSHD	PUSH-LOCATION
PWD	GET-LOCATION
R	INVOKE-HISTORY
REN	RENAME-ITEM
RM	REMOVE-ITEM
RMDIR	REMOVE-ITEM
SLEEP	START-SLEEP
SORT	SORT-OBJECT
TEE	TEE-OBJECT
TYPE	GET-CONTENT
WRITE	WRITE-OUTPUT

Aliases are a convenient construct, and although PowerShell has many built-in aliases you can create your own. To do so, use the SET-ALIAS cmdlet as follows:

```
SET-ALIAS gi -VALUE GET-ITEM
```

This would make gi an alias for GET-ITEM.

PowerShell has the interesting feature that the Alias object is a .NET assembly or provider that can be viewed as if it is the file system drive ALIAS:. You can move to the ALIAS: drive using

SET-LOCATION ALIAS: and examine the contents using the GET-CHILDITEM ALIAS: command. To create an alias for launching a program like Notepad, you would enter this command:

```
SET-ALIAS NP C:\WINDOWS\SYSTEM32\NOTEPAD.EXE
```

Then you simply enter **NP** at the PS prompt to launch that text editor. The REMOVE-ITEM ALIAS NP would delete that alias.

Execution Policies

With all the facilities that PowerShell puts into the hands of its users, you might wonder what's to stop the evildoers from using that program to gain access to your system and modify it in ways you might not appreciate. PowerShell runs under a policy that Microsoft calls "Secure by Default." That is, you have to specifically unlock PowerShell features to get them to run on your system or anyone else's system. There simply is no way to run a script on a system that has not been unlocked; the PowerShell program can start up, but it won't even run a user's profile file.

To allow scripts in PowerShell to run, you need to enable what is called an *execution policy*, which defines under what level of security an operation is allowed. The four levels of execution are:

Restricted   No scripts or profiles can run. This is the default level.

AllSigned   Only scripts that are signed can run if you allow them. You can deny their execution if you don't recognize or trust the source.

RemoteSigned   This policy will allow scripts that come from other applications such as Microsoft Office, Outlook, Messenger, or Microsoft Mail to execute when the script and configuration file is signed by a trustworthy source.

Unrestricted   With this setting, PowerShell will run all scripts. Scripts that originate in other applications will post a warning before they execute.

To view the current execution policy, enter:

```
GET-EXECUTIONPOLICY
```

To set security, use the command:

```
SET-EXECUTIONPOLICY <level_name>
```

The SET-EXECUTIONPOLICY benefits from the -WHATIF and -CONFIRM parameters, which will show you the new level before it sets it, and will confirm that the level was set after the operation is complete. Also note that the SET-EXECUTION cmdlet requires an administrator privilege to execute.

To sign a script, you will need to either create a certificate and place the authenticode signature on that certificate, or use a certificate from a trusted source that is already signed and can be placed on your script. Use the SET-AUTHENTICODE and GET-AUTHENTICODE cmdlets to sign your scripts and the MAKECERT cmdlet to create certificates.

Scripts

PowerShell is an interactive command-line environment. When you enter a command at the prompt, that command is executed immediately and the output is displayed in the PowerShell window. You can also send output to a file or printer, or pipe the output to another cmdlet. If there are commands or a sequence of commands that you use, you can store those commands in a PowerShell script. A PowerShell script is a text file with the .PS1 file extension. You execute a script by entering `<path>\<scriptname.ps1>` at the prompt. The path must be a fully qualified path, but the .PS1 extension is optional.

In PowerShell, you must set an execution policy that allows a script to run. Scripts won't run unless you validate them, and you can use a digital signature as part of that validation. To learn more about digital signing, enter the command GET-HELP ABOUT_SIGNING.

PowerShell supports WSH scripts, and while both offer access to COM automation objects, PowerShell has the ability to provide an interactive command session.

Microsoft maintains a library of PowerShell scripts that you can find at

```
http://www.microsoft.com/technet/scriptcenter/default.mspx
```

Figure 8.7 shows this PowerShell script's home page.

FIGURE 8.7
Microsoft maintains a PowerShell script library. Be sure that the script you choose is Windows Server 2008 compatible before using it.

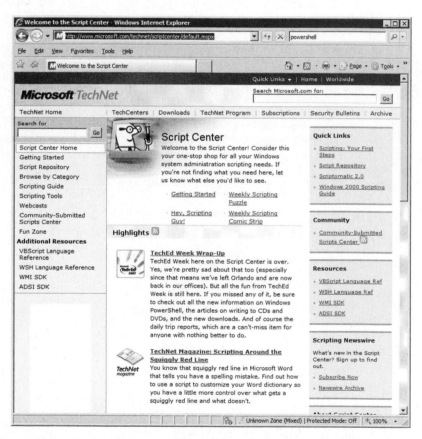

If you are familiar with VBScript or want to translate VBScripts to Windows PowerShell scripts, you can find the translation guide "Converting VBScript Commands to Windows PowerShell Commands" at

```
http://www.microsoft.com/technet/scriptcenter/topics/winpsh/convert/default.mspx
```

PowerShell scripts can be used to retrieve Terminal Server properties. You can use scripts to list service properties, accounts, client settings, logon settings, network adapter settings, permission settings, and session and terminal settings, among other parameters. You can download sample scripts from

```
http://www.microsoft.com/technet/scriptcenter/scripts/msh/ts/
default.mspx?mfr=true
```

Summary

In this chapter, you learned about Microsoft's new scripting and command-line environment called PowerShell. With PowerShell you can access the Windows rich object model and get those objects to perform actions and services for you. PowerShell is Microsoft's new administrator tool, and its use as the underlying command environment means that many future server applications are simply front-ends for PowerShell commands. When you use PowerShell, powerful commands come under your control, letting you query and modify both your local system as well as systems on your network.

In the next chapter, you will learn about the many new security features in Windows Server 2008 and how to use them to make your network more secure. Among the many new security features are the Internet Protocol Security (IPsec) standard, new methods for authentication, and cryptographic support. Windows Server 2008 offers new techniques for working with network shares, as well as new methods for securing network services such as DHCP and VPN from attack. Through NAP, it is possible to only allow access to "healthy" clients, thus further strengthening your network's security.

Chapter 9

Security

In Windows Server 2008 security is job one. Security enhancements permeate all of the Windows Server 2008 subsystems. You can't launch a program on Windows Server 2008 without running into the User Account Control (UAC), which escalates privileges temporarily. UAC is a feature that is part of Windows Server Hardening, and it's meant to protect vital services, the Registry, access to system files, and certain aspects of network access from unauthorized use.

Much of what's new in security is aimed at making the server footprint smaller. The intent of the new Server Core role is to dramatically lower the "attack surface" of Windows Server 2008 by removing the user interface from Windows. Server Core requires command-line management, but chances are that once a server is configured in this role it will be a production system and won't require much attention. The whole idea of roles and components is to deploy only those systems you need, which also makes Windows Server 2008 a hardened target while improving server performance.

Good security is a little like good insurance: you don't need it until you need it. Users may leave newly installed applications unprotected simply by accepting the default password. Security vulnerabilities tend to accrue over time. This version of Windows Server introduces the Security Configuration Wizard (SCW), a multipurpose wizard that walks you through the enforcing of a strong security policy. This wizard is described in detail in this chapter, and you will find many of the new security features in Windows Server 2008 highlighted in the wizard. The SCW isn't just for setup—it's something you can run at any time.

Security Overview

Windows security is multilayered and hinges on a number of mechanisms and challenges that confront any potential intruder. The basic concept behind security is that of allowing only authenticated access to resources through a mechanism called the Challenge-Handshake Authentication Protocol (CHAP). The formal specification for CHAP as it's defined for use on the Internet is part of the RFC 1994 protocol for Point-to-Point Protocol (PPP), but the mechanism has been part of operating systems for quite some time.

In a CHAP authentication, the following steps are performed:

1. A link is established between the client and server in which the client is the system that requests resources. The link could be from a peer in a peer-to-peer network as well.

2. The server responds with a challenge to the client that the client identify itself.

3. The client presents its credentials, which could include a system identification number (SID) for a client whose system is part of a domain, along with a user ID and password for domain access.

The identification presents the Machine account, as well as the User account. However, there are processes such as web connections where the machine account isn't required, and in those cases a one-way hash or MD5 checksum can be sent to the server where it must be decoded to be allowed.

4. The server examines the response to see if the machine is in the domain and if the SID matches the one on record. The server then checks the User account information against the Windows Security Account Manager (SAM) database.

   For connections that aren't domain based, the server would check the hash or checksum against its calculation for a match.

5. If the match is made, the server authenticates the client and allows the connection.

6. Every so often, the authenticator reissues a slightly different challenge, forcing the client to respond with the correct credentials.

Microsoft's version of this authentication is called MS-CHAP.

NOTE Microsoft's Security Central website at www.microsoft.com/security/default.mspx features links to security updates, tools for users and developers, and white papers on topics such as the Trustworthy Computing initiative that Microsoft began nearly five years ago with the Windows 2000 platform. The TechNet security home page for IT administrators can be found at www.microsoft.com/technet/security/default.mspx.

Starting with Windows Server 2003 and continuing with Windows Server 2008, Microsoft has worked at instituting authentication based on the Kerberos network protocol, which isn't point to point like CHAP. In Kerberos the client-server model employs a trusted third party and uses symmetric key cryptography to pass encoded messages between client and server. It is now a three-tiered approach. Kerberos communication is protected against eavesdropping and against what are called *replay attacks*, in which packets are intercepted and manipulated. Kerberos uses a set of session tokens (based on random calculations) that are for the onetime use of communication in either direction. Sometimes tokens are time stamped as another way of narrowing the validity of the token and making them harder to intercept and manipulate.

What's New in Security

Microsoft breaks down security into the following four general areas, each of which has had some improvements made to it for Windows Server 2008:

Desktop, Device, and Server Management   Security access lists (SACLs) are an object's security descriptors; they provide access to the object. The centralized installation and configuration of applications, resource monitoring and reporting, patch management, system security through standardized configurations, mobile device management, UAC, and security management and reporting are all technologies that support server management.

Network and Edge Protection   To harden networks you use technologies such as security zoning, network firewall and web proxies, Secure Sockets Layer virtual private networks (SSL VPNs), IPsec domain isolation, network-level VPN, and intrusion detection and protection.

You've already seen one of the more interesting technologies for network security called Network Access Protection (NAP) in Chapter 5. NAP is a policy-based system that evaluates systems connecting to your network for their security "health" and isolates those clients that don't meet a set of requirements. Other security improvements in Windows Server 2008 included the addition of Internet Protocol security (IPsec).

Identity and Access Management   This category includes Active Directory; single sign-on or account management over multiple authentication authorities; trusted domains; identity mechanisms for AAA services such as centralized connection Authentication, Authorization, and Accounting services; and the Identity Lifecycle Manager, which builds metadirectory and user provisioning on the Microsoft Identity Integration Server (MIIS).

Data Protection   Mechanisms for data protection include host-based firewalls, malware and antivirus software, information rights management, file and disk encryption (EFS and BitLocker), network traffic encryption (IPsec and VPN); backup, restore (Windows Backup), and replication (DFS); stronger application stream protection through better transport protocols; and centralized removable device management.

The Security Configuration Wizard

Windows Server 2008's new Security Configuration Wizard (SCW) guides you through a set of security policies decisions that will be applied to computers and users on your network. The SCW creates security policy templates. The wizard evaluates the services running on your computer, and checks your firewall security settings, open ports, server roles, and current Registry settings. It then closes unneeded ports, turns off unnecessary services, turns on security auditing, and performs other tasks to make your system more secure. The resulting settings are stored in an XML file that you can open and edit in the SCW.

You can also use the command-line tool SCWCMD to work with certain aspects of the SCW. Templates that you create on one computer can be applied to other systems on the network using the SCWCMD TRANSFORM command to create the necessary Group Policy Objects (GPOs). Remember that in a domain the GPO security policy will usually take precedent over any Registry settings applied by the SCW. Thus to apply the SCW as a domain policy, you use SCWCMD TRANSFORM to apply your security GPO over Active Directory Domain Services (AD DS). SCWCMD does not work with anything other than security templates.

Microsoft's SCW is meant to solve the problem of inexperienced administrators installing roles and services and not securing their server afterwards. The SCW can be run after any significant change is made to services and applications. You don't need to perform the steps in all of the sections of the wizard; you can use the Skip This Section button at the start of each section to move to the next set of settings.

To launch the Security Configuration Wizard, do one of the following:

◆ Click Start ➢ Administrative Tools, and then select the Security Configuration Wizard command.

◆ Type **SCW** in the Start Search text box of the Start menu; then press Enter.

The first step of the Role is the welcome screen shown in Figure 9.1.

FIGURE 9.1
The Welcome to the
Security Configuration Wizard screen

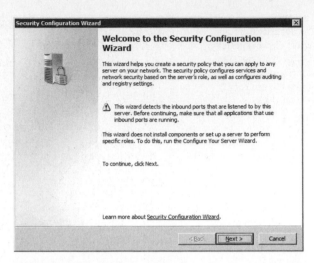

Make sure all of your server's applications are running and that the computer is in its fully functional state—the wizard is meant to analyze a system in its working state so as to best secure it.

Role-Based Services

The Role-Based Services steps of the SCW can be set up as follows:

1. Click the Next button on the first Welcome screen to go to the second step.

2. On the Configuration Action screen, click the Create a New Security Policy radio button (the default), then click Next.

   If you want to edit an existing security policy or substitute another security policy, select one of the other radio buttons: Edit an Existing Security Policy, Apply an Existing Policy, or Rollback in the Last Applied Security Policy. You will need to provide the path to the security policy file for these options.

   You can create security policies that are in place for different time periods, when different applications are running, or for whatever purpose you have in mind. You can run the wizard again at a future time to alter your security policies.

3. On the Select Server screen, enter the name of the server you wish to apply the security policy to, or click Browse to enter the server name and its path; then click OK.

   If you don't already have a Security Configuration Database, then the Processing Security Configuration Database step creates one. The server is scanned for installed roles, roles in use, services, and IP addresses and subnets that are defined on the server.

   To view that database, click the View Configuration Database button on the Security Configuration Viewer screen. Figure 9.2 shows the SCW Viewer application that appears when you click that button. The database is a set of XML files found at %SYSTEMROOT%\SECURITY\MSSCW\KBS, combined into a single server-specific MAIN.XML file that you see summarized in Figure 9.2.

FIGURE 9.2

The Security Configuration Viewer application lets you view the security settings applied to each of a server's different roles.

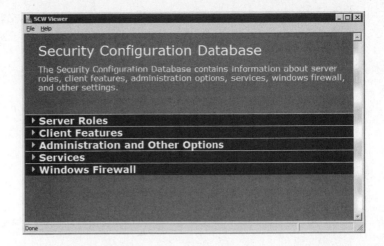

NOTE You must have local Administrator access on the server you wish to apply a security policy to.

4. Click Next to view the Role-Based Service Configuration screen, then click Next again to view the Select Server Roles screen, shown in Figure 9.3.

The Role-Based Service Configuration part of the wizard applies settings to the different roles that you already have installed on your server. If you install additional roles, you need to configure these settings again. The View list box allows you to look at uninstalled roles, selected roles, or all roles. Services that aren't required by roles and features are disabled, unless you indicate otherwise.

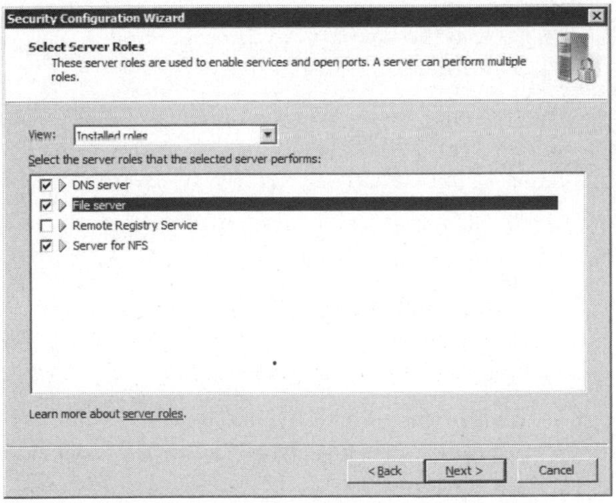

FIGURE 9.3

The Select Server Roles screen lets you secure the different installed roles on your selected server.

5. Select the server roles you wish to secure; then click Next.

The wizard populates the Select Client Features screen shown in Figure 9.4, and when you expand each selection you get an explanation of what the client feature does, as well as any required services (also called dependencies).

FIGURE 9.4

The Select Client Features screen allows you to apply security settings on a feature-by-feature basis. The expanded role offers an explanation of the feature's purpose and its dependencies.

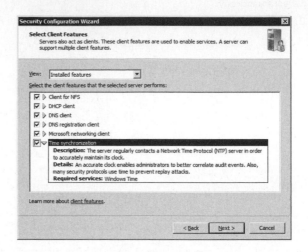

6. Click on the checkbox(es) of the features that you wish to secure, then click Next to view the Select Administration and Other Options screen, shown in Figure 9.5, the seventh step of the wizard. Select the options you wish to secure, and then click Next.

FIGURE 9.5

The Select Administration and Other Options screen is used to open ports for the services on this list, or to close the ones that aren't enabled.

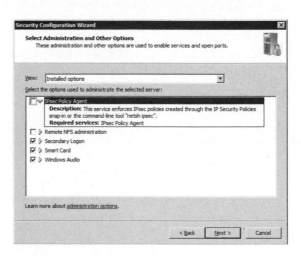

7. On the Select Additional Services screen shown in Figure 9.6 are listed all services in the Services control panel. Disable any services that you don't require the server to run; then click Next.

The services on the Select Additional Services screen are the same listed the Services control panel. The wizard gives you the opportunity to enable services that aren't mapped directly to a role recognized by the Security Configuration Database.

FIGURE 9.6
This screen displays the services that are installed on your server and which ones will start automatically.

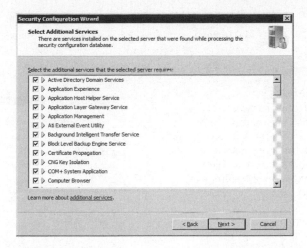

8. On the Handling Unspecified Services screen, you are asked for the policy to effect when a server running a service that isn't specified by policy is encountered. Your choice is either Do Not Change the Startup Mode of the Service (the default) or Disable the Service.

9. After you click Next, you will see a Confirm Service Changes screen. Click Next again to end the Role-Based Services portion of the wizard.

Network Security

The Network Security steps of the SCW enforce a set of rules that apply to the server firewall, network services, and allowed IP addresses. The first screen of Network Security is shown in Figure 9.7. Note that this screen has a Skip This Section checkbox should you wish to move to the next section of the wizard (the Registry Settings section).

FIGURE 9.7
The Network Security settings enforce policy on your firewall, network services, and IP addresses.

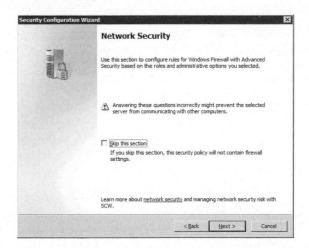

The Network Security steps of the SCW are as follows:

1. On the Network Security screen, click Next to go to the first page of settings—the Network Security Rules screen shown in Figure 9.8. Or click Skip This Section and then Next to proceed to the Registry Settings Section of the SCW.

FIGURE 9.8

The Network Security Rules open or close ports of the Windows Firewall to specific service traffic, based on the network protocols used.

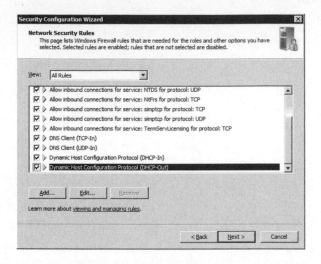

2. The next screen shows the rules that the Windows Firewall will observe. These rules open ports and enable inbound and/or outbound traffic for that protocol over that port. Enable or disable these rules as required, but be aware that when you do, the services that the protocol traffic supports will be impacted. If you expand a rule, you'll see detailed information about the protocol and port, something similar to Figure 9.9.

FIGURE 9.9

When you expand the protocol, you get detailed information on the programs that use them and on the associated ports.

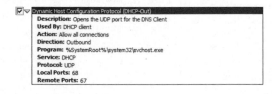

3. Click the Edit button to open the detailed multi-tab Edit Rule dialog box shown in Figure 9.10. Many of the settings in this dialog box are predefined and can't be changed, but the scope of allowed IP addresses that can access the port by this protocol is one very significant security setting that can be allowed. So be sure not to miss this dialog box in your transit through the wizard.

4. Click Next to finish the Network Security section of the SCW and move to the Registry Settings section.

Of course, you could open the Windows Firewall to enable these settings, but the wizard is a convenient place to take care of these settings in the context of the other settings on which they depend, and they offer quite a bit of valuable hand-holding.

FIGURE 9.10

You can set a scope for protocol communication in the Edit Rule dialog box that is one of the most effective security settings.

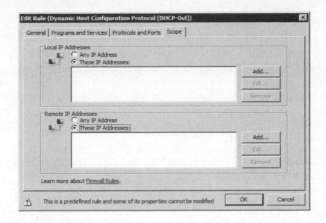

Registry Settings

The purpose of the Registry Settings is to provide the means to digitally sign communications from the selected server to another server. Figure 9.11 shows the first page of the Registry Settings section of the SCW. As you go through the Registry Settings, you enforce the following:

♦ Actions relayed to authentication on SMB (usually file access) communications

♦ Authentication methods used with user accounts for both outbound and inbound traffic

♦ How to handle incoming authentication requests from users without local accounts coming from legacy Windows systems

Let's take a closer look at the steps involved.

FIGURE 9.11

The first page of the Registry Settings section of the SCW. This section enables the authentication mechanism for secure communications between servers.

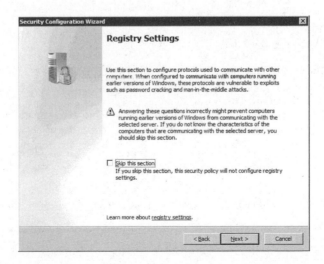

To enforce Registry Settings related to authentication:

1. Click Next to view the Require SMB Security Signatures screen shown in Figure 9.12. You can enforce minimum requirements on legacy Windows systems and on Windows Mobile devices. You can also enforce that all file and print traffic be digitally signed, provided that the server has enough remaining CPU capacity to service the request. Select your settings and click Next.

   The registry key containing SMB authentication is HKLM\System\CurrentControlSet\ Services\LanManServer\Parameters\RequireSecuritySignature.

FIGURE 9.12
Authentication of SMB traffic can set minimum client connection properties and can enforce signing for file and print traffic.

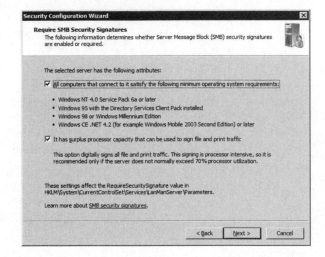

2. The Outgoing Authentication Methods screen allows you to enforce three different types of authentication mechanisms:

   ◆ Domain accounts

   ◆ Local accounts on the remote computers

   ◆ File sharing passwords on Windows 95, Windows 98, or Windows ME

   You can enable any or all of these mechanisms. The associated Registry key is HKLM\System\CurrentControlSet\Services\Control\LSA\LMCompatibilityLevel.

3. The steps you see next depend on your selections, but if you enabled Domain Accounts the next screen is called Outbound Authentication Using Domain Accounts. Here you can enforce the minimum client connection properties:

   ◆ Windows NT 4.0 Service Pack 6a or later operating systems

   ◆ Clocks that are synchronized with the selected server's time clock

   If you enabled Local Accounts, an identical page appears with these same settings for clients connecting using local accounts. If you have selected to allow file sharing passwords on legacy systems, you don't see the Outbound Authentication page, but instead are taken to the Registry Settings Summary page.

4. Click the Next button to end the Registry Settings section of the SCW.

Audit Policy

The Audit Policy section of the SCW creates security events that are written to the Windows Server 2008 Security log. The pages in this section let you define which security events you wish to monitor. Unlike other security policy settings in the previous sections of the SCW, the audit policy can't be rolled back using the SCW. You can remove these policies in the Group Policy Editor.

NOTE Auditing security events can place a load on server resources, including processors, memory, and hard drive space. Only enable auditing if your server has sufficient space, memory, and processing capabilities so that it isn't affected negatively by these activities. Audit loading increases with the number of connected users, the number of processes being run, and other factors.

To set the audit policy in the SCW:

1. Click Next on the Audit Policy screen to view the System Audit Policy screen, shown in Figure 9.13.

Three policy categories are offered: Do Not Audit, Audit Successful Activities, and Audit Successful and Unsuccessful Activities. I recommend that you turn on auditing for successful and unsuccessful activities, as both are required to fully assess security violations.

FIGURE 9.13
On the Security Audit Policy screen, you can enable both successful and unsuccessful security events.

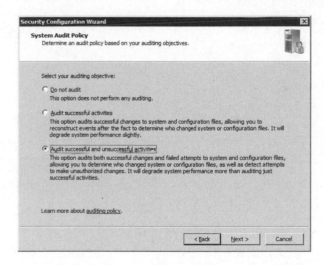

2. When you click Next, you see the Audit Policy Summary screen, shown in Figure 9.14.

This screen is strictly informational and cannot be changed. However, it does indicate that the settings are saved into the SCWAUDIT.INF security template. If you wish to change these settings or view which settings are being audited, open the Auditing Security Template (ASCAUDIT.INF), which you will find at %WINDIR%\Security\MSSCW\KBS.

FIGURE 9.14
The Audit Policy
Summary screen is a
confirmation of your
settings.

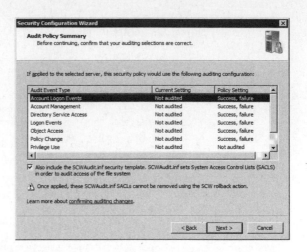

3. Click Next to go to the Save Security Policy screen; then click Next again to view the Security
   Policy File Name screen, as shown in Figure 9.15. Name the XML file and its location, then
   click Next again.

FIGURE 9.15
The Security Policy
File Name page is a
confirmation of your
settings.

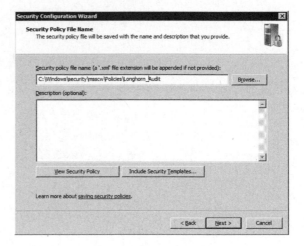

Completing the SCW

You can click the View Security Policy button (see Figure 9.15) to open the SCW Viewer that you
saw earlier in Figure 9.2. Additional security templates can be included at this point.

1. The Apply Security Policy screen lets you do one of the following:

   ◆ Apply Later (run this wizard again to apply this security policy at a later time).

   ◆ Apply Now (when you click Next, the wizard applies the security policy to the selected
     server).

   The first setting creates the security template file, and you can apply the setting at another
   time. You might apply later if you intend to use the settings on another system, or if you're

using these settings for a group of servers. The second setting enforces your settings immediately.

2. Click Next to complete the wizard.

If you decide to apply the security template at a later time, rerun the SCW. On the second screen of the wizard, called Configuration Action, select the Apply an Existing Security Policy radio button and specify the security policy file in the Existing Security Policy File text box (see Figure 9.16).

FIGURE 9.16
To apply an existing template, run the SCW and at the second screen specify the template file to use.

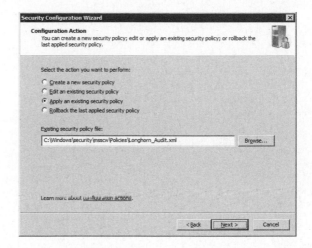

Windows Firewall with Advanced Security

Windows Firewall with Advanced Security combines what were previously two different functions:

- Windows Firewall
- Internet Protocol security (IPsec)

Gone are the IP security policies and IP Security Monitor that were part of Windows Server 2003/XP and Windows 2000.

To launch the Windows Firewall with Advanced Security MMC, click Start ➢ All Programs ➢ Administrative Tools, and then select the Windows Firewall with Advanced Security command.

The Windows Firewall appears as shown in Figure 9.17.

Windows Firewall with Advanced Security brings some of the best features of the Microsoft Internet Security and Acceleration Server into Windows Server 2008, but in a simplified fashion. Windows Firewall filters all IP traffic, both IPv4 and IPv6. It defines three sets of access policies:

Domain Profile   Apply to any computer connecting to Windows Server 2008 using domain authentication

Private Profile   Apply to computers that connect to the server without the use of domain authentication but on a private network

Public Profile   Apply to computers connecting from an external subnet

FIGURE 9.17
The Windows Firewall with Advanced Security lets you create rules that restrict or allow network traffic.

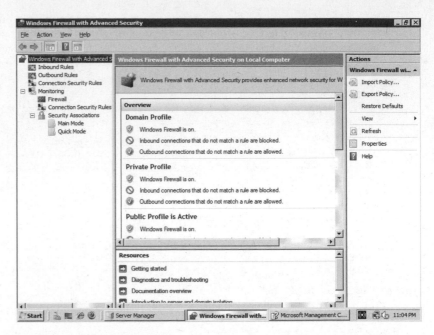

Each connection has a firewall profile applied to it, and the public profile should be the most restrictive of the three. Firewall profiles are saved to files with the .WFW (Windows FireWall) extension, with all three sets in a single file. You can use the Import Policy and Export Policy commands on the Action panel or menu to save or open a firewall profile. You can also import the policy into a Group Policy Object and use the Group Policy Object Editor (GPOE) to modify and apply those settings.

Firewalls operate using a set of rules that you define. Rules can be applied to a LAN, VPN, remote access, ports, protocols, users and groups, and even network address access requests. There are three types of rules:

Rules for Incoming Traffic   Unless incoming traffic conforms to certain rules on the firewall, that traffic is blocked. Rules you can enforce include allowed port numbers, IP addresses and subnets, and access to applications or services on servers, among other things. Unless you create a rule, traffic is, by default, disallowed, and out of the box the server is hardened.

Rules for Outgoing Traffic   Outgoing traffic is allowed, unless the traffic conflicts with rules that disallow it or the packets are nonstandard. Rules are applied in this order: default profile, an allowed connection type, a blocked connection type, and an authenticated bypass or rule that overrides the block rules.

Connection Security Rules   The firewall rules you create allow or deny traffic through the firewall. However, firewall rules do not authenticate the traffic in any way. To ensure that communications are secure, you create connection security rules, and those rules use IPsec to ensure that the two computers sending and receiving the traffic.

The Advanced Security portion of the new firewall refers to the protection of IP traffic using the IPsec protocol, which provides an authentication for both the sending and receiving computers. As an option, IPsec can encrypt its communications. You create the IPsec authentication rule by clicking the Connection Security Rules node of the Firewall tree control, which is located in the Monitoring section.

The IPsec protocol uses a key exchange technology to provide authentication that the data being sent is secure. For IPsec to operate, both computers have to have this network protocol installed and running locally, both must have a common authentication method, and both must be able to share the same shared session key. Windows Firewall with Advanced Security uses the Diffie-Hellman (D-H) algorithm for key exchange, which applies a hash function to the key before communication with the other party.

The Monitoring section of Windows Firewall with Advanced Security is used to view which profile is active, as well as the settings that the profile has. The Firewall page monitors all firewall rules, those that are in the active profile, and those that have been applied by GPOs. If any communications use IPsec authentication, they are displayed in the Connections Security Rules section. Security Associations refer to the secure connections made between each of the two nodes in an IPsec connection.

Network Connection Security

Although the Windows Firewall with Advanced Settings MMC and the Windows Firewall itself allow you to create inbound and outbound rules as well as define secure connection rules (in the MMC only), you can also set security on each network connection. Network connections use dial-up, broadband (Point-to-Point Protocol over Ethernet [PPPoE]), or VPN connections.

To require authentication and encrypt dial-up, PPPoE, or VPN data communications, do the following:

1. Open the Network Connection folder and right-click on the connection you want to modify.

2. Select the Properties command, then click the Security tab.

3. Select Typical (Recommended Settings), then select Validate My Identity as Follows.

4. Select one of these radio buttons:

   ◆ Automatically Use My Windows Logon Name and Password (and Domain If Any)

   ◆ Require Data Encryption (Disconnect if None)

   ◆ Require Data Encryption (Disconnect if None)

NOTE Only the Require Data Encryption selection creates secure traffic.

5. Click OK to enforce your settings.

Table 9.1 shows you the settings that are possible for this form of network security.

TABLE 9.1:   Security Settings for Dial-Up, PPPoE, or VPN Connections

VALIDATE IDENTITY	USE WINDOWS LOGON	REQUIRE DATA ENCRYPTION
For Dial-up and Broadband (PPPoE) connections		
Allow Unsecured Password	Unavailable	Unavailable
Required Secured Access	Available	Available
Use Smart Card	Unavailable	Available

TABLE 9.1: Security Settings for Dial-Up, PPPoE, or VPN Connections *(CONTINUED)*

VALIDATE IDENTITY	USE WINDOWS LOGON	REQUIRE DATA ENCRYPTION
For VPN Connections		
Require Secured Password	Available	Available (on by default)
Use Smart Card	Unavailable	Available (enabled by default)

Access Control List Security

Many objects you find in the Windows GUI, such as disks, folders, shares, and so forth, have security set as part of their access control list (ACL). You can set security by doing the following:

1. Right-click on the disk, folder, share, or file desired.

2. Select the Properties command from the context menu.

3. Click the Security tab; you should see a dialog box that looks like Figure 9.18.

FIGURE 9.18
The Security tab for a
network share

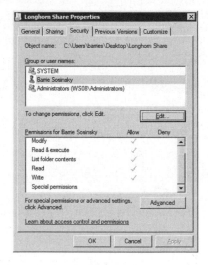

4. Select group or user names that you wish to provide access to in the top list box, then apply the permissions desired in the Permissions list.

   You can use the Edit button to add users and groups and specify associated permissions. The Security tab and the Permissions dialog box (which appears when you click the Edit button) are nearly identical to the one you saw in Windows Server 2003/XP.

5. Click the Advanced options to set Permissions, Auditing, Owner (ship), and the Effective Permissions in the Advanced Security Settings dialog box (optional).

6. Click OK twice to enforce your settings.

Summary

In this chapter, you learned about the security mechanisms that Windows Server 2008 uses to establish secure network connections and to control the kind of network traffic allowed. A new set of management tools allows you more streamlined control over security features. New in Windows Server 2008 is a detailed Security Configuration Wizard that can help you establish a strong security policy. The Windows Firewall has now been integrated with IPsec, allowing traffic to not only be allowed but authenticated as well.

In Chapter 10, we'll take a further look at different types of network connectivity from clients to Windows Server 2008. Microsoft has always sought to be the control console for a heterogeneous network of clients. There are numerous network services available for Macintosh, Unix, Linux, and mobile clients in Windows Server 2008 that need to be installed and enabled in order to make these systems function on a Windows network.

Chapter 10

Clients, Interoperability, and Printing

Microsoft wants Windows Server 2008 to be the center of your networking world. Of course, they want Windows Server 2008 to be surrounded by Windows clients, but rarely is that exclusively the case. Given the open source nature of Linux, and the strong and sometimes dominant roles that Unix applications and Microsoft desktops play, Windows must accommodate these clients as well. In this chapter, we'll consider the different levels of support offered to clients.

Windows Server 2008 also offers a new print architecture as well as a new printer management framework. Some significant new features offer better control over print servers, more and finer control over printer policy, as well as options such as Internet printing and Vista client print rendering that take advantage of the capabilities built into Windows Server 2008.

Windows Server 2008 and Vista: "Better Together"

Is Windows Server 2008 justification for upgrading your clients to Vista? Microsoft sure hopes so. As with the Windows Server operating systems that came before it, certain new features of Windows Server 2008 are only possible when you have Vista as a client. From more automated deployment options to Group Policies such as Network Access Protection (NAP), and more, only an enlightened client such as Vista can take full advantage of them. Microsoft refers to a client that fully exploits a server platform as an "enlightened client," or when a little less functionality is available, as a "gifted child." Windows Server 2008 would be an enlightened client, while Vista 2008 R1 would be a gifted child.

Better Management

"Better Together" is Microsoft's slogan for Windows Vista's enhanced client status on a Windows Server 2008 network. It makes sense that two operating systems built on the same core would share features that aren't possible with older, "down-level" clients such as Windows XP, 2000, and the now-unsupported Windows 98 clients. Indeed, throughout this book I've mentioned that you could create this or that policy only when you had the unique combination of Windows Server 2008 and a Vista client.

The shared Windows cores that Windows Server 2008 and Vista have means that Microsoft can use a single Windows Update and Service Pack model for both. This should be a convenience when managing the upgrade paths for both operating systems. Additionally, Vista uses the full range of services of the Windows Server 2008 server, and its Vista client shares the same policy model and event model. One example of where Vista's capabilities come into play is in NAP, where Vista clients can be fully accessed as to their network "health" and the security policies in place. Vista clients can perform event forwarding to Windows Server 2008 that is useful in determining the condition of the client.

More Features Readily Available

Most of the aforementioned features allow you to better manage Vista clients on Windows Server 2008. However, some features give Vista a greater availability in certain areas as well. For example, Vista can make print servers more scalable by performing remote or client-side rendering. Other required server resources such as cached objects can similarly be cached on the client side and be available to local users even when the server is not. The cache then updates when Windows Server 2008 and Vista reconnect.

Another advantage of Vista as a client of Windows Server 2008 is that scripts and applications can run on both systems and use the transactional file systems described in Chapter 6 to ensure that the transactions either fully succeed or fail and roll back to their previous known good state.

Quality of service (QoS) policies can be more fully implemented on Vista and Windows Server 2008 together, and enable applications or services to have guaranteed network bandwidth available to them. QoS can control not only bandwidth but the actual data being transferred. Many QoS systems will perform deep-packet inspection to determine the priority of a certain type of traffic to be transmitted.

Faster Communications

Vista clients and Windows Server 2008 share the new TCP/IP stack that was a major new feature of the Longhorn core. Therefore, Vista clients are likely to have better speed and more secure access to other Vista clients and Windows Server 2008 systems than down-level Windows systems (see the section "Down-Level Compatibility" later in this chapter). IPv6 on both client and server should also make it easier to switch over to this new network addressing scheme. IPv6 is both more scalable and more reliable than IPv4.

TCP/IP wasn't the only network transport that was rewritten. Vista clients can make full use of the new Server Message Block (SMB) 2.0 protocol, which is used for connecting to file shares over high-latency connections. SMB is the protocol that is commonly referred to as "Windows Networking," and version 2.0 provides a mutual authentication scheme and a message signing capability for improved security. SMB is the preferred method for accessing storage on a Windows network, so these changes are very significant. In certain instances, there are reports that SMB data can be sent and received up to 4,000 times faster with SMB 2.0 than was previously possible.

Another improvement is the ability of Vista clients to connect by remote access to the network through the HTTP gateway service and have remote applications execute in their own windows as if they were a local application. The only way to tell that the application is remote is to examine the Properties dialog box of the application that was launched.

Down-Level Compatibility

Down-level clients is the term used by Microsoft for versions of the operating systems that are still supported but at a lower feature set level than Vista. Windows Server 2003 and Windows XP Pro generally can use most of the Windows Server 2008 feature set, and Windows Server 2000 and Windows 2000 Professional are the clients with the least support. Any client older than Windows 2000 is considered unsupported. That doesn't necessarily mean you can't connect them to Windows Server 2008, but it does mean that many new features won't work and that you are on your own. Systems that have been "sunsetted" include Windows Server NT (all versions), Windows 98, and prior versions of the desktop. Refer to Table 10.1 for a comparison of the capabilities of different Windows clients that work with Windows Server 2008 features.

TABLE 10.1:   Windows Clients Compatibility Chart

FEATURE	VISTA/2008	XP/2003	2000/SERVER	WINDOWS98	NT4
.NET Framework	Y/Y	Y/Y	Y/Y	Y	Y
64 bit support	Y/Y	N/Y	N/Y	N	N
BDD Deployment	Y/Y	Y/Y	N/N	N	N
Full Volume Encryption	Y/Y	Part/Part	N/N	N	N
Internet Printing	Y/Y	Y/Y	Y/Y	Y	Y
IPv6	Y/Y	Y/Y	Part/Part	N	N
Network Access Policy NAP	Y/Y	Y (SP3) /N	N/N	N	N
Network Location Awareness	Y/Y	Y/N	N/N	N	N
PowerShell client	Y/Y	Y/Y	N/N	N	N
RDP 6.0	Y/Y	Y/Y	N/N	N	N
Remote Console	Y/Y	Y/Y	Y/Y	N	N
WMI Support	Y/Y	Y/Y	Y/Y	Y	Y

Mobile Clients

The most important improvement related to managing mobile clients on Windows Server 2008 has been the addition of the Network Access Protection (NAP) policy and infrastructure (described in detail in Chapter 5). That infrastructure was put into place primarily to protect networks from penetration or infection from laptops brought into the network from outside.

To enable mobile devices to work on NAP, you will need to create rights account certificates (RACs) and use licenses for applications that conform to the Active Directory Rights Management Services (AD RMS) standard. To enable certification of mobile clients, follow these steps:

1. Open Windows Explorer and go to the folder containing IIS. By default this is `C:\INETPUB\WWWROOT_\WMCS\CERTIFICATION`, but it can be changed.

2. Right-click on the `MobileDeviceCertification.asmx` file and select the Properties command from the context menu.

3. Select the Security tab, then click Add. Add the mobile system's AD machine account and the AD RMS Service Group.

4. In Permissions for Groups, enable the Allow for Read and Allow for Read & Execute permissions; then click OK.

5. Restart IIS in the Server Manager, or by using the `IISRESET` command at the command prompt.

With these settings in place, the mobile client will be discovered automatically by AD RMS when it connects to the network.

Macintosh Interoperability

In terms of significant new features for Macintosh clients, Windows Server 2008 seems to have less support for the Macintosh than previous versions. While Microsoft has a vital Macintosh development group, most of their efforts seem to have gone into Microsoft Office and desktop applications than into significant network client support. If you create a NAP infrastructure and policy set on your Windows Server 2008 network, Macintosh (and Unix) systems will be put on the restricted network because they lack the requisite health certificates, for example.

With a Macintosh client, you get the following:

◆ Access to the Internet

◆ Addressing through DHCP, DNS, access file shares, printers, and open terminal sessions to Windows Vista and Windows Server

◆ Membership in the Active Directory Computer account as a Primary Group member (usually Domain Users logging on to the Windows network using Services for Macintosh [SFM])

…and that's about it. Most of the advanced networking features are limited to Windows clients. These same services are also available to POSIX (Portable Operating System Interface) clients such as Unix and Linux.

You get Internet access by setting the TCP/IP addressing, gateway, and DNS servers in the Macintosh TCP/IP Control Panel. The Macintosh Safari browser can act as an Active Directory Federation Services (ADFS) client, provided that JScript (Microsoft's version of JavaScript) is turned on in the browser.

Although many Macintosh networks still use AppleTalk to find resources, TCP/IP is used as the transport for most connections. Since Windows XP, support for the AppleTalk protocol has been removed from the Windows operating system. So if you need to run SFM, you have to load it onto a Windows Server 2003 system, as it is unavailable in Windows Server 2008.

Macintosh clients can make use of the new SMB protocol built into Windows Server 2008 to more efficiently address shared storage, and Microsoft recommends that you convert and upgrade network printers and file servers to SMB, which has Macintosh support as well as Windows support.

The one significant improvement offered to Macintosh users is through terminal services. Microsoft has finally revised their Macintosh version of the Remote Desktop Protocol (RDP) version 6 protocol for Mac OS X, shown in Figure 10.1. The utility is called the Microsoft Remote Desktop Connection Client for Mac 2.0. The Mac client:

◆ Is a universal binary

◆ Connects to Vista Business and Vista Ultimate

◆ Has better printer support and supports Macintosh printers that aren't PostScript printers, as was the case for the previous RDP client

◆ Offers dynamic screen resizing so that you can switch from a session window to full-screen mode in a session

◆ Provides an improved user interface that is more Mac-like

The Mac RDP Client can run multiple sessions on the Macintosh, but may require the third-party utility RDC Launcher (`http://osx.iusethis.com/app/rdclauncher`) in order to instantiate additional sessions. Each new connection runs inside its own windows on the Mac OS X desktop. Each connection can be saved as an RDP file so that the session can be reestablished using the same settings.

FIGURE 10.1

The new Remote Desktop Connection Client 2.0 for Mac OS X brings some improvements in functionality to Mac users, but lacks some of the new remote connection features that the Windows version offers.

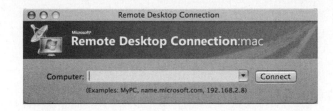

The Macintosh RDP client has some significant limitations compared to the Windows version, most particularly its lack of support for the new Terminal Server Gateway.

Unix Interoperability

Unix and Unix applications play an important role in many enterprise deployments. You only have to consider the dominant role that Apache web servers have on the Internet to understand why accommodating these servers and clients is an important characteristic of any server platform that desires to be the management platform for a heterogeneous network. To serve as the domain, name, identity, or address server in a large enterprise, it is essential to be able to provide these services to as many different operating systems as possible. If Microsoft doesn't provide these capabilities, then competitors such as Novell (who has a very strong eDirectory product) or Sun (which has a strong storage asset management position) will gladly displace Windows servers. Windows Server 2008 continues a trend in heterogeneous networking of improving Unix interoperability.

Windows Server 2003 used the add-on product Services for Unix (SFU) to provide access to network-attached storage (NAS) for Unix and Windows clients so that they can connect to the shares and files on the storage server. In Windows-based NAS solutions, Microsoft has an original equipment manufacturer (OEM) version of the Windows Server operating system, the Windows Storage Server OS, that has specifically been tuned for storage services. The Storage Server OS is based on Windows Server 2003, and each OEM vendor modifies the bundled SFU in their NAS appliances in a proprietary manner. In Windows Server 2003 R2 Microsoft put the various SFU subsystems directly into the operating system.

Windows Server 2008 contains the following services for Unix interoperability:

Services for NSF   The Microsoft Services for NFS allows Unix clients using the NFS protocol to access network shares. With this service installed, you see a Sharing tab when you open the folder's Properties dialog box.

Identity Management for Unix   This service turns on the Network Information Service (NIS) with Windows Server as the Master Server in the directory service. Unix clients use NIS to distribute system configuration data such as usernames and hostnames. NIS is a Sun technology that is licensed to all other Unix vendors.

Subsystem for Unix Applications   This subsystem lets you run compatible Unix applications natively on a Windows client or server.

Identity Management for Unix

Identity Management for Unix is a Windows Server 2008 role service, and is installed as part of the Add Role Services wizard (described in more detail a bit later). Two components of Identity Management for Unix are Server for Network Information Services and the Password Synchronization feature that is new to Windows Server 2008.

Server for Network Information Services exports NIS domain assignments to Active Directory, mapping users and hostnames to User accounts and Machine (System) accounts. By creating a unified namespace, a Windows server can manage both Windows and Unix client and server access to network resources. The mapping scheme used is RFC 2307 compliant and allows both Unix and Linux clients to access AD using LDAP directly.

The Password Synchronization feature allows Unix users to modify their password on their Unix system and have that change be recorded in Active Directory using the NIS mapping. The NIS service stores passwords as part of account identification. Password Synchronization is supported for the following operating systems: IBM AIX 5L version 5.2, HP-UX 11i, Red Hat Linux 8 and 9, and Sun Solaris 7 and 8.

When a password is modified on Unix, the PASSWD program calls the pluggable authentication module (PAM) to register the change. Password Synchronization has a Web module for each of the supported Unix/Linux OSs listed earlier. That Web module then encrypts the password and sends it to the Password Synchronization Server, where it alters the appropriate Windows user accounts, either domain or local. Passwords changed on Windows are encrypted by the Password Synchronization service and sent to the Unix server as a background process called the single sign-on daemon.

To install Identity Management for Unix, do the following:

1. Open the Server Manager and click on the Roles node in the tree control.

2. Scroll down to the Role Services section and click the Add Role Services link.

    The Add Role Services wizard opens, as shown in Figure 10.2.

FIGURE 10.2
To add Identity
Management for
Unix, which turns on
an NIS mapping ser-
vice, use the Add Role
Services wizard.

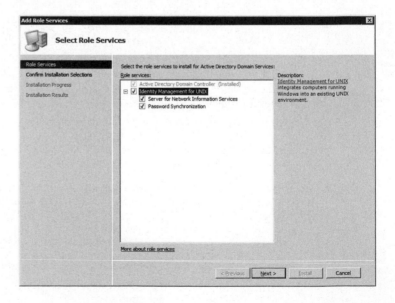

3. Select the Identity Management for UNIX checkbox (its subselections should be checked by default), then click the Next button.

You can disable either the Server for Network Information Services or the Password Synchronization services, but it is usual to enable both for this function.

4. Complete the steps of the wizard.

5. Restart your server to complete the installation.

Identity Management for Unix is managed using an MMC console either through the Server Manager's Active Directory Domain Services section or through a stand-alone console. You can open the console by doing any of the following:

◆ Open the Server Manager, scroll to the Active Directory Domain Services section, and click Microsoft Identity Management for Unix.

◆ Click Start ➤ All Programs ➤ Administrative Tools, ➤ Identity Management for UNIX.

◆ Click Start ➤ Run (or press Windows+R), enter **IDMUMGMT.MSC**, and then press Enter.

Subsystem for Unix Applications

Subsystem for Unix-based Applications (SUA) is the latest version of the Interix module that was part of Windows Service for Unix 3.5. Using SUA it is possible to have a Unix operating system run on top of Microsoft Windows. Among the services provided for Unix applications are 300 Unix commands, Unix file-naming conventions, shells, scripts, job services, and Unix compilers. As shown in Figure 10.3, SUA does not run as a Unix emulator; it is a native POSIX subsystem and runtime environment that runs on top of the Windows kernel. Since this is a native subsystem, Unix applications run with the kind of performance that you would expect from native Unix running on the same hardware platform.

SUA runs Unix scripts natively, but requires that any application that runs in the environment be ported from Unix to Windows, which requires that you recompile the application. Recompilation is something you would have to do if you wanted to run an application from one version of Unix to another in any case. Since SUA is built to have signaling in Unix contained in the Unix stack, the number of changes required to recompile Unix applications is generally modest.

Microsoft believes that SUA will have the most benefit for the following applications:

◆ Database connectivity

◆ 64-bit hardware support

◆ Visual Studio support for Unix semantics and facility in debugging Unix-based applications

As shown in Figure 10.3, Windows and Unix have their own stack and appear to be separate. However, through the SUA subsystem an application can be managed as either a SUA process or a Windows process. A Unix application that can access Windows APIs is referred to as mixed mode. To install SUA:

1. Open the Server Manager and click on the Server Manager node in the tree control.

2. Scroll down to the Features Summary section and click the Add Features link.

The Add Features Wizard opens as shown in Figure 10.4.

3. Enable the Subsystem for UNIX-Based Applications check box, then click the Next button.

4. Complete the steps of the wizard.

FIGURE 10.3
The SUA architecture runs the Unix operating system above the Windows kernel.

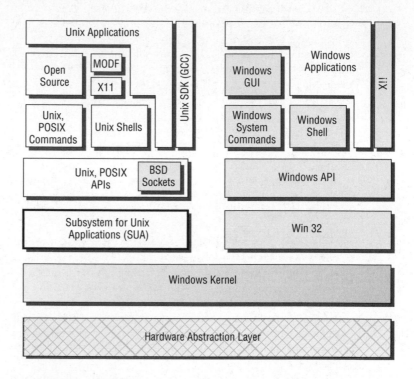

FIGURE 10.4
To add SUA, use the Add Features Wizard. This feature lets Windows run certain Unix applications.

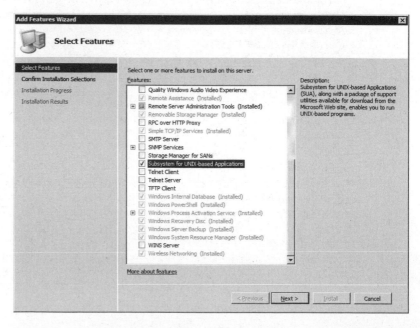

Network Printing

Network printing is a significant part of most enterprise networks. Depending on how a network is set up, print servers are usually the second or third most popular server type, only behind file services and backup servers. Therefore, more efficient use of network printers offers a great opportunity to capture savings and create efficiencies. Windows Server 2008 offers a new print architecture based on .NET and the Windows Presentation Foundation (WPF), a new print management role, as well as numerous new features based on policies, Internet printing, Unix and Macintosh printer support, and other aspects of Windows Server 2008. The following sections highlight some of the new print features.

The XPS Print Architecture

Windows Server 2008 has the new XML Paper Specification (XPS) print architecture, which improves printer and print server performance in addition to a number of new options for remote printing across a network. This new architecture is backward compatible with older Windows applications and printer drivers, making the addition of Windows Server 2008 as a print server seamless. The new features can be added on to Windows Server 2003 R2.

XPS manages the entire document printing process. The XPS print job uses a powerful set of XPSDrv printer drivers and a more efficient print queue; it is modular and self-contained. All Windows-compatible applications can use XPS. These drivers add the capability to perform print job accounting and quota management as part of the driver. You can also include background graphics such as watermarks, as well as other custom features.

To take full advantage of XPS, an application must use .NET Framework 3.0 and WPF. However, even applications that aren't written for .NET can print with this new subsystem. XPS shipped with Vista. The XPSDrv architecture can also be installed on Windows Server 2003 print servers and supports Win32 applications as well as the Point and Print functionality to Windows XP systems.

Windows Server 2008 is the first Microsoft server to support the new XPS print path natively. The XPS document format is used throughout the path from the application to the printer. The XPS-Drv printer driver is a modular system that can be shared by different applications. This means that the print driver components can be reused.

Windows Server 2008 pushes out the print processing to enlightened clients such as Vista, which can greatly improve the performance of Windows Server 2008's Print Services role by distributing the load. This makes XPS much more scalable than the older print subsystem. Another effect of the system is that by rendering pages at the client the returned print job is in a Page Description Language (PDL) and less data is returned. The print spooler on Windows Server 2008 uses RPC for client/server communications. The Windows Server 2008 print spooler requires fewer threads of execution for RPC, which can lead to significant performance improvements in medium and large print systems.

XPS Document is a format that is written based on a fixed layout. It delivers high-quality print output because the new standard isn't based on the older Graphics Device Interface (GDI) routines. Therefore, XPS documents can manipulate graphics in alternate color spaces, and the routines used to generate this format rely on more efficient and new graphics libraries. XPS Document is the Microsoft implementation of the XPS and Open Packaging Conventions (OPC) format and is based on XML and ZIP according to an industry standard. The print standard is open, cross-platform, and royalty-free, and provides higher WYSIWYG output.

Add a Printer

Adding a printer to Windows Server 2008 is similar to the same function in previous versions of Windows:

1. Click Start ➤ Control Panel, and then select the Printers command.

2. Double-click the Add Printer item in the Print Management Console.

   The Add Printer wizard appears, as shown in Figure 10.5.

3. Select either Add a Local Printer or Add a Network, Wireless or Bluetooth Printer and complete the wizard.

Windows Server 2008 supports wireless printing from devices as part of the Web Services on Devices (WSD) initiative, which in turn is part of Windows Rally (see `www.microsoft.com/whdc/rally/rallywsd.mspx`). A Devices Profile for Web Services is a lightweight subset of the web services protocols. It uses core web services to dynamically discover, subscribe, and communicate with wireless devices securely. On Windows Vista the Web Services on Devices API is available to connected devices as a client and server.

FIGURE 10.5
The Print Management Console in Windows Server 2008 has been improved, as has the Add Printer wizard.

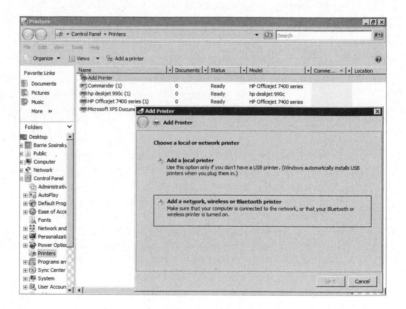

Print Services Role

The Print Services role in Windows Server 2008 allows you to manage both print servers and printers. It creates a central management framework that allows you to create a logical entity called a Print Server and assign, monitor, and control printers across a network using that server. Print Services may not be required for printing to a small number of printers, but you will certainly want to install the Print Services role when you manage many printers.

The Print Services role adds the Print Management Console, which offers a number of new features that weren't part of the previous servers. A feature called Printer Migration allows you to migrate print servers from Windows Server 2003 (and prior Windows operating systems) to Windows Server 2008. You can use the Print Management Console to manage printers connected to Windows 2000 and later systems.

To install the Print Services role:

1. Open the Server Manager, click on the Roles node, and click Add Roles to start the Add Roles Wizard.

2. Enable the Print Services checkbox, then click Next as shown in Figure 10.6.

FIGURE 10.6

You install the Print Services role by using the Add Roles Wizard.

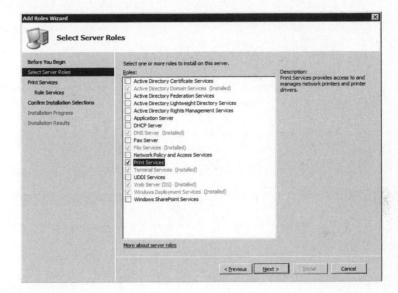

3. Enable or disable LPD Service or Internet Printing, as desired (see Figure 10.7), then click the Next button and complete the wizard.

To finish the installation, you have to reboot your server.

FIGURE 10.7

Print Services include the Print Server, UDP Server, and the Internet Printing features.

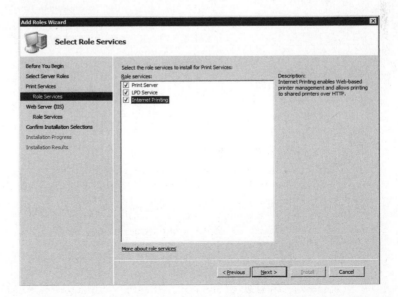

If you are supporting Unix servers or client, install the LPD or Line Printer Daemon service. This print server provides print services for Unix systems.

The Add Printer wizard's Network Printer option contains a feature called Internet Printing that lets a client print to either local or Internet printers using the Internet Printing Protocol (IPP). This feature lets you print from a client's web browser provided that the Internet Information Server is running on Windows Server 2008. Internet Printing requires that you run the following IIS services: HTTP Redirection, ASP, ISAPI Extensions ISAPI Filters, Tracing, Basic Authentication, Windows Authentication, and IIS 6 Metabase Compatibility. If any of these services are missing when you enable the Internet Printing feature, the Add Roles Wizard will prompt you to add them before it will let you install Internet Printing.

Once you've installed Print Services, you can view the Print Management Console in any of the following ways:

♦ Click the Print Services node in the Server Manager

♦ Click Start ➤ All Programs ➤ Administrative Tools, and then select the Print Management command.

♦ Enter **\WINDOWS\PMCSNAP\FNPRINTERS.EXE** at the command line.

In the first instance you view the Print Management Console in the Server Manager, while the other two open Print Management in its own MMC console, as shown in Figure 10.8.

From the Print Management node you can add printers to the local print server or add and remove print servers from the console. Although printers are autodiscovered on your subnet, you can force Print Management to search for printers on other print servers (computers). You can also migrate print servers from one system to another using the Printer Migration Wizard or at the command line using the PRINTBRM command.

FIGURE 10.8
Print Management allows you to manage discovered printers on your subnet or browse other available networks for printers. Using the menu, you can manipulate the print queue, set print policy, and more.

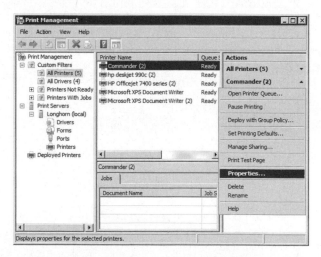

In large enterprises there can be hundreds of printers, so applying a filter allows you to view only the printers you desire. Filters can be dynamic and use conditions that are evaluated when the console refreshes. You can also set a filter to alert an administrator by e-mail when the printer has any status other than Ready. You can list or remove printers from Active Directory by using the List in Directory or Remove from Directory commands in the context menu of a print server.

Printers can be deployed as a result of a Group Policy Object (GPO) stored in Active Directory. To alter this policy click the Printers node of the print server you want to deploy and select the

Deploy with Group Policy command (which appears in Figure 10.8). Group Policy deployments can be specified for users on Windows 2000, and by machine connections for XP systems or later.

Since Print Management controls deployment, it also makes sense that there is a printer driver management feature in the console. To add and remove print drivers, right-click on the Drivers node and select Manage Drivers. That command launches the Add Printer Driver Wizard, which walks you through the process. The wizard allows you to add different drivers as a function of operating systems, as shown in Figure 10.9.

FIGURE 10.9
You can add and manage printer drivers through a couple of similar wizards accessed from the Drivers node of a print server.

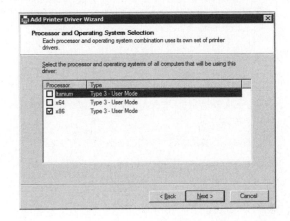

Summary

Windows Server 2008 has its feature set fully expressed when Vista is a client, and increasingly less so as older versions of the Windows operating system are connected to Windows Server 2008. There's been a considerable amount of heterogeneous client support built into Windows servers over the years, with particularly strong support of Unix and Linux systems that tend to play significant roles in many enterprise network deployments. This version of Windows Server adds a new Unix subsystem that allows Windows to run ported applications on top of the Windows kernel. For Apple Macintosh, fewer new features are offered. Services for Macintosh has been abandoned, with TCP/IP and SMB the preferred connection methods. However, a new terminal server RDP client for Macintosh lets those systems connect to Windows Server 2008 and Vista.

In this chapter we looked at the new print architecture based on .NET and the Windows Presentation Foundation. Using a new document format called XPS, Windows can better render print jobs and more efficiently distribute the print processing load. A new Print Management Console lets you create and manage print servers and queues, and provides access to print policy objects in Active Directory.

In Chapter 11 you'll learn about the new features built into Windows Server 2008, such as improved network load balancing, multipath I/O, cluster support, storage management, and policy-based resource management system.

Performance Enhancements

Windows Servers are widely deployed in some very large systems worldwide, and this is an area of technology that Microsoft pays particular attention to. In this chapter you will learn about systems for achieving reliability and high levels of accessibility. Among the topics covered in this chapter is the Windows System Resource Manager (WSRM), which lets you set a policy for how a server's resources are allocated.

Technologies allow enterprises to both scale out their systems as well as scale up. In *scale-out deployments*, more servers are added to improve the ability of the group of servers to manage the load. Network load balancing is a technology that helps manage scale out, and is particularly important in areas such as websites and telecommunications where the processes are I/O bound. In *scale-up deployment*, fewer and more powerful servers are added to improve capacity. Microsoft Cluster Server is an example of scale up.

As servers scale, it becomes increasingly important that more efficiencies be wrung from them. Several of the technologies described in this chapter are meant to help you better allocate your resources. WSRM is a machine settings–based policy engine that allows you to define rules for system loading and works best on a server-by-server basis. Network load balancing allows traffic to be routed to many servers all performing the same task.

One of the most anticipated new features in Windows Server 2008 is server virtualization. Microsoft's new virtualization technology has the potential to completely alter how increasingly powerful servers can be sliced and diced so that they serve more roles and so that each server is efficiently utilized. The new hypervisor architecture puts virtualization into its own layer of the Windows Server operating system, and will allow completely new approaches to server management.

The Windows System Resource Manager

In Chapter 7 I briefly touched on the Windows System Resource Manager (WSRM) as a component of the Server Manager. WSRM is a policy-based console that allows you to assign server resources to applications or services. WSRM originally was a downloadable extra for Windows Server 2003 Enterprise and Datacenter Editions, but has been rolled into Windows Server 2008's console. The program also shipped with those prior additions on the CD for both the 32-bit and 64-bit 2003 versions.

To open the Windows System Resource Manager:

1. Open the Server Manager, expand the Diagnostics node in the tree control, and then click on Windows System Resource Manager.

2. In the Connect to Computer dialog box shown in Figure 11.1, select the computer you wish to manage. You can select the local computer or a remote computer that you have administrative rights on.

If you are connected to a system, you can click the Connect to Computer link in the Actions panel or select that command from the Action menu to connect to and manage a different system.

FIGURE 11.1
WSRM lets you set performance policies on your local server or on remote servers.

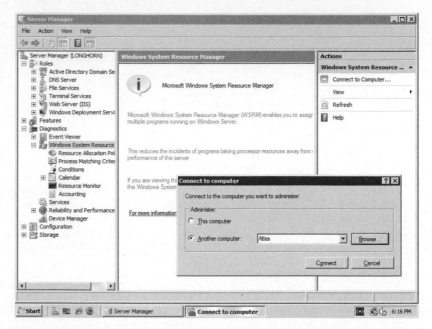

WSRM is used to ensure that, when a server is under significant workload, no application is locked out completely from system resources. When WSRM is enabled, it manages the processor load when Windows Server 2008 is running at 70 percent full utilization or more. For a dual-processor, dual-core processor system the 70 percent loading would require that the total of all four cores be running at 70 percent or more. There are a number of other policies you can set that limit access to system resources, including access to memory by process, user, or session, or as an IIS Application Pool (the collection of applications that define the capabilities of an IIS website—discussed in depth in Chapter 13). WSRM has a calendar scheduling function, as well as the ability to control logging for SQL Server and for Microsoft Cluster Server.

To enforce system policies, WSRM needs to be running, and is therefore configured as a service. You can open the Services console from the Administrative Tools folder, but the ability to stop and start WSRM is also in the Server Manager WSRM console itself.

When WSRM loads, it displays the console shown in Figure 11.2. What you are looking at is a rather inelegant expression of the WSRM Properties dialog box. If you double-click anywhere in the central pane you will open the Management tab of that dialog box, shown in Figure 11.3. The links correspond to the various tabs and their settings in the dialog box, with the exception of the WSRM Help link, which opens the online help system.

The WSRM Properties dialog box provides basic policy control out of the box. The Management tab allows you to change the state from Running to Stopped, enable and disable the Calendar, and set the Resource Allocation policy. Policies that you apply to the Calendar run automatically when their allotted time occurs.

FIGURE 11.2
WSRM allows you to control system resources, set schedules, log events, and set alerts in an MMC console.

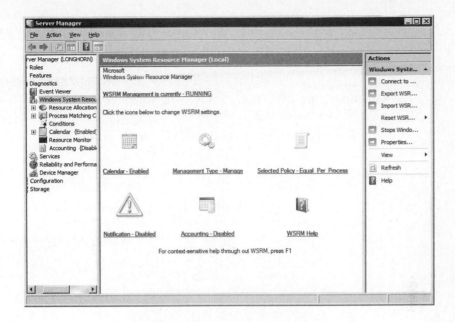

FIGURE 11.3
WSRM Properties dialog box.

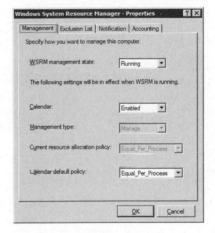

WSRM comes with four built-in resource management policies, as well as some custom policies that you can use to specify which processes or resources are controlled by the policy. The four built-in policies are:

Equal_Per_Process   This policy divides processor usage by the number of processes and assigns that amount of processor capacity to each. Processes necessary to run the server and its services take precedence over these assignments.

Equal_Per_User   Each user is assigned an equal processor capacity.

Equal_Per_Session   Each connected user gets an equal share of processor capacity.

Equal_Per_IISAppPool   Here any resources that can be accessed by IIS are divided by the website equally.

Custom policies include:

Process Matching Criteria (PMC) This allows you to assign applications and services that are managed by a set of rules you define.

You can also assign what is called the processor affinity, where different PMCs can be applied to different processors on the managed server. When processor affinity is used to assign resource allocation, WSRM only considers the processor specified for its loading and does not consider the loading of other processors.

Resource Allocation Policies (RAPs) Here processor and memory are assigned to processes according to the PMC that you specified.

Exclusion Lists You can choose to excluded applications, services, users, and groups from WSRM management.

RAPs can be applied using the Calendar so that they turn on at a single event or at recurring times. You can also specify that certain events—such as a change in the amount of memory or processors or a server going offline—force WSRM to switch to another RAP.

To set a resource policy, do the following:

1. Click on the Resource Allocation Policy node and then click on one of the four built-in policies you wish to enforce.

2. As an example, to set Equal_Per_Process you would click on that node and then select the processes you want to manage from the list of processes that appears in the details pane. Each managed process, as shown in Figure 11.4, can be part of the resource allocation pool, but most often a process match is applied that limits the number of managed processes to just a few. Figure 11.4 shows the Equal_Per_Process pane.

FIGURE 11.4
Resource allocation can be set on a process basis.

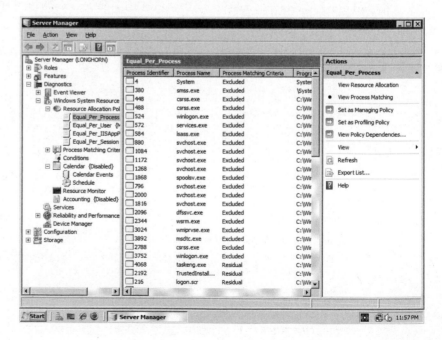

3. Click on View Resource Allocation to view the process matching criteria and the CPU% used by each, or click the View Process Matching link to view each process's consumption of resources by process IDs.

4. Click Set as Managing Policy.

5. Confirm that the calendar can be turned off.

High Availability and Fault Tolerance

High availability (HA) is a measure of the percentage of the time that a system is running. Saying a system has HA implies that a system is up and running nearly all the time. Fault tolerance (FT) means that a system is capable of surviving the loss of one or more critical components while still retaining functionality. The two terms often get confused, but they have entirely different meanings.

Take the Hubble Space Telescope as an example. Hubble shipped with six gyroscopes and needed three for normal observations. As gyroscopes failed, NASA found a way to maintain functionality by taking some of the operational gyros and moving them to stabilize the telescope to keep their observations running. That's the essence of FT—the ability to recover from system failures through redundant systems. It's not HA because there have been times when the telescope has been offline while being upgraded and serviced.

The traditional measurement of availability is referred to as *powers of nines*. If the system must support an enterprise e-mail database such as Exchange, then perhaps 99.5 percent uptime is satisfactory. That would mean that about one day a year the system would be unavailable. For a site like eBay, for example, going down one day would result in tens of millions of dollars in loss, and perhaps a much more substantial loss to their stock price. eBay might require a system with five nines (99.999 percent) uptime, or an outage of five minutes a year. A hospital emergency ward monitoring and responding to critical-care patients might require an even higher reliability. Table 11.1 summarizes reliability rates.

TABLE 11.1: Reliability Rates

POWER OF NINES	UPTIME	DOWNTIME	EXAMPLE OF WHAT'S POSSIBLE	CLASSIFICATION
Two nines	361.60 days/ year	3.65 days	Part can be mailed priority or overnight.	Good availability
Three nines	364.89	9.13 hours	Local service visit or expedited regional visit.	Enterprise application-level availability
Four nines	365.21	53.47 minutes	Spare part on site can be replaced.	High availability
Five nines	365.24	5.34 minutes	You can perform a system reboot.	Very high availability
Six nines	365.246	13.15 seconds	A system can fail over to another system.	Mission critical

Fault tolerance is straightforward: build in redundant parts and a method for failover. Scale-out using a network load-balanced server farm is one approach. To make something highly available, you need rapid failover to redundant systems and highly reliable redundant systems. Microsoft Cluster Server (MSCS) is an example of a Microsoft HA solution.

Since Windows 2000, Microsoft has endeavored to make Windows servers more fault tolerant and more available. Every version has included new plumbing for redundancy, new software to manage server systems for FT and HA, and even new versions of the Windows Server operating system, of which Windows Datacenter Edition (2000 and beyond) and now Windows Server Core (see Chapter 14) are two good examples. In the sections that follow, you will learn about Windows Server 2008's advancements in the area of reliability and highly available services.

Network Performance and the TCP Offload Engine (TOE)

When you analyze the performance of servers connected at high speed to anything else, you observe that the processors spend a lot of time processing the data required to make traffic flow over the network. That's true for server-to-storage communications, and it's why the industry has developed special adapters with application-specific integrated circuits (ASICs) that offload storage networking traffic. A problem occurs in server-to-server situations when servers are part of a cluster or part of a server farm. Large fan-out, which is typical of web applications, turns server network I/O into a performance bottleneck. The processing load to manage web clients is one of the reasons why web applications scale out by using many low- or medium-powered servers in a server farm, rather than scaling up as large database applications.

As Ethernet has gotten faster and moved into Gigabit Ethernet (GigE) and toward the 10 GigE range, it is replacing the proprietary interconnect media that has been used for high-speed data transfer. An example of one of these application technologies is Alacritech's (www.alacritech.com) Scalable Network Accelerators for Windows Servers. Using Microsoft's Network Driver Interface Specification (NDIS) 6.0, which supports the Chimney Offload architecture and is part of Windows Server 2008, some applications can have their network processing run at 90 percent without offload, while with TOE they run at 5–10 percent in some instances.

NOTE Space precludes a fuller explanation of TCP offload, and in particular the Microsoft TCP Chimney feature that NDIS in Windows Server 2008 supports. A white paper on how this technology is supported in Windows is available at http://www.microsoft.com/whdc/device/network/tcp_chimney.mspx.

When looking at high-speed interconnect NICs or high-speed Ethernet performance from an ASIC that is onboard a motherboard, you should check if it has support for TOE. It's somewhat expensive to implement now, but will get considerably cheaper over time.

Network Load Balancing and NLBS

Network load balancing (NLB) is the name given to a service that analyzes network traffic or a protocol such as TCP/IP and routes traffic to one of a group of servers based on a policy. NLB can be implemented in hardware, as is the case for F5 Networks' BIG-IP (www.f5networks.com) director (or router), or it can be a software service such as the one that is part of Windows Server 2008. NLB works best for applications where the dataset being manipulated is small and has a low rate of change, and where the data doesn't have much of a memory footprint. Transactions of this type are called *stateless transactions*.

NLB distributes the workload given to set of systems in order to increase system utilization, efficiency, and scalability. NLB creates a virtual server with a single logical name and a virtual IP address. Nodes in the cluster retain their system name, but requests to the NLB server are routed to a set of virtual IP addresses maintained in a map table on the load balancer. Most NLB servers are multihomed, which means they have two or more network interface cards in them.

When a server fails in a server farm, the load balancer redistributes the load in order to keep the system vital. NLB adds to the fault tolerance of large systems, especially when the resources found on the failed server are replicated on another system or systems. A feature allows Microsoft's Network Load Balancing Services (NLBS) to automatically rejoin the failed node when it detects that the system is back online. This same feature makes it easier to remove a node from service when it needs maintenance.

A load balance service accepts requests, and then maps those requests to services running on member servers. Many different types of NLB servers may be deployed in enterprises, including HTTP, SSL (various types), DNS, FTP, and NNTP, among others. The most common of these are HTTP NLBs, which create the server farms that make modern large websites manageable. Other examples of NLB systems are content caching, compression, firewall traffic, and content analysis. Content control often uses deep-packet inspection technology for bandwidth, spyware, or virus control. When an NLB is used to manage geographically distributed traffic, the service is sometimes referred to as either Global Server Load Balancing (GSLB) or Global Traffic Management.

Windows added their NLBS to Windows Server starting in Windows Server 2000, and has improved the service in every version of Windows Server since then. Figure 11.5 shows the feature being added in the Add Feature wizard.

FIGURE 11.5
Network Load Balancing is a feature that you can add using the Server Manager's Add Features wizard.

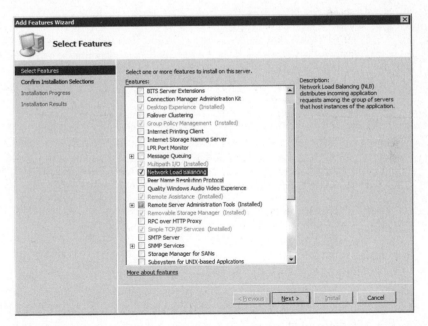

The current version is a TCP/IP load balancer and supports up to 32 nodes. NLBS allows you to control the load-balancing behavior of one or more nodes using a set of IP port management rules. Rules you can enforce include:

◆ Specify rules for a single port or group of ports.

◆ Block network access by type to an IP port of a node.

♦ Enable the Internet Group Management Protocol (IGMP) to manage switch-flooding operations for multicast communications.

♦ Log actions and changes in the Windows Event log.

♦ Direct application traffic to a particular node.

To create a cluster, you will need to supply the following information:

♦ The server's parameters: the name for the NLBS host and IP address

♦ The virtual name for the cluster and its virtual IP address

♦ The traffic rules that you want NLBS to enforce

To create an NLB cluster:

1. Click Start ≻ Administrative Tools, and select the Network Load Balancing Manager command, or enter **NLBMGR** at a command prompt.

   The Network Load Balancing Manager appears, as shown in Figure 11.6.

FIGURE 11.6
The Network Load Balancing Manager lets you set up and manage server farms and clusters.

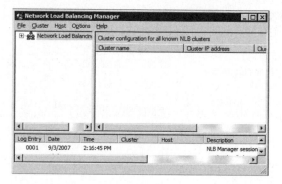

2. Right-click on Network Load Balancing Clusters and select the New Cluster command.

3. Enter the hostname, click the Connect button, and select the network interface you wish to use for NLB in the Interfaces Available for Configuring a New Cluster list box, as shown in Figure 11.7.

4. In the Host Parameters dialog box (Figure 11.8), select a value in the Priority (Unique Host Identifier) pull-down and the IP addresses that are used to communicate with the network (not the cluster).

   The host parameter is a unique ID for each host. As NLBS assigns traffic to the cluster, any traffic that isn't part of a port rule is routed to the lowest-priority host.

5. On the Cluster IP Addresses dialog box (Figure 11.9) click Add, then enter the IP address and subnet mask, specify an Internet name (optional), and set the cluster operations mode; then click the OK button followed by the Next button.

   The same IP values should be used on all Terminal Server nodes, and an Internet name is not required for that type of cluster.

FIGURE 11.7
To create a cluster you must specify the host as well as the network interface used to communicate with the nodes (hosts).

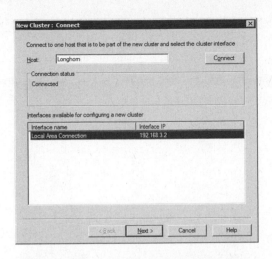

FIGURE 11.8
On this screen, you set host parameters and specify the IP addresses on the host that aren't part of the cluster.

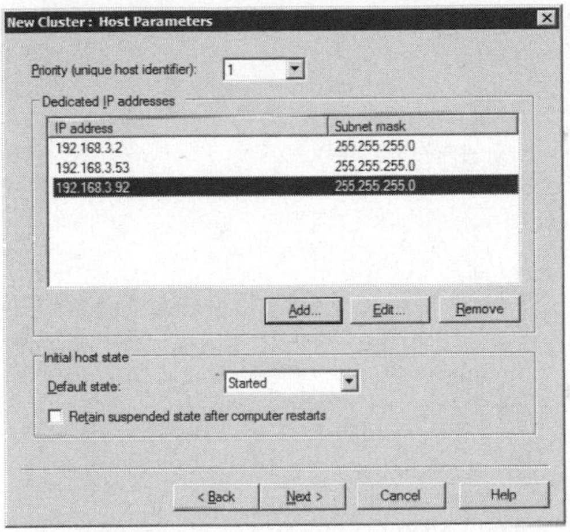

FIGURE 11.9
The addresses added in this step are used by cluster nodes to communicate with the host.

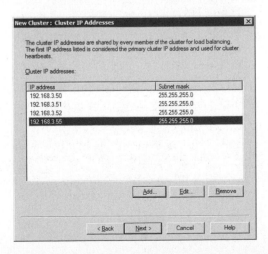

6. On the next screen, enter the cluster parameter information, as shown in Figure 11.10.

Unicast assigns the MAC address to the NIC for a node, allowing the node to participate in the cluster using a virtual IP address.

FIGURE 11.10
The cluster parameters

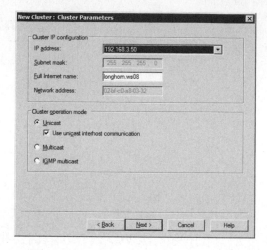

7. On the Port Rules screen, click the Add button to create a rule. In the Add/Edit Port Rule dialog box (Figure 11.11), specify the address(es) traffic will be sent to, the port range, the protocol, and filtering mode options, then click OK to create the rule.

Since specific ports are attached to specific protocols, you have fine control over which traffic goes to which server(s). The Multiple Host option under Filtering Mode specifies that this type of port rule be distributed to the cluster. If you select an Affinity radio button, None applies to the use of the session directory; Single is when you don't use the session directory; and Network uses the first available cluster node.

Take particular note of the Load Weight parameter, which allows you to set a custom loading distribution. The Load Weight value can be between 0 and 100. A value of 0 (or zero) suppresses traffic to the node(s) specified. The Equal Load Distribution parameter is combined with Load Weight to calculate the amount of load that each node will receive. The Equal parameter assigns a load weight of 50. You set the Load from the New Cluster Port Rules dialog box (Figure 11.11) using the Edit button with that node selected.

8. When you have created the rules you desire, click the Finish button to create the cluster.

If you decide to edit rules or add hosts to/remove hosts from the cluster after its creation, you can do so from the context menu of the cluster in the Network Load Balancing Manager. Use the Cluster Properties or the Add Host to the Cluster command.

Many of the changes in NLBS for Windows Server 2008 are internal and are meant to support new features. Microsoft has added full IPv6 support, as well as support for the new NDIS 6.0 network driver and its lightweight filter model. You can load-balance both native IPv6 as well as IPv6 over IPv4 network traffic.

FIGURE 11.11
Port rules can be configured to route traffic to different node(s), set a traffic loading, or fully balance traffic.

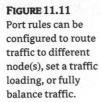
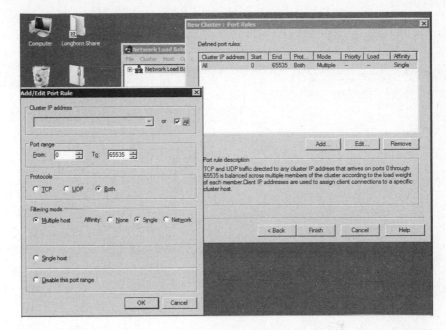

FIGURE 11.11
Port rules can be configured to route traffic to different node(s), set a traffic loading, or fully balance traffic.

Windows Server 2008 consolidates the management of load balancing into the Network Load Balancing Manager. The Network Connections tool that was used to manage NLB clusters in Windows Server 2003 is no longer used. In instances where NLBS detects a denial-of-service (DoS) attack, it can use a callback interface to notify administrators that an attack is in progress so that appropriate modifications can be made. Load-balanced Microsoft ISA Server makes use of this security feature.

There are also several new management features in NLBS 2008. The WMI `MicrosoftNLB` namespace adds both IPv6 and IPv4 address objects, as well as a `NodeSetting` class that stores their properties in `DedicatedIPAddresses` and `DedicatedNetMasks` objects. These settings support a new feature that allows NLBS to assign multiple IP addresses to a client node of the server.

Fail-over Clusters

Although Microsoft calls network load-balanced servers "clusters," most people think of Microsoft Cluster Server (MSCS) when they think of clusters. In Windows Server 2008 the term "server cluster" has been supplanted by the term "fail-over cluster," which is at least descriptive if not entirely correct. Figure 11.12 shows how a two-node fail-over cluster operates. The following network connections are operating here:

- A heartbeat connection over a fast IP or Virtual Interconnect Architecture (VIA) network to detect whether a node is online and to initiate fail-over when a heartbeat isn't detected.

- A high-speed storage connection to the quorum, or witness, disk (which I'll explain in a moment), as well as to shared storage that clients connect to. If shared storage is on a storage area network (SAN), that storage must be exclusively owned and managed by the cluster.

- A redundant set (two or more) of Ethernet connections to clients and the management console.

FIGURE 11.12
Fail-over in a two-node cluster

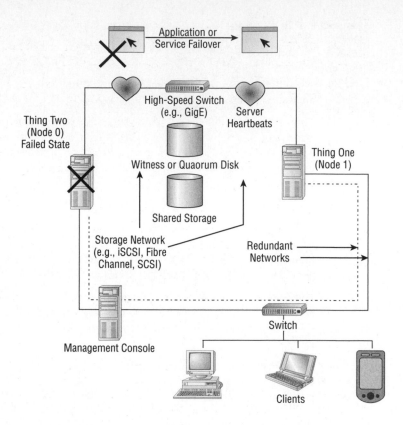

NOTE When a SAN is used by the cluster with MSCS and when using SCSI as the interconnect protocol, the changes in Windows Server 2008 require that SCSI conform to the SCSI Primary Commands-3 (SPC-3) standard and support persistent reservations. Additionally, the storage miniport driver needs to work with the Microsoft Storport storage driver.

NOTE More importantly, the cluster's storage must be isolated from other servers either by zoning or logical unit number (LUN) masking. LUNs map physical disks and RAID sets as volumes to an alias that abstracts the physical location of storage to a client. Multiple volumes can be defined in a LUN. A LUN is masked from other servers by security access settings at the domain or server level.

MSCS also requires identical servers in the cluster. The servers must have the same processor and be the same brand, model, and version so that all drivers are matched.

The quorum disk (referred to now as a "witness disk" in Microsoft documentation) contains the cluster configuration database. In a two-node cluster, the configuration of the quorum disk is Node and Disk Majority, as is the case for any even node cluster (cluster with $2x$ members, where $x >= 1$). This configuration maintains the cluster configuration database on both nodes as well as the quorum and will continue to operate the cluster as long as two out of the three databases are available. Both the quorum disk and the shared storage disk must be configured as basic disks using NTFS.

Several significant changes have been made to fail-over clusters in this server upgrade:

◆ The configuration interface has been simplified, as has the process for creating a fail-over cluster. The Create Cluster wizard is scriptable and can be automated.

◆ A validation system is included that determines a server's condition and whether storage and networking configuration has been added.

Three sets of diagnostic tests—System Configuration, Network, and Storage—are provided. The System Configuration test verifies that a cluster server is running a compatible operating system and service pack. The Network test checks for the existence of two working network interfaces, which define the redundant pair of Ethernet subnets. The Storage test measures the response to SCSI commands, in addition to testing a simulated set of cluster operations.

◆ A configurable quorum is included that controls the heartbeat and fail-over of the cluster.

A quorum in this new version is no longer the single point of failure. In previous versions, the cluster used either the quorum resource model or the majority node set model, or a combination of the two. Now when a quorum disk isn't detected by the cluster, the cluster can carry on as long as the cluster configuration database on both nodes is accessible.

◆ Better methods are featured for storage communications, including connections via SCSI (SAS), Fibre Channel, and iSCSI. The new SCSI connections eschews the use of SCSI bus resets, retaining disk connections at all times. Disk maintenance can now be done on connected disks as well.

◆ IPv6 has been integrated, both from node to node in the cluster as well as from node to clients.

◆ DNS only addressing is included, eliminating the need to account for NetBIOS and WINS. This makes it easier to route SMB traffic to storage.

◆ Subnet restrictions have been relaxed; it is now possible to locate cluster nodes on different IP subnets. This makes it much easier to create clusters that span large distances or to work with different units of an enterprise.

MSCS is more powerfully controlled by WMI or by using command-line or PowerShell commands. Among the diagnostics you can apply to fail-over servers for troubleshooting are Event Tracing for Windows.

To create a fail-over cluster:

1. On node 1 of the cluster you are creating, open the Server Manager and in the Features Summary section, click the Add Features link.

2. In the Add Features wizard, enable the Failover Clustering feature, then click the Install button.

3. Go to node 2 and repeat Steps 1 and 2 so that both nodes now have the Failover Clustering feature installed and running on them.

4. Click Start ➢ Administrative Tools ➢ Failover Clusters Management to open the utility shown in Figure 11.13.

FIGURE 11.13
Microsoft's new validation utility will determine if the nodes that you want to use in your cluster have the necessary components.

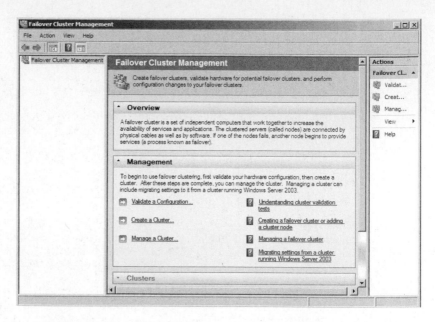

5. Click on Failover Cluster Management in the tree node (left) to highlight it, then click the Validate a Configuration link in the Management section of the center pane.

   The Validate a Configuration wizard appears, walking you through the steps needed to test server requirements. A summary page appears when the wizard is complete.

6. On the Summary page, either click View Report or click the Finish button.

   To view the configuration report after the wizard closes, go to: %SystemRoot\Cluster\ Reports\Validation Report date and time.html.

7. After the validation is complete, with the Failover Cluster Management node selected click Create a Cluster in the Management section of the center pane.

8. Enter the following information into the wizard: the cluster servers, the logical name (network) of the cluster, and the address assignment.

9. On the Summary page, either click View Report or close the wizard.

With the fail-over cluster established, you will need to assign shared storage to the cluster, assign services that will run on the cluster, turn those services on, and make a share available to clients. Windows Server 2008 continues this process using the High Availability wizard.

To configure a two-node server fail-over cluster's services and storage:

1. Click Start ➤ Administrative Tools ➤ Failover Cluster Management ➤ Manage a Cluster. The High Availability wizard appears.

2. If the cluster is missing, right-click on Failover Cluster Management, click Manage a Cluster, and then highlight the cluster you intend to modify.

3. Open the cluster node, and for servers that will not use IP networking to access storage, open the Networks node, right-click on the network, and select the Properties command.

4. Enable the option Do Not Allow Cluster to Use This Network; then click OK.

5. Highlight Services and Applications; then in the Actions pane, click on the Configure a Service or Application link.

The Select Service or Application screen appears, as shown in Figure 11.14.

FIGURE 11.14
The High Availability wizard lets you add a range of services to your cluster. You can select one or more of these services.

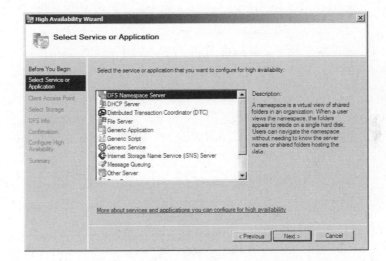

6. To create a highly available file server, select the File Server service, then click Next.

7. Give the clustered file server its network name and addressing, and assign the storage volumes to the cluster file server.

8. After the wizard completes, the Summary page offers you a report of the wizard's actions using the View Report feature. To close the wizard, click Finish.

You can then add shared storage using the Create a Shared Folder wizard that was described in detail in Chapter 6. Once everything is in place, you should test that fail-over works the way you expect it to.

To manually create a fail-over:

1. Right-click on the clustered file server and then select the Move This Service or Application to Another Node command.

2. Click on one of the other nodes, and when prompted for confirmation, click the Yes button.

The service should change status in the Management (center) pane.

Virtualization and Scaling

In Chapter 1, in the section "Virtualization and the Hypervisor" you learned about the Viridian project and the resulting Microsoft server virtualization technologies from an architectural perspective. Some of the promised virtualization technologies that are part of Windows Server 2008's internal architecture are enabled by the hypervisor add-on to Windows Server 2008--now branded as Hyper-V. Hyper-V adds a modest additional cost to Windows Server 2008, and provides the enablement of many of the technologies described in the sections that follow.

Virtualization is an important area to enterprises because it allows organizations to:

◆ Maximize the usage of their servers

◆ Test and isolate applications in virtual machines or "sandboxes"

◆ Consolidate different servers onto a single physical system

◆ Eliminate conflicts and improve application compatibility

◆ Fail over in order to preserve business continuity

◆ Provide a means to run legacy applications

All of these reasons have made virtualization an increasingly important area of technology for processing, storage, network assets, and just about any other hardware component that is expensive and in demand. From Microsoft's standpoint Windows Terminal Server is a virtualization of presentation (display) technology, Virtual PC, and Virtual Server virutalize hardware (systems), and SoftGrid (now Microsoft Application Virtualization is virtualized applications in their own runtime.

Virtual PC and Virtual Server

Single-processor CPUs have almost entirely been replaced in server systems by multicore CPUs for several good reasons. As clock speeds have gone up and transistor and interconnect line sizes have diminished, it has become more efficient to scale by packaging more processing units into the same-sized package. The trend presages an era of super-parallel computing that will surely arrive. Since it will take a complete rewrite of our software to fully leverage this hardware trend, it may take a full decade for this to be fully realized. The first place to look for advances in multiprocessor computing is the operating system, and server virtualization is an important step on this road.

Microsoft entered the virtualization software space when they purchased Connectix's Virtual PC products and hired the software team that managed it. Microsoft Virtual PC was introduced in 2006 as a free product running on Windows, while discontinuing support for the Macintosh version (which would have required a development effort in order to port to the new Intel-based Macs that were being rolled out at the time). The thinking makes sense as you can run Windows on Intel Macs and use Virtual PC there. Virtual PC 2007 emulates PC hardware platform with the following characteristics:

◆ Pentium 4 32-bit processor

◆ Intel 440BX chip set

◆ SVGA VESA graphics card with up to 16MB of VRAM

◆ AMI BIOS

◆ SoundBlaster16

◆ DEC 21041/21140 Ethernet NIC

Microsoft Virtual Server 2007 will only use emulation for guest operating systems that don't recognize the new hypervisor or its drivers.

NOTE You can download Microsoft Virtual PC 2007 by going to http://www.microsoft.com/ windows/products/winfamily/virtualpc/default.mspx. It provides a means to test products in a virtual environment. You can find Microsoft Virtual Server 2005's home page at http://www.microsoft.com/windowsserversystem/virtualserver/default.aspx.

Microsoft Virtual Server is the server version of Virtual PC, and was part of Microsoft's Connectix acquisition. The first version of Virtual Server to appear was Virtual Server Enterprise Edition (which is freely downloadable and runs on XP and Windows Server 2003). The second version that appeared was Virtual Server 2005, which is currently at version R2 SP1 and can run on either the Intel VT or AMD Virtualization platforms. Virtual Server R2 SP1 is also a free download from http://www.microsoft.com/technet/virtualserver/software/default.mspx.

In the 2005 R2 SP1 release, Microsoft added virtual server clustering, 64-bit support, iSCSI clustering for guest-to-guest virtual operating systems (including Linux) across physical systems, better hyperthreading, and PXE boot support. For 64-bit servers, Virtual Server can run more than 64 virtual machines (VMs), so the limit of 32 VMs applies to 32-bit servers only. Virtual Server management tools have been based on either an IIS interface or using the Windows VMRCplus client tool, whereas the tool included with Windows Server 2008 is an MMC snap-in that is part of the Server Manager.

Virtual Server 2007

Microsoft's Windows Server 2008 virtualization feature rolls Virtual Server into Windows Server 2008 as a server role. I trelies on the Hyper-V technology to isolate hardware resources from the operating systems that run above it. A hypervisor that runs directly on top of hardware is referred to as a Type 1, or native, virtual machine. When the hypervisor runs on top of the operating system kernel (as was described briefly in Chapter 1), it is referred to as a Type 2, or hosted, virtual machine.

The hypervisor in a Type 1 Virtual Machine Manager (VMM) can either be:

◆ Monolithic, or "fat," and include hardware drivers in the hypervisor itself. This architecture is faster than the thin hypervisor, but requires that Microsoft create a new driver model for the operating system. It is judged to be somewhat less secure than a thin model because any OS can get access to devices.

◆ Microkernel, or "thin," with the drivers moved into each of the supported operating systems. The thin model uses the existing driver model and is more secure because only the parent has access to device management, but it is a little slower. Figure 1.9 in Chapter 1 shows a depiction of this model, which is reproduced in part in Figure 11.15.

Figure 11.15 shows the difference between these two structures. Microsoft has chosen a microkernel hypervisor with a parent OS (Windows Server 2008) containing a virtualization stack and guest or child operating systems running in their own separate virtual machine. That's the model depicted on the right side of Figure 11.15.

In the thin hypervisor model the parent (or root) partition manages the resources that are assigned to each of the guest operating systems, allowing the management tools running in the parent to assign memory, disk resources, and other hardware resources to each child OS. Each guest OS runs in its own address space and is assigned one or more virtual processors, but the size of those resources is managed by the parent OS. System functions such as managing devices through PnP are also performed by the virtualization stack in the parent virtual machine. You can think of the virtualization stack as an extension of the hypervisor; the stack manages and creates the child partitions, as well as exposing the API that allows management applications to access the virtual machinery.

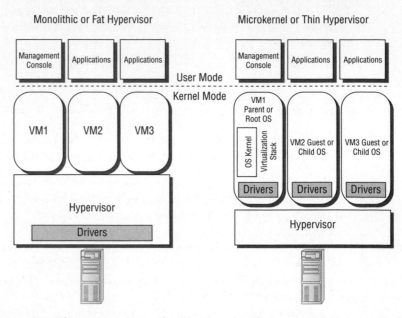

FIGURE 11.15
Two different models of a Type 1 VMM

Hypervisors have long been the pride and joy of hackers, along with rootkits. A hypervisor loads before the operating system does and runs in the Ring 1 part of a processor where its processes aren't part of any of the mapped address spaces. Rootkits are programs that load before the operating system and modify system security of a system module so that they can run in the background without being detected. In order to run in Ring 1, the hypervisor relies on hardware routines built into the processor that manage the interrupts (so that the hypervisor can communicate with the processor) and that manage the security of the communications. In Intel VT processors, the technology is called Execute Disable (XD), and in AMD-V processors the technology is referred to as No Execute (NX).

The parent partition in Windows Server 2008 contains both the Longhorn kernel and the new Virtual Service Provider (VSP). Windows Server 2008 will be installed in the Windows Server 2008 server core on 64-bit systems only. There are advantages to running Server Core in that it has a smaller footprint and attack surface. Indeed, Microsoft expects that Virtual Server 2007 will be one of the main uses for Server Core and recommends that you install this role on any server core that you deploy.

The VSP also makes some new capabilities available to Virtual Server 2007 that weren't possible in previous versions. Whereas Virtual PC and Virtual Server 2005 both used emulation to create the specifications for a virtual machine, the VSP runs a set of worker processes within the parent VMM's virtualization stack for each of the virtual machines. The kernel of the parent partition communicates with virtual machines through the VMBus, which is a set of specialized drivers that can route requests from guests to the parent and data from the parent to the guest.

Guest operating systems running in a VMM may or may not be aware that they are running on top of a hypervisor. When they are aware, they are called "enlightened guests" and can use the VMM interface to communicate with the parent OS. Windows Server 2008 is an enlightened guest and can run a Virtual Service client for the VSP. Enlightened guests, as you may remember from Chapter 10, are the more recent versions of client operating systems that implement advanced features of the client/server architecture and services.

Windows Vista is aware of the drivers in use by the VMM and is "partially enlightened." Other operating systems are unaware of the hypervisor and its drivers and require emulation in order to run. Microsoft, in partnership with XenSource, is building a VSC/VSP coupling that should allow Linux to run as an enlightened client when the next version of Windows Server Virtualization (WSV) ships.

With WSV's feature set still being decided, here are the features that are slated to be part of the initial release:

◆ Only a 64-bit version of Windows Virtual Server 2008 will be released.

◆ 64-bit virtual machines. By contrast, Virtual Server 2005 R2 didn't run on 64-bit OSs.

◆ Virtual machines can have over 32GB of memory assigned to them.

◆ Support for NAT, policy-based resource management, snapshots, and Shadow Copy Service,

◆ Cluster support allowing virtual machines to be installed on a cluster as if it was a single system.

◆ The Virtualization Management Console is an MMC snap-in, instead of the Web UI used in VS 2005 R2. This is role in Windows Server 2008, displayed in the Server Manager and available as an individual utility in the Administrative Tools folder.

◆ System Center Virtual Machine Manager (SCVMM) is Microsoft's enterprise-class virtualization management tool for Active Directory–based management of a large number of virtual servers. It is slated to ship in the third quarter of 2008. The beta contains physical-to-virtual (P2V) and virtual-to-physical (V2P) migrations. Users can create virtual machines through self-service provisioning. SCVMM will be sold as a stand-alone program, as well as a component of System Center. Since System Center is used by SMS and MOM virtualization will be a feature you can manage from these systems.

◆ Licensing will be unchanged, allowing one licensed instance of Windows Server 2007 Enterprise Edition to host four guest operating systems on Windows Server 2008. Hosting more than four guest OSs on Enterprise Edition requires additional licenses. Each license for Volume Snapshot Service (VSS) on Datacenter Edition allows the parent OS to run an unlimited number of guest OSs.

Microsoft has left the following planned features for its virtual machine technology out of its first release of Windows Server 2008:

◆ Hot addition of memory, processors, and NICs

◆ Live migration of virtual machines between physical servers

◆ Support for a maximum of 16 processor cores only (for example, a server with four quad or eight dual-core processors)

Other unsupported features include clustering of virtual machines, clustering of the physical server, compacting of virtual hard disks, and the backup of guest operating systems using VSS. A guest operating system (Windows Server 2003 and Windows Server 2008) that can install the Integration Services can perform volume backups. Other limitations include the restriction that a domain server cannot be installed on a guest OS that is installed on a virtual machine running on a host system that is a domain controller.

Perhaps the best-positioned software in the virtualization area at the moment is VMware (http://www.vmware.com). VMware Server has many of the features that Microsoft was forced to cut, including the ability to move virtual machines from one physical server to another and to create a snapshot of the virtual machine that you can roll back to—not to mention their very significant VMotion technology, which allows the transfer of virtual machines from server to server while that server is running so that there is no downtime involved.

It's clear that Microsoft won't overtake VMware before the end of 2009, but future versions of Microsoft's technology might close the gap. To compete with Microsoft's free download offer, VMware also offers a free download of its server product (`http://www.vmware.com/download/server/`).

VMware has published a white paper claiming that "Microsoft does not have key virtual infrastructure capabilities (like VMotion), and they are making those either illegal or expensive for customers; Microsoft doesn't have virtual desktop offerings, so they are denying it to customers; and Microsoft is moving to control this new layer that sits on the hardware by forcing their specifications and APIs on the industry." Included in this document are explanations with supporting details of some of these specific areas, which you can read at `http://www.vmware.com/solutions/whitepapers/msoft_licensing_wp.html`. That white paper generated some interesting trade press, as well as a response (`http://blogs.technet.com/windowsserver/archive/2007/02/25/Where-we_2700_re-headed-with-virtualization.aspx`) from Mike Neil, general manager of Microsoft's virtualization strategy. This is clearly going to be a very interesting area of technology to watch over the next couple of years.

Windows Server Virtualization

Microsoft included a subset of the Virtual Server technology in Windows Server 2008 starting with the RC0 release in the beta cycle. To install this technology, which is available on the 64-bit version of Windows Server 2008 only, you need to have a processor with virtualization support. On Intel Xeon processors, that support is labeled VT; on AMD Opteron processors, that technology is branded as Pacifica. Both of these processor families require that you turn on virtualization in the server BIOS.

RC0 required that two system patches be installed from the `percentWinDir percent/WSV` directory. With those patches applied, Windows Server Virtualization (WSV) is installed as a role inside the Server Manager; the first screen in the Add Roles wizard for Server Virtualization is shown in Figure 11.16.

FIGURE 11.16
Windows Server Virtualization is a role that must be installed using the Add Roles wizard.

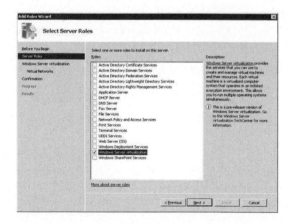

The Add Roles wizard requires the following steps for Windows Server Virtualization installation:

1. Start the Add Roles wizard.

2. Fill out the information and confirmation page shown in Figure 11.16, and click Next.

3. Select your virtual network interfaces, as shown in Figure 11.17, and click Next.

FIGURE 11.17
A virtual server must have an assigned virtual network interface, which is defined in the Add Roles wizard.

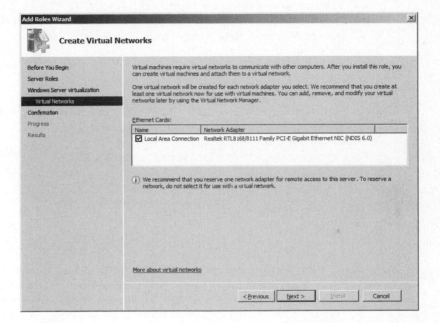

4. Click Yes when the wizard asks you to confirm. The next screen displays the progress of the installation.

5. The final screen of the wizard asks you to restart the server in order to complete the role installation.

With the role installed, the next step is to create a virtual machine inside Windows Server 2008:

1. Open the Server Manager, click on the Windows Server Virtualization node, and then click on the Virtualization Services node.

2. Click the Connect to Server link in the Actions pane, or select that command from the Actions menu.

3. In the Select Computer dialog box (see Figure 11.18), specify whether you want to connect to the local computer or to another computer on your network.

FIGURE 11.18
You can connect to a
local server or to a
remote server and
create your virtual
machine in that
location.

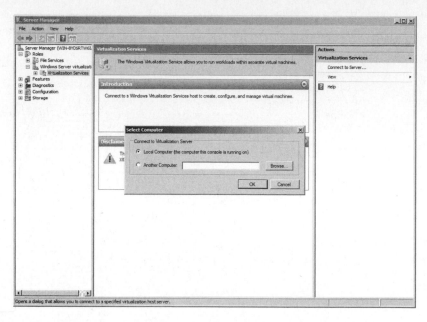

4. Click the New link in the Actions pane and select the Virtual Machine command to launch the New Virtual Machine Wizard.

5. After displaying an informational Before You Begin screen and the Name and Location screen, the wizard will prompt you for the amount of system memory you wish to allocate to the virtual machine, as shown in Figure 11.19. Enter the amount and then click Next.

FIGURE 11.19
On the Memory screen
of the New Virtual
Machine Wizard,
enter the amount of
memory you will allo-
cate to the new VM.

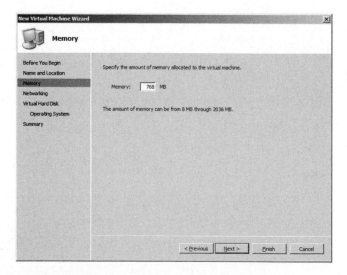

6. Select the network interface on the Networking screen; then click Next.

7. On the Virtual Hard Disk Name and Location screen, click the Create a New Virtual Hard Disk radio button (the default); then enter a name, location, and size for the hard drive.

You can also specify an existing hard drive, or attach the hard drive to the virtual machine after you create it using the other two radio buttons, as shown in Figure 11.20.

FIGURE 11.20

This screen lets you create or specify disk storage for your virtual machine.

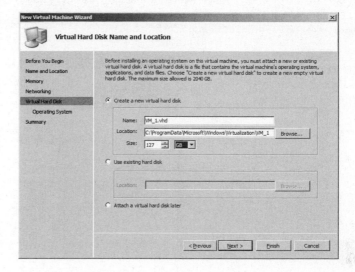

8. On the Operating System page, specify the location of the guest operating system's installation files. You can also choose to install the guest operating system after you create the virtual machine.

9. The Summary page displays the progress of the installation (see Figure 11.21), showing the creation of the DVD drive (at this point in the installer).

10. Click the Finish button when the installation is complete to close the wizard.

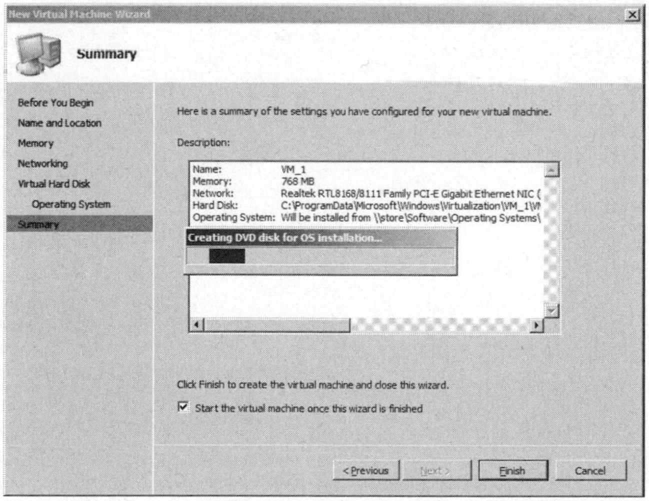

FIGURE 11.21

The Summary page of the New Virtual Machine Wizard

At this point you have a completely configured virtual machine and you've installed a guest operating system. You will want to configure the virtual machine settings using the Settings command for that virtual machine in the Server Manager. Figure 11.22 shows the specification of the boot order; Figure 11.23 shows the selection of the number of processors that the virtual machine can use, with a limit of 8.

FIGURE 11.22
The boot order for a virtual machine is set in the Settings dialog box.

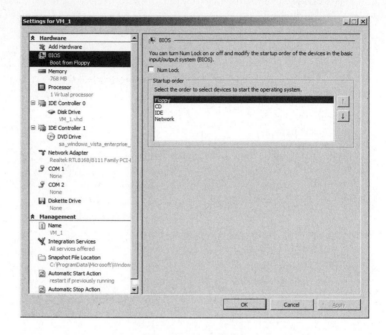

FIGURE 11.23
Settings for a multi-core processor virtual machine.

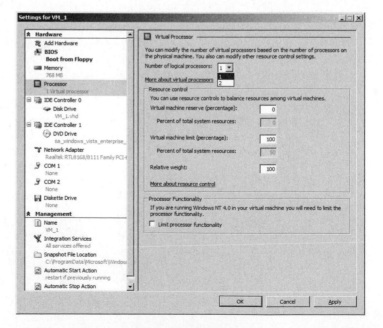

While in the Settings dialog box check that your Network Adapter setting is correct. Also, if you require a certain MAC address, enter it in the Static Address Settings boxes. Virtual machines let you create a user-definable MAC address, or you can use a dynamic or machine-assigned MAC address (the default).

The Windows Virtual Machine Integration Service runs a set of integrations services such as operating system shutdown, time synchronization, data exchange, a heartbeat service, as well as backup through the VSS service. You can turn any or all of them off in the Integration Services settings shown in Figure 11.24. In the management section, you can also control what happens when the virtualization service either starts up or stops in terms of what actions are to be taken.

FIGURE 11.24

Integration Services are a set of virtual machine services that the guest operating system can run; you can turn these services on or off.

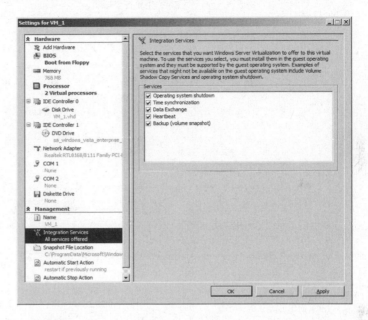

Automatic shutdown ensures that the guest OS is stopped when the host system has to shut down or restart. The startup options are used when the host system starts up again to determine if the virtual machine should be restarted. For a Vista client, you can hibernate the guest OS when the server shuts down or terminate the session.

A guest system can be installed either from a DVD/CD installation disc, from an ISO image file, or from a network installation share. Once the operating system is installed, you will want to install the Virtualization Guest Components in order to have the services described here run in the guest operating system. Only Windows Server 2008 or Windows Server 2003 will run the Integration Services. Although you can install Vista, that guest operating system does not provide Integration Services.

Dynamic Systems Initiative

Before we leave the topic of performance and scaling, it is worth mentioning that Microsoft has started a business initiative for virtualization technologies called the Dynamic Systems Initiative (DSI). Initiatives are what Microsoft does when it wants to impact a broad area of technologies by acquiring partners. An example of a previous effort along these lines was Microsoft's BizTalk's initiative, which supported industry-oriented XML schema for Electronic Data Interchange (EDI). Microsoft started their BizTalk initiative in 2000.

Dynamic Systems Initiative (`http://www.microsoft.com/business/dsi/default.mspx`) is Microsoft's vision of using applications that can be self-managed to dynamically respond to current workloads. For example, under DSI a set of web servers (physical and virtual) would respond to increased workload by adding more resources to existing servers, or by deploying additional virtual servers when and where they were needed—Microsoft refers to this as *infrastructure optimization*. The three elements of Microsoft's strategy are design for operations, knowledge driven management, and virtualized infrastructure.

DSI as it stands now consists of the following:

◆ Partners creating applications using Visual Studio and the .NET Framework

◆ Deployment of applications on Vista and Windows Server 2008

◆ Virtualization with Virtual PC and Server

◆ Management with the System Center (`http://www.microsoft.com/systemcenter/`) products, including MOM, Configuration Manager, Capacity Manager, Reporting Manager, and SoftGrid Service Desk (which was recently acquired by Microsoft—to read about SoftGrid Application Virtualization products go to `http://www.microsoft.com/systemcenter/softgrid/default.mspx`).

◆ The Forefront security and policy automation tool (`http://www.microsoft.com/forefront/default.mspx`)

◆ Microsoft Identity Lifecycle Manager

If DSI holds true to form, then its website will be a good place to go to investigate the current state of Microsoft's virtualization portfolio, as well as a resource center for the products mentioned in this list. At the moment the white paper that you can access from the site is more a marketing manifesto than a technological realization.

Summary

In this chapter you learned about Microsoft's enterprise offerings for large management server solutions. These offerings include new software, new methods for connecting systems, as well as a number of significant changes to the Windows operating system that allow you to create virtual servers.

In the next chapter you will learn about the changes in another enterprise category: Windows Terminal Server. Windows Server 2008 introduces a number of significant improvements to Terminal Server. Microsoft has delivered a new terminal client, and now Terminal Server sessions run on a client desktop as if they were local on the system. With a new Terminal Server Gateway, web delivery of applications, and a new tunneling mechanism, Microsoft has made it easier to connect to a Terminal Server, as well as safer too.

Chapter 12

Terminal Server

Windows Terminal Server is one of the most popular server configurations that Microsoft offers, and it is widely deployed in the enterprise. With such a large installed base, this role of Windows Server 2008 received a lot of development in this version. Many new features in Terminal Server should appeal to current users, and companies and administrators seeking to minimize their hardware and administration costs will find there's much to recommend it.

Core services have been reworked, the Remote Desktop Protocol (which transports client/server I/O) has been revised, and the Vista "User Experience" has been extended to this platform (if you have Vista as a client). The most notable new features in Terminal Server relate to its use as an application platform. Remote applications now run as if they were running locally on a client's system—something that Microsoft calls TS RemoteApp. Gone is the confusing desktop within a desktop. TS Web Access, a "role service" of Terminal Server, allows users to launch a remote application from a web page. It's easier to connect to Terminal Server, security has been improved, and with TS Gateway, clients can connect through a firewall to applications on a LAN.

It behooves you to pay attention to the way that Windows Terminal Server can serve up remote applications, because this is the new model of applications delivered as a service that Microsoft hopes will replace current versions of Microsoft Office and many other of its current applications. Here application usage is money, probably Microsoft will use a model more akin to your cellular phone companies than a simple pay-as-you-go model.

In the coming era of massive parallel computing, Terminal Server may be a technology that has seen its peak. The addition of processor virtualization support into multicore CPUs means that future servers may run instances of the Windows operating system isolated into a single core. However, terminal servers and their architecture will probably bridge the old technology of the past 20 years to the technology of the future. So there likely are ten more good years left in the terminal server game. Truly, Windows Terminal Server is a product with one foot in the future and one foot in the past.

Footprints of the Past

Terminal servers go back to the time of the first mainframes when keyboards and monitors were first introduced as I/O devices. A terminal, or "dumb terminal" as they were first called, contained little or no processing. Terminals were connected to a mainframe where processing was done by a communications hardware and software protocol that gave the terminal a node or address that data could be sent to and taken from. The bi-directional communications path was called the channel.

The first large-scale implementation of terminals was in the American Airline SABRE airline reservation system introduced in 1960. That system was upgraded to 12 IBM System/360 mainframes in 1972, which supported video terminals (VTs) all over the United States. The first monochrome terminals were green screens, and they appeared in the late 1960s. Green VTs worked using the green

P1 phosphor. The most famous green screen was the one that shipped with the original IBM PC (model 5150), the CTR (model 5151). Green screens or the P3 amber phosphor screens that replaced them stayed in use until the mid-1980s. You can still find graybeards like myself who refer to "green screen" applications when they talk about terminal clients.

Green screens have become legendary. When you see the green-ghosted images of the mainframe source code in the *Matrix* film trilogy, they want you to connect that image to a powerful controlling mainframe. The green ghosting was screen afterglow, which if left static long enough turned into permanently burned-in images. There were many monitors with C:\> (the DOS C prompt) or with a burned-in rectangular box (the original cursor) found in those days, and although they're no longer necessary all of the screen savers of today were solutions to that problem long ago.

VTs were often connected by RS-232 serial devices, the original connection that modems used. Some motherboards still ship with RS-232, but the standard is rapidly being abandoned—supplanted mostly by Ethernet. Among the software transport protocols that RS-232 can now support is TCP/IP, Telnet, SSH, or other Local Area Transport (LAT) protocols. All of the original VT applications were low-bandwidth, character-based systems. Terminal services on Unix became very popular; the X Window System developed at MIT in 1984 was the latest graphical generation of the technology.

In the 1970s and 80s, terminal technology migrated down onto minicomputers, which were actually midrange systems that were physically smaller but very powerful. DEC's PDP and VAX series, Data General's Nova, Prime Computer's Prime 50 series, HP's HP3000, and IBM's midrange computers were systems of this type. It was natural, then, that as IBM developed their next-generation graphical operating system, OS/2, the idea of terminal servers would be quite appealing. Therefore, when OS/2 was under development at IBM some of the developers wanted IBM to build that OS as multiuser system. Since IBM thought that this might cannibalize their sales in their midrange line, the company was naturally reluctant to do so.

The Citrix Contribution

Windows terminal services can trace their roots to IBM OS/2 developer Ed Iacobucci starting up a company called Citrus, which was later renamed Citrix (Citrus + Unix). In 1989, Citrix released MULTIUSER, based on OS/2 code licensed from Microsoft. That product didn't sell, which led the company to adapt the technology to support MS-DOS and Windows 3.1. In 1993 Citrix released WinView, which became popular. When the company released WinFrame in 1995 (a stand-alone product that ran on Windows NT 3.51), Citrix had a hit on their hands and 500,000 licenses sold.

Here's where the story gets a little cloudy. In 1997 Microsoft realized that WinFrame was competing very successfully with the Windows NT Server operating system and taking sales away from Microsoft. Microsoft withdrew their NT license from Citrix and began to create their own version of WinFrame. The Microsoft teams working in Redmond and France (Microsoft acquired Prologue Software) found that Windows NT 4.0's incorporation of the graphics API into the kernel limited the ability of their terminal server to five concurrent users, at a time when Citrix WinFrame could support as many as 200 concurrent users. Microsoft found that they were up against Citrix's session space patent, which shared kernel memory and isolated user sessions in a manner that mimicked how user mode processes work.

So, Microsoft and Citrix cut a deal. Iacobucci and the Citrix lawyers flew to Redmond and spent a month there hammering out a cross-licensing agreement. Microsoft gave Citrix the rights to license Windows Server source code and Citrix gave Microsoft the rights to use the session space technology created by John Richardson at Citrix. Additional aspects of the original five-year agreement have shaped Citrix since then and defined what Windows Terminal Server could be. Citrix agreed not to ship a Windows server to Windows client terminal server product, but retained the enterprise-level terminal services that would support non-Microsoft clients. Microsoft agreed to not to compete with Citrix in non-Windows application delivery. You can read about the original agreement on Microsoft PressPass at

```
http://www.microsoft.com/presspass/press/1997/may97/hydrapr.mspx
```

After the agreement Citrix continued to use their proprietary Independent Computing Architecture (ICA) transport protocol, while Microsoft products went on to acquire a company called T.share and develop their product into the RDP transport protocol that Terminal Server uses today. Thus, although Citrix and Microsoft share technologies, the products of each company aren't interoperable with the other company's products. However, the agreement held up through the development of Windows Server 2000 and 2003, with Citrix having access to server source code and Microsoft maintaining the benefits of having a strong independent software vendor (ISV) relationship. In 2004 Microsoft and Citrix extended their agreement for five more years. Over the past few years Citrix has been the Microsoft ISV of the Year, and in 2007 Microsoft named Citrix their first-ever Global ISV Partner of the Year. Citrix was a co-developer of Terminal Server 2003, and probably made important contributions to Terminal Server 2008.

It's important to understand the relationship that Citrix and Microsoft have, because it not only defines Terminal Server's current state and boundaries but the platform's future directions as well. Citrix continued to develop their remote access server technology adding additional capabilities to WinFrame and marketing it as MetaFrame. As Citrix began to support operating systems other than Windows they further renamed the product to Citrix Presentation Server and porting their suite onto other platforms. You'll find versions of Presentation Server. Presentation Server is available for Solaris, HP-UX, and IBM AIX, thus supporting heterogeneous clients in a way that Microsoft Terminal Server will not. Presentation Server is particularly powerful at publishing applications to clients and web launching of applications, both of which are key features in this new version of Terminal Server. The terms of the Citrix license requires that Presentation Server clients have a Windows Server client access license (CAL) since Presentation Server runs on Windows, as well as a Terminal Server connection CAL.

Not So Thin Anymore

Terminal services may have started green and dumb, but with Windows Terminal Server it is no longer so. Terminal Server has often been referred to as "thin client/server technology." This refers to a generation of clients that run a lightweight operating system, such as Windows CE or Debian GNU Linux, and that have a little memory (often flash memory). Many are diskless. Thin clients are systems that can display a browser window, or an X11 display (for X Window), and support the Citrix ICA or the Microsoft RDP transport protocols as well as TCP/IP. Most often the vendors of these devices support both ICA and RDP in order to broaden their utility.

A thin client is a marketing term that has no standardized definition. In the past these devices were often called "graphics terminals." Sometimes these devices are the size of a cable modem and are attached to monitors; other times they are part of a monitor, or even a laptop. I've even seen one packaged into a keyboard. Several vendors make thin clients, including Wyse Winterms (see Figure 12.1), Neoware Appliances, HP Compaq t-series, and many others. Many thin clients are based on embedded operating systems such as Windows XP Embedded or Windows CE .NET.

Thin clients are systems with little or no processing capability short of graphics display. In most cases the BIOS of these systems is loaded without being modified, but since many clients support multiple operating systems this definition doesn't reflect the current state of things. Although thin clients are a successful niche market, the reality is that the vast majority of thin clients are hosted software that runs on top of standard PC hardware. Software-only clients often run various forms of Linux such as PXES Universal Linux Thin Client, Pilotlinux, or BeTwin.

FIGURE 12.1
The Wyse V90 Win-term is an example of a thin client. The size of a paperback, this Winterm runs Windows Embedded and connect via Citrix ICA or Microsoft RDP to a terminal server.

FROM THE WYSE PRESS PHOTO LIBRARY.

A "fat" client, also called a thick client, is a system that has processing capabilities and memory, and that category would include standard PCs. As it becomes easier to centrally manage PCs, and as the application delivery model also becomes more centralized, there is increasing pressure by vendors such as Microsoft to move to a service delivery model. The idea is that if Microsoft can deliver the Vista experience on a PC in a Terminal Server session, then that mode of delivery offers considerable advantages to an enterprise. Central management, better security, and more efficient use of licenses and resources are now extended to systems that have fewer server requirements, significantly better multimedia performance, better client software support, and much faster network performance. Although users might not like the idea of their software running on a remote system and being less customizable, if the experience is seamless their objections diminish. And it is very clear that one of the major goals of Terminal Server 2008 was to greatly improve the user experience a fat client would have.

From Microsoft's viewpoint, the fat client terminal services model presents an opportunity to move to a more predictable service-based model where revenues are regular and predictable. There's no need to go to the expense of creating and marketing large version upgrades such as XP or Vista when your service lets you roll out improvements as they become available.

If you want a Windows Terminal Server experience that adds the Vista features, you'll need a Vista client to support it. You can get high-resolution, dual monitor support, the Desktop Experience (a.k.a. Aero), and many more of the UI improvements with this version of Terminal Server.

Microsoft has improved service redirection in Terminal Server. If you plug in a camera or media player, your terminal session now can use Plug and Play to mount that device. You'll need to have a camera that uses the Picture Transport Protocol and a media player that can use the Picture Transfer Protocol, but support for these protocols is widespread. Terminal Server can also redirect devices that use the Microsoft Point-of-Service (POS) that was introduced in .NET 1.11.

So clearly Microsoft's main goal in improving Terminal Server has been to improve the way fat clients interact with the server. Along with improvements that a user can see and feel, there are performance improvements built into Terminal Server that improve system performance. In Terminal Server 2003 when large print jobs started or there were other processes that required large data transfer, bandwidth that was assigned to the KVM components (keyboard, video, and mouse) of the client would often be assigned to support the data transfer. In a fat client, their system would then become sluggish. Terminal Server 2008 offers a new system of process priorities that enforces a certain minimum level of performance to KVM devices that minimizes this problem. A new version of the Remote Desktop Connection, version 6.0, has been released to support this new functionality.

However, it is in the delivery of applications to clients that Terminal Server has made the most advances. Citrix has long offered their clients the ability to launch remote applications or publish applications, browser launching of applications, and other application delivery services. It seems likely that Citrix contributed to many of these new capabilities, and if not directly, through the influence of their product suite.

I believe that the ability to run "remote applications" as seamlessly as the same application running on a local client is the most significant improvement in this version of Terminal Server. Gone is the confusion that faced many users of previous versions of Windows. A single sign-on capability is also a feature available on the Citrix platform in the Citrix Password Manager, another fat client feature that is part of Terminal Server. The new remote access technology in Terminal Server, TS Gateway, creates an encrypted connection to the terminal server, and is reminiscent of the kind of connection that Citrix's acquisition of GoToMyPC offers to users for directly connecting to their desktop (but without the window-in-a-window). It's interesting and possibly significant that these two similar technologies do the same thing but don't compete with each other.

In the end few people are going to care where the code was written, or who inspired which feature. What matters is whether these new features will keep Terminal Server vital and competitive with advances on other platforms and with other technologies. It's a good chance that they will. With this general introduction to terminal services, let's turn our attention to the details of the major changes in Windows Terminal Server 2008.

How Terminal Server Works

Terminal servers work because they take as much of the operating system as they can and create a common pool that each instance can reference and use. This common code leaves only user mode application-specific memory that must be managed on a per-user and a per-session instance. So if a server has enough memory, the additional processing power necessary to support an additional user or session is rather minimal. A large departmental server, perhaps with a eight-way processor, can support as many as 50 user sessions for productivity workers, and many more for low-memory single applications such as an electronic cash register or automated teller (ATM) machine.

The magic that is a terminal server is defined in large part by the creation of a new form of memory address space that takes the pool of common operating system code and attaches to it a session ID. The event queue manages access to common memory so that one session ID doesn't bump into another and so that when a session ends, the memory that it is using is released. Figure 12.2 shows a schematic of the Windows Server 2008 Terminal Server architecture. Notice that there are two separate areas:

System space   The System space is the common pool of system processes that is used by each session for underlying services. At the bottom are I/O drivers, in the middle in kernel mode are TCP/IP and protocol drivers, and at the top are a set of different managers, all running within the Terminal Server service.

Session space   The Session space consists of individual user environments, each isolated from one another and processing independently. The Logon service, which consists of the UI (`Explorer.exe`), and the Windows Manager interface, along with the running applications, are all separate from the pooled system memory processes.

Notice also that both System space and Session space with independently managed memory addresses both have user mode and kernel mode components. It is the element of session objects and process and memory isolation that makes Terminal Server 2008 such a stable environment.

FIGURE 12.2
The Windows Server 2008 Windows Terminal Server architecture

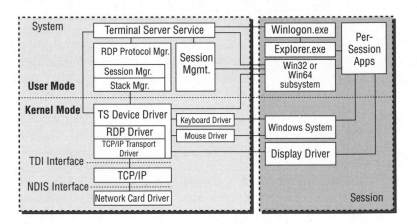

Core Improvements

The improvements in Windows Terminal Server 2008's core functions affect improvements in the transfer protocol, the support for additional .NET functionality, high-function user desktop experiences, and more powerful peripheral access and control. Some of these changes are obvious to users, but other changes are not.

One of the important new tools to manage Terminal Server 2008 is the Terminal Server section of the Server Manager, shown in Figure 12.3. This management tool allows you to add roles, check connections, get reports and statistics, manage sessions, install and perform licensing, and many more tasks. Throughout this chapter we will return to this tool again and again.

FIGURE 12.3
To manage and control your terminal server(s), go to the Terminal Server section of the Server Manager.

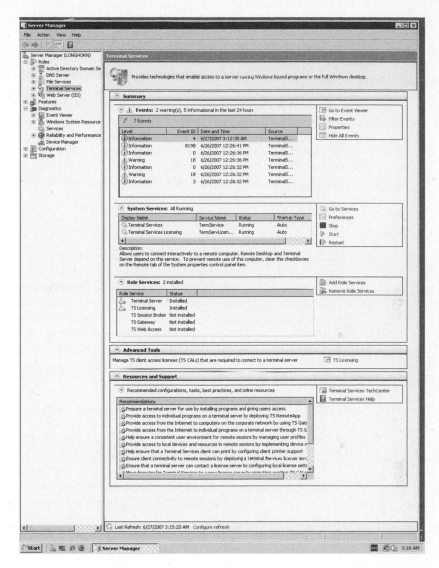

If you have a Vista client or a Windows Server 2008 server, then RDP 6.0 is part of your distribution. If you want to connect to a Terminal Server 2008 server with a Windows XP SP2 or Windows Server 2003 SP1 (or greater) client, you will have to download this software from the Microsoft Download Center at:

```
http://go.microsoft.com/fwlink/?LinkId=79373
```

Software features that require the Windows Server 2008 core won't be available to these older operating systems, but most new features will be. In some instances you will be prompted to upgrade your client, but it is best practice to upgrade all of your clients when you deploy your Terminal Server 2008 servers. For example, the Vista User Experience (which mostly includes the new Aero interface) is a Windows Server 2008 core feature. It isn't supported on early systems.

In terms of speed, it doesn't appear that this version of Terminal Server or the Remote Desktop client have greatly improved. However, there have been some tweaks that should result in improved performance in spite of no change in data throughput rate. In previous versions of RDP when there were large file transfers occurring between the client and the server, the KVM components would become sluggish until the file transfer was completed. Microsoft has tuned this process so that there is always a certain minimum level of bandwidth allowed for KVM in a session. The default number was 70 percent of the bandwidth. This version of RDP allows you to modify the percentage of your bandwidth that will be assigned to KVM; you might use a lower percentage for a high-bandwidth connection and a greater percentage for a low-bandwidth connection.

The feature of tuning your bandwidth is called display data prioritization. If you want to adjust the default bandwidth ratio from its default value of 70%/30%, you can do so in the Registry. The 30% value controls the bandwidth of printing, file transfers, clipboards, and other data processes that require wire transfer.

To adjust the display data prioritization ratio:

1. Click Start and in the Run/Search text box enter **REGEDIT**; then press the Enter key.

2. Open the following key:

   HKEY_LOCAL_MACHINE\SYSTEM\CurrentControlSet\Services\TermDD subkey

3. If this is the first time you open this key, right-click the TermDD key, then select New ➢ DWORD (32-bit) Value, enter **FlowControlDisable**, and click OK. This creates the FlowControlDisable subkey.

4. Repeat step 3 and create the FlowControlDisableDisplayBandwidth, FlowControlChannelBandwidth, and FlowControlChargePostCompression subkeys.

   When complete, the Registry Editor will look like Figure 12.4.

FIGURE 12.4
The RegEdit subkeys used to alter the display data prioritizations

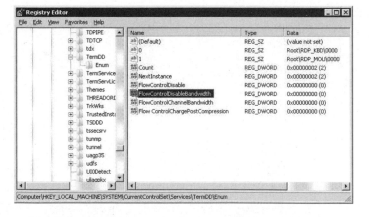

5. To set the relative priority for virtual channels (print, file transfers, clipboard, etc.), set FlowControlChannelBandwidth value (the default is 30). The maximum value available is 255.

6. To disable display data prioritization, set FlowControlDisable to 1 (the default is 0); then requests are on a first-in, first-out order.

7. To set the relative priority (display and input data versus other processes), change the `FlowControlDisableBandwidth` percentage (the default is 70 for %). A maximum value of 255 is available.

8. To enable any new settings, restart Terminal Server.

Display data prioritization is the ratio of the `FlowControlDisplayBandwidth` and `FlowControlChannelBandwidth`. For values of 50 and 100, the ratio would be 50/100, or 0.5, versus the default ratio of 70/30, or 2.33. Use the `FlowControlChargePostCompression` key to alter the balance of compression versus post-compression bytes. A default of 0 means that any display data prioritization is based on uncompressed data only.

The Single Sign-On

A single sign-on service applies the password and user ID that you enter at logon to other services once that logon is authenticated. Sometimes this is done through a trust relationship (which is an allowed pass-through authentication from one domain to another), and other times it is part of a service that different authentication mechanisms subscribe to. This is a valuable add-on service that is often offered as a separate product in many network management products. This version of Terminal Server adds single sign-on for users with domain accounts so that their logon using either a password or a hardware device (such as a smart card or key) provides access not only to their terminal server but to other remote resources as well.

Single sign-on is popular with administrators because it means less management to keep their users connected. With enterprise (what Microsoft refers to as line-of-business [LoB]) applications often deployed on terminal servers, this mechanism will become increasingly popular by eliminating the need for secondary logons as part of the user's session.

To participate in Terminal Services single sign-on, you must connect a Vista client or Windows Server 2008 Server to a Terminal Server 2008 server. The user accounts must have rights to the terminal server, the client machine account must be part of the domain, and the terminal server must be part of the domain; if not, the administrator must be able to add these authentications prior to the single sign-on session.

To enable single sign-on, you must enable authentication on the server as well as set a Group Policy. To enable single sign-on, do the following:

1. Open Terminal Services Configuration in the Server Manager of the terminal server. Or click Start ➢ Run, type **TSCONFIG.MSC**, and then click OK.

2. Right-click RDP-Tcp in the Connections section, then select Properties.

3. On the General tab, make sure that the Security Layer has Negotiate or SSL (TLS 1.0) enabled; then click OK.

4. On the Vista or Windows Server 2008 remote client, click Start and enter **GPEDIT.MSC** in the Start Search text box; then press Enter.

5. Click Credentials Delegation in the Computer Configuration, Administrative Templates, System section.

6. Double-click on Allow Default Delegating Default Credentials, then in the Properties dialog box select the Settings tab. Choose Enabled and then Show.

7. Click Add in the Show Contents dialog box, then in the Add Item dialog box, type **termsrv/ <servername>** in the Enter the Item to Be Added box. Then click OK.

Large Monitor Support

The ability to create custom display resolutions is now supported, bringing Terminal Server 2008 clients the capability to use wide-screen and high-resolution displays. In past versions of RDP, the highest display resolutions available were 1600×1200 at a 4:3 display resolution ratio. This is the aspect ratio used by NTSC TV monitors in standard mode (from RCA's original TV specification).

This version of RDP allows you to run wide-screen resolutions commonly used to display movies. Wide-screen resolution ratios of 16:9 (the most common) and 16:10 (less common) are available to you; resolutions of 1680×1050 or 1920×1200 are also available provided your display adapter and monitor are capable of displaying these modes. A maximum resolution of 4096×2040 can be achieved with a RDP 6.0 client, which is best used for multimonitor displays.

To support a custom display size:

1. Navigate to and open your .RDP file in Notepad or another text editor.

2. Alter these two settings for the size of the display:

   ```
   desktopwidth:i:<value>
   desktopheight:i:<value>
   ```

3. To change the settings directly from a command prompt, type **MSTSC.EXE /w:<width> /h:<height>** and then press Enter.

The value of these settings can be 1680×1050, 1920×1200, or whatever your monitor can support. It is often the case that a monitor has the lowest resolution in the display subsystem. If your graphics card has enough video memory to support Vista Aero (256MB), then these higher resolutions are most likely supported.

For example, an ATI Radeon 9600 SE, which is a last-generation AGP 8X video card, is capable of supporting resolutions up to 1920×1080. That's not too bad for a video card that has a 64-bit memory interface and 128MB Double Data Rate (DDR) frame buffer (memory). A higher-end card such as the Radeon X1950 (which is a 512MB GDDR4 PCI-X card) will run all digital resolutions up to 2560×16003 and analog resolutions up to 2048×14363. Yes, those numbers 16003 and 14363 are not a mistake. This is a *Crossfire-capable* card, which means that you can connect two cards together to get even more powerful performance, although not quite twice that of an individual card.

This higher-end (but by no means the highest-end) card can support resolutions that no monitor can come close to. As a result many gamers run two large wide-screen displays one next to the other in their games without any loss of image quality even at high frame rates and with sophisticated shading, texturing, and rendering.

Large monitor support for Terminal Server 2008 clients opens this technology to a whole new range of users: graphics professionals, desktop publishers, video production, just about anyone who needs this kind of image quality and performance. Combined with Microsoft's DirectX 10 rendering technologies, Terminal Server 2008 clients become a full participant in these endeavors.

Monitor Spanning

Monitor spanning is what you see when you go into an electronics store and see a wall of monitors all playing part of a picture. It is much more common for people to set up dual-monitor systems (or even a third) monitor in an effort to extend their desktop across a much larger angle and size. Indeed, the sense of realism with two large monitors as well as the improvements in productivity make this a lovely setup for any computer professional to have.

This approach works best when the monitors can display the same resolution. Monitors can be spanned horizontally (in rows), but vendors do not make displays that span monitors vertically. The maximum monitor resolution for all monitors in a span is 4096×2048.

To enable monitor spanning, do the following:

1. Open the `.RDP` file in your text editor.

2. Modify the following values:

   ◆ If `<value>` = 0, monitor spanning is disabled.

   ◆ If `<value>` = 1, monitor spanning is enabled.

3. Alternatively, you can enter this at the command prompt: **`MSTSC.EXE /SPAN`**.

Managing Terminal Server with Windows System Resource Manager

For enterprises with large number of client connections to Windows Terminal Server, managing the connections can be a major problem. Terminal Server 2008 provides a means through the Windows System Resource Manager (WSRM) to control how terminal server CPU and memory are allocated to applications, services, and the processes running on the server. Control over these factors provides a more predicable terminal server environment where you can manage multiple applications for multiple connected clients at a single management point.

WSRM is a service that you can install as part of the Windows Server 2008 Administrative Tools set. After you install the service, you can access the MMC WSRM console by choosing Start ➢ Administrative Tools ➢ Windows System Resource Manager. You have individual control over computers and their resource allocation policies. Among the important settings are:

◆ `Equal_Per_User`

◆ `Equal_Per_Session`

These policy settings even out resource allocation so that one user or setting cannot hog the terminal server resources. Microsoft recommends that you collect statistical data on resource usage before you implement these policies (especially `Equal_Per_Session`) as the results may impair the performance of essential connections.

To view the Windows System Resource Manager, select that utility in the Server Manager. Figure 12.5 shows this utility and the `Equal_Per_Process` policy.

FIGURE 12.5
Use the Windows System Resource Manager to set Terminal Server usage policies.

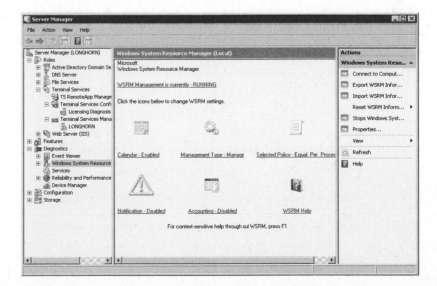

Themes and Desktop Experience Pack Support

The Desktop Experience consists of the Aero interface, new desktop theme support, Windows Media Player 11, and the Windows photo management support tools. Although most administrators won't turn on Desktop Experience for their server, they may want to do so for their terminal clients. You will want to make sure that clients have the necessary requirements to support Desktop Experience, which is a video card with at least 256MB of video RAM.

To install Desktop Experience in the terminal server environment:

1. Select Start ➢ Administrative Tools ➢ Server Manager if the Server Manager isn't open on your screen.

2. Click Add Features in the Features Summary section.

3. Enable the Desktop Experience checkbox in the Select Features section; then click Next.

4. Verify your selections on the Confirm Installation Selections page, then click the Install button.

5. You will be prompted to restart your system on the Installation Results page; click Close, select Yes, and your server will restart.

After the server desktop appears, you can verify that the Desktop Experience has been installed by seeing whether Windows Media Player operates, or by examining the Features Summary section of the Server Manager to see that Desktop Experience is listed as being installed.

The Windows Aero interface (http://www.microsoft.com/windows/products/windowsvista/features/experiences/aero.mspx)—with its translucent windows, the Alt+Windows stacked windows display that shows the flip screen feature, and the taskbar with buttons that are thumbnail window representations of your open windows—is part of the Desktop Experience but is called "Desktop Composition." To enable this part of Desktop Experience, you will need to turn on the Theme service, as follows:

1. With Desktop Experience enabled, select Start ➢ Administrative Tools ➢ Services.

2. Right-click Themes in the Services pane and select the Properties command from the context menu.

3. Select the General tab and change the Startup Type to Automatic; then click the Apply button.

4. In the Service Status section, click Start to initiate the Themes service, and then enable automatic service starting by clicking OK.

NOTE   The Aero interface or Desktop Experience does not need to be running on a Windows Terminal Server in order to support those features on the client.

Once themes are enabled, you will need to configure the parts of the user experience that you want your terminal server to provide. You do this in the Terminal Server 2008 Control Panel, as follows:

1. Select Start ➢ Control Panel ➢ Appearance and Personalization.

   If you don't see Appearance and Personalization, your system may be in Classic View. To switch to the new view go to the Control Panel folder and use the link in that dialog box to make the change.

2. Select Personalization, then select Windows Color and Appearance.

3. Enable any of the following Desktop Experience features:

◆ Select the Appearance tab, select Effects, and enable Show Windows Contents While Dragging if you want this feature to appear on your clients' desktops; then click OK twice to enable this selection.

◆ Click the Display Settings and select the Monitor tab. In Colors, select Highest (32 bit), then click OK if you want to enable full color on a client desktop.

◆ To turn on accessibility features, in the See Also section enable Ease of Access, then enable Make It Easier to Focus on Tasks in the Explore All Settings section.

◆ To enable animation features in the accessibility settings click on the Use Computer Without A Monitor section. There you can disable the settings Turn Off All Unnecessary Animations (When Possible) in the Adjust Time Limits and Flashing Visuals section.

4. Click the Save button to enable your selections.

You will also need to enable Desktop Composition on the client side as follows:

1. Select Start ➢ All Programs ➢ Accessories ➢ Remote Desktop Connection.

2. Click Options in the Remote Desktop Connection.

3. Click the Experience tab; then enable the Themes and Desktop Composition checkboxes.

4. To make the connection and check settings, click the Connect button.

5. While in the client (Vista), use the local settings to modify the aspects of Desktop Composition that you desire.

Font smoothing using ClearType and Font Smoothing are an example of a technology that you might want to turn on in a remote client. You can enable this in a client session by opening the Appearance and Personalization control panel and enabling the Use the Following Method to Smooth Edges of Screen Fonts checkbox, then selecting ClearType. You can open this control panel from the Start menu, or by right-clicking on the desktop and selecting it from the context menu.

With ClearType enabled, you must open the Remote Desktop Connections Options dialog box. Select Start ➢ All Programs ➢ Accessories ➢ Remote Desktop Connection and then click the Options button. On the Experience tab, click on Font Smoothing and any of the other features that interest you. Figure 12.6 shows the RDP client-side Options dialog box.

FIGURE 12.6
The Remote Desktop Connection client's Desktop Experience settings for RDP 6.0

Terminal Service Remote Applications

A Terminal Services RemoteApp (TS RemoteApp) is an application server platform for remote clients. The RemoteApp service name has been trademarked by Microsoft, and is a new feature in Windows Server 2008. To run a remote application you need to connect to a Terminal Server 2008 with an XP SP2, Vista, Windows Server 2003, or Windows Server 2008 system using the RDP 6.0 TS Client and connection protocol. Remote applications run in the UI as if they were local applications, and can only be recognized as a remote application when you look at their Properties dialog box. Microsoft envisions that TS RemoteApp will be useful not only to remote users but to branch offices, to LoB applications, as a method for application deployment, and for roaming users.

However, TS RemoteApp also defines a new way to deliver services to all sorts of clients: kiosks, small footprint devices such as phones and PDAs, and computer appliances such as thin-client stations. Beyond all of these possible uses, TS RemoteApp is a prototype platform for a coming era of application services. Remote applications may be ushering in a completely new era of service delivery.

Remote applications can be distributed to clients by:

♦ Providing access to a specially prepared web page through TS Web Access.

♦ Deploying remotely as a .RDP file

♦ Installing from an .MSI package, possibly deployed by a network management package such as SMS.

♦ Using Simple mode. In this mode RemoteApp makes the programs available on a terminal server or a group of terminal servers appear to all users on a TS Web Access web page without customizing the web page by user.

♦ Using Active Directory mode. Here RemoteApp deployment uses TS RemoteApp Manager combined with an Active Directory Group Policy for software distribution where the administrator defines which controls a remote user can see and operate.

Figure 12.7 shows the mechanism by which Terminal Server 2008 deploys and manages RemoteApps.

FIGURE 12.7
The RemoteApp deployment technology

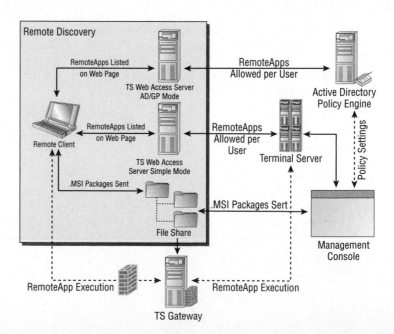

Active Directory RemoteApp Deployment

Active Directory mode has some distinct advantages and some distinct disadvantages as well over Simple mode. In Simple mode the entire desktop of a terminal server can be made available to a remote user. For Active Directory mode, the deployment is more complex and does not allow full access to the terminal server desktop (but decreases security risks). Active Directory mode does provide application access filtering by user account, and will be used to distribute .RDP and .MSI packages that allow a user to run RemoteApp without having to visit a TS Web Access web page.

To create an Active Directory deployment, you must first install Terminal Server and the RemoteApp programs, and then enter the remote connection settings.

To install Terminal Server, use Server Manager to add the Terminal Server role service. The installation will ask you for the authentication method, the licensing mode, and the user groups that will have access to the terminal server.

You can install a program from the distribution disc or from a package in the UI. Use the CHANGE USER / INSTALL command at the command line to escalate your privileges for application installation, and then use CHANGE USER / EXECUTE to exit the Installation mode.

To minimize the number of open remote sessions running on your terminal servers, install program suites such as Office, as well as any program that requires another program both on a single terminal server. If you believe that two programs are incompatible with each other, place them each on different terminal servers.

In staging your applications, keep in mind the capacity of your terminal server to support concurrent remote user connections and plan accordingly. Terminal Server 2008 can be placed into server farms, and through Network Load Balancing (NLB) can have capacity added to any RemoteApp access.

Then follow these steps:

1. On the terminal server, open the TS RemoteApp Manager and add the RemoteApp programs to the Web Access.

2. Configure the global deployment settings for those applications.

3. Add the machine account for the TS Web Access server to the TS Web Access Computer group.

4. Create installation packages for the programs you wish to remotely deploy.

5. Set an Active Directory Domain Services (AD DS) Group Policy software distribution.

6. Within the AD DS, add the RemoteApp program to the TS Web Access server list.

You can create an installation package in the TS RemoteApp Manager Actions pane by selecting the Create Windows Installer Package command, which launches the RemoteApp Wizard. On the Specify Package Settings page, you will be prompted with Enter Location to Save Packages for the .MSI package you are creating.

Clearly this procedure is a lot of work to provide access to an application for a few people. However, if you are rolling out a deployment for hundreds of people, then AD deployment of RemoteApp is the way to go. It is no longer necessary to use deployment software such as SMS, LANDesk, or OpenView to deploy RemoteApp installation packages. You can also put the package into a network share and let your remote users have access to that share when they connect to your LAN.

Remote Connections

The remote connection is enabled on the terminal server when the Terminal Server role service is installed on the server. As part of the procedure in the previous section on AD deployment, you will need to add users and groups that can access the server and the RemoteApps on that server.

To configure remote connections:

1. Click Start ➤ Run, enter **CONTROL SYSTEM** into the Open box, and click OK.

2. Under Tasks (on the left side of the screen), click Remote Settings.

3. The System Properties dialog box opens; on the Remote tab (the default), set either of the two following properties:

   ◆ Allow Connections from Computers Running Any Version of Remote Desktop (Less Secure): This is the default option, and allows remote clients of any type to access the RemoteApp.

   ◆ Allow Connections Only from Computers Running Remote Desktop with Network Level Authentication (More Secure): This option enables domain authentication of remote clients and requires RDP 6.0.

4. Add users and groups to the allowed connecting clients by clicking Select Users and then adding the desired users and groups.

   The local Administrator group has access to the terminal server by default, and is not listed in this dialog box.

5. Click OK to close the System Properties dialog box and enable your selections.

You can also use the TS RemoteApp Manager's RDP Settings to create custom settings. Among the settings that can be specified are display settings, redirection for storage, I/O devices and other resources, and the client's User Experience settings. This is one instance where the Global Settings for Terminal Server's .RDP connections take precedence over the local settings. The TS Manager's Actions panel also allows you to export your RemoteApp settings, or import settings from a settings data file.

RemoteApp Configuration

You will need to set up an application to make that program available to remote users. Not all programs are compatible with RemoteApp technology, so first check to see if the program you want to deploy has any issues running remotely on a terminal server. (You can do this by searching the Knowledge Base.) Once you create the distribution package, you will need to add the program to the list of allowed applications in the TS RemoteApp Manager. This administrative tool is installed as part of the Terminal Server role.

To enable a RemoteApp, do the following:

1. Select Start ➤ Administrative Tools ➤ Terminal Services ➤ TS RemoteApp Manager (Figure 12.8) to open that console.

2. Click Add RemoteApps in the Actions panel. The Welcome to RemoteApp Wizard appears, as shown in Figure 12.9.

FIGURE 12.8
The RemoteApp Manager utility

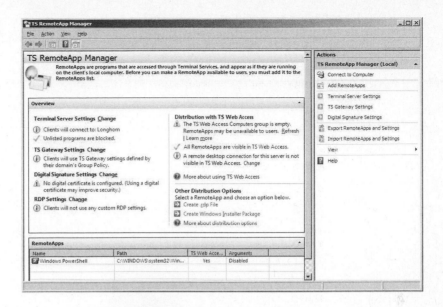

FIGURE 12.9
The RemoteApp Wizard

3. Click Next on the Welcome page, then in the Choose Programs to Add to the RemoteApps list, check the boxes next to each program that you want to enable.

Any program that is enabled will appear on the Terminal Server's All User Start menu. You can also specify additional programs by browsing for them and specifying that program's executable (.EXE) file and location.

4. To set RemoteApp properties, select the program name, click Properties (Figure 12.10), and then click OK when finished. You'll use these options in the dialog box:

◆ Modify the displayed program name in the RemoteApp Name text box.

◆ Alter the path to the executable file in the Location text box.

◆ Set the access property by enabling (the default) or disabling the RemoteApp Is Available Through the TS Web Access option. For RemoteApps that you are deploying as packages, you may want to disable this option.

◆ To modify the way a program runs, you can specify command-line switches, or disable all command-line switches.

◆ Alter the default program icon by clicking Change Icon and selecting a different .ICO file.

FIGURE 12.10
The RemoteApp Wizard Properties page

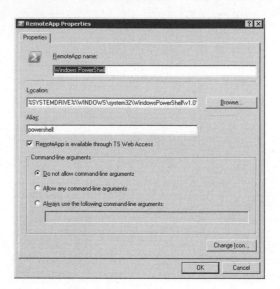

5. When all properties are set, click Next, verify the values on the Review Settings page, and then click the Finish button. At this point your application should appear on the RemoteApps list as available to your clients.

Just as you use the TS RemoteApp Manager to add programs to the TS Web Access RemoteApps list, you use this same utility to change the deployment settings of a RemoteApp as well as remove any RemoteApp from the displayed list. To change the properties of a RemoteApp or delete it:

1. In the TS RemoteApp Manager, click the program name.

2. Again click the program name in the Actions panel.

3. Select Properties to view and alter the RemoteApp's properties.

4. Select or deselect the Show in TS Web Access or Hide in TS Web Access option to add or remove the RemoteApp from the list.

5. Alternatively, click Remove to delete the application from the list entirely.

When you delete the application you are deleting the .RDP connection files or the .MSI package that you deploy. You will be asked to confirm the deletion. Deleting the application from the list does not uninstall the application from the terminal server.

It is possible to set the deployment settings for all RemoteApps programs, what Microsoft refers to as *global deployment settings* within the TS RemoteApp Manager. Any settings that you specify will be ignored by any installation package that you create for RemoteApps with a different setting. That is, global deployment settings apply to default values and are overridden by local settings.

The TS RemoteApps Manager has some other critical server-level settings that you will want to configure:

◆ Terminal Server Settings gives you access to the Connection tab for the Terminal Server (by clicking the Change link). On that page you can modify the RDP port number, server authentication methods, and rename the server.

◆ The Desktop Access settings let you enable the Make a Remote Desktop Connection to This Terminal Server Available in TS Web Access option, which adds a link for the terminal server desktop to the TS Web Access web page.

◆ For the Access To Unlisted Programs setting you can choose:

◆ Block Remote Users from Starting Unlisted Programs. Remote Users Will Only Be Able to Start RemoteApps That You List. (Recommended): This ensures that a remote user cannot start any program that isn't on your approved list from an RDP file.

◆ Allow Users to Start Both Listed and Unlisted Programs: This lets users start any program that they want from an RDP file. Microsoft cautions administrators to not use this setting as it represents a security risk.

NOTE Keep in mind that the client systems running Windows XP SP2 and Windows Server 2003 will need to connect to the terminal server by Secure Sockets Layer (SSL) and therefore will require that you have an SSL certificate installed on the terminal server.

In addition to general terminal server settings, you can control various aspects of the TS Gateway from within the TS RemoteApp Manager. Refer to the section "The Terminal Server Gateway Console" later in this chapter. You can allow remote clients to automatically detect and connect to the TS Gateway, or you can specify the settings that clients use.

TIP To view a list of public certification authorities that are part of the Microsoft Certificate Program, go to http://technet2.microsoft.com/windowsserver2008/en/library/ 61d24255-dad1-4fd2-b4a3-a91a22973def1033.mspx?mfr=true.

RemoteApp Security

To further secure RemoteApps, consider signing your .RDP files with a digital certificate. This technology adds a cryptographic key to the connection file that allows the certificate authority to verify that the RemoteApp's publisher is known and identifies that publisher. To sign .RDP files on Windows Server 2008, use a Server Authentication certificate (SSL certificate), or use a Code Signing Certificate. You can use the same SSL certificate that you establish for your terminal server or TS Gateway for signing your RemoteApp .RDP files.

Whether or not a certificate is required for a RemoteApp to run is something that can be configured by an administrator as part of a Group Policy. To control whether a signed .RDP connection is always allowed from a specific publisher or whether applications without a certificate are disallowed, open the Local Group Policy Object Editor in the Computer Configuration and User Configuration node. You will find the setting enabled at `Administrative Templates\Windows Components\ Terminal Services\Remote Desktop Connection Client`. For this policy setting you can choose:

- Specify SHA1 Thumbprints of Certificates Representing Trusted .RDP Publishers: An SHA1 is a Secure Hash Algorithm 1 key for verifying that the certificate is valid with the CA (Certificate Authority).

- Allow .RDP Files From Valid Publishers and User's Default .RDP Settings: Here any `.RDP` with a valid certificate, not just the ones you specify by thumbprint will be accepted.

- Allow .RDP Files from Unknown Publishers: This is the setting that basically disables this security feature.

Terminal Services Web Access

Terminal Services Web Access, or TS Web Access, allows users to launch a RemoteApp from within their browser. TS Web Access is a role service within the Terminal Services role. When users open a web page on the TS Web Access server, they are presented with a page containing the program icons of the programs that they can launch. A user can launch one or more of these programs and the programs run on the server but are displayed on the user's monitor.

TS Web Access has some major advantages over programs running on a client system. Since the program launches from a single web page, deploying an application requires one installation and one deployment. The TS Web Access web page is a customizable ActiveX Web Part, which means that it can be incorporated into other web pages or into a Microsoft Windows SharePoint Services website. There are three methods you can use to deploy a Web Part:

- Deploy the Web Part in the TS Web Access web page (which is the default).

- Deploy the Web Part in a web page to which you add the Web Part ActiveX.

- Deploy the Web Part in a SharePoint Services page.

TS Web Access can be deployed on any Windows Server 2008 server that has IIS 7.0 on it. It does not have to be deployed on a Terminal Server. TS Web Access has the following requirements:

- A Windows Server 2008 system that runs Microsoft Internet Information Services (IIS) 7.0.

- Supported clients include: Vista, XP SP2, Server 2003 SP1, and other Windows Server 2003 Servers.

- Remote Desktop Connection version 6.0 client, which contains the TS Web Access ActiveX control.

When users navigate to the web page containing the TS Web Access Web Part, they see a list of RemoteApps that are dynamically updated by the service. The list can contain applications that run on one terminal server or a group of terminal servers. A distributed distribution of applications is made available through a Group Policy software rule. Users don't have to have RDP 6.0 running on their computer when they launch the application from the browser. The connection is established and provisioned automatically.

During the connection process the user will see the I Am Using a Private Computer That Complies with My Organization's Security Policy checkbox in the bottom-right corner of the TS Web Part. If the user is connecting from a public computer, that checkbox should be cleared, and the option of saving connection credentials on that computer will be disabled.

NOTE To make RemoteApps available over the Internet using TS Web Access, use TS Gateway to create secure connections between the Terminal Server client and the server itself.

Although you can launch applications from any IIS server, the application that launches must be on the Terminal Server that contains that program. If a single Terminal Server is the data source, then the list of programs is displayed to all current users. When the data source is Active Domain Services (AD DS), then the TS Web Part deploys the RemoteApp program packaged with an `.RAP` file contained within an `.MSI` installer package to the client. These packages are created in the TS RemoteApp Manager MMC snap-in, and are enabled as part of a software distribution Group Policy. The ability to dynamically update a website with a list of available remote applications is new in this version of Terminal Server.

The Terminal Server Gateway

Terminal Services Gateway, or TS Gateway, is another of the new role services that are part of the Terminal Services role. The service creates a secure connection in a terminal server session between a remote user and a corporate or private network that allows the remote user to run RemoteApps without having to create a VPN connection. The list of available remote programs that a user sees can be customized for each specific user.

There are three ways to set up the TS Gateway service:

◆ As the remote access point for a LAN

◆ As the access point where clients are validated by a Network Access Protection (NAP) policy service or a RADIUS server

◆ As an SSL connection bridge that is part of an Internet-facing demilitarized zone (DMZ) or edge network

Gateway Connections

In the most common method used to start the RemoteApp using the TS Gateway, a user navigates to the web page containing the Web Part ActiveX and then clicks the program icon. The program launches on the server and appears on the user's desktop at the remote location. But this isn't the only method. Clients can also launch an RDP file that has been provided to them, or they can click a RemoteApp program icon that has been placed on their system. The file and program icons can be part of a deployment solution in an enterprise.

Should the user start two or more remote programs, each terminal server that contains a running program establishes its own user session and connection to the remote user. In this regard the remote user isn't any different than a local user connecting to programs on two different terminal servers.

The process of a connection is as follows (refer to Figure 12.11):

1. The user initiates the connection.

2. An SSL tunnel is established between a TS Client and the TS Gateway, and the client's connection is authenticated.

3. The TS Client requests a connection to the desired resource.

4. The client's system is verified as conforming to the Network Access Protection (NAP) policy and the user's credentials are authenticated.

5. An SSL connection is created between the client and the TS Gateway, and an RDP connection is created by the gateway (and monitored) between the TS Gateway and the desired resource.

6. The TS Client begins a user session on the Terminal Server resource, which then validates the request of the user access based on domain requirements.

7. The RemoteApp communicates through the TS Gateway using RDP through port 3389, and the TS Gateway communicates using RDP packets encapsulated in an SSL session through port 443.

FIGURE 12.11
The most common way to set up a TS Gateway connection places the gateway between the client and LAN and further between two firewalls.

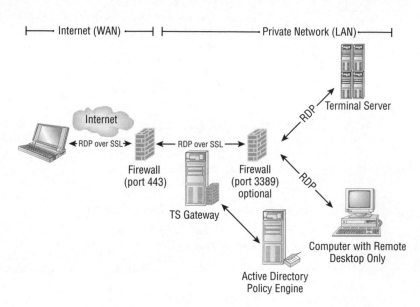

Once the communications is established, it is bi-directional. There are some aspects of the gateway that are worth noting. First, the gateway provides both hardware and software protocol isolation. Traffic always goes through the gateway. Second, the client is authenticated in different ways at several steps in the process. It is very difficult for an unauthorized user to compromise this system, since it is secured as a multistep process.

When a user launches a RemoteApp and creates a remote session, the program appears on that user's desktop and behaves as if it is a local application. Users can minimize, maximize, and restore as they would any other application. The client does not have to have Remote Desktop Connection version 6.0 on the system; when the program launches, the client software is provisioned and a secure and encrypted RDP-over-HTTPS connection is established. The ActiveX is part of the RDP client. The security model of the connection comprehensively supports all internal network security mechanisms that are already in place.

TIP You can define both a Terminal Services Resource Authorization Policy (TS RAP) and a Terminal Services Connection Authorization Policy (TS CAP) for the TS Gateway using the Authorization Policies Wizard.

To work properly, the TS Gateway must provide remote users with a means of connecting through firewalls and across Network Address Translation (NAT) devices. RDP uses port 3389 for its connection, which is blocked by default at the firewall as a security method. Since TS Gateway uses RPD over HTTPS, the remote traffic communicates with the local network through the firewall on port 443 and establishes an Internet connection on that channel using an HTTP Secure Sockets Layer/Transport Layer Security tunnel. Thus the TS Gateway circumvents the problem that ordinary RDP traffic would have connecting to a private LAN through the firewall. Figure 12.12 shows the configuration you might use for a TS Gateway coordinating with a health policy service.

FIGURE 12.12
When a gateway connects to a NAP server, the remote user connection topology might be configured as shown here.

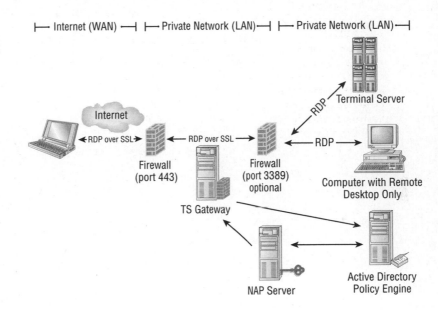

Gateway Requirements

The TS Gateway service has the following requirements:

- ◆ TS Gateway must be installed on a Windows Server 2008 server.

- ◆ That server must be running IIS 7.0 Server, and the Remote Procedure Call (RPC)-over-HTTP proxy service must be enabled on that web server.

- ◆ You must have an SSL certificate in place for the TS Gateway server (you do not have to have a CA infrastructure in place if you have an external trusted certificate).

- ◆ The client connecting to the service must be using either Windows Vista or XP, Windows Server SP1 (or later), or another Windows Server 2008 system.

- ◆ If you require that clients be authorized by system, user, and group, your TS Gateway will have to be part of a domain running the Active Directory Domain Services.

- ◆ You must define a set of Resource Authorization Policies (TS RAP) and Connection Authorization Policies (TS CAP) for the gateway after you install the gateway role service. TS RAP provides authenticated access for Terminal Server clients to network resources.

Network Access Protection Policies

Network Access Protection (NAP) is a security policy method that is part of Windows XP SP2, Vista, and Windows Server 2008. The policy can require that specific software versions be present in a client, that all security patches be in place, and that there be other computer security settings in effect in order to establish a connection. The set of settings are commonly referred to as a "health policy." The NAP system is composed of NAP clients, NAP policies (at the server), and NAP enforcement points, which are often part of network edge systems on a DMZ.

A DMZ is a subnet that is screened from the main network. It must be successfully authenticated against before further access is allowed. The connection between the remote client and a screened subnet (also known as a perimeter network) is usually an SSL connection. If you set up a perimeter network, the network topology may look something like Figure 12.13. The DMZ shown is populated with a TS Gateway between two firewalls. In this scenario the TS Gateway is inside the corporate network and validates the requests with Active Directory. A Health Policy Server isn't used.

FIGURE 12.13
In a perimeter network, the TS Gateway is deployed internally behind the corporate firewall.

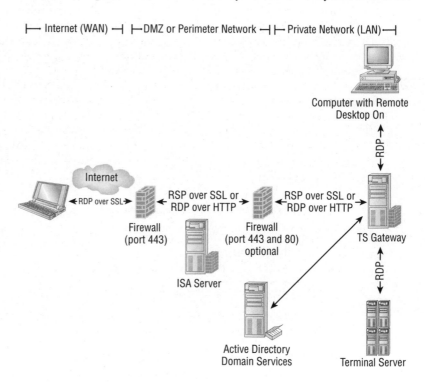

NOTE You can find information about setting up an Industry Standard Architecture (ISA) Internet-facing server for a TS Gateway, configuring the service, and more in the "TS Gateway Server Step-by-Step Setup Guide" that you can download from http://go.microsoft.com/fwlink/ ?LinkID=85872.

NAP enforcement points can be:

◆ NAP-enabled routers

◆ DHCP servers

- ISA servers or proxy servers

- VPN servers

All of these NAP enforcement points rely on what is called the Health Registration Authority (HRA) to authenticate connecting clients. These are computers (typically Windows Server 2008 systems) that enforce the Health Policy Server (HPS). An administrator can set the health policy of the network to enforce certain aspects of the client's configuration.

NOTE To read more about NAP on Microsoft's website go to `http://www.microsoft.com/technet/network/nap/default.mspx`.

For example, connection can be denied to a client found running without the latest virus update or the latest system patch. The client obtains a client certificate from the CA that it meets or exceeds the minimum health requirements of the service, and then that client can remotely connect to the local network and its resources. If clients don't meet the established requirements, they can be connected to a restricted part of the network or denied access to the network entirely. The restricted network can be set up to contain a "remediation server," which is a system that contains the resources necessary to update clients so that they can conform to the health policies. A subsequent request for client access would then be allowed.

Another example of a network policy and access service is a Remote Authentication Dial-In User Service (RADIUS) server, which have been in wide use in remote access applications for many years. If you have a RADIUS server, the TS Gateway can use the Network Policy Server (NPS) service to validate the remote connection in place of a NAP server. RADIUS servers can have a TS CAP defined that provides authenticated access to storage, management policies, and validation of remote clients. If you already have VPN or dial-up remote access configured through a RADIUS server, you may want to configure TS Gateway to use this service.

The Terminal Server Gateway Console

You configure your remote access policies for the gateway in the TS Gateway Manager MMC snap-in, as shownpreviously in Figure 12.8. That snap-in lets you assign the following access rights:

- Resources that users and groups can connect to

- The authentication method, be it password, smart card, or both

- That the remote computers are known to Active Directory by their machine ID, and that they can be validated

- Whether or not the client's requests can be redirected to other shares or devices

- Whether the connection must use NAP for a security provision

The TS Gateway Console provides information about the state of any active connection that the service has allowed. To view remote connections using the TS Gateway service:

1. Open the TS Gateway console.

2. Click the TS Gateway node.

3. Click Monitoring.

The Results pane that appears contains information about the various connections. Among the data displayed are the following:

◆ Connection ID

◆ User ID

◆ User name

◆ Connection duration

◆ Idle time

It is possible for the remote client to directly specify the address of the resource or remote application terminal server that they wish to connect to by directly entering the address into their browser. The address that they enter must be a fully qualified domain name (FQDN) containing the name of the Terminal Server server and the TS RemoteApp. The request is translated by the TS Gateway into a NetBIOS name and passed onto the Terminal Server application server. If a NetBIOS name is specified by the user, the request will fail. To enable the use of both NetBIOS and FQDN names by a user, the remote access policy in the TS Gateway console should allow both types of name resolution. For example, `TSRemoteAppServer` and `TSRemoteAppServer.DomainName` `.com` would both have to be listed in the computer group.

It is not required that you have the TS Gateway service running on a Terminal Server. Keep in mind that if you do install the TS Gateway on a Terminal Server 2008 server, any RAPs that you define during installation will not apply to the computer group you specify during installation. That is, the Allow Access to All Computers option in the installer will not apply to this server. You can verify that this is true by opening the TS Manager Gateway console and displaying the Properties dialog box for the Terminal Server RAP that was the result of the installation. The Computer Group list does not display this computer group. Therefore, to allow the TS Gateway access as part of the computer group, first install the Terminal Server role, and then install the TS Gateway separately later. You can also manually alter the RAP.

Session Broker

The TS Session Broker is a new feature in Windows Server 2008. It is a role service that lets users reconnect their session to a particular server in a server farm of load-balanced terminal servers. The TS Session Broker creates a compound Session ID based on several pieces of session state information. Part of the ID contains the name of the server as well as the particular user ID and session ID that the authorization request was associated with. The Session Broker is a less restrictive form of load balancing and is meant for terminal server farms in the two-to-five server range. Only Windows Server 2008 servers can participate in this form of session management. Larger server farms should consider using the Windows NLB solution.

TS Session Broker only requires that you have a DNS service running and that each member of the TS farm has its IP addressed registered in the DNS database. TS Session Broker works somewhat like NLB in that incoming sessions are assigned to the first IP in the range, and to the next one (should that IP address fail to respond quickly enough). For a server with a substantial load, TS Session Broker will direct new sessions to a server with lighter loads.

TS Session Broker offers two new features that you'll find valuable. You can assign a weighting factor to each server in the pool using the Terminal Server Configuration tool. The settings are located on the General tab of the RDP-Tcp connection. The second part of the policy will reconnect to the specific server in case a user disconnects.

You can find the TS Session Broker Policy at

```
Computer Configuration\Administrative Templates\Windows Components\Terminal
Services\Terminal Server\TS Session Broker\TS Session Broker Load Balancing
```
Settings for this policy are:

Enabled   New sessions are load balanced, and existing sessions are redirected to the server the session is running on.

Disabled   Users with a new session log on to the terminal server that they connect to.

Not Configured   When not configured, the terminal server's connection policy is controlled by other services. By default, this setting is left as not configured.

Terminal Server Licensing

Windows Terminal Server has a license management system, TS Licensing, that manages the Terminal Server client access licenses (CALs) and users. All previous versions of Terminal Server had license utilities, but in Windows Server 2008 the license utility has been reworked and has many new features. The new License utility supports Terminal Server 2008, Terminal Server 2003, and Terminal Server 2000.

When the Terminal Server role service is installed, the server is running an instance of the Windows application environment. From the standpoint of licensing, Microsoft treats the connection as an instance. You have the choice of attaching a TS CAL to either a user or to the connection.

To manage licenses, you install the TS Licensing role server. The license server manages the pool of terminal servers you have as well as the TS CALs. Two terminal server connections for administrators are part of the server and do not require connection licenses. To assign a CAL to a client, the terminal server must be able to communicate with the licensing server. The licensing server can be located on a terminal server, a domain server, or a dedicated server (for large organizations).

The TS Licensing service has very few transactions, so it is rare to dedicate an entire system to it. According to Microsoft, the licensing server is active only during a request, and the license database adds only 5MB for each 6,000 CALs that are managed. You can use the licensing server for administration, tracking, and reporting, as well as for purchasing new licenses.

Two modes are available for TS Licensing:

Per User   Each user account must have his or her own license. Per-user licensing is only supported in a directory and must have the Active Directory Domain Service available.

Per Device   Each named client is assigned a license.

To initiate TS Licensing:

1. Open the Server Manager and click on Terminal Server in the left-hand pane.

2. Scroll down to the Advanced Tools section, then click TS Licensing.

   The Activate Server wizard shown in Figure 12.14 appears.

FIGURE 12.14

Initiate TS Licensing using the Activate Server Wizard.

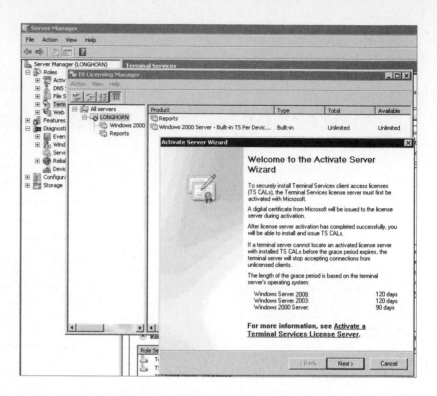

Summary

In this version of Windows Terminal Server, Microsoft has added a number of features that add the Windows Vista user experience to remote clients. A new kind of application called a RemoteApp puts a remotely run application into a window on the remote desktop that runs inside the remote user's standard desktop. That feature alone will lower the amount of training that administrators will have to give their users.

Remote access to the Terminal Server's applications has been greatly enhanced. A technology called Windows Terminal Server Web Access allows an application to be launched from a web page icon. When coupled with the new TS Gateway feature, users from anywhere in the world can connect through the gateway securely without having to use VPNs.

In the next chapter, we'll have a look at Internet Information Services, version 7.0. This core service supports many of the server services in Windows Server 2008 and has enhanced security and management features.

Chapter 13

Internet Information Services

Internet Information Services (IIS; formerly called Internet Information Server) version 7.0 is a completely restructured version of Microsoft's popular web server. The entire application has been reworked as a set of over 40 modules, some of them core services, and each is accessible with its own API. You can extend IIS with additional modules from third-party developers, as well as configure a custom installation to perform the tasks your website requires.

Along with a new architecture Microsoft has migrated the management function of IIS to an MMC snap-in that is part of the Server Manager. Event logging, role service installation and configuration, tracing, and new diagnostic tools can all be accessed through this new console. IIS has a new Windows Management Instrumentation (WMI) provider and is more easily automated. The interface brings the management of IIS and ASP.NET together in the same application. Settings and configurations are now stored in XML globally and at the site and folder level, making it easier, faster, and safer to change configurations on the fly. It is also now possible to manage remote websites through external firewalls.

IIS 7.0 is a completely new product, and it is the perfect example of what Microsoft was trying to achieve in terms of integrated management with the Longhorn core. We got a glimpse of what IIS 7.0 could be with Vista, but with Windows Server 2008 IIS is able to display its full capabilities.

Core IIS Changes

Internet Information Services has gone through seven versions since it was first released (as Internet Information Server) with Windows 3.51 as an add-on. Version 7.0, which is an add-on to Vista and a role for Windows Server 2008, is the eighth. This version of IIS will also install on Windows Server 2003.

Microsoft has renamed IIS as Internet Information Services to emphasize that IIS provides core internetworking services: the HTTP and HTTPS network protocols. Whether you consider IIS a server—that is, a computer running a service or a service running on a computer—there's no argument that IIS is an important core component in Windows Server technology. Actually, starting with version 7.0 IIS is no longer one core component; it is several modular components. Microsoft has rewritten IIS so that a new core web server engine can have individual modules added to it, as required by the task at hand.

The IIS modules that are now part of Windows Server 2008 are in the areas of:

- Common HTTP features
- Application development
- Health and diagnostics
- Security

- ◆ Performance
- ◆ Management tools
- ◆ FTP Publishing Service

NOTE Microsoft has created a new information portal for IIS at `http://www.iis.net/default.aspx?tabid=1`, with a TechCenter, download section, forums, blogs, and more.

Indeed, if you install the Web Server as a role on Windows Server 2008, the installation creates a list of 37 individual components that are role services that you can install for IIS; some are installed by default as part of the core service. These modules are listed individually in the Role Services section of the Web Server (IIS) of the Server Manager, as shown in Figure 13.1. Refer to Table 13.1 later in the chapter for an explanation of the various modules.

Figure 13.1 illustrates that the management application for IIS 7.0 is now an MMC snap-in to the Server Manager and is no longer a separate application, as it was with version 6.0. The configuration of ASP.NET is now integrated into the management interface. Modules can be loaded as needed either globally or on a per-site basis. By installing only the modules you need, you greatly lower the attack surface of IIS, lower the processing requirements, and improve performance and reliability.

FIGURE 13.1
The 37 modules that ship with IIS 7.0 in Windows Server 2008 can be viewed as a set of role services in the Web Server (IIS) section of the Server Manager. Only a few of these modules are installed by default.

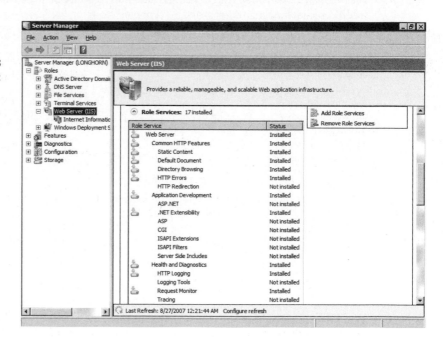

Sites and Applications

With Windows Server 2008 you create websites that are containers for web applications organized into a pool, that have a unique IP address and port, and that have option host headers on `HTTP.SYS` to listen for requests. Each website has a default web application, although there can be more applications that are used as well.

To give websites more flexibility and the ability to scale, IIS supports the concept of *virtual directories*. A virtual directory is one that is mapped by a pointer to a physical directory in another location. When you use a virtual directory, the name becomes part of the web application's address. Websites are published using either the XCOPY command or (more typically) FTP over a Secure Sockets Layer (SSL).

IIS 7.0 introduces a radical new architecture for the web server; that of a minimal core to which only required functionality is added, as needed. This approach, which will become the main architectural model for which Windows itself will be architected means that IIS has a new set of modular APIs, modules, security functions, and so forth, that will be described in the sections that follow.

IIS Modular APIs

Whereas past versions of IIS exposed the capabilities of the IIS through the ISAPI API, this monolithic API has been replaced with module APIs. Requests for access to services go directly to IHTTPMODULE for a module written in the .NET Framework, or to the module itself if it is written in another programming language.

The modular nature of IIS 7.0 allows you to pool applications together into groups (Figure 13.2). The benefit of creating application pools is that it creates a process boundary in which worker processes (W3WP.EXE) are shared by the applications in the pool. This has performance benefits, in addition to isolating faulty processes from one group so that other groups are unaffected. This organizational scheme also works well from the standpoint of future processor architectures as it is an efficient means for utilizing multicore processors.

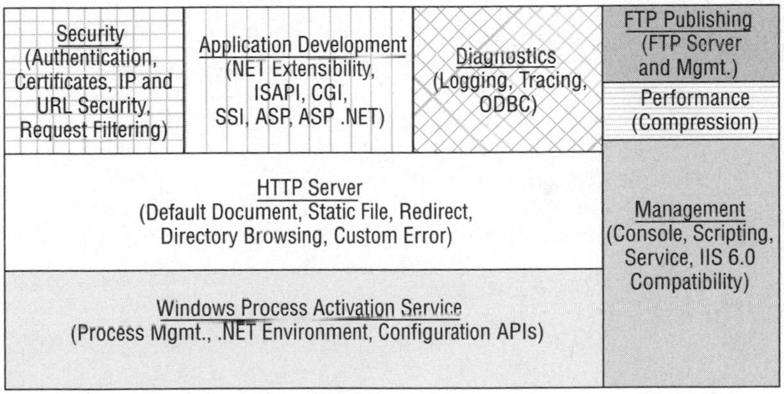

FIGURE 13.2
The modular nature of IIS 7.0 is evident in this functional topological diagram. Core services are separated from the web browser, as are other optional components.

Application pools can run in either integrated mode or in ISAPI mode; each mode handles incoming requests differently. In integrated mode, requests to web applications use IIS and ASP.NET to process the request. In ISAPI mode, the requests go to ASPNET_ISAPI.DLL and the managed code is processed in the same way it was in IIS 6.0.

Windows Process Activation Service

The Windows Process Activation Service (WPAS) manages IIS 7.0's application pools and the worker processes which they spawn. When you install the Web Server role, WPAS is installed as a required (default) feature. WPAS includes the process model, as well as configuration APIs and the hooks into the .NET environment. WPAS manages HTTP requests, as well as some of the other transport protocols.

WPAS is the service that actually instantiates worker processes. When a protocol listener detects incoming traffic, WPAS matches the protocol to the ones installed. It then looks at the queue to see which processes are running and, if there is a match, assigns the request to the worker process for processing. If no match is found, WPAS starts a worker process for that request.

You can view the properties of the application pool and some of the settings from the process model in Figure 13.3. The link Set Application Pool Defaults in the Actions panel leads you to the Application Pool Defaults dialog box.

FIGURE 13.3
The properties of the process model for an application pool are exposed in the Application Pools section of the IIS Manager.

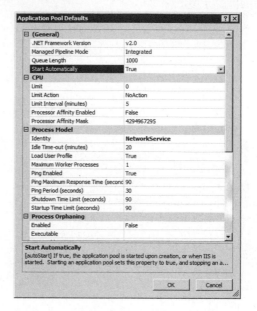

To manage worker processes, WPAS reads and updates configuration information for sites, applications and pools, global configuration, HTTP logging, and other settings. Not only does WPAS start the worker process, but it also monitors its progress, terminates processes when necessary, and restarts a process with new inputs when needed. To view worker processes that are currently running, follow these steps:

1. Open the IIS Manager and use the Features view to scroll to the Health and Diagnostics section.

2. Double-click the Worker Processes button. IIS Manager will then list all of these processes for you in the central details pane.

WPAS takes what was once an HTTP-only service and generalizes it so that it can service other protocols. WPAS replaces what was once a function of the WWW process.

Any applications that host Windows Communications Foundation (WCF) services can now have their processes managed by WPAS. IIS 7.0 also relies on WPAS to perform message-based activation using the HTTP protocol.

IIS 6.0 had a monolithic pipeline that offered little flexibility for modifying or optimizing processes and that was based on IIS and ASP.NET. For example, a request that comes into IIS 6.0 is handed off to the ISAPI extension `ASPNET_ISAPI.DLL`, where the process is fulfilled and the data is returned to IIS. The process involves two communications streams: one forward and one back.

IIS 7.0 handles requests very differently. In its "classic mode" IIS 7.0 uses the same mechanism just described for IIS 6.0. In the "integrated mode" ASP.NET and IIS are in the same pipeline.

Configuration Store

IIS 6.0 used a metabase for its configuration store. While it is still possible to use the metabase to manage IIS 6.0 websites, the default configuration store in IIS 7.0 are XML files. At the moment only the FTP server settings in IIS 7.0 are still stored in an IIS 6.0 metabase. There are several configuration files for IIS 7.0:

◆ APPLICATIONHOST.CONFIG contains system configuration data in two separate setting groups. The System.applicationHost section has site, applications, application pools, and virtual directory settings. You will also find settings for protocols other than non-HTTP, but not at the moment for FTP. The System.webServer section stores security, compression, and logging settings for sites, applications, directories (physical and virtual), and files.

◆ WEB.CONFIG (root) has configuration settings for each different website, as well as the applications and directories (both physical and virtual) that are part of each site.

◆ WEB.CONFIG (application) stores the same settings as the root version of this file, but applied to a specific website as either the content or the application themselves.

The system is similar to the one developed for ASP.NET's configuration, and indeed you can combine the IIS and ASP.NET configuration settings into a unified store. You will find the configuration files at %WINDIR%\SYSTEM32\INETSRV.

There is an order of precedence to the settings in the three files listed. When someone with appropriate privileges such as the server administrator makes changes to the APPLICATIONHOST.CONFIG file, those changes are inherited by WEB.CONFIG files beneath it. If you define a setting in the root WEB.CONFIG file, it overrides the settings in the APPLICATIONHOST.CONFIG file. Similarly, settings in the local or application level WEB.CONFIG can override the root version of the file.

Changes can also be made to website or application owners through Windows logon—even for users who have no Windows credentials at all. The changes that are made can be locked down to prevent them from being changed, and most of the settings in the APPLICATIONHOST.CONFIG file are locked.

You can edit configuration files using the IIS Manager GUI, a text editor or XML editor, through a WMI script, or programmatically with the IIS 7.0 configuration API.

Modules

Modules are a set of small programs or routines that process requests of a certain type. One module might authenticate an incoming request; another might support a certain protocol. Well over 40 modules ship with Windows Server 2008, as indicated in Table 13.1.

Some modules are native modules and others are manual modules. The difference is that native modules register at the server level and use native code DLLs that process the request for a specific purpose. Once a native module is registered, it can be instantiated at the site or application level as required and the work the module does is at that level only. Managed modules are those that access managed code. They run alongside native modules, and allow you to request content using those features. Forms are an example of managed code.

TABLE 13.1: Internet Information Services 7.0 Modules

ROLE SERVICE	MODULE NAME	DESCRIPTION	RESOURCE LIBRARY
HTTP Modules			
HTTP Errors (Default)	CustomErrorModule	Sends default and configured HTTP error messages when an error status code is set on a response.	INETSRV\CUSTERR.DLL
HTTP Redirection	HTTPRedirectionModule	Supports configurable redirection for HTTP requests.	INETSRV\REDIRECT.DLL
Syntax Checker	OptionsVerbModule	Provides information about allowed verbs in response to OPTIONS verb requests.	INETSRV\OPTIONS.DLL
Protocol Support	ProtocolSupport Module	Performs protocol-related actions, such as setting response headers and redirecting headers based on configuration.	INETSRV\PROTSUP.DLL
Request Forwarder	RequestForwarder Module	Forwards requests to external HTTP servers and captures responses.	INETSRV\FORWARD.DLL
Tracing	TraceVerbModule	Returns request headers in response to TRACE verb requests.	INETSRV\TRACE.DLL
Security Modules			
Anonymous Authentication	AnonymousAuthentication Module	Performs Anonymous authentication when no other authentication method succeeds.	INETSRV\AUTHANON.DLL
Basic Authentication	BasicAuthentication Module	Performs Basic authentication.	INETSRV\AUTHBAS.DLL
Client Certificate Mapping Authority	CertificateMapping AuthenticationModule	Performs Certificate Mapping authentication using Active Directory.	INETSRV\AUTHCERT.DLL
Digest Authentication	DigestAuthentication Module	Performs Digest authentication.	INETSRV\AUTHMD5.DLL

TABLE 13.1: Internet Information Services 7.0 Modules (*CONTINUED*)

ROLE SERVICE	MODULE NAME	DESCRIPTION	RESOURCE LIBRARY
IIS Client Certificate Mapping Authentication	IISCertificateMapping AuthenticationModule	Performs Certificate Mapping authentication using IIS certificate configuration.	INETSRV\AUTHMAP.DLL
Request Filtering (Default)	RequestFilteringModule	Performs URLScan tasks such as configuring allowed verbs and file extensions, setting limits, and scanning for bad character sequences.	INETSRV\MODRQFLT.DLL
URLAuthorization Module	URLAuthorizationModule	Performs URL authorization.	INETSRV\URLAUTHZ.DLL
Windows Authentication	WindowsAuthentication Module	Performs NTLM integrated authentication.	INETSRV\AUTHSSPI.DLL
IP and Domain Restrictions	IPRestriction Module	Restricts IPv4 addresses listing the ipSecurity list in configuration.	INETSRV\IPRESTR.DLL
Content Modules			
CGI	CGIModule	Executes CGI processes to build response output.	INETSRV\CGI.DLL
CGI	FastCGIModule	Supports FastCGI, a high-performance alternative to CGI.	INTESRV\IISFCGI.DLL
Distributed Authoring Versioning	DavFSModule	Sets the handler for Distributed Authoring and Versioning (DAV) requests to the DAV handler.	INETSRV\DAVFS.DLL
Default Document (Default)	DefaultDocumentModule	Attempts to return default document for requests made to the parent directory.	INETSRV\DEFDOC.DLL
Directory Browsing (Default)	DirectoryListing Module	Lists the contents of a directory.	INETSRV\DIRLIST.DLL
ISAPI Extensions	ISAPIModule	Hosts ISAPI DLLs.	INETSRV\ISAPI.DLL

TABLE 13.1: Internet Information Services 7.0 Modules (*CONTINUED*)

ROLE SERVICE	MODULE NAME	DESCRIPTION	RESOURCE LIBRARY
ISAPI Filters	ISAPIFilterModule	Supports ISAPI filter DLLs.	INETSRV\FILTER.DLL
Server-Side Includes	ServerSideInclude Module	Processes server-side includes code.	INETSRV\IIS_SSI.DLL
Static Content (default)	StaticFileModule	Serves static files.	INETSRV\STATIC.DLL
Compression Modules			
Dynamic Content Compression	DynamicCompressionModule	Compresses responses and applies GZIP compression transfer coding to responses.	INETSRV\COMPDYN.DLL
Static Content Compression	StaticCompressionModule	Performs pre-compression of static content.	INETSRV\COMPSTAT.DLL
Caching Modules			
File Cache	FileCacheModule	Provides user mode caching for files and file handles.	INETSRV\CACHFILE.DLL
HTTP Cache	HTTPCacheModule	Provides kernel mode and user mode caching in HTTP.SYS.	INETSRV\CACHHTTP.DLL
Site Cache	SiteCacheModule	Provides user mode caching of site information.	INETSRV\CACHSITE.DLL
Token Cache	TokenCacheModule	Provides user mode caching of username and token pairs for modules that produce Windows user principals.	INETSRV\CACHTOKN.DLL
URL Cache	URLCacheModule	Provides user mode caching of URL information.	INETSRV\CACHURI.DLL
Logging and Diagnostic Modules			
Custom Logging	CustomLoggingModule	Loads custom logging modules.	INETSRV\LOGCUST.DLL

TABLE 13.1: Internet Information Services 7.0 Modules (*CONTINUED*)

ROLE SERVICE	MODULE NAME	DESCRIPTION	RESOURCE LIBRARY
Failed Request Tracing	FailedRequestsTracingModule	Supports the Failed Request Tracing feature.	INETSRV\IISFREB.DLL
HTTP Logging (Default)	HTTPLoggingModule	Passes information and processing status to HTTP.SYS for logging.	INETSRV\LOGHTTP.DLL
Request Monitor (Default)	RequestMonitorModule	Tracks requests currently executing in worker processes and reports information with Runtime Status and Control Application Programming Interface (RSCA).	INETSRV\IISREQS.DLL
Tracing	TrackingModule	Reports events to the Microsoft Event Tracing for Windows (ETW).	INETSRV\IISETW.DLL
Managed Support Modules			
.NET Environment	ManagedEngine	Provides integration of managed code modules in the IIS request processing pipeline.	MICROSOFT.NET\FRAMEWORK\V.2.0.50727\WEBENGINE.DLL
Configuration APIs	ConfigurationValidation Module	Validates configuration issues, such as when an application is running in Integrated mode but has handlers or modules declared in the SYSTEM.WEB section.	INETSRV\VALIDCFG.DLL
Managed Support Modules			
Anonymous Identification	AnonymousIdentification	Manages anonymous identifiers, which are used by features that support anonymous identification such as ASP.NET profile.	SYSTEM.WEB.SECURITY.ANONYMOUSIDENTIFICATIONMODULE
Default Authorization	DefaultAuthentication	Ensures that an authentication object is present in the context.	SYSTEM.WEB.SECURITY.DEFAULTAUTHENTICATIONMODULE

TABLE 13.1: Internet Information Services 7.0 Modules (*CONTINUED*)

ROLE SERVICE	MODULE NAME	DESCRIPTION	RESOURCE LIBRARY
File Authorization	FileAuthorization	Verifies that a user has permission to access the requested file.	SYSTEM.WEB.SECURITY .FILEAUTHORIZATIONMODULE
Forms Authorization	FormsAuthentication	Supports authentication by using Forms authentication.	SYSTEM.WEB.SECURITY .FORMSAUTHENTICATIONMODULE
Output Cache	OutputCache	Supports output caching.	SYSTEM.WEB.CACHING .OUTPUTCACHEMODULE
User Profiles	Profile	Manages user profiles by using ASP.NET profile, which stores and retrieves user settings in a data source such as a database.	SYSTEM.WEB.PROFILE.PROFILEMODULE
Role Manager	RoleManager	Manages a RolePrincipal instance for the current user.	SYSTEM.WEB.SECURITY .ROLEMANAGERMODULE
Session	Session	Supports maintaining session state, which enables storage of data specific to a single client within an application on the server.	SYSTEM.WEB.SESSIONSTATE .SESSIONSTATEMODULE
URL Authorization	UrlAuthorization	Determines whether the current user is permitted access to the requested URL, based on the user name or the list of roles that a user is a member of.	SYSTEM.WEB.SECURITY .URLAUTHORIZATIONMODULE
URL Mapping	UrlMappingsModule	Supports mapping a real URL to a more user-friendly URL.	SYSTEM.WEB.URLMAPPINGSMODULE
Windows Authentication	WindowsAuthentication	Sets the identity of the user for an ASP.NET application when Windows authentication is enabled.	SYSTEM.WEB.SECURITY .WINDOWSAUTHENTICATIONMODULE

TABLE 13.1: Internet Information Services 7.0 Modules (*CONTINUED*)

ROLE SERVICE	MODULE NAME	DESCRIPTION	RESOURCE LIBRARY
Management Tools			
IIS 7 Management Tools	IIS Management Console	Infrastructure to manage IIS 7's UI, either for a local or remote web server HTTP traffic. For SMTP or FTP, however, you need to use IIS 6 Management Console.	
IIS Management Scripts and Tools	IIS Management Scripts and Tools	Programmatically manage IIS 7 using commands in a command window or a script. Useful for running batch files or when you want a low overhead to manage IIS.	
Management Service	Management Service	Infrastructure to configure IIS 7.0 user interface, IIS Manager, and remote management.	
IIS 6 Management Capability	IIS 6 Metabase Compatibility	Infrastructure to query and configure the metabase so that you can use applications and script from earlier version of IIS that used Admin Base Object (ABO) or the Active Directory Service Interface (ADSI) APIs.	
IIS 6 WMI Compatibility	II6 WMI Compatibility	Enables WMI scripting interfaces to manage and automate tasks for IIS 7 web servers using the WMI provider. This includes the WMI CIM Studio, WMI Event Registration, WMI Event Viewer, and the WMI Object Browser.	

TABLE 13.1: Internet Information Services 7.0 Modules (*CONTINUED*)

ROLE SERVICE	MODULE NAME	DESCRIPTION	RESOURCE LIBRARY
IIS 6 Scripting Tools	IIS 6 Scripting Tools	Uses IIS 6 scripting inside IIS 7, allowing use of ActiveX Data Objects or Active Directory Service Interface (ADSI) APIs. These tools require the Windows Process Activation Service API.	
IIS 6 Management Console	IIS 6 Management Console	Infrastructure for administering remote IIS 6.0 servers.	
FTP Publishing Service	FTP Server	Provides infrastructure to create an FTP site using the FTP protocol and client software. FTP uses TCP/IP to distribute files in a similar way to how HTTP does, and is useful for uploading and downloading files as it has faster transfer speeds.	
FTP Management Console	FTP Management Console	Provides infrastructure to manage an FTP site. IIS 7 uses IIS 6 Management Console for FTP local and remote servers.	

NOTE Of the modules loaded with IIS by default, only the modules necessary to support installed IIS server role service are actually accessed. You can remove many of these modules (outside the core ones) if you aren't going to use the role features that use them.

Each of these modules has a handler associated with it. Handlers are written in either native or managed code, and are used to process a request for services for the module that they are associated with. When a request is handled, it is passed on to the resource that is mapped to the handler, such as a CGI or ASP file. When you remove a module, you can remove the handler as well. Handlers are specified in the Handler Mappings list.

Security

The modular nature of IIS 7.0 has the effect of isolating one site from another as well as one application pool from another. When you create a new website, it comes with its own personal application pool. Process isolation means that even if one site is compromised, additional sites shouldn't be. Each application pool is its own network service, and each service is referencing its own configuration file, isolated from the other running web instances.

Surprisingly, IIS 7.0 doesn't install security authorization as part of the default Windows Server 2008 installation. Security must be added later. The one and only security module installed by default is the RequestFilterModule. This module takes a set of filters you specify, such as file extensions, verbs, character strings, required character length, and malformed URLs, and blocks these requests. Gone from IIS 7.0 is the URLScan add-on, which was part of IIS 6.0; it is now part of the default installation. For more information on using RequestFilterModule, which has no management tool other than hand-editing the configuration files directly, go to http://www.iis.net/default.aspx?/tabid=2&subtabid=25&i=1040.

It's important to note that none of the authentication modules are installed by default. You need to also add an authentication method(s) as a role service after the fact so that anyone who attempts to access the web server is forced to identify themselves. Authorization limits the access of IIS 7.0 resources users and groups to files or directories, applications or sites, and computer, domain, or sites. IIS 7.0 also supports the creation of *roles*, which are groups of users to whom security authorization may be given. Access to resources can be restricted on the basis of the domain or IP address of the requesting party. Restriction lists allow you to apply inheritance rules to what can be accessed.

The four available authentications methods offered as add-ons are:

♦ Anonymous authentication

♦ Windows authentication

♦ Basic authentication

♦ Digest authentication

You can set up these different authentication methods (provided that you have installed the IIS 7.0 web server) by going to Authentication in the Security section of the IIS Service Manager.

Through Forms, you can use the redirected logon authentication method. .NET provides a means for authenticating user access to the web server. You can also authenticate clients using certificate mapping to an Active Directory user account, as well as use IIS certificate mapping as an alternative where client certificates are mapped to a user(s).

IIS is now an extensible framework application, so the types of authentication mechanisms that may ultimately be available to you may be different than the four types listed earlier. They can even be modules that you create yourself, or ones that you purchase from third parties. Also keep in mind that you need to install supporting modules if you decide to use one of these authentication mechanisms.

Install and Setup

When you install the Web Server (IIS) role, you install a minimal set of modules. This keeps the footprint of the server small for better performance and security. The following features are part of this core installation:

◆ **Common HTTP**. Static Content, Default Document, Directory Browsing, and HTTP Errors.

◆ **Health and Diagnostics**. HTTP Logging and Request Monitor

◆ **Security**. Request Filtering.

◆ **Performance**. Static Content Compression.

◆ **Management Tools**. IIS Management Console.

This is a very sparse set of services. It doesn't even have the basic authentication mechanism installed. Unless the web server is running in a core server role, you'll probably want to add many more features—especially security features—to your installation.

You can add IIS 7.0 to your Windows Server 2008 installation by using the Add Roles Wizard of the Server Manager. To add the web server, you must either be a local administrator or have Web Server Administrator credentials. To install IIS, open the Server Manager, click the Add Roles link in the Roles Summary section, and follow the steps of the Add Role Wizard. The default installation applies a minimum set of role services. To install the Web Server role service, use the Add Role Services link shown in Figure 13.1.

You can also install the various Web Server roles and its role services from the command line. To install IIS from a script using the PKGMGR command, you can edit the following command to include just those modules you wish to install. (Table 13.1 describes in more detail the purpose of each of these modules):

```
>start /w pkgmgr /iu:IIS-WebServerRole;IIS-WebServer;IIS-CommonHttpFeatures;➡
IIS-StaticContent;IIS-DefaultDocument;IIS-DirectoryBrowsing;IIS-HttpErrors;➡
IIS-HttpRedirect;IIS-ApplicationDevelopment;IIS-ASPNET;IIS-NetFxExtensibility;➡
IIS-ASP;IIS-CGI;IIS-ISAPIExtensions;IIS-ISAPIFilter;IIS-ServerSideIncludes;➡
IIS-HealthAndDiagnostics;IIS-HttpLogging;IIS-LoggingLibraries;IIS-RequestMonitor;➡
IIS-HttpTracing;IIS-CustomLogging;IIS-ODBCLogging;IIS-Security;IIS-
BasicAuthentication;➡
IIS-WindowsAuthentication;IIS-DigestAuthentication;IIS-
ClientCertificateMappingAuthentication;➡
IIS-IISCertificateMappingAuthentication;IIS-URLAuthorization;IIS-RequestFiltering;➡
IIS-IPSecurity;IIS-Performance;IIS-HttpCompressionStatic;IIS-
HttpCompressionDynamic;➡
IIS-WebServerManagementTools;IIS-ManagementConsole;IIS-ManagementScriptingTools;➡
IIS-ManagementService;IIS-IIS6ManagementCompatibility;IIS-Metabase;IIS-
WMICompatibility;➡
IIS-LegacyScripts;IIS-LegacySnapIn;IIS-FTPPublishingService;IIS-FTPServer;IIS-
FTPManagement;➡
WAS-WindowsActivationService;WAS-ProcessModel;WAS-NetFxEnvironment;WAS-
ConfigurationAPI
```

When you complete an installation, you install a default website at `http://localhost/`, which is shown in Figure 13.4.

FIGURE 13.4
The default website is installed on the local-host and uses port 80, the well-known HTTP port. The links take you to www.iis.net.

Management

IIS 7.0 has four main tools used to provision and configure the web services:

Server Manager   In the Server Manager, you can see an overview of your websites, install or remove role services, view the event log (if you have installed that service), determine system service states, and view IIS Manager.

Internet Information Services (IIS) Manager   Since the IIS Manager is an MMC snap-in, when you install the IIS Management Console role service it can be opened in its own console view. The command that opens IIS Manager is found in the Administrative Tools folder.

TIP   Any role service that isn't installed won't show up in the IIS Manager. If you are managing other websites where that feature was used and you haven't installed the supporting role service, you won't be able to manage that feature. Therefore, consider installing additional role services for features that you expect to appear locally or remotely.

Administration API   The `Microsoft.Web.Administration` API allows you to provision, access, and diagnose XML configuration files and server objects.

Command-Line Administration   The `APPCMD.EXE` command is the command-line version of the IIS Manager and is described in more detail in its own section later in this chapter.

The IIS Services Manager

The IIS Services Manager opens in a browser window that shows either the Features view (see Figure 13.5) or the content view. As you develop websites and add web pages, images, and other items to the website, you will want to manage them in content view.

FIGURE 13.5

The IIS Services Manager is where you can create websites, manage content, and use the various applications and features that you have installed. It is shown here in the Features view.

You can use the IIS Manager to view any IIS 7.0 website that you can connect to. Individual wizards guide you through the process of:

◆ Specifying server connections

◆ Specifying the site connection details

◆ Specifying application connection details

◆ Providing credentials

◆ Specifying a connection name

Chances are that you will spend most of your time managing IIS 7.0 websites inside the IIS Manager.

CREATE A WEBSITE

There are several places in Windows Server 2008 where you can create a website. You can do so from the command line as well as from the management consoles. However, the IIS Manager is a convenient place to create a website and manage its properties. Let's take a brief look at how this is done and what some of the options are.

To create a website in the IIS Services Manager:

1. Right-click on the Sites node of the Connections pane (the left hand pane in the manager window), then select the Add Web Site command from the context menu, as shown in Figure 13.6.

FIGURE 13.6

To create a new website, use this command for Sites in the IIS Services Manager's Connections pane.

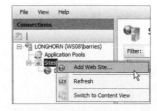

2. In the Add Web Site dialog box that appears (Figure 13.7), enter the name of the website, the physical location for the site's files, the connection properties (or binding), and click OK.

The website is created and then listed in the Connections pane.

FIGURE 13.7
The Add Web Site dialog box lets you enter basic properties for your new website.

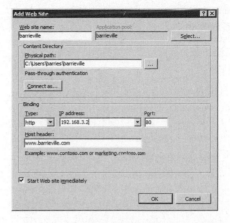

3. If you want to share the folder containing the website, click the Edit Permissions link in the Actions panel. A standard Windows Server 2008 folder properties dialog box appears that contains Sharing and Security tabs, Previous Versions (Shadow Copy), and so forth.

4. To edit the bindings, click the Bindings link in the Edit Site section of the Actions panel.

5. To edit the location of the files and the connection properties, click the Basic Settings link in the Actions panel.

You cannot rename the website or its application pool; however, you can create a new website and move the content from another site into that site.

If you need to manage IIS 6.0 websites, install the management tools as a role service for IIS 6.0. You can also remotely manage sites provided that the Management Service server role has been installed and is running. Figure 13.8 shows you these additional role services in the Web Server section of Server Manager.

FIGURE 13.8
Additional role services are required to manage IIS 6.0 and remote websites.

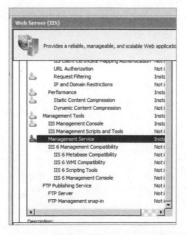

SITE DELEGATION

To manage IIS 7.0, you need to be an administrator. You can't make changes in the IIS 7.0 console, use the command line, change configuration files, or access IIS 7.0 settings through WMI without having this level of authority. To make it easier to administer websites, IIS 7.0 has three administrative role groups:

Web Server Administrator   A Web Server Administrator is a member of the local Administrators group or a domain administrator for that server's domain. This group can create and modify not only the web server itself, but also sites, application pools, directories (physical and virtual), and files.

A Web Server Administrator can delegate authority to Web Site and Web Application administrators so that they can perform administrative tasks. The Web Server Administrator still retains control over the web server and can deny certain site and application settings that the Web Server Administrator doesn't want to delegate.

Web Site Administrator   Web Site Administrators have access to features that are based on the site or sites that they control. Certain features and configurations can be locked by the Web Server Administrator, which places limits on what a Web Site Administrator can do. Usually Web Site Administrators can modify the website they have been delegated, applications, directories (physical and virtual), and files contained in that website.

Web Site Administrators can delegate some of the features of the website to Web Application Administrators.

Web Applications Administrator   Web Applications Administrators have the ability to modify applications that have been delegated to them either by the Web Server or the Web Site Administrator. They face the same restriction on their actions that Web Site Administrators do in that a Web Server Administrator can lock certain features and configurations so that they can't be altered. Web Applications Administrators can modify the action of the application that has been delegated to them, as well as the directories (physical and virtual) that are used by the applications, in addition to any files that are contained in those directories.

The delegation of features in websites and applications is on a feature-by-feature basis. In the management console it is possible to deny access to a setting; also, a higher-level administrator can control whether the lower-level administrator can see that setting at all. When you establish a default setting, that setting is applied by inheritance to all of the objects lower in the Web Service hierarchy. For example, a Web Server Administrator who applies a setting at the server level can have that setting apply to all sites and applications.

It is also possible to set a custom delegation setting, which acts like an exception and applies only to the object it was set on. A custom setting applied to a website might apply to that site only. Feature delegation can be on a read/write or read-only basis. You can also use the Remove Delegation option (to lock down objects below in the hierarchy) or the Reset to Inherited option (which returns the delegation settings to their default condition).

APPCMD.EXE

The APPCMD.EXE command is a CLI tool for managing web servers, applications and pools, configuration settings, modules, directories, and tools. This command is stored in the %WINDIR%\ SYSTEM32\INETSRV directory, along with its XML configuration file APPCMD.XML. Figure 13.9 shows you the help for APPCMD.EXE at the overview level. To get help for specific features, use the command **APPCMD <OBJECT-TYPE> /?**, where **<OBJECT-TYPE>** is **SITE, APP, VDIR, APPPOOL, CONFIG, WP, REQUEST, MODULE, BACKUP,** or **TRACE**.

FIGURE 13.9
The APPCMD command lets you create, modify, and manage websites. It is the command-line equivalent of the IIS Manager.

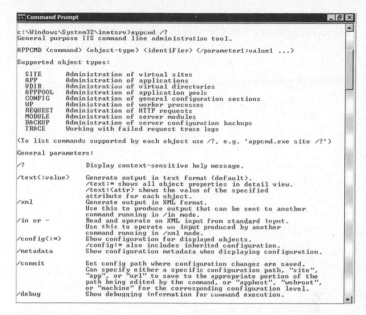

The APPCMD command replaces what was a rat's nest of script in IIS 6.0 with this one command. For example, you can use the APPCMD command to create a completely new website. The exact syntax of the command is:

```
APPCMD ADD SITE /NAME: "SEVENFRIENDLYCATS" /ID:3
```

The command above the ID was set to 3 because this was the third website on the server after Default and BARRIEVILLE.

NOTE   For more information on using APPCMD, go to the IIS.NET article on the subject at http://www.iis.net/articles/view.aspx/IIS7/Use-IIS7-Administration-Tools/Using-the-Command-Line/Getting-Started-with-AppCmd-exe and the article on Tech-Net at http://technet2.microsoft.com/windowsserver2008/en/library/ec52c53b-6aff-4d76-995e-3d222588bf321033.mspx?mfr=true.

WMI PROVIDER

Another way to manage IIS 7.0 from the command line is to use scripts that use the services of the WMI provider. This service is added to IIS when you install the IIS Management Script and Tools role service. Although a WMI provider shipped with IIS 6.0, the provider in IIS 7.0 switches the service over to the XML configuration data store. Older scripts using WMI are sometimes incompatible with IIS 7.0's provider.

The new WMI provider streamlines the object model into two separate groups:

◆ Classes that manage IIS objects including sites, applications, application pools, and so forth

◆ Classes that manage the configuration of IIS features such as ASP.NET and the .NET Framework mostly in the form of Configuration sections

Through the use of WMI you can create, modify, stop, start, and delete website, as well as create and modify website objects. WMI enumerates object types and provides the mechanisms by which these objects may be manipulated. To learn more, see `http://www.iis.net/articles/view.aspx/IIS7/Use-IIS7-Administration-Tools/Scripting-IIS7/Managing-Sites-with-IIS7-s-WMI-Provider`.

Summary

In this chapter you learned about the radically new version of IIS 7.0 that ships with the Windows Server 2008. Windows Server 2008 brings this new technology to full realization by providing a server platform on which you can create and manage websites locally and remotely.

IIS 7.0 is a framework on which different functional modules are applied. In the IIS Manager you are now able to manage both IIS and ASP.NET from the same console. Management functions have been greatly consolidated, and a number of wizards make the job of site management much easier to perform.

The new architecture of IIS 7.0 ushers in a new era at Microsoft where future operating systems and the enterprise appliations that run on them will be built on a small core to which you add only the functions you require. The next version of the Windows desktop, the project named Vienna, will start with a MinWin core. This approach solves so many problems related to right-sizing, improving security, enhancing portability, and distributing applications smoothly that it isgan extremely elegant solution. Modular products should give Microsoft manifold advantages going forward.

In the next chapter you will learn about the new Server Core version of Windows Server. Server Core eliminates the Windows GUI, leaving only applications and services running on the server. Server Core can be a file server, domain server, DNS server, or DHCP server, but additional versions are being considered. Server Core is meant to be a more secure, better-performing version of Windows Server 2008, and requires a whole new management style and toolset to run.

Chapter 14

Server Core

Oddly one of the most talked about new features in Windows Server 2008 isn't new at all, and in a sense isn't Windows either. Windows Server 2008 Server Core is a stripped-down version that runs server roles: file server, domain controller, DNS, and DHCP services among others. Server Core runs in an environment that is less than 20 percent the size of a standard installation. You can use it to run Microsoft Cluster Server, Network Load Balancing, Windows Backup, Subsystem for Unix-based Applications (SUA), Removable Storage Management, SNMP, and BitLocker drive encryption, for example. You should expect to see more capabilities for Server Core in the future.

Server Core doesn't run the graphical components of Windows, so when you boot to the operating system you see a command prompt. In fact, you get to the command prompt rather quickly—which may surprise you. The operating system supports local logon, Remote Desktop, Web Services for Management (WS-Management), and the Windows Remote Shell (WinRS). The latter two are execution environments that are available on Vista or Windows Server 2008. When you connect to a Server Core system, all you see is a command-line window. You can manage a Server Core remotely with the MMC by accessing the Server Core snap-ins, but there's only a little "Windows-like" capability remaining. You can get to the Task Manager and see alert boxes, and that's about it.

Server Core represents a radical departure for Microsoft away from its reliance on the GUI as a management platform to a server that is lightweight and likely to be more stable, higher performing, and more secure. Fewer server subsystems mean a smaller attack surface (fewer targets), fewer patches applied, and fewer equipment requirements. At least that's the expectation. If Server Core ends up being a success, you can expect to see this configuration rolled out for many more of the roles that Windows Server 2008 supports. Server Core will force you to do nearly everything in Windows in new ways, and many people won't like that. However, if you are comfortable working at the command line, know or appreciate scripting, and have been keeping up to date with subjects like Windows Management Instrumentation (WMI), this is an area of technology where your skills can shine.

Server Core Basics

Server Core is a feature-reduced minimal installation of Windows Server 2008, installed as a role for Windows Server 2008 Standard, Enterprise, and Datacenter Edition. Server Core can be installed in the following server roles:

- ◆ Active Directory (AD)
- ◆ Active Directory Lightweight Directory Services (AD LDS)
- ◆ DHCP Server
- ◆ DNS Server

- ◆ File Server
- ◆ Media Services
- ◆ Print Server

Server Core is meant to serve the role as a stable and low-maintenance infrastructure platform. Although it comes with management tools and utilities, and can support third-party agents, it is not an application server. That is, you wouldn't use Server Core to run Exchange, Oracle, or any other server application because it is missing the required GUI necessary to support these products. You can run third-party applications that run as a server as long as they are designed to operate and be administered without any graphical components.

You can manage Server Core locally from the command prompt or remotely using the Windows Terminal Services RPD protocol. Certain tools that make limited use of the Windows GUI, such as Task Manager, as well as utilities that rely on Remote Procedure Calls such as DCOM, can run remotely. You can use WS-Management and WinRS to perform remote command execution. These utilities are part of Vista and Windows Server 2008.

Included in Server Core are the following:

- ◆ Hardware Abstraction Layer

- ◆ Device drivers for basic components such as disks, NICs, video, and other devices

- ◆ Security and WinLogon

- ◆ Networking subsystem and NAP client

- ◆ File System

- ◆ Inter-application communication protocols such as RPC and DCOM

- ◆ SNMP

- ◆ Plug and Play

- ◆ Windows Firewall and IPsec

- ◆ Remote Desktop and RDP 6.0

- ◆ WMI and scripting

- ◆ WinRM and WS-Management

- ◆ Event, counters, logging, task scheduling, Task Manager (TASKMAN), and the Registry Editor (REGEDIT)

NOTE   Server Core installs two shims, or code layers, between applications and the Windows API. The first shim is the `RegEditImportExportLoadHive` that lets RegEdit import and export Registry hives. The second shim is called the `NoExplorerForGetFileName` and allows the Open (GET) and Save (PUT) operations to work in applications such as Notepad. This second shim posts a rudimentary standard file dialog box that has the features that were in Windows in the very earliest days (such as Windows 3.1).

NOTE A shimming engine can be used by the Application Compatibility Toolkit (ACT; see Chapter 2) to apply these shims to other applications so that they can open and save files. To use the ACT this way you need to copy the %SystemRoot%\AppPath\SysMain.SDB (or its AppPatch64 folder equivalent) database from Server Core to the Windows Server 2008 system that has ACT on it and then edit the database to accommodate the application. Then copy the modified database back to Server Core and install it using the %SystemRoot%\System32\SDBINST.EXE application.

For a listing of the DLLs included in a Server Core installation, refer to Table 14.1.

TABLE 14.1: Server Core DLLs by Feature

FEATURE	DLLs	SERVICE
Active Directory	ACTIVEDS.DLL	Active Directory Service Interfaces (ADSI)
	NTDSAPI.DLL	Domain controller and replication management
Installation	CABINET.DLL	CAB file management
	IMAGEHLP.DLL	Portable Executable (PE) extraction
	MSI.DLL.	Windows installer
	SETUPAPI.DLL	Microsoft Windows Setup
	SXS.DLL	Manifest Logging
DHCP	DHCPSVC.DLL	DHCP
DNS	DNSAPI.DLL	DNS
Networking	AUTHZ.DLL	Secure RPC
	HTTPAPI.DLL	HTTP
	IPHLPAPI.DLL	Internet Protocol Helper (IP Helper)
	MGMTAPI.DLL	SNMP management
	MPR.DLL	Windows Networking (WNet)
	MPRAPI.DLL	RAS and router administration
	MSWSOCK.DLL	Winsock
	NETSH.EXE	NetShell
	RPCRT4.DLL	RPC NDR engine

TABLE 14.1:   Server Core DLLs by Feature *(CONTINUED)*

FEATURE	DLLs	SERVICE
	RTUTILS.DLL	Remote RAS tracing
	SECURITY.DLL	Remote RAS security
	SNMPAPI.DLL	SNMP
	TRAFFIC.DLL	QoS traffic control
	WINHTTP.DLL	HTTP
Security	ADVAPI32.DLL	HTTP authentication and credential management
	CREDUI.DLL	Credential management
	CRYPT32.DLL	Windows Cryptographic service
	CRYPTDLL.DLL	Cryptographic Manager
	CRYPTNET.DLL	Secure channel (X.509 certificates)
	CRYPTUI.DLL	Credential management
	NETAPI32.DLL	Microsoft network operations
	SCHANNEL.DLL	Secure channel (X.509 certificates)
	SECUR32.DLL	Windows Security library functions
	WINTRUST.DLL	Catalog functions
Server Clustering	CLUSAPI.DLL	Clustering API
	RESUTILS.DLL	Clustering utility functions
System Services	CLFSW32.DLL	Log file management
	DBGHELP.DLL	Debugging helper
	DCIMAN32.DLL	Graphics support
	FLTLIB.DLL	Minifilter management
	FLTMGR.SYS	Minifilter management
	GDI32.DLL	Graphics support
	KERNEL32.DLL	Windows system kernel
	MSTASK.DLL	Task scheduler
	NTDLL.DLL	Windows internal

TABLE 14.1:   Server Core DLLs by Feature *(CONTINUED)*

FEATURE	DLLs	SERVICE
	OLE32.DLL	Object management
	OLEAUT32.DLL	Object management
	PDH.DLL	Performance monitoring
	POWRPROF.DLL	Power management
	PSAPI.DLL	Performance monitoring
	PSTOREC.DLL	Protected storage interface
	SFC.DLL	Windows File Protection
	SRCLIENT.DLL	System Restore functions
	USER32.DLL	User objects
	USERENV.DLL	User profile support
	VERIFIER.DLL	Performance monitoring
	VERSION.DLL	Versioning information
	VSSAPI.DLL	Volume shadow copy
	WINSTA.DLL	Windows internal
User Interface	MLANG.DLL	Multiple language support
	MSCTF.DLL	Text Services Framework (TSF)
	SHELL32.DLL	Shell functions for opening web pages and files
	SHLWAPI.DLL	Function library for UNC and URL paths, registry entries, and color settings.

Source: Windows Developer Network (http://msdn2.microsoft.com/en-us/library/ms723876.aspx)

Server Core strips the base installation of Windows Server 2008 down from about 6GB to about 1GB. Although the default services list is about 40 entries, essential services such as outgoing HTTP, Windows File Protection, Windows Installer (for .MSI files, etc.), Windows Firewall, IPsec, the Event Log, Performance Monitor, counters, licensing, and others are on that list.

The following major Windows components are not part of a Server Core installation:

Windows Shell   Windows shells, Windows Explorer, the Windows Desktop, Start menu, and all browsers such as Microsoft Internet Explorer are not available.

Graphical Windows Applications   These include Outlook Express, WordPad, Paint, Media Player, just to name a few. Notepad is available, but only in a feature-limited version. To open Notepad, enter **NOTEPAD.EXE** at the command prompt.

.NET Framework   No .NET managed code is allowed, which means that PowerShell will not run on the first release version of Server Core. All running code must use the native Windows APIs. A rewritten version of .NET Framework is expected to be added to a future version of Server Core. Since your interaction with Server Core is through a remote administration session, you can use PowerShell on your local system even though it won't run on Server Core.

Control Panel   The CONTROL.EXE file does not run by itself. To work with control panels, you will need to specify the individual control panel itself, and only a few of those control panels are enabled for Server Core.

Peripheral drivers   Server Core doesn't support sound or printers.

Microsoft Management Console   You can't run the MMC locally, but you can access the settings used by the MMC for different snap-ins remotely.

Installing Server Core

Server Core is installed using the same installer that you use for any other version of Windows Server 2008. Server Core installation requires a clean install from media or a network share. Server Core is available for both the x86 and x64 versions of Windows Server 2008 Standard, Enterprise, and Datacenter Editions. Although Server Core doesn't support many of the features that Enterprise and Datacenter Editions offer, you do get the higher processor limits moving to both, as well as the Datacenter assurance program for system reliability.

To install Server Core on a local system:

1. Insert the media into the server's optical drive. Setup should proceed automatically.

2. Select Server Core as the version you wish to install in the dialog box; then click Next, as shown in Figure 14.1.

FIGURE 14.1
There are three kinds of Server Core that you can choose from the Windows installer: Standard, Enterprise, and Datacenter.

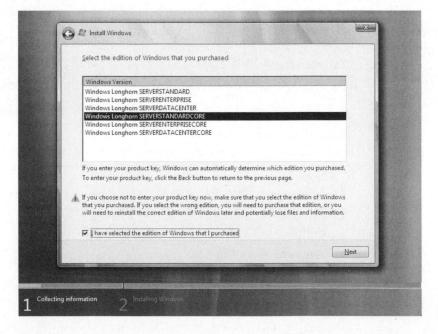

3. Complete the installation as instructed.

The Windows Server logon screen will appear when installation is complete, as shown in Figure 14.2.

FIGURE 14.2
There's little to indicate that Server Core is different from any other version of Windows Server based on the logon screen alone.

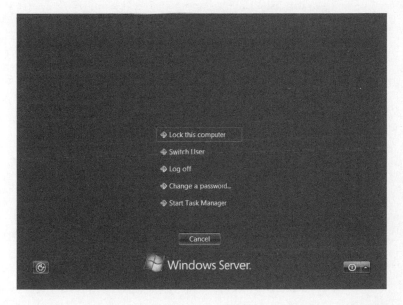

You can use the Windows Preboot Execution Environment (PXE) to install Server Core from media or from a network share using an answer file that you can create using Windows System Image Manager. With the UNATTEND.XML answer file either on the local drive or a network share, you can use that file to drive a Server Core installation. Chapter 2 described these technologies in some detail, and the same techniques are applied in this instance.

To perform an unattended (automated) installation of Server Core:

1. Insert the Windows PE disk and go to the command prompt.

2. Change directories to the drive or share containing the installation files.

3. Type the command **SETUP /UNATTEND:<PATH> \UNATTEND.XML**, then press Enter.

Setup should run to completion.

Once Server Core is installed, you will need to configure your system. The following steps need to be performed:

1. Assign the Administrator password.

2. Assign a static IP address if desired (optional); otherwise the default dynamic DHCP address is retained.

3. Join a domain (optional).

4. Activate Server Core.

5. Specify which ports on the Windows Firewall should allow network traffic.

Server Core's installation on a system that already contains the Windows operating system, say another version of Windows Server, is performed in both an interesting and thoughtful manner. The installer upgrades your installation by putting all of your previous operating system's files into a folder labeled <*01dOS*>.OLD so that you can access the files. It then proceeds to write all of the new files to disk, replacing anything that was operationally part of your previous installation—that is, all boot files, INI files, configuration parameters, and the directory into which all of the files are written are all new. You don't have a situation where the WINDOWS, SYSTEM, or SYSTEM32 folders contain a mixture of old and new files. Essentially this is a fresh installation that archives your older files. There's no option made in the installer to roll back the installation if you change your mind, although third-party software enables you to do so with some extra effort.

Server Core Management

Server Core is meant to be managed either from the command prompt or remotely. The following services are available for management by utilities, scripts, or agents:

- Command-line execution. (See the section "Command-Line Commands" later in this chapter.)
- Remote access through RDP and terminal services.
- Windows Management Instrumentation.
- Remote access to MMC snap-ins using RPC or DCOM.
- Task Schedule utility for job creation and management.
- Event logging and forwarding.
- SNMP event trapping.
- WS-Management and WinRS for remote command-line execution.

Although Server Core is missing most of Windows Server GUI functionality, there is enough functionality in the product to support some of the important management tools that you are used to. You can open Task Manager from the command prompt, as is shown in Figure 14.3, by pressing Ctl+Alt+Esc. However, for the most part management of a Server Core will largely be done at a command prompt or through an MMC, and will likely be performed remotely employing Server Core as a headless (without a monitor) system.

Command Prompt Management

The first time you log in, you will be asked to create an Administrator password. Then the command prompt window shown in Figure 14.4 opens. If you want to open another command prompt window locally, follow these steps:

1. Press Ctrl+Alt+Del.

2. Type the administrator account ID (if necessary) and password; then press Enter.

   The command prompt window then appears, as shown in Figure 14.4.

FIGURE 14.3

You can open the Windows Task Manager from a command prompt onHServer Core.

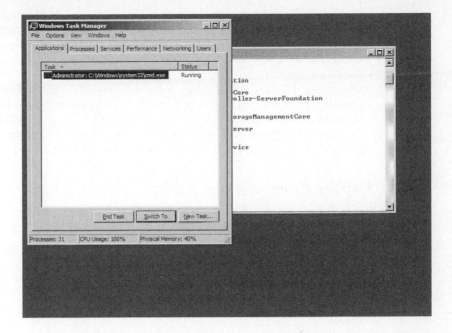

FIGURE 14.4

When you log in locally to Server Core, this command prompt window is the only window you see.

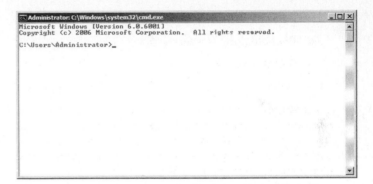

If you close your command prompt, you can use the Task Manager to reopen it:

1. Display Task Manager on your Server Core.

2. Select File ➤ New Task to display a Run-like dialog box.

3. Enter **cmd** in that box and click OK.

   Figure 14.5 shows these two minimal graphic utilities.

FIGURE 14.5
You can launch a command prompt from the Create New Task dialog box of Task Manager—which is not a Run dialog box but access to a shim.

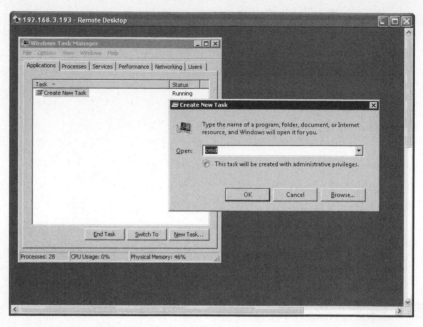

With LOGOFF, any processes or applications that you left running will continue to execute. You can log on again and start a session using the current state of those processes or application. If you want to end a session with no further processing, exit or terminate those applications and processes before logging off.

Enable Remote Connections

You can't access a new installation of Server Core from another system until you turn on Remote Desktop Administration; and you will have to do so locally. So this is one of the very first tasks you want to perform once you've logged in the first time and set the Administrator's password. To get a remote command prompt, you use the Windows Terminal Server Remote Desktop. Remote Desktop Administrative mode on Server Core allows Server Core to accept incoming connections.

To enable remote desktop sessions on Server Core, at the Server Core command prompt, type:

```
CSCRIPT C:\WINDOWS\SYSTEM32\ SCREGEDIT.WSF /AR 0
```

then press Enter.

The SCREGEDIT.WSF Windows Scripting file has a number of important roles. You can use the following switches:

◆ /AU to enable or disable Automatic Updates

◆ /CS to allow Terminal Service connections from downstream clients

◆ /IM to enable remote management of IPsec

◆ /DP to set the order of the DNS SRV records and /DW to set up DNS SRV weightings—both of which you would might want to use if you were setting up Server Core as your domain server

- ◆ /CLI to display a list of common tasks that you can perform from the command line

- ◆ /? to display the online help for the sc script itself

Be certain that when you use any of these switches that you change to the SYSTEM32 directory (CD C:\WINDOWS\SYSTEM32\) and that you precede the command with the CSCRIPT Windows Scripting Host command processor.

To connect to Server Core from a remote system:

1. Click Start ➤ Run, type **MSTSC**, and click OK. Alternatively, open the Remote Desktop Connection from the Start menu.

   The Remote Desktop Connection dialog box appears.

2. Enter the name of the Server Core (or the IP address), then click the Connect button.

3. Enter the Administrator account and password.

   The command prompt window then appears as the terminal server session.

4. Should you wish to change the administrator password, enter **NET USER ADMINISTRATOR** *.

5. When you are finished, you can close your session with the LOGOFF command.

Windows Remote Shell is another means for executing commands on Server Core using Vista or Windows Server 2008 as the remote systems. Just like with Remote Desktop Administrative mode, you need to enable incoming Remote Shell connections on Server Core using the following command-line command:

```
WINRM QUICKCONFIG
```

Then with Windows Remote Shell enabled, you can open a command prompt on your remote command and issue a Windows Remote Shell command from that computer's command prompt. The syntax for a command issued remotely in that case is as follows:

```
WINRS -R:<ServerCoreName> <CommandToExecute>
```

Network Settings

With remote administration turned on, you can continue on locally to configure network settings. If you enter **IPCONFIG /ALL** while you are local at the server and then write down the DHCP setting that Server Core has, you can move to a remote system for further administration.

The first time through is a good time to activate your server. To activate Server Core locally, enter **SLMGR.VBS -ATO**.

When you move to a remote system, open the Remote Desktop Connection and enter the IP address into the Connection text box. You'll be prompted for the Administrator's password, and after authentication you'll see what passes for the desktop on Server Core—the command prompt window. To activate remotely:

1. Type **CSCRIPT SLMGR.VBS -ATO** *<ServerName> <UserName> <PASSWORD>*, then press Enter.

2. Then type **CSCRIPT SLMGR.VBS -DID** and take note of the computer's GUID that is returned in output; press Enter.

3. Complete activation by entering **CSCRIPT SLMGR.VBS -DLI** *<GUID>*, and press Enter.

   Check that the Licensing status is returned as Licensed (activated) in the output.

If you want to change the Administrator's password, type **Net User Administrator** *. The purpose of the asterisk is to suppress the display of the password that you type twice to make the change. One task you might want to perform is to set a static IP address so that you always know that your remote connections to Server Core will succeed.

To set a static password:

1. Type **NETSH INTERFACE IPV4 SHOW INTERFACES** and press Enter.

   An "interface" is just another name for a network connection, and can be an address for hardware (your NIC) or for a virtual interface such as the Loopback Connector (a virtual machine).

2. Type **NETSH INTERFACE IPV4 SET ADDRESS NAME=<*IDX*> SOURCE=STATIC ADDRESS=<*IPAddress*>**, where *IDX* is the interface ID. Then press Enter.

   If you perform these tasks remotely, then your connection will drop out if the IP address changes and you will have to reconnect.

3. Enter **IPCONFIG** to confirm your static address assignment.

Figure 14.6 shows an example of this setting.

FIGURE 14.6
Use this procedure to set a static IP address on Server Core.

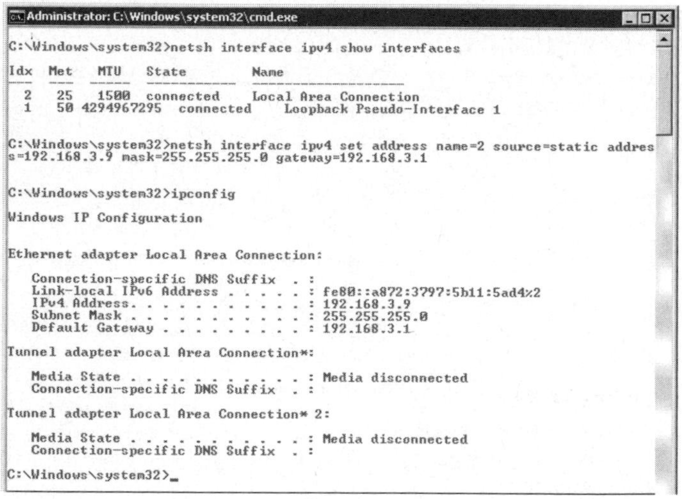

You will also need to set the DNS server address in order to be able to resolve network addresses (IP). To assign a DNS server, type **NETSH INTERFACE IPV4 ADD DNSSERVER NAME=INTERFACEID ADDRESS=<*IPofDNSServer*> INDEX=1**; then press Enter.

Notice the Index number, which was set to 1. The Index sets the order of DNS servers, so if you want a secondary DNS server, run this command again with the next address and use **Index=2**.

You can at any time switch back to a DHCP address using the following command:

```
NETSH INTERFACE IPV4 SET ADDRESS NAME=<IDX> source=DHCP
```

Hostname and Domain

To find your system's name, you use the HOSTNAME command. Unless you want to remember the gobblygook that Setup returns for a randomly assigned hostname (mine was WIN-QQJ3WW83B2Z), you'll want to give your server a name you can remember. To rename your server, enter:

```
NETDOM RENAMECOMPUTER <SetupAssignedName> /NewName <GivenName>
```

then press Enter.

Although Microsoft has eliminated reboots for IP address changes, installation of services, and a number of other functions that used to require a reboot, it is necessary to reboot a server after a name change so that the system is forced to represent its credentials to prevent spoofing. As you can see in Figure 14.7, if you use HOSTNAME again the system still has the SetupAssignedName until the reboot is performed.

To reboot the computer, use the SHUTDOWN /R command. There are many switches for this command, which can be used to log off, shut down, abort a shutdown, place a system in hibernation, set a timeout period, and force all applications to terminate before a shutdown. Windows posts the friendly dialog box shown in Figure 14.8 for you before shutting down.

FIGURE 14.7
NETDOM RENAME-COMPUTER is used to give your system a friendly name.

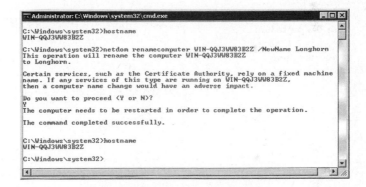

FIGURE 14.8
Windows posts an alert box after you issue a reboot command using the SHUTDOWN /R command.

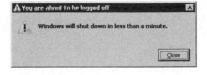

The final task for network settings is to join a domain. In most instances Server Core will not be used as a domain controller. Should you wish to remotely install a secure server, it is recommended that you use the Read-Only Domain Controller role instead. To join a domain:

1. Enter the following command: **NETDOM JOIN COMPUTERNAME /DOMAIN:DomainName / USERD:UserName /PASSWORDD:***.

   The extra D in the word PASSWORDD is not an error and is required for the command to work properly. Remember, the asterisk simply suppresses the display of the password you enter.

2. Add your domain user account to the local administrator group using the command **NET LOCALGROUP ADMINISTRATORS /ADD** *DomainName\UserName*.

3. If you are local, you can use Ctrl+Alt+Del to go back to the logon screen and then click the Restart button. For a remote session reboot, you will need to use SHUTDOWN /R as before.

Server Core Roles

Unless you intend using your Server Core installation for anything more than command-line practice or to impress your Unix buddies, you'll need to install a role on Server Core that actually does something useful. Remember, Microsoft didn't create Server Core to be an application server, so it's not meant to run your favorite enterprise application. What it's meant to do is to run Windows Server 2008 services. The key to working with Server Core roles is the OCSETUP command. Before moving to that command, you should enter the OCLIST |More command to view the Server Roles that are available for installation. Figure 14.9 shows the beginning of the output of this command, which runs several screens long—too long to reproduce in full here.

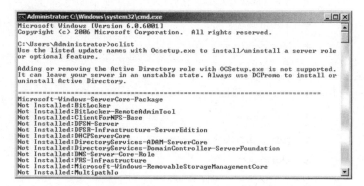

The OCSETUP *<RoleName>* command is used to install a role on Server Core. When you enter this command at the command prompt, the role installs. You may be required to restart the system to complete the installation if the Windows Package Manager posts the dialog box shown in Figure 14.10.

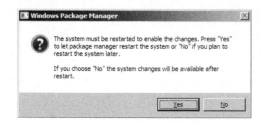

The following roles are available with the current version of Server Core Enterprise Edition:

◆ BitLocker

◆ BitLocker-RemoteAdminTool

- ClientForNFS-Base

- DFSN-Server

- DFSR-Infrastructure-ServerEdition

- DHCPServerCore

- DirectoryServices-ADAM-ServerCore

- DirectoryServices-DomainController-ServerFoundation

- DNS-Server-Core-Role

- FailoverCluster-Core

- FRS-Infrastructure

- IIS-WebServer Roll

- Microsoft-Windows-RemoveableStorageManagementCore

- MultipathIo

- NetworkLoadBalancingHeadlessServer

- Printing-ServerCore-Role

- Printing-LPDPrintService

- QWAVE

- ServeForNFS-Base

- SNMP-SC

- SUACore

- TelnetClient

- WAS-WindowsActivationService

- WindowsServerBackup

- WINS-SC

The list that's actually returned by OCLIST drills down to specific role services, giving you a hierarchy of role services and features, so that if you examine something like IIS, 48 lines of categories and items are returned.

OCSETUP is the Windows Package Manager installation command. You can display the command-line options available for OCSETUP by entering the OCSETUP /? command, as shown in Figure 14.11. Notice that the command for installing a role or role service only requires the name of the service as the input to the command. Should you want to uninstall a service or role, you can use the /UNINSTALL switch for that purpose.

FIGURE 14.11

The switches for the OCSETUP command are displayed in a dialog box as a response to the /? switch.

Setting Up a Print Server

If you have a server role without dependencies, you can add the role directly. For the Printing role the command OCSETUP Printing-ServerCore-Role does the trick. When you execute the command, the Package Manager opens the dialog box shown in Figure 14.12, which asks you to reboot the server to complete the installation.

FIGURE 14.12

Many roles require that you reboot your server in order to install the package.

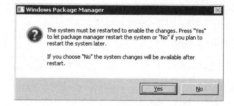

> **NOTE** The package installation command is case sensitive, so prior to running an installation use the OCLIST command to obtain the exact spelling to enter for the OCSETUP command.

Some services are dependent on other services. If you want to create a print server, you need to add the LPD Print Server role. That role depends on the Printing-ServerCore-Role to run successfully. Service roles are not automatically installed when you install a role in order to keep the footprint of Server Core low. To add LDP Print Server, you'd enter the OCSETUP Printing-LPDPrintService command.

A file and print server will not work properly unless you open the appropriate ports on the Windows Firewall. Although there are a number of ways of managing the Windows Firewall, the NETSH FIREWALL SET SERVICE FILEANDPRINT ENABLE command allows you to quickly do so from the command line. When the command runs successfully. Server Core posts the message OK in the command prompt window and returns you to the prompt. At this point you have a functioning print server to which you can add printers and configure their use.

There are a number of scripts for printer management in the Windows\System32\Printing_Admin_Scripts\en-US directory that you can use to configure printers. To use these VBScripts you first have to enter the CSCRIPT command to start the Windows Hosting Shell command interpreter.

For example, to view, delete, or add printer drivers you would use the CSCRIPT PRNDRVR.VBS command with the appropriate switches. Figure 14.13 shows you the help output of the Printer Driver script without any switches specified.

FIGURE 14.13

A set of scripts found at Windows\System32\ Printing_Admin_ Scripts\en-US lets you control printers from the command line.

Printer management scripts in the Printing_Admin_Scripts directory include:

NET PRINT   View or control a print job or the queue.

PRINT   Print a text file.

PRNCNFG.VBS   View the configuration information for a printer.

PRNJOBS.VBS   Pause, cancel, list, or resume a print job.

PRNMNGR.VBS   Set the default printer; add, list, or delete printer connections.

PRNPORT.VBS   Manage printer ports; add, delete, list, and configure TCP/IP Printer ports.

PRNQCTL.VBS   Manually pause or resume a printer, or clear the printer queue. You can also print a test page.

PUBPRN.VBS   Add or publish a printer in Active Directory.

Microsoft Management Console Management

You can connect to Server Core using the MMC. If you are connecting to Server Core from another member of its joined domain, then you only need present an Administrator account and its password from the domain to load snap-ins remotely. If the system you are connecting from isn't a member of the same domain, you will need to present the local Administrator and password for Server Core to get started.

To open Server Core MMC snap-ins remotely:

1. Open a command prompt on the remote system and enter the following command if you can't present domain credentials:

   CMDKEY /ADD:<ServerCoreName> /USER:<UserName> /PASS:<Password>

   The /PASS switch allows the password you entered to be accepted without confirmation.

2. Open the MMC snap-in from the Administrative Tools folder or by entering the command for that console at the command prompt.

   For example, you can enter **COMPMGMT.MSC** to open the Computer Management console or **EVENTVWR.MSC** to open the Event Viewer console.

3. In the tree control, right-click on the top-level node and select Connect to Another Computer from the context menu.

4. Enter the name of the Server Core in the Another Computer text box, then click OK.

   The MMC for Server Core then appears, and you can use the consoles to manage various aspects of Server Core.

The MMC offers a consolidated means for working with the various snap-ins of Server Core on remote systems. On another Windows Server 2008 system or on Windows Vista, you can open the Print Management console and add the Server Core system to that console. Chapter 10 describes how to work with the Print Management console and shows you how to add drivers using the Driver Installation wizard. The steps for installing a printer from the MMC are as follows:

1. Open the Print Management console and add the Server Core to your Print Servers list.

2. Right-click on the Drivers node in the tree control and select Add Driver to start the Driver Installation wizard.

3. Install the print driver(s) you need to support connected systems that will print to the printer share.

4. To confirm the driver installation on Server Core, open the Server Core console and change to the `Printing_Admin_Scripts` directory (as described in the previous section, using the CD command); then enter **CSCRIPT PRNDRVR.VBS -1**.

   The output returned will list your installed printer driver.

5. Add a port for your installed printer and name the port (optional).

6. Name the printer and create the printer share in the wizard.

7. Test-print from a remote system.

Don't forget that any service you run on Server Core will not be able to be managed remotely or indeed be operational until you open the appropriate firewall ports. You can do this with the following command in the Server Core console:

```
NETSH ADVFIREWALL SET ALLPROFILES SETTINGS REMOTEMANAGEMENT ENABLE
```

Command-Line Commands

The first place to look for command-line help is the SCREGEDIT.WSF script that you ran previously to turn Remote Desktop Administration on. That command's /CLI switch returns enough information to help you get your system set up the first time you log into the system. Since the output of this script's help for CLI is so useful, I've reproduced it for you here (see Listing 14.1). Keep in mind that SCREGEDIT.WSF is a script and that Microsoft will undoubtedly be modifying it over time. So when the time comes you should rely on what you see on your monitor and not necessarily what's outlined here, particularly for additional content. See also Table 14.2, "Command-Line Utilities for Server Core Management."

LISTING 14.1:   SCREGEDIT.WSF /CLI Output

```
C:\Windows\system32>cscript scregedit.wsf /cli
Microsoft (R) Windows Script Host Version 5.7
Copyright (C) Microsoft Corporation. All rights reserved.

To activate:
    Cscript slmgr.vbs -ato

To use KMS volume licensing for activation:
    Configure KMS volume licensing:
        cscript slmgr.vbs -ipk [volume license key]
    Activate KMS licensing
        cscript slmgr.vbs -ato
    Set KMS DNS SRV record
        cscript slmgr.vbs -skma [KMS FQDN]

Determine the computer name, any of the following:
    Set c
    Ipconfig /all
    Systeminfo.exe or Hostname.exe

Rename the Server Core computer:
    Domain joined:
        Netdom renamecomputer %computername% /NewName:new-name /UserD:domain-u
sername /PasswordD:*
    Not domain joined:
        Netdom renamecomputer %computername% /NewName:new-name

Changing workgroups:
    Wmic computersystem where name="%computername%" call  joindomainorworkgroup
 name="[new workgroup name]"

Install a role or optional feature:
    Start /w Ocsetup [packagename]
    Note: For Active Directory, run Dcpromo with an answer file.

View role and optional feature package names and current installation state:
    oclist

Start task manager hot-key:
    ctrl-shift-esc

Logoff of a Terminal Services session:
    Logoff
```

To set the pagefile size:
      Disable system pagefile management:
            wmic computersystem where name="%computername%" set AutomaticManagedPa
gefile=False
      Configure the pagefile:
            wmic pagefileset where name="C:\\pagefile.sys" set InitialSize=500,Max
imumSize=1000

Configure the timezone, date, or time:
      control timedate.cpl

Configure regional and language options:
      control intl.cpl

Manually install a management tool or agent:
      Msiexec.exe /i [msipackage]

List installed msi applications:
      Wmic product

Uninstall msi applications:
      Wmic product get name /value
      Wmic product where name="[name]" call uninstall

To list installed drivers:
      Sc query type= driver

Install a driver that is not included:
      Copy the driver files to Server Core
      Pnputil -i -a [path]\[driver].inf

Rename a Network Adapter:
      netsh interface set interface name="Local Area Connection" newname="Private
Network"

Disable a Network Adapter:
      netsh interface set interface name="Local Area Connection 2" admin=DISABLED

Determine a file's version:
      wmic datafile where name="c:\\windows\\system32\\ntdll.dll" get version

List of installed patches:
      wmic qfe list

Install a patch:
      Wusa.exe [patchame].msu /quiet

```
Configure a proxy:
     Netsh winhttp proxy set [proxy_name]:[port]

Add, delete, query a Registry value:
     reg.exe add /?
     reg.exe delete /?
     reg.exe query /?


C:\Windows\system32>
```

TABLE 14.2:   Command-Line Utilities for Server Core Management

TO DO THIS...	...USE THIS COMMAND
Activate the server	SLMGR.VBS –ATO locally, CSCRIPT SLMGR.VBS –DLI *\<GUID\>* remotely.
Set a new admin password	Type **NET USER ADMINISTRATOR ***.
Display or alter physical address translation	Enter **ARP** at the command prompt.
Manage automatic updates	To view your settings, enter **CSCRIPT SCREGEDIT.WSF /AU /V**. To enable automatic updates, enter **CSCRIPT SCREGEDIT.WSF /AU /4**. To disable automatic updates, enter **CSCRIPT SCREGEDIT.WSF /AU /1**. Group Policies are a good method for setting the behavior of automatic updates on Server Core.
Manage disk partitions	Use DISKPART to manage disk partitions.
DNS	Enter **NSLOOKUP** to view or modify DNS server assignment.
Domain: Join or unjoin	To join: **NETDOM JOIN %SystemName% /DOMAIN**:*\<DomainName\>**\<UserName\>* **/PASSWORD**: *\<NewPassword\>*. 1. To unjoin: **NETDOM REMOVE**. 2. Restart the system to enforce your changes.
Domain: View current	Enter **SET** at the command prompt.
Domain: Create a domain controller	Run **DCPROMO** and supply an unattended installation text answer file.

TABLE 14.2: Command-Line Utilities for Server Core Management *(CONTINUED)*

TO DO THIS...	...USE THIS COMMAND
Drivers: Add or remove	1. To add a driver for Plug and Play hardware, copy the driver to *%HomeDrive%\\<DriverFolder>*. 2. Enter **PNPUTIL -I -A %HomeDrive%\\<DriverFolder>\\ <DRIVER>.INF** at the command prompt. 3. Plug in your hardware device to have it recognized. 1. To list drivers, enter **SC QUERY TYPE=DRIVER**. 2. Then enter **SC DELETE <ServiceName>**.
Error Reporting	To view current error reporting settings, enter **SERVERWEROPTIN /QUERY**. To automatically send detailed reports, enter **SERVERWEROPTIN /DETAILED**. To disable error reporting, enter **SERVERWEROPTIN /DISABLE**.
Event Logs: List	Enter **WEVTUTIL EL** to list the event logs.
Events: Clear a log	Enter **WEVTUTIL CL <LogName>** at the command prompt.
Events: Export a log	Enter **WEVTUTIL EPL <LogName>** at the command prompt.
Events: Find or Query	Enter **WEVTUTIL QE /F:SearchString <LogName>**.
Event: Trace logs	Use the TRACERPT command to parse Event Trace Logs, including log files from the Performance Monitor and other real time event loggers. It can generate dump files, and report files and schemas.
Events: Trace sessions and performance logs	Use the LOGMAN command to create, start, stop, query, delete, update, import, and export data from performance logs.
Firewall	To enable remote management of a firewall, enter **NETSH ADVFIREWALL FIREWALL SET RULE GROUP="WINDOWS FIREWALL REMOTE MANAGEMENT" NEW ENABLE=YES** at the command prompt. Group Policies are a good method for setting the behavior of Server Core and firewalls.
File system: Manage	To administer the file system use the FSUTIL command.
File: Compact	Use the COMPACT command to compact a file.
File: Manage open files	Use the OPENFILES command to administer open files.
File: Ownership	To take ownership of a file use the ICACLS command.
File: Signature	To verify a file signature use the SIGVERIF command.
Group: Add to local system	NET LOCALGROUP <GroupName> /ADD

TABLE 14.2:   Command-Line Utilities for Server Core Management *(CONTINUED)*

TO DO THIS...	...USE THIS COMMAND
International settings	Use CONTROL INTL.CPL to change a Server Core's international settings.
IP Address: Set a static address	1. Enter IPCONFIG/ALL to view interface MAC addresses and DHCP assignments. 2. Enter **NETSH INTERFACE IPV4 SHOW INTERFACES** to view the interface list. 3. Enter **NETSH INTERFACE IPV4 SET ADDRESS NAME** *<InterfaceID>* SOURCE=STATIC ADDRESS=*<NewStaticIPAddress>* GATEWAY=*<GatewayAddress>*. The interface ID should be on the interface list. 4. To confirm your address assignment, enter **IPCONFIG /ALL**. The address should be returned, and DHCP should be set to No.
IPsec settings	Enter **NETSH IPSEC** to retrieve IPsec settings.
Mount points	To manage volume mount points use the MOUNTVOL command.
NAP settings	Enter **NETSH NAP** to view the Network Access Protection.
Network Connections: NetBIOS over TCP/IP (NBT)	Enter **NBSTAT** at the command prompt.
Network Connections: TCP/IP	To view or modify TCP/IP network connections enter **NETSTAT** at the command prompt.
Network Connections: Trace hops	Enter **TRACERT** at the prompt.
Page file	To enable: **WMIC PAGEFILESET WHERE NAME="***<Path/FileName>***"** SET INITIALSIZE=*<InitialSize>*,MAXIMUMSIZE=*<MaxSize>*. This command sets the path and name to the page file and sets the initial and maximum size of the file in bytes. To disable: **WMIC COMPUTERSYSTEM WHERE NAME="***<ComputerName>***" SET AUTOMATICMANAGEDPAGEFILE=FALSE.**
Performance counters	Use the RELOG command to extract performance counter logs into delimited file formats.
Performance data	Use the TYPEPERF command to return performance data to the command window or save it to a log file.
Proxy server bypass	To allow traffic from this Server Core through a proxy server, enter **NETSH WINTTP SET PROXY** *<ServerName>*:*<Port Number>*BYPASS-LIST="*<LOCAL>*".
Proxy server configuration	Enter **NETSH WINHTTP SET PROXY** *<ServerName>*:*<Port Number>*.

TABLE 14.2: Command-Line Utilities for Server Core Management *(CONTINUED)*

TO DO THIS...	...USE THIS COMMAND
Process or application: List	Enter **TASKLIST** at the command prompt.
Process or application: Terminate	1. Enter **TASKLIST** and find the process ID (PID) of the process or application you wish to terminate. 2. Enter **TASKKILL /PID <PID #>** at the command prompt.
RAID	To manage software RAID, use the DISKRAID command.
Rename domain system	NETDOM RENAMECOMPUTER *%ComputerName%* / NEWNAME:*<NewComputerName>* /USERD:*<DomainName\UserName>* /PASSWORD:*<Password>*
Rename workgroup system	NETDOM RENAMECOMPUTER *<ComputerName>* / NEWNAME:*<NewComputerName>*. Renames require a restart.
Routing	To view or alter the local routing table, enter **ROUTE** at the command prompt.
Routing: Multicast router settings	Enter **MRINFO** at the command prompt to view the configuration of a multicast router.
Services: List	Enter either **SC QUERY** or **NET START** to return a list of running services.
Services: Start or stop	To start a service, enter **SC START** *<ServiceName>* or **NET START** *<ServiceName>*. To stop a service, enter **SC STOP** *<ServiceName>* or **NET STOP** *<ServiceName>*.
Shadow Copy	To manage Shadow Copy, also called the Volume Snapshot Service, use the VSSADMIN command.
Log off, shut down, or reboot	Use the SHUTDOWN command with /L to log off, /F to force a shutdown, with /R to reboot, and with /S to shut down.
System information	To get system information use the SYSTEMINFO.EXE command. Note that WINVER.EXE will not work on Server Core.
Task Manager	Enter **TASKMGR** at the command prompt; the Task Manager dialog box appears. Alternatively, press Ctrl+Alt+Del.
Time: Change	Use the CONTROL TIMEDATE.CPL command to change the time zone.
Updates	To add an update type **WUSA** *<UPDATE>***.MSU /QUIET**. 1. To remove an update, enter **EXPAND /F:*** *<UPDATE>***.MSU C:\TEST**. 2. Open the following file in a text editor: C:\TEST\ *<UPDATE>*.XML. 3. Change the instance of INSTALL with REPLACE, then save the file. Then enter **PKGMGR /N:***<UPDATE>***.XML** to complete the removal.

TABLE 14.2: Command-Line Utilities for Server Core Management *(CONTINUED)*

TO DO THIS...	...USE THIS COMMAND
User: Add or remove from local Administrators group	To add type NET USER `<DOMAIN>\<USER NAME>` /ADD `<NewPassword>`. To remove type NET LOCALGROUP ADMINISTRATORS /DELETE `<DomainName>\<UserName>`.
Volume: Defragment	Use the DEFRAG command to defragment a volume.
Volume: Convert to NTFS	Enter CONVERT `<VolumeLetter>` /FS:NTFS at the command prompt.

Server Core is meant to be management framework "friendly." Most agent-based management packages run as a background service and don't display an indication of their presence. Provided these agents install using an MSI package they should work on Server Core, although any requiring .NET won't. Most enterprise antivirus packages should run on Server Core as well. Check to see if the "Designed for Windows Server 2008" logo is part of the package, because that testing will also certify compatibility with Server Core. It is always worth checking with the software vendor for their compatibility requirements as well.

Summary

Server Core offers an interesting new possibility of creating high-performance, highly secure infrastructure servers. As Microsoft develops this new type of Windows server it may well be that a GUI client will emerge that will make it easier for Server Core to be managed by those of us who have relied on Microsoft's GUI for their configuration. You should expect to see new scripts, new services, and a more refined version of Server Core to eventually emerge.

This chapter also completes our exploration of Windows Server 2008. In the chapters you have read I have highlighted what is new so that you could dive right in and add to the skills you have already have. I hope you have enjoyed reading about the next generation of Windows servers as much as I have writing about them for you.

Index

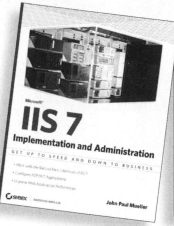